SO ORDERED

Ann Branigar Hopkins

Foreword by Mary Roth Walsh

So Ordered

MAKING PARTNER

THE HARD WAY

University of Massachusetts Press
Amherst

Copyright © 1996 by
Ann Branigar Hopkins
All rights reserved
Printed in the United States of America
LC 96–19645
ISBN 1–55849–051–5
Set in Adobe Melior
Printed and bound by Braun-Brumfield, Inc.

Library of Congress Cataloging-in-Publication Data

Hopkins, Ann Branigar, 1943–
    So ordered: making partner the hard way / Ann Branigar Hopkins; foreword
by Mary Roth Walsh.
    p.   cm.
    Includes index.
    ISBN 1–55849–051–5 (cloth : alk. paper)
    1. Hopkins, Ann Branigar, 1943–   —Trials, litigation, etc.
2. Price Waterhouse (Firm)—Trials, litigation, etc.
3. Sex discrimination in employment—Law and legislation—United States.
4. Women executives—United States–Biography.   I. Title.
KF3467.H66   1996   ·
344.73'01433'092—dc20
[347.304144133092]
                                                                96–19645
                                                                CIP

British Library Cataloguing in Publication data are available.

This book is published with the support and cooperation of the University of
Massachusetts Boston.

To the memory of my mother,
Tela Chiles King

Contents

Foreword ix

Preface and Acknowledgments xvii

Heritage 1

Apprentice 14

Marriage 29

Miners 33

Children 1 43

Citizens 57

Stability 59

Indians 62

Children 2 69

Transition 76

Hernia 81

Diplomats 84

Therapy 101

Journeyman 103

Fidelity 115

Master 120

Message 137

Failure 140

Ipecac 145

Idiot 147

Huron 152

Litigant   156

Unemployment   165

Hopkins v. Price Waterhouse   170

Nepal   174

Trial 1: Getting Ready   191

Trial 1: Monday   207

Trial 1: Tuesday   214

Trial 1: Wednesday   223

Trial 1: Thursday   232

Trial 1: Friday   240

Dyslexia   243

Discrimination   252

Desertion   255

Appeal 1   261

Coping   265

Constructive Discharge   273

Custody   279

Price Waterhouse v. Hopkins   290

Divorce   297

Evidentiary Standards   303

Healing   308

Trial 2: Wednesday   320

Trial 2: Thursday   337

Reading   347

Partnership   349

Order   356

Poetry   361

Appeal 2   367

Celebration   375

Reaffirmation   377

Briefcase   380

Epilogue   383

Index   399

Foreword

MARY ROTH WALSH[1]

I met Ann Hopkins for the first time in 1993 when I invited her to participate in a conference on "Glass Ceilings in High Places" co-sponsored by my research center and the Harvard Law School. I discovered that she had written an account of her lawsuit against Price Waterhouse and I offered to help her find a publisher. I was happy to do this because I am a specialist in professional women's coping and negotiation strategies and I was fascinated with her account. I suspected that others would also enjoy reading her version of events because there was so much media coverage of her legal case. Now, I am pleased that Ann Hopkins and her book will be reaching a larger audience. I think she has much to tell us about the changing roles of women in the late twentieth century.

In the following pages, Ann Hopkins tells us how it felt to take a business giant to court and win. Stories such as Hopkins relates in this book have to be told because working women are still being left out of the business history books. I was not suprised to find that a recently published 441-page history of Price Waterhouse makes no mention of

[1] Mary Roth Walsh, Ph.D., is a University Professor and Professor of Psychology at the University of Massachusetts, Lowell, where she is also Director of the Women in the Workplace Research Center. She has published three books with Yale University Press: *"Doctors Wanted: No Women Need Apply," Psychology of Women: Ongoing Debates*, and *Women, Men, and Gender: Ongoing Debates*.

the Hopkins case, even in a footnote, despite the fact that *Price Waterhouse v. Hopkins* is considered a landmark legal case.[2] Moreover, there is a great deal of misinformation circulating about Hopkins in professional circles. In the past year I have heard numerous accounts of what happened to her career, ranging from rumors that she never worked again to a report that she returned to Price Waterhouse as the company's director of affirmative action.

Ann Hopkins's legal victory is significant because it marks the first time that a federal court ordered a firm to grant a partnership to a plaintiff as a remedy for discrimination. As Elizabeth Spahn, a law professor at the New England School of Law, points out, *Price Waterhouse v. Hopkins* is a landmark legal case in the modern history of sex discrimination law because it marks a break with earlier cases where discrimination was so blatant that it was easy for plaintiffs to prove gender bias.[3] After losing those early court cases, employers developed a more sophisticated defense against charges of discrimination. In what is known as a "mixed motive case," employers argued that even if discrimination had occurred, they also had legitimate reasons for not hiring or promoting someone. In other words, employers argued that they would have made the same decision even if the process had not been tainted by some element of discrimination. Consequently, plaintiffs in such cases were then faced with the difficult task of proving that sex discrimination was the *only* reason they were not hired or promoted.

The Price Waterhouse decision changed all of this by declaring that it was enough for the plaintiff to show that discrimination was a motivating factor in the employer's decision-making process. In the Hopkins case, the "mixed motive" concept was very clear. Price Waterhouse claimed that Hopkins was "lacking in interpersonal skills." As it turned

---

[2] Edgar Jones, *True and Fair: A History of Price Waterhouse* (London: Hamish Hamilton, 1995). Ann Hopkins is the subject of a 1991 Harvard Business School case study (Case No. 9-391-155), a best-seller with more than 10,000 copies sold in five years (personal communication, Mary Lou Walsh, May 16, 1996). The law index cites at least sixty articles on Ann Hopkins and I consulted a substantial number of these articles in addition to news reports on her case.

[3] Elizabeth Spahn, personal communication, April 20, 1996. I am also indebted to Elizabeth Bartholet and Mona Harrington for their comments; to Patricia Flynn and Tjalda Belastock for their generous sharing of scholarly resources; and to Catherine Madsen for her research assistance.

out, some of the partners had a strange set of standards, declaring that Hopkins needed a course at charm school and advising her to walk, talk, and dress more femininely and to wear make-up and jewelry. But Hopkins's autobiography is more than a tale of a court battle, dramatic as that story is. I think readers can gain perspective on their own lives by reading this book. Although it is unlikely that any of us will see our names attached to a Supreme Court decision, there is much in Hopkins's life from which we can learn, including how to cope with personal and career disruptions. Corporate America's current fascination with downsizing has created an age of uncertainty in which many workers run the risk of being cut adrift from what they thought was a secure job or career. Certainly all of us, at one time or another, will find ourselves in workplace or personal situations that seem beyond our control.

Ann Hopkins's case, with its revelations about how personnel decisions are often made, helps explain the durability of the "glass ceiling." In 1996, ten years after two *Wall Street Journal* writers coined the term, less than 5 percent of the country's top business executives are female. Employment discrimination has clearly followed women as they climbed the corporate ladder. Where once discrimination issues were largely fought at the hiring stage, today's plaintiffs are more apt to be challenging promotion and partnership decisions.[4]

Over the years, a number of researchers have tried to explain the relatively small number of female leaders. In the process, behavioral scientists have offered new and sometimes conflicting theories, such as fear of success, fear of failure, low self-confidence, career-family conflict, low-status aspirations, and women's communication styles. Popular writers have picked up on these theories and have been quick to offer instant "solutions," ranging from assertiveness training and dressing for success to adopting a male style of communicating.[5] The message they send is clear. There is something wrong with women and if they want to get ahead, they need to fix themselves. But as we learn from this book,

[4] Kari Aamot-Snapp, "Putting Teeth into Minnesota's Employment Discrimination Law: A Legislative Proposal Defining Gender Stereotyping," *Minnesota Law Review* 79 (1994): 224.

[5] Mary Roth Walsh, *Psychology of Women: Ongoing Debates* (New Haven: Yale University Press, 1987), and Mary Roth Walsh, *Women, Men, and Gender: Ongoing Debates* (New Haven: Yale University Press, 1996).

when Price Waterhouse decided not to offer her a partnership, Ann Hopkins did not conclude that she had to fix herself.

When it became clear that Price Waterhouse was not going to reconsider her case, Hopkins resigned and filed a lawsuit, charging that the firm's unwillingness to promote her to partner violated Title VII of the Civil Rights Act of 1964. Her timing could not have been better. A few months after she left Price Waterhouse, the Supreme Court ruled for the first time, in *Hishon v. King and Spalding* that Title VII covered advancement to partnerships. Although Betsy Hishon, a candidate for partnership in a law firm, eventually settled her case out of court, she cleared the way for the Hopkins case to go forward.

Price Waterhouse v. Hopkins is an unusual case because the Supreme Court was asked for the first time to examine carefully the role of gender stereotyping in an employment discrimination situation. Although social science research had played an important role in *Brown v. Board of Education* (1954), the case that found segregation in the public schools unconstitutional, Hopkins's suit marked the first time that it was used in a sex discrimination complaint argued before the Supreme Court.[6] The significance of her case was underscored by a recent survey of the nation's top CEOs demonstrating that preconceptions and stereotypes of woman's role were the greatest barriers to women's advancement in the corporate world. Like Hopkins, other women were thought by business leaders to be weak in interpersonal skills. "The most common lament of top management men," one consultant observed, was that women were "too shrill . . . too aggressive . . . too hard edged."[7]

Henry Higgins might hope for "a woman to be more like a man" in *My Fair Lady,* but he clearly would find little support in the offices of the country's business leaders. American companies are full of bosses who brag about being "pitbulls," but blanch at the thought of a hard-nosed female executive. Hopkins's case dramatizes the double bind faced by

[6] Susan T. Fiske, Donald N. Bersoff, Eugene Borgida, Kay Deaux, and Madeline E. Heilman, "Social Science Research on Trial: Use of Sex Stereotyping Research in Price Waterhouse v. Hopkins," *American Psychologist* 46 (October 1991): 1049. For discussion of the debate that developed over this testimony and the American Psychological Association's amicus curiae brief, see Walsh, *Women, Men, and Gender.*

[7] Jaclyn Fierman, "Why Women Still Don't Hit the Top," *Fortune,* July 30, 1990, p. 46; Joann S. Lublin, "Women at Top Still Are Distant from CEO Jobs," *Wall Street Journal,* Feb. 28, 1996, pp. B1, B7. A detailed copy of the 1996 report on CEO jobs can be obtained from Catalyst, a non-profit research group, 250 Park Ave., South, New York, N.Y. 10003-1459.

many professional women who must walk a narrow line between appearing to be too feminine and too businesslike. On the one hand, if women behave according to the female stereotype that calls for them to be passive, docile, and noncompetitive, they run the risk of being passed over for promotion because they lack characteristics associated with leadership positions such as assertiveness and dominance. On the other hand, if they depart from the female image, they run into the criticism that Hopkins experienced.

Ironically, while Hopkins's case was winding its way through the court system, Brenda Taylor, an assistant state attorney in Broward County, Florida, was also criticized by her supervisor because of the way she dressed. Only in this instance, it was not because she was too masculine, but because she appeared too feminine. In fact, her boss told Taylor, who preferred to wear designer blouses, ornate jewelry, tight-fitting skirts, and spike heels, that she looked like a "bimbo." When Taylor complained to the federal Equal Employment Opportunity Commission, she was fired.[8]

The task of Hopkins's lawyers and expert witness Susan Fiske, a social psychologist, was to convince the court that gender stereotyping played a major role in Price Waterhouse's decision not to grant Hopkins a partnership. Fortunately, her lawyers had plenty of ammunition because, in addition to the advice given to Hopkins to be more feminine, previous women candidates for partner at Price Waterhouse had been criticized for, among other things, being too much "like one of the boys," being a "women's libber," and reminding a male partner of "Ma Barker."[9] Nevertheless, a man was promoted to partner at Price Waterhouse, despite being criticized for acting like a "marine drill sergeant."[10] Evidence for the salience of gender in the decision-making process was also found in the comment of one partner who declared that he did not see why women were being proposed for partnerships when they were not even suited to be senior managers. Significantly, no one at Price Waterhouse called him to task for his remarks.

Susan Fiske's assignment was to explain to the court the kind of

[8] R. Lacayo, "A Hard Nose and a Short Skirt, *Time*, Nov. 14, 1988, p. 98.

[9] Martha Chamallas, "Obvious Case of Sex Discrimination," *Des Moines Register*, December 13, 1988, p. 10A.

[10] Sheryl McCarthy, "Sex Bias Case Going before Supreme Court," *Newsday*, November 9, 1988, p. 4.

workplace conditions that encourage stereotyping and to identify the indicators that reveal the existence of stereotyping in Price Waterhouse's evaluation process. She pointed out, for example, that stereotyping is most likely to occur when an individual is one of a "few-of-a-kind" in an otherwise homogeneous environment, exactly the situation in which Hopkins found herself, the only woman among the eighty-eight candidates in a company with just a handful of female partners. Fiske also explained that stereotyping is more likely to occur when the evaluative criteria are ambiguous and subject to personal interpretation. Objective criteria, such as the amount of new business generated, are relatively immune to stereotyping and it was in this area that Hopkins received the highest marks from her evaluators. In contrast, in the subjective area of interpersonal skills she experienced her most damaging ratings.[11]

The lawyers and Susan Fiske were obviously persuasive. Nevertheless, the case dragged on for more than seven years with Price Waterhouse appealing each new decision in Hopkins's favor. The district court and the U.S. Circuit Court of Appeals agreed that unconscious sex discrimination had played a part in Hopkins's rejection. At that point, the burden of proof shifted to Price Waterhouse to demonstrate by "clear and convincing evidence" that it would have rejected Hopkins's candidacy even if there had been no negative stereotyping. After hearing Price Waterhouse's appeal, the Supreme Court agreed with Hopkins's position, noting that "an employer who objects to aggressiveness in women but whose positions require this trait places women in an intolerable catch 22: out of a job if they behave aggressively and out of a job if they don't. Title VII [of the Civil Rights Act] lifts women out of this bind."

But the case was not over. Although the Supreme Court agreed with the lower courts that Price Waterhouse had been motivated in part by discriminatory stereotyping, it found they had erred in requiring the firm to prove its case using "clear and convincing" evidence. Instead, the Court declared, Price Waterhouse had only to refute Hopkins's charges by a "preponderance of the evidence," a lower standard of proof. But this was Price Waterhouse's last gasp. On May 14, 1990, U.S. District Judge Gerhard Gesell (the son of the noted developmental psychologist Arnold Gesell) announced that the firm had failed to prove

---

[11] Fiske et al., "Social Science Research on Trial," pp. 1050-51.

its point. The judge went on to order Price Waterhouse to grant Hopkins a partnership and pay her back wages.

Price Waterhouse v. Hopkins sent shock waves through business and professional circles. According to Theodore St. Antoine, an expert on labor and employment law at the University of Michigan, "the court set down a pretty significant general principle that you can't treat a woman different from a man simply because you have this old-fashioned notion of what kind of lady-like decorum ought to be exhibited by a woman rather than a man. I think it will lead to some healthy soul-searching."[12]

Unwilling to wait for such introspection by the nation's CEOs, a number of states have incorporated the court's prohibition against stereotyping in *Price Waterhouse* into their employment discrimination laws. Moreover, Congress went beyond the original Supreme Court decision by declaring that once a plaintiff demonstrates that discrimination was a motivating factor in an employment decision, she is entitled to relief. This supersedes the Price Waterhouse decision that an employer could avoid liability in a mixed-motive case by demonstrating that the same employment action would have been taken if the discriminatory factors had not occurred.[13]

I think that millions of women can celebrate Hopkins's victory because it shows that one can stand up to discrimination in the workplace. Not everyone will win and certainly few, if any, will make history as Ann Hopkins did, but progress often consists of incremental steps rather than quantum leaps forward. We are all indebted to her for her courage and perseverance. Years earlier, Ann Hopkins's mother gave her this advice: "When you walk into a room, walk in as if you owned it."[14] Ann Hopkins doesn't own Price Waterhouse, but she certainly has earned her piece of the firm.

---

[12] Eric J. Wallach, "Businesses Fear Case May Bring Courts into Partnership Matters," *National Law Journal*, Sept. 24, 1990, p. 18. St. Antoine is quoted in Pamela Mendels, "She Didn't Get Her Partnership," *Newsday*, June 30, 1990, p. 62.

[13] Aamot-Snapp, "Putting Teeth into Minnesota's Employment Discrimination Law," p. 222; Michael A. Zubrensky, "Despite the Smoke, There Is No Gun: Direct Evidence Requirements in Mixed-Motive Employment Law after Price Waterhouse v. Hopkins," *Stanford Law Review* 46 (1994): 970.

[14] William Glaberson, "Determined to Be Heard: Four Americans and Their Journeys to the Supreme Court," *New York Times Magazine*, October 30, 1988 p.37.

Preface and Acknowledgments

A journalist once told me that most interesting stories are about issues between parties with opposing views, strongly held. He planned to write what he hoped would be an interesting story about a lawsuit. The issue was discrimination in an employment decision—admission to the partnership. The parties to the litigation were me and my firm, Price Waterhouse. That the litigation took many years attested to the strength of the opposing views.

The story he wrote appeared in the *New York Times Magazine* in 1988, around Halloween, when the U.S. Supreme Court heard arguments on *Price Waterhouse v. Hopkins.*

During seven years in the courts and in the five years since the litigation ended, hundreds of people have asked me to discuss discrimination or issues related to discrimination litigation. Plaintiffs and potential plaintiffs, representatives of the media, college students and faculty, the professionals I work with, and other groups interested in discrimination issues asked for advice, counsel, comment, or just a hearing for their stories or points of view.

Some assumed, even published, that I was a lawyer or an accountant and I have been variously characterized as victim, villain, heroine, pioneer, zealot. I am none of these. I am, however, the first person to be admitted to a partnership by a court order. I am a legal landmark, albeit a reluctant one.

I wrote this story in response to an oft-heard suggestion, "You should write a book." The book is my side of a story. It is about me and my seven years in litigation with my firm. I wrote it as a general response to the many questions people posed to me about me, my firm, and our litigation.

We—the firm and I—are both less than perfect. But neither of us is the villainous character that the media has described. And from what I know about other firms that compete in the marketplace where I work, I would rather be a partner at Price Waterhouse than an employee or a partner with any of the competing firms.

The story is about the judicial process and the issues as I saw them through the eyes of a layperson and a plaintiff. It speaks to or about people, psychology, and the law.

I am indebted to my partners, some past and some present, for the opportunity to tell this story. It owes its happy ending to Doug Huron and Jim Heller, first my attorneys and foremost my friends. The story is shorter than it might have been but for the perseverance of Betsy Hishon in her litigation with King and Spaulding. If she had not started into the courts in 1978, my litigation might have been years longer. For her tenacity I am grateful—I tired of litigation long before it ended.

To Ruth Hopper, my neighbor of eighteen years, and Tela, Gilbert, and Peter Gallagher, my children, I owe my sanity. Ruth held my hand and my head through many years of emotional ups and downs. My children, the focus of my attention, prevented me from being obsessed with the judicial process.

The confidence and optimism of my siblings, Susan Wilmer, John Hopkins, Cathy Hopkins, and Sheila Gallagher, cheered me on and carried me through events whose outcomes, viewed by others, were devastating. My friends, especially Mary Curzan, Toni and John Gibbons, Susan Riley, Vera Schneider, and Carol Supplee stood by me, comforted me, and advised me.

The family's financial survival during seven years of litigation was largely due to the loyalty of my clients at the U.S. Department of State and, in the later years, to my employer, the World Bank. I worked hard for Roger Feldman, Toni Gibbons, Bob Lamb, Howard Renman,

W. David Hopper, Bob Picciotto, and George West, to name only a few. I hope I earned their confidence. I certainly appreciated it.

By commitment to their work and my children, my children's teachers lightened my load. Joanne Dondero and the staff of the Oakland School in Charlottesville, Virginia, helped Peter learn to read. Kevin White and Greg Ruffer of Gonzaga College High School in Washington, D.C., showed Gilbert what success looked like and why values matter.

Dozens of people helped convert memories, recollections, and notes to the printed page. I thank the readers, writers, and poets in my life— Sally Keene Craig, Julie Randall, Sandy Comenetz, and Sandy Kinsey. The story owes its order, organization, and cohesiveness to Maggie Stephenson. Her humor, candidness, and editing skill helped me turn an unruly pile of words into a manuscript.

Finally, I offer my regards to Mary Roth Walsh and Paul Wright who pushed the story to publication. If the story has value, credit many. Errors are mine.

SO ORDERED

Heritage

I am a Texan. The land in Texas grows black-eyed peas and cotton and pinto beans, but you have to work at it. I love freshly shelled black-eyed peas and cotton jeans. Polyester is offensive to the touch. Chili made with kidney beans is something other than chili. I am a Texan and have worked at it, whatever it was.

I was born in 1943 on Galveston, an island fifty miles south of Houston. My father and his brother were born there. My paternal grandparents, although not born on the island, lived there for the better part of half a century.

My mother was born in East Texas—more specifically Troupe, near Tyler, in the vicinity of Dallas. My maternal grandmother was named Smith, one of twelve children, most of whom lived and raised families in or around Dallas.

One of my great-uncles held a Smith family reunion in Dallas one summer when I was about five. Three generations attended. At least fifty people, mostly from Texas, enjoyed Mexican food in a lovely rose garden. The children of my generation were all cousins.

Most of the family was named Smith, but with interesting first names: Tela, Frances, Julius, Junius. Many members of the family had the same first name because of a tradition of naming the children of one generation after members of an older generation.

It was hard to identify who was who by name, first or last. The family differentiated among the various same-named members by initials or

1

middle names. My mother, for instance, was named after her aunt Tela O. Hinkle, who raised her. She was born Tela Maurine Chiles but was known through her early life as Tela Maurine or TM. This, among other things, differentiated her from her aunt TO. My daughter is named and called Tela Margaret.

My father was John William Hopkins, named after his father whom I never knew—he died a few years before I was born. I was told that my grandfather was from Virginia and went to Transylvania College and the University of Virginia. He was apparently an attorney, graduated first in his class, and gave his valedictory address in Greek. As the story goes, he went to Houston shortly after the turn of the century when it was a railhead and cow town of about thirty thousand.

On one of the first of his few days in town, a bunch of cowboys rode in and shot up the place. He decided that Texas was too rough for him and was headed back to Virginia when someone suggested that he go see beautiful Galveston Island. He never left Galveston. He never practiced law, but he was on the board of regents of the University of Texas, wrote arithmetic textbooks for the state, was the superintendent of schools in Galveston, and was an officer of the American National Insurance Company.

I was devoted to my grandmother, Grace Branigar Hopkins. Her maiden name is my middle name and my uncle's name, although everyone called him Barney. I think of Mom Moo, a nickname from infancy, every time I sign my name, which I always sign in full. We were intimate friends; I in my youth, she in her old age. In addition to the first few years of my life, I spent every summer that I was in the United States until I went to college in 1961 with her. I visited her for long periods each year thereafter until she died in her eighties.

I treasure family. My summers in Galveston with my grandmother taught me the value of roots, of stability, of families connected one to another by friendships among members of three generations. I loved and was fascinated by the members of the first of these generations, almost all of whom came to Galveston from somewhere else.

The men, most of whom died before I was born or when I was very young, started as lawyers and grocers and bankers and clerks. I remember only a few of them individually and then only vaguely. My recollection of them as a group, conveyed by what their widows said over card tables, was of prominence and dignity. By the time I heard the stories about them, they were judges or men whose families owned chains of grocery stores, banks, cotton compresses, and insurance companies.

The women were an eccentric, self-sufficient, poised, occasionally cantankerous lot, none of them cut from the same mold. As a child, I called most of them Miss Mable or Miss Mary or the like. Some I later addressed by their proper titles and surnames. None was ever addressed by first name only, although I knew many for thirty or more years.

During my summers in Galveston, two or three times each week, I made a run in Mom Moo's Buick to pick up the card group and deliver them to one of the clubs or Victorian homes where the members regularly played bridge or canasta. I usually got three sets of detailed instructions even though I knew the way by heart and each of the players lived within fifteen blocks of the others. Most of them lived in huge gingerbread Victorian houses that, while still elegant in my time, must have been spectacular in their prime.

When the women got too old for the houses to be manageable, some of them moved into apartments, as did my grandmother, or into more modern brick houses on the west end of town. One of my favorites, Miss Mary Hutchings, simply covered the furniture, had an elevator installed, and lived quite pleasantly in a few rooms of her own house.

The place was something straight out of *Great Expectations.* It suited Miss Mary nicely though. She cut her own hair and continued to wear her mother's clothes, sometimes unaltered, until they wore out. She traveled everywhere. Some summers I missed her when I went to call because she was off in Africa or Asia. Although she probably could have afforded a private plane, she always traveled coach class. "The people you meet in coach are so much more interesting," she once told me.

My grandmother always flew first-class. She was uncomfortable traveling as the result of a couple of hip replacements, one of which she had so late in life that she had to lie about her age to get a physician to perform the surgery. She walked with an elegant, dark, highly polished wooden cane until a couple of broken arms convinced her to use a walker. The aluminum walker embarrassed her; she thought it undignified. She herself was incapable of being undignified.

I loved the old lady. Even in my twenties, I called her Mom Moo. With few exceptions, however, everyone else called her Mrs. Hopkins. Only intimate family and people with whom she played cards for decades called her Grace.

I grew up with Victorian formalities and I appreciated them, enjoyed them. I wore white gloves and hats when the occasion called for it, learned ballroom dancing, went to debutante balls. In my youth I learned about the proper disposition and placement of napkins, forks, spoons, and knives, some of which (ice cream forks, for example) I have seldom seen since.

I was only a little better acquainted with the men of my mother's generation than with those of my grandmother's. Mom's generation of men was away at war. She and her female contemporaries were brides and first-time mothers together in Galveston. Over the years, I spent summers as a member of the third generation and, as I matured, eventually became friends with that second generation.

In most cases, Mom's friends and I are on a first-name basis. Prints of the prominent homes and historical buildings of Galveston hang on the walls in my dining room, a wedding gift from one second-generation friend. Pickles and olives are served every Thanksgiving and Christmas in the gift from another.

I am an army brat. My father joined the army to serve in World War II. He and I were never close, maybe because I was almost three by the time he returned from the Pacific. The man in my life as an infant and a toddler was my Great-uncle Julius, whom I followed around and called "Man" before I learned to love him for the person he was.

Jobs were scarce after the war. Dad and many of his friends stayed in the army and made careers of it, so we traveled a lot. My sister and brother were born less than two years apart on different army bases in the States. In 1949 we were ordered to Germany. My father was assigned to command a battalion in the Fulda gap up along the East German border.

There were no convenient Pampers to pollute the environment back then, and it took twenty-four hours to fly to Europe the first time we went. Mom made it seem easy, but it must have been terribly difficult. My brother was a baby; I was five; my sister was in between.

Milk and water were sometimes contaminated. In Europe in the late forties, people actually died from tuberculosis and typhoid fever. Mom boiled all the water. To this day I shun milk products, probably because they were prohibited when I was a kid. I learned to speak German and English simultaneously. I never had a choice. There were few English-speaking children where we lived. I had to speak German or play alone.

When I was in third grade, there were only five American children of school age at the post. The school we attended was located sixty kilometers away in Bad Herschfeld in the basement of the bombed remains of an old building, grades one through twelve, thirty-six students, two teachers. We rode to and from school on the train under the protective eye of a member of the military police. If I stayed late for Girl Scout meetings, an MP drove me home in an army-green Volkswagen. I originally thought the teenaged MPs, who carried rifles, were protecting us from the local population. When the commanding general's son pulled the emergency brake and brought the train to a dead stop, I learned that they were actually protecting the Germans. The five of us had to write "I will not pull the emergency brake on the train" a thousand times.

After three years in Germany we moved in 1952 to Fort Leavenworth, Kansas. My father was first assigned to and later became an instructor at the War College there. I never figured out what a "war college" was. We had a garden plot down near the Missouri. We planted tomatoes, cantaloupes, cucumbers, lettuce, radishes, and carrots. The cantaloupes seemed to have no taste, probably because for a Texan the only good cantaloupes in the world are grown on the Pecos River.

We had a series of black-and-white Boston terriers—all named Taffy or Tuffy, depending on sex. Everywhere I went I was followed around by a very protective dog. If I waded up to my knees in Missouri river mud, the dog sloshed up to his neck in it.

I never managed to teach the dog to clean up before going into the house. Mom always cleaned up. My father was the disciplinarian. When we stepped out of line we were whipped with a belt or a riding crop. But the dog watched out for us. My sister once escaped a sound thrashing because one of the Tuffys or Taffys attempted to remove the seat of my father's pants.

There was a polio epidemic while we were at Fort Leavenworth. As I recall it, three thousand cases were diagnosed. I remember the braces and the wheelchairs. Mom returned to her profession as a nurse and went to work at the hospital. She worked rotating shifts: seven to three for a while, followed by three to eleven, followed by eleven to seven. Every day she washed, starched, and ironed her uniform and hat, its shape specified by the nursing school she had attended.

I was concerned when Mom occasionally came home with blood on her normally spotless white uniform. Usually it was the result of a severed umbilical cord that got loose—Mom worked in labor and delivery. My father disapproved of my mother's working: "Officer's wives don't work" was his view.

I had to take home economics in school—only the boys could take shop. I got a D in spite of the fact that I had been well trained at home. My mother kept a spotless house, was a superb cook, set a lovely table, and taught all of us what to do. I also learned a lot about cooking from my grandmother's help, all of whom were black, all of whom were beautiful, all of whom were my peers when we were in the kitchen.

None of them used a book. Both Mamie and Georgia made biscuits that I am still unable to replicate in spite of the fact that each gave me a recipe: "Miss Ann, what you have to do is add a glug of" this to a "dollop of" that, etc. Over many years, I have listened carefully enough to the sounds of the ingredients hitting containers, to know what a glug and dollop are. To this day, however, I am unable to produce the same mouth-watering biscuits that were served daily in my grandmother's house.

Anyway, I got a D because my red felt circle skirt was egg-shaped, and I ironed on the wrong side of the ironing board. The products of my ironing effort always looked good, but I never seemed to put the iron down in the "right place" when it was not in use. I never in my life wore a circle skirt and I still iron on the wrong side of the board.

After War College in 1957, my father was attached to the Military Advisory and Assistance Group at the American Embassy in Bonn. We lived in Plittersdorf, which is near Bad Godesberg in the vicinity of Bonn. The German police rode vehicles that were, in concept, big tricycles with boxes over the back wheels. The American embassy was bounded on two sides by cherry and pear farmers. Bonn was then, as it is now, one of the more prominent American foreign service posts.

I was mischievous. Because Mom failed to comprehend German, or so I thought, I delighted in translating for her when one of my siblings, usually my brother, got into trouble. I vividly recall translating the comments of the irate German police when my brother let the air out of the three-wheeled vehicle tires or got chased by an enraged, shotgun-carrying farmer protecting his cherry orchard. It turned out that Mom understood just fine without the benefit of my translation.

As an officer's wife, Mom entertained, and she entertained according to all the rules and protocols appropriate to the occasion. I must have been thirteen one sunny afternoon when she was having what looked like half the diplomatic corps to play bridge. I had been collecting things in the garden and putting them in a shoe box. When I came into the house the bridge party was at a lull. Someone, I believe it was the Belgian ambassador's wife, engaged me in conversation over the contents of my box. I can still remember the look on Mom's face when I opened the box and introduced the ambassador's wife to my newly acquired green garden snake.

I learned to be independent, probably at the expense of considerable anxiety on my mother's part. She seemed less than terrified, however, when she put me on a plane going from Germany to London the summer of 1958. Her parting words were, "In case of war or other emergency, go to the nearest American consulate or embassy. Don't lose your passport. I love you."

I made the trip from Frankfurt to London to Cardiff and on to the northern coast of Wales where the rest of the Girl Scouts were convened at an international scout camp. We were a diverse group. More than five languages were spoken by the couple of dozen of us. With a little effort, we communicated, in a primary or secondary language or through an intermediary using a common language. In a period that ended in what was known as the "Berlin Crisis," I managed to get where I was going and back with confidence and without worrying too much about how much trouble I could get into.

I went to the American School on the Rhine along with children of diplomatic families from all over the world. That school only went through ninth grade so I had to go to Frankfurt to boarding school in tenth. Although Elvis Presley was stationed in Frankfurt about that time, I never saw him.

For some reason that I never understood, my father cut short his tour in Bonn. We returned to the States, in the middle of the school year, just before Thanksgiving. We went to live in Alexandria, a suburb of Washington, D.C. After a bout with pneumonia, I finally showed up at the only civilian school I ever attended just after New Year 1960.

In academic circles, World War II had apparently not yet ended—I had to take French because German was not offered. The public schools were being integrated, making for a difficult time. The crowds of nonblack teenagers parted like the Red Sea under the influence of the Lord when the four black students walked the halls to change classes.

I was unquestionably an outsider. In a school where there was no Girl

Scout troop, I was curb bar, the Girl Scout equivalent of an Eagle Scout in the Boy Scouts. The conventional loafers, denim skirts, cotton shirts, and school jackets that I had worn in the military dependents' and diplomatic families' schools in Europe were nothing like the preppie attire worn in the States. Mom and I cried a lot over my difficulties coping with sororities and cheerleaders and snobbery and bias. But we muddled through.

I went to work Saturdays and three nights a week at the local library. The job diverted my attention from the unpleasant social scene at school and provided me with a peer group in the form of the half a dozen or so other pages who worked with me. My boss was a woman named Joey Biero. She was young enough to be a friend and just enough older than I to be a role model during my teenage years.

We must have driven her crazy with our stunts, the most notable of which was running a forgery operation in the book labeling and repair shop in the back of the library. We altered Virginia driver's licenses, which in that day were photostats. Carefully done pinpoint erasure and white-ink replacement of the birthday for those under eighteen guaranteed the holder access to any bar in Washington. We also fabricated some very official-looking library employee identification cards that served a similar purpose. When our activities came to her attention, we caught hell. Joey was not one to mince words.

After eighteen different schools, including three high schools, I graduated, high in my class, in the summer of 1961. It never occurred to me not to go to college. Education was something prized by both of my parents.

I never knew until after he died that my father missed graduating from the University of Texas by a few credits. My mother, who never mentioned her B.A. from Baylor because it was in nursing, made it clear that a college education was as important to my generation as a high school diploma was to hers.

Sight unseen, I attended the college of my mother's choosing. One of Mom's best friends, Jane Shirley, also a Texan, attended Hollins College for a couple of years in the thirties. Mom and Jane were brides and mothers together, but not in Galveston. Jane's husband, Jack, and my father graduated from New Mexico Military Institute in Roswell. Everyone met and married at about the same time. I was the same age as Jane and Jack's daughter, Susan, who had applied to Hollins for early admission. Jack and my dad both retired from the army in Washington.

For a while, we all lived in the same apartment building. Mom and Jane thought it would be wonderful to have their children go off to college together and develop into the best of friends. Susan and I have gotten to know each other better over the years since we left college, but we barely knew each other at Hollins.

I was visiting in Galveston the summer before I was scheduled to start college. I thought I was going to Sophie Newcomb College, now a part of Tulane University. Mom Moo told me that Uncle Barney, who was a petroleum engineer with one of the huge oil companies, had been promoted and would be moving out of New Orleans to the Philadelphia area. Mom was reluctant to have me in the Deep South, that far away from home, without a relative nearby. One day I got a letter from her telling me that I was going to Hollins, a small, southern, liberal arts, women's college in Virginia.

Although where I went to college was a matter of little interest to me, going to only one college was very important. After all the elementary and secondary schools I had attended, I was determined to love whatever college I started out in. What I studied was also important. My mother lobbied hard for literature, history, art, and philosophy. I declared a mathematics major six weeks into my freshman year.

I took only those literature and history courses required by the core curriculum. All the time I had for extra courses I filled with chemistry and German literature. I carried a D in the required course on the history of Western civilization, partly because it was hard, but mostly because I did not like the reading. I finally read a lot of the texts when my interest in history picked up during and after graduate school.

Over the last ten or twenty years, based on a singularly unstatistical survey of the women I have met, I have concluded that most interesting women attended women's colleges. I believe that Hollins, as a women's college, played an important role in my development. I was educated free of the social pressures that coeducation created in many similarly intellectually immature women of my age.

I learned to depend on myself and on the analytical integrity of an answer to a question or a solution to a problem before I was taught to depend on or defer to members of the opposite sex or their point of view. I was limited in what I could do only by the number of hours in a day. I sang in the choir, worked in the theater, managed the business of the newspaper, and worked in the Head Start program. I ran for but was never elected to office, although I was selected for *Who's Who in American Colleges and Universities.*

As a student I excelled in areas that I pursued with interest and enthusiasm. If the subject did not interest me, I got average results. I came within a hair of failing physical education for lack of interest in reading, let alone memorizing, the American Red Cross water safety instructors' text.

Most of my friends studied literature, history, philosophy, art, and music. Through them I met William Golding, Howard Nemerov, Robert Penn Warren, Eudora Welty, and other prominent literary figures of the day, sometimes at readings or lectures, but more often at the home of Julia Van Ness Randall. Sometimes known as Mrs. Sawyer, remnant of a former marriage, sometimes Julie, she was the resident Mozart lover, eccentric, poet, and teacher of subjects literary.

Julie always had several, usually ill-trained or untrainable, beagles or West Highland white terrier-like dogs running around the place. I frequently found the literary figures to be as incomprehensible as the dogs were incorrigible. In my adulthood, my dogs have, however, always been named, by the Randall dog-naming convention, after literary figures—in fact after the same literary figure, George Sand, that way the name applies regardless of the sex of the dog.

I stayed with Julie when I returned to Hollins many times after graduation to revisit fond memories and enjoy the enduring beauty of the place. Julie retired and returned to live where she had her roots, in Baltimore, where we saw each other several times each year. When development began to encroach on her environmental and psychological space, she moved to the Bennington area in Vermont where she had gone to college. I continue to visit her there on my way to or from my sister's family place in central Vermont. Julie is my daughter's godmother.

Like many of my contemporaries in the midsixties, I did not know what to do for a living as graduation neared. The women I spent most of my time with in my junior and senior years included a Danforth, a Wilson, a Fulbright, and more than the usual proportion of Phi Beta Kappas. In pursuit of academic quests, they were all headed to graduate school. That course of action relieved them of the burden of résumé writing and shifted the paperwork to the faculty, who had to write letters of recommendation. For lack of a better plan, I decided to go to graduate school.

My faculty adviser was a man named Claude Thompson who was only a few years older than his students. We all believed that it was to increase the perception of chronological distance between himself and us that he always addressed us as Miss. Until the day I graduated, he referred to me as Miss Hopkins. Thereafter he called me Ann, in spite of the fact that everyone else called me Hoppy.

I idolized Mr. Thompson. He wore granny glasses without realizing that they were in style and smoked a pipe through a thick, broomlike black mustache. We worried that he might bite through the pipe when he clenched his teeth to show his annoyance at our performance on tests or homework. He had the most professorial appearance of anyone I ever met in the halls of academe, but he was anything but absentminded. He had a most unusual accent: a blend of Oklahoma drawl from his place of origin and a Yale twang acquired at the university.

I presented myself in his office one day to announce, as if it were a life-altering decision, that I had decided to go to graduate school. Furthermore, I wanted to go to Yale I told him. "Mees Opkins," he began, "whereas Ah have no doubt but that you can get into Yale, Ah am equally certain that you will nevah get out." He followed up with a question that implied a recommendation: "Would you considah Texas or Indiana?" To escape the family umbilical cord, I decided to go to Indiana University.

In the meantime, my mother left my father shortly after I graduated from college. I drove her nonstop from Washington to her new home in central Florida in my brand-new 1965 Volkswagen, a graduation present from my grandmother. My mother went back to work until she married Gilbert Wesmore King, a retired army officer, in 1967. The family called him Gil. My older son is named Thomas Gilbert and is called Gilbert.

I drove on to Galveston to spend the summer before graduate school. It was the last time I saw my grandmother. One of the great sadnesses of my life was that I was on a camping trip in northwestern Canada, between my two years in graduate school, when she died. I found out about her death, after the funeral, through the efforts of the Royal Canadian Mounted Police. My mother called the Mounties who eventually contacted me after posting notices on bulletin boards at the entrances to national parks all over Canada.

I earned my master's degree in mathematics at Indiana, but I hated every academic minute of it—what I studied had no perceivable relation to real-world activities required to get something useful done. As I approached the end of my formal education in the summer of 1967, however, I still had no notion of how to get a job.

Mr. Thompson was scheduled to take a sabbatical the academic year that began in the fall of 1967. I jumped at the offer to teach his courses for the year he would be away. I taught at Hollins that one year. I was the youngest member of the faculty and had, as students, women who had attended college with me two years earlier.

The familiarity of the loving and lovely bucolic setting and the intellectual challenge of remaining one lecture ahead of my very bright students made my year of teaching a positively memorable experience, but teaching was not my calling. I took a job with IBM.

In the summer of 1968 before I started work, my brother John and I, along with a couple of college friends of mine, went on a camping trip. Our planned destination was Alaska. We started in Florida with Mom and my stepfather, Gil, proceeded up the East Coast, and across Canada. It was cold and rained much of the time. After a soggy but successful fishing stint in Moraine Lake, north of Banff, we struck south in search of drier, warmer weather. Until the ice chest was empty, we ate fish broiled over a campfire two meals a day as we worked our way down the West Coast, through Death Valley and the Grand Canyon and finally into Texas.

In a beat-up, green Volkswagen bus, we descended with my Pekingese dog, George, on my Uncle Julius and Aunt Frances Smith in Dallas. We had a great time running around in blue jeans and boots. When Brother John and I told them that we planned to drop in on relatives in Houston and friends in Galveston, they simultaneously suggested that we pick up some more "appropriate" clothes.

I am not sure that my "cousins" Lyndall and Gus Wortham were really blood relations. She was my grandfather's niece. She seemed to be of the age to belong to my grandmother's generation, maybe a little younger. Over my formative years, she flitted into and out of my life like Auntie Mame, but without the stylistic flair of Rosalind Russell. She dropped in on my family when we lived in Europe, and I did the same to her whenever I was in Houston.

In University Park in Houston, our entourage pulled into the driveway and George hopped out. We were greeted by Robert, the butler. When we declined his offer to take our bags—all our stuff was packed up in knapsacks—he showed us to our rooms. After showering and bedecking ourselves in the appropriate clothes that Frances and Julius had suggested, we presented ourselves before Lyndall in the sunroom. "Robert tells me that we are not having dinner at the Houston Country Club as planned," she said.

We used Gus and Lyndall's place as an air-conditioned base of operations for crabbing trips to Galveston. The household staff was relieved when Brother and I told them we had boiled, stripped, and iced the crabs on the beach. They helped us pick crabs in the kitchen and cleaned up the mess behind.

Gus was more of a legend in my life than he was a close friend. As a kid, I found his straight-faced, quiet manner of speaking, when he spoke, to be a little scary. Gus was a prominent business executive with an insurance company in Houston. Early one morning at breakfast, I asked him for his advice and counsel on how to be successful in business. He and I were alone at a formally set table that would easily have accommodated another dozen people—Lyndall never got up before midday.

In response to my query, he reached back fifty years. "When Ah was a young man," he drawled softly, "mah daddy wanted me to study the law and he sent me off to the university. But the university didn't want me to study the law and sent me home. So mah daddy sent me back to the university to study the liberal arts. The university didn't want me to study the liberal arts either. So Ah went back to mah daddy's ranch to punch cattle. Ah guess the thing that contributed most to mah success in business is that when mah Daddy died in the early thirties, he left me $10 million—cash." He grinned. I laughed. So much for education.

Apprentice

To everyone's sorrow, John F. Kennedy did not live to see his objective achieved: putting a man on the moon in ten years. The aerospace business boom of the sixties that resulted from the nation's effort to meet that simple objective was my opportunity to stop drifting around in academia and go to work in the real world.

I was unaware that IBM was the acronym for the International Business Machines Corporation when I scheduled an appointment with the recruiter who was interviewing mathematics and statistics majors at Hollins. It was only by Archimedean revelation that I signed up: IBM was recruiting my students, ergo they could recruit me. Eureka!

Although I had never met a programmer, I believed that for a mathematician to be a programmer was comparable to a concert pianist playing an upright in a bar. Two weeks into IBM's four-month basic programmer training, I overcame that ignorant, arrogant prejudice.

Graduate school had been hard and I struggled to get through, but I went to classes for fewer than four hours each day, including the course I taught to earn the twenty-six-hundred-dollar-stipend I received as a teaching assistant. Even with daily assignments, preparation for routine exams, and studying for comprehensives and language competency tests, I could usually count on two or three hours each day to sit around over a beer with friends or have people by the apartment for dinner.

The IBM classroom training ran eight hours each day. Nights and weekends, for as long as we could stay awake, we did our class assignments or worked on technical exercises at the computer facility.

As a moral commitment, I worked hard enough to survive in graduate school: had I flunked out, future generations of applicants from Hollins might have been rejected. I worked a lot harder at IBM, however, to earn the $202 per week I was paid and to make sure that I still had a job when the training was over.

After training, going to work on a project for a paying customer seemed like a vacation. I worked eight-hour days, measured by the clock on which I punched in and out. I had no choice but to limit my work day in the office to eight hours. The first time a manager observed that I was still at my desk after normal business hours, I was affectionately shooed away from work because, I was told, I was classified as a nonexempt employee. Apparently that meant that IBM might be accused of staff abuse if I were in the office more than the prescribed number of hours, even if I wanted to be there out of sheer exuberance. I just took my work home. The problem was solved shortly when I was promoted to an exempt labor category—then I could work for however long I chose.

My father died in 1969 while I was working for IBM. I called the office and said he had died and I would not be at work for a while, nothing more—not my father's name, not where I was going. I went back to Galveston for the funeral. Somehow IBM determined where the funeral was and thoughtfully sent birds of paradise. The flowers and a man I had never met and whom I have never seen since arrived at my father's funeral. The man handled the situation tastefully and disappeared appropriately. I was tearfully impressed.

IBM was under contract to the National Aeronautics and Space Administration (NASA) to support a group of satellites with computer systems and related analysis. My Federal Systems Division, located in Riverdale, Maryland, had two or three hundred people working on that contract. Basically what our group did was support scientific and weather satellite missions.

Other NASA and contractor people did all the work that resulted in liftoff; my group worked with NASA to figure out where the satellites were, what they were doing and seeing, what commands had to be sent to make them move the right way, and where they were going to land or burn up when gravity took its inevitable toll and they hit the atmosphere.

We built and operated the computer systems that resulted in the weather showing up on the evening news. We supported the launches of frogs and monkeys, but no people. We made sure that the scientists who studied solar flares or went looking for black holes or tried to map the moon got the data that they needed. It was neat stuff and there were never enough people to do it.

IBM had recruited us from all over the country. We had been educated as musicians, linguists, mathematicians, physicists, engineers, and the like. We were male and female, black, white, yellow, and red. We wore business suits, blue jeans, mustaches, beards, long hair, and crew cuts. (Pantsuits were only initially and only mildly controversial.)

I had the impression that the demand for technical people so far exceeded the supply that our group might have included green chimpanzees wearing tennis shoes had they been technically qualified. To this day, I fail to understand the view of IBM as a group of blue-suited, white-shirted, uptight conservatives. My view of the culture was captured by an expression frequently used by Frank Hughes, my first IBM manager: "Let the wild ducks fly."

My office mate, like myself, was educated as a mathematician and had a master's degree. Alva Butcher was a tall, slender, Fulbright Scholar, homecoming queen from the Northwest. Although she and I were, for all practical purposes, theoretical physicists apprenticed to IBM's Ph.D. chief scientist, we had vague titles that sounded like senior associate systems analyst. We pushed equations.

It was a good thing that we hit it off personally from the start because equation pushing was a lonely business. We spent little time with anyone other than each other. She reviewed my equations and I reviewed hers. Occasionally the chief scientist reviewed all the equations. We had lots of intellectual fun but little of the gratification that comes from seeing results.

We never knew if the mathematical models we developed were of any use. It was pretty hard to determine because our equations described things that were close to immeasurable. Some of the equations, as an example, modeled the effects of the pressure of molecules that were radiated by the sun and bombarded onto the surface of satellites that orbited reasonably close to the earth.

Satellites in near-earth orbits are dramatically affected by the earth's gravitational field, somewhat affected by the earth's magnetic field, and barely affected by solar radiation pressure. If, therefore, one of the near-earth orbiting satellites moved in some unexpected, peculiar manner, we never knew if it was because we made an error or because gravity or magnetism overpowered the situation.

The rapport that developed at work carried over into our personal lives. Alva and her husband, Bruce, lived not far from me in College Park. We regularly found ourselves together at their place or mine for dinner. We all liked simple modern furniture, classical music, and good conversation. They had traveled widely as members of the Peace Corps. We differed on matters of faith. I was a Presbyterian, from a long line of Presbyterians; they were both practicing Roman Catholics.

Bruce was an attorney, educated in the liberal arts tradition, who had no great interest or background in the details of matters technical or mathematical, but who would and could debate any subject from any point of view. Furthermore, he loved debate per se.

I sometimes believed he pushed intellectual argument to the point of irritation, particularly Catholic theology, but he was easy to forgive on that point because he was kind, supportive, and generally well intentioned. When I learned how to duck Catholic issues, we managed to avoid theological debates and engage in conversations on a wide range of more interesting subjects.

Eventually Alva and Bruce gave their beat-up old Ford to the Catholic church and moved back home to the Northwest, by train because Bruce had a diagnosable anxiety about flying. Alva came back to my wedding (by train). She and Bruce have a large number of children. I still talk to her by phone every few months. Over the years, she has greatly furthered my understanding of my dyslexic son by recounting her experiences with hers.

The loss of their company was not compounded by the loneliness of being an equation pusher. By the time Alva left IBM, I had become a project manager on one of the satellite support systems.

Project management and teamwork were what kept all those wild ducks flying toward the same destination and landing on the same intermediate ponds. The imbalance between supply and demand for technical people created an even greater imbalance in the number of people able to manage technical activities. Although I was inexperienced, IBM gave me a project to manage, partly because I was bright, but largely because there was no one more experienced available.

What I lacked in personal experience, I made every effort to overcome with the experience and insight of others: I read. I read every internal IBM publication I could find on project management. I subscribed to *Business Week,* the *Wall Street Journal, Forbes, Fortune,* and the *For-*

tune book-of-the-month club. If I liked a management book written by an author, I read everything else he wrote. I became well informed about management long before I became skilled.

This project management stuff was fun I thought. The six or seven of us on the team all had different skills, no one of which would get the job done alone. Everything that each of us did affected the others. If the system that we put together crashed and burned, the individual brilliance of each of us would be subsumed in the flames of the failure. My job was to do whatever it took for the team to meet its objectives.

As a team, we had to compensate for the weaknesses of each individual and thereby make the team stronger than any of its members. My team quickly discovered my most obvious and glaring weakness: I was unable easily to add, let alone subtract, multiply, or divide. This glaring weakness related to conventional number skills was a crippling inadequacy in the computer field where the numbers were usually expressed in binary (base two) or, worse, in hexadecimal (base sixteen).

To compensate for my numerical inadequacy, my people did two things. First, they relieved me of responsibility for most work that required numerical calculations and then checked the occasional calculations that I made. Second, they presented me with a hexadecimal calculator, taught me how to use it, and insisted that it remain on my desk next to the conventional calculator. I compensated by exercising inordinate care whenever I had to do arithmetic.

NASA put the follow-on work to the contract on which I had become a fledgling project manager out for competitive bids. IBM lost. I was young, ambitious, and nearsighted. When Frank Hughes left IBM to join the new contractor, Computer Sciences Corporation (CSC), I agreed to join him on the condition that I could take a couple of months off when we got settled in our new jobs. It seemed like a good idea at the time, but I later regretted the decision on several occasions after comparative experience taught me that IBM was a remarkably progressive, flexible organization, especially given the 240,000-person behemoth that it was in my day.

When Frank and I started to work under the new contract, we were a department of two with requirements for a staff of seventy or eighty. Few IBMers were inclined to bail out of Big Blue, as it was known, to join the competition. We soon discovered that raiding IBM staff was like trying to attract rats to a sinking ship. So I learned how to recruit. We were able to put together a team of wonderful people.

By the time we saw the end of recruiting in sight, it was early summer 1971. I packed up George and the camping gear and headed north again. It took almost a month to get to Alaska. The weather was better than it had been on my camping trip with Brother. Although I had five flat tires on the round-trip over the Denali Road to Mt. McKinley, the trip north was generally uneventful; not so the trip back south.

More than a hundred miles south of Fort St. John in northern British Columbia I encountered a boulder three or four feet wide. Dislodged from the hillside, it had rolled onto the road where I hit it as I came around the curve that hid it from my sight. The impact of car on stone removed the boulder from the road and left the two front wheels of my Chevy Nova treading air. George and I worked our way through the rear window with the help of an ax stowed with the camping gear on the back seat.

Although it was dusk, it was late. As I scrounged around to find stuff to build a fire to make smoke to summon the Mounties, I was picked up by what had to be the only other car on the road for fifty miles. In the wee hours of the morning, my rescuers dropped me at the Mountie Station in Fort St. James, a tiny town near the border between British Columbia and Alberta. I could tell from his demeanor and body language that the duty Mountie regarded me as undesirable. (I did look a little ratty.) George saved the day by wandering around the barrier counter that separated me from the Mountie, whimpering wistfully, and wagging her Pekingese tail. The Mountie made reservations for me at the local hotel, drove me there, and escorted me to my room.

It was a more than a week before the Chevy was declared a total wreck. The body shop had to send a crane to pull the car out and bring it back to town. Then it was hunting time: the time when the body shop owners stocked the family freezers. The insurance claims adjuster, in conjunction with my insurance company, had to study the excise tax consequences of junking the car in Canada. When all the details were settled, the body shop owners gave me a ride to Edmonton, Alberta, where I got a flight home.

I decided not to buy another car. Being carless was no problem at CSC. I lived across the street from the office in Silver Spring. Grocery store runs and routine errands I handled by bicycle. When that became tedious, I bought a 70-cc Suzuki motor scooter, which I eventually upgraded to a motorcycle.

For the eighteen months I spent at CSC, I worked for Frank Hughes. I modeled my management style on his. He was a terrific manager and team builder. As a Ph.D.-dropout in crystal physics, he could speak credibly with the Ph.D.'s on the staff. He was an orphan, had been in reform school, and had always fended for himself, but he assumed the Big Blue image that he valued: short, well-groomed hair, white shirt, dark suit, black shoes. The diversity of education, image, and background made it easy for him to deal with a wide range of working levels from key punch (data entry) operators to NASA executives.

He rolled up his shirt sleeves and worked with his people. He treasured and took care of them. Good performers were promoted to the next level as quickly as they could handle it. Consistent failure to perform resulted in removal, by transfer or termination.

He was fair. When I observed that Yangja Kim, a Korean woman with very good performance ratings, was paid five thousand dollars per year less than all the rest of the staff at her level, he had it fixed. She got a startling raise to twelve thousand dollars. She and I became friends to the extent that I attended her wedding, and she presented my daughter Tela with a baby spoon and fork at birth. She has listed me as a reference on her employment applications over the years. Based on the last one that I completed, she now works for the federal government.

Frank's clients trusted him. One of his Ph.D.'s wrote an uninterpretable academic report, several hundreds of pages long and consisting largely of equations. It failed to answer the central question that the client, Roger Werking, wanted addressed. Roger clearly expressed his dissatisfaction, expletives undeleted. Frank made no excuses, blamed no one, accepted responsibility for the problem. He and Roger agreed that if Frank would insert a single page at the front of the report that correctly answered the question, Roger would pay for the report. Frank declared that he would never again embarrass Roger with a rambling academic exercise. Absent trust, there might have been a lawsuit. The Ph.D. disappeared from the department.

Frank surrounded himself with smart people who were comfortable disagreeing with him. As a group, the members of Frank's department were generally not reluctant to express themselves to each other. When I summarized my assessment of Mike Rosen at the end of an interview by telling him that he "had tremendous potential" and we were going to offer him a job, his flatly stated response was "potential can only be measured in physics." I was startled. He was blunt but right. Nevertheless, he was hired and got terrific results. I learned to count on him to provide the ungarnished truth to technical questions. Mike and his wife are in the San Francisco area now. I still think fondly of him when word about his current work drifts back through the grapevine.

Most of us were young, gung ho for what we did, and occasionally oblivious to all around us. During testing of one system, a member of the staff tested screen processing by playfully displaying a message on the launch monitor referring to his team manager as "a prick." No one realized the message was picked up by closed-circuit television and displayed all over the Goddard Space Flight Center until the client, amused, suggested that we select better test messages.

To guide the young turks, there were a few older, wiser, more mature professionals around. They typically had gray, thinning hair, quiet dispositions, and titles like "project scientist." I had seen them in the mission control room on half a dozen occasions when satellites were launched. They usually sat quietly, in a straight-backed chair, with a clipboard supported by one leg crossed over the other. Slide rule in one hand and pencil in the other, they doodled equations on the clipboard, fiddled with the slide rule, and then repeated the process. After a few hours their absence was noticeable, but they never seemed to have any discernible role in the launch-related activities.

Although I worked in various capacities with a lot of satellites, I was responsible for only one, the first of the series of Small Astronomy Satellites. The series was nicknamed SAS, as in sassy. As the first in the series, my particular SAS was hyphenated with an A to become SAS-A. The major instrument on SAS-A was a mathematically simple but technologically very sophisticated star sensor, so named because it noticed energy related to stars that passed through its field of vision as it spun around on the satellite.

SAS-A was scheduled to be launched from the Nairobi platform in the Indian Ocean off the coast of Africa, as it happened on my birthday, a week before Christmas. Because of political unrest in Africa and concerns about sabotage, the satellite was apparently shipped to the launch site in crates labeled in a language other than English.

The satellite was eventually renamed Uhuru, a Swahili word meaning "peace." The NASA project officer was in Africa overseeing the liftoff and in close communication with the primary tracking station there. The secondary tracking station was in Quito, Ecuador. My team was in a control room at the Goddard Space Flight Center near Washington.

We were scared to death. Our job was to interpret the data relayed to us by the primary and secondary tracking systems, to compute where the star sensor was pointing, to predict where the star sensor would be pointing over the next orbit or so, and to figure out what commands had to be relayed back to the satellite to keep it pointing in the right direction. We had built and tested all the computer systems from scratch. If something went wrong with any of the many new elements of our system, we would be responsible for a multimillion-dollar piece of space junk. At all costs, we had to avoid the sun. If the delicate star sensor caught sight of the sun, it would burn out, go blind, and the mission would be over.

Assuming that a lot of other people did their jobs and there were no major equipment blowups, the first critical point where the sun would be a threat was when the satellite went into its initial orbit around the earth. If all went as planned, the star sensor should be safely scanning in a plane perpendicular to the line of sight to the sun.

We could never count on conformance to plan, however, so immediately after launch there would be a scramble to compute the initial pointing direction. If anything went wrong with the data traveling in waves around the world or with the primary, secondary, or backup computer systems that processed it, we could be in serious trouble. That was where the quiet, seasoned project scientist came in. If all else failed, he computed the answer with his slide rule and pencil. He was the ultimate backup.

A second critical point occurred any time we tried to maneuver the satellite to change the field of vision of the star sensor. Sending a command back through the tracking stations and to the onboard computer was complicated. Even more complicated was the trial and error algorithm that figured out when and for how long to turn on the coils that changed the satellite's magnetic field. It was the interaction of the onboard magnetic field with that of the earth that changed the satellite's orientation. A member of our team, Stan Croyden, would have to worry about that when the time came for the first maneuver.

Tom King, the public voice of Apollo was all I could think of. Here I was, Ann Branigar Hopkins, the voice of SAS-A—actually, only half the voice. John Snyder, the number-two person on the team, was the other half. Our situation was not quite as glamorous as Tom King's had seemed to me. Instead of nationwide television coverage, we had two squawk boxes, one connected us to Quito and the other to the liftoff folks in Africa. The launch clock that Apollo's television audience never saw but that Tom King frequently referred to was a computer monitor hung from the ceiling. In light-gray numbers on a dark-gray background, minutes to liftoff were listed with tasks in terse text next to them.

John and I idly observed that we had 120 minutes to liftoff as we nervously hung around the monitor. The operations team were all assembled, seated in front of their respective computer terminals. Stan was pacing around somewhere, ready to crank up his trial and error control system if SAS-A started out pointing in the wrong direction. We waited. I had a project checklist that specified when and what each member of the team was supposed to do. My checklist started at forty-five minutes and counting.

Africa squawked something unintelligible. Quito squawked for a repeat. There was something wrong with the launch clock. Expletives squawked from everywhere as the launch clock dropped to twenty minutes and counting. For one brief moment, I panicked. We were twenty-five minutes behind schedule coming out of the starting gate.

John stayed cool. In the years that we worked together, I never saw any overt signs of concern in John. He was a few years younger than I, pale complected, medium height, approaching skinny. His full head of straight, wispy, dirty blond hair tended to curl evenly up from his collar when he needed a haircut, like he did then. We had worked long hours for weeks. John was cerebral around computers; he always put his hands in his lap, stared at the information displayed on the terminal, and thought about what he was doing before he touched the keyboard. Even then, he reread what he typed before he hit the enter key. He was careful.

John sat down in a hurry to crank up the system. NASA had changed versions of the operating system on the computer the night before. The control language that John typed produced an unexpected error message. As he meticulously reviewed what appeared on the screen, the only sign of stress was the increased rate at which he smoked Camels.

Unable to do John's job, I was powerless even to help. I focused on staying out of John's way by getting the rest of the team back on the scheduled track while John reviewed error messages.

"How about a cup of coffee?" John asked lightly ten minutes later as he hit the enter key and everything cranked up the way it was supposed to. We communicated the end of the crisis with an unspoken eyeball-to-eyeball look recognizable only to us, a couple of friends who had worked together closely in trying times.

The project scientist went home without using his slide rule that day.

John and I worked sixteen hours a day in shifts that overlapped four hours on each end. At the end of his first shift, John retired to what was known as the bomb shelter, where he sacked out for eight hours on one of several cots arranged in rows, each cot neatly covered with an olive-green army blanket.

By the time John returned, less than completely refreshed, Stan was at work with a light pen and his trial and error program, plotting curves that zigged and zagged across a computer monitor to represent the motion of the satellite. A touch of the light pen told the computer program which commands to use and which to ignore. When Stan decided on a set of commands to be sent to SAS-A, John and I agreed on the operational procedures to be followed to execute them. With that my shift ended.

It was my turn to retire. I asked John where to go, followed his instructions to the bomb shelter, fell onto the nearest empty cot, and slept soundly. On awakening, I went looking for a vending machine. Roger Werking joined me as I drank a cup of very hot, overly salty, yellow flecked with green parsley specks chicken soup from a paper cup.

"I don't know how to explain this," he said sheepishly, "but you spent the night in the wrong bomb shelter." All I could do was laugh as Roger explained that there were both boys' and girls' bomb shelters and that the security force had been upset at discovering my presence on one of the cots in the bomb shelter normally reserved for males.

"No problem, Roger. Tonight, I sleep in the girls' bomb shelter." That, however, was easier said than done. When the time for my next respite arrived and I inquired about the location of the girls' bomb shelter, I was referred to the security force.

It took almost an hour to contact security, arrange for an escort to the sleeping quarters, sign in, and receive instructions on how to get out at the end of my increasingly shorter naptime. I was securely locked in. To get out the next morning the process was reversed: I called security; the guard came and let me out; I signed out; and so on.

John wondered first why I was grumpy, and second why I was late.

For the remainder of my tenure as the voice of SAS-A, I slept in the boys' bomb shelter—I was just going to have to take my chances of being raped, and security was just going to have to humor me. Uhuru was a success and was written up in *Scientific American* as one of the first experimental missions to confirm the existence of black holes.

When aerospace began its decline, I got out as did most of us. John works for an insurance broker in Baltimore. He and his wife raise horses in their spare time. Stan earned a law degree and went to work for the federal government. Roger went to work for one of NASA's contractors.

"What's a Big Eight?" I asked Tom Carter. I envisioned a college football conference. Tom had scheduled a job interview for me with one of the Big Eight. After more than five years in the aerospace end of the computer industry, beginning with the prominent, first-class International Business Machines Corporation and moving to progressively smaller, outfits, I was looking for a job. The year was 1974.

Tom Carter was a recruiter whom I had used to hire dozens of data processing professionals in the years after I left IBM. It seemed logical that he should help me find a new position. I wanted out: out of aerospace, out of small business, and out of sleazy beltway bandits, as the here-today-gone-tomorrow government contractors that ringed the Washington beltway were called. I had told him so. His charge from me was to find a first-class company, not involved in aerospace, that would give me a chance to manage projects to develop computer systems.

Tom was patient with my naïveté and ignorance as he explained that the Big Eight were eight international accounting firms, all partnerships, which, taken as a group, audit the financial statements of "just about any corporation a prudent investor would ever buy stock in." When the largest corporations in the world hired professional firms to build computer systems, they frequently selected from among the Big Eight. Touche Ross and Co. (the Co. stood for copartners, not company) was one of the Big Eight and Tom had arranged an interview for me on Saturday at eight in the morning. Could I go, he asked. The die was cast.

The Friday night poker game with the gang from the office ended at about two in the morning. When I got up I needed a shower to help bring the world into focus. From what Tom had said, conservatism was the word for the day, so I put on a black knit Saks Fifth Avenue suit with gold buttons and silk leopard-patterned lining and a conservative blouse and stepped into appropriate, scuff-free, black Ferragamo's. I dragged my snowmobile suit and motorcycle helmet out of the closet, zipped and snapped myself in, and took the Rock Creek Parkway downtown. Fortunately, it was not raining. I hated riding the motorcycle in the rain.

I have always been compulsive about being on time so it was an anxious ride. Although I lived in Washington and had lived there for several years, I never worked downtown and I did most of my chores and socializing in the Maryland suburbs. To my relief, it only took ten minutes to get downtown and find the area around the Touche offices at Eighteenth and K streets. It was deserted at half past seven, and I had no trouble finding a parking lot. Normally, I would have parked at the curb. Under the circumstances, however, I was concerned that I might be spotted by some member of my future employer as I shed my motorcycle gear on the street. I parked in the lot and left the bike and related paraphernalia under the supervision of an amused parking lot attendant.

A pleasant young woman greeted me in the reception area of the Touche offices in the heart of downtown where the firm occupied several floors. She provided me with a schedule that showed times and names of interviewers in columnar format. The times ran nonstop in thirty-minute intervals until noon. There were no titles for the interviewers. They were, by their names, all men. I took a seat in the reception room with two other women and a couple of men and waited, but not for long. Precisely according to schedule, the doors of the reception area opened and each of our columnarly specified interviewers introduced himself.

A well-groomed, carefully dressed man in a dark suit and tie, wing tips, and a white shirt escorted me down a narrow hall with boxes of business files neatly stacked on both sides, to a small office with standardized but tasteful furniture and fixtures. He expressed a genuine desire to give me any information that I needed for the interview process. Speaking as if he had told the tale before, he identified the Big Eight by name: Arthur Andersen, Arthur Young, Coopers and Lybrand, Ernst and Whinney, Haskins and Sells, Peat Marwick and Mitchell, Price Waterhouse, and Touche Ross. He then described the consulting hierarchy at Touche. In ascending order, there were associates, senior associates, managers, and partners. That was it. The exhaustive list of professional positions included only four titles.

He explained that the business area of an individual was sometimes used as a modifier of the position title to explain what the individual did—tax associates did tax work; audit associates did audit work; consulting associates did consulting work. He also explained that partners were not employees. They owned the partnership that employed everyone else. As a detail, he observed that a partner who had not earned a CPA was technically entitled a principal and was prohibited from signing certain audit documents. The distinction was lost on me but I concluded that most people who had ownership interests in the partnership and did consulting work were principals, not partners. No matter what they were called, partners or principals, they held the risks and opportunities, assets and liabilities of the partnership. They were owners.

He also explained a whole new vocabulary. Touche Ross and Co. was not the partnership or a company, it was the firm. There was no such thing as a customer—the Big Eight equivalent was a client. A client did not hire a Big Eight firm, we were engaged, occasionally retained by our clients. Jobs or contracts were referred to as projects or engagements. It all sounded a little stuffy to me. But I incorporated the new terminology into my vocabulary. After a while it came out naturally.

The interviewers changed with the precision of the Buckingham Palace Guards according to the interview schedule. Although no one stood up and left in midsentence, it was clear that they were keeping to a timetable and did not intend to waste their time or mine by moving me from office to office. I sat in the same office all morning as the interviewers changed.

Because I had run out of intelligent-sounding, riskless questions with the first interviewer, I spent most of the next two or three interviews responding to questions. I described how IBM had recruited me and a number of my students on campus at Hollins. We discussed the nuances of FORTRAN, basic assembler language, machine language, and operating systems that IBM taught me in three or four months of basic programmer training. In the interview context I found it hard to explain my work as a theoretical physicist developing mathematical models to predict the motion of scientific and weather satellites for NASA. It was easier when we got past the more technical aspects of computer systems and started discussing management. I had read every book I could find on management and had been managing teams of people that developed computer systems for several years.

The men who were interviewing me managed projects. Many of the projects were related to computer systems and required selecting, organizing, and supervising analysts, designers, programmers, and other professionals to develop computer systems that did the right thing and got finished within time and budget constraints. The only difference between them and me was that they worked largely on business systems and I had worked largely on scientific systems. I started to see the job fit and hoped that they also did.

Tom Carter had not told me anything about the interview process. I should have asked. As I wondered who the decision maker was and what I could do to enhance my chances of joining the firm, the final interviewer arrived and introduced himself as Bill Atkins. He had a riveting manner, never lost eye contact, focused on whatever subject he was discussing, and dragged you back to the point whenever you tried to change the subject on him. He was all business and very serious, but he had a mercurial smile and expressive eyes that reminded me of a mischievous child. I liked him, and although all the titleless interviewers appeared to me to be about the same in terms of size, shape, dress, demeanor, age, and style, there was something noticeably different about Bill. After responding to a few of his questions, I decided to ask him who the decision maker was, how I was doing, and what he thought.

I was a little startled when he evasively told me that after the interviews were over, all the interviewers would get together and vote. Because the votes were still out, he said, how I was doing was imponderable. That did not resolve the decision maker question. I wondered how ties were broken. Bill, however, looked like a man not to be pushed, so I backed off. Instead, I asked him how he thought I was doing. I do not remember his response, but an hour later I had a job at Touche Ross and Co.

I started to work at Touche in March 1974. My first project for the firm was a payroll and personnel system for one of the regulatory banking agencies in town. The partner on the job was Bill Atkins. He was actually a principal—an owner who was not a CPA—but he had the distinction of being called "the Owner."

I was assigned to an office, called the bull pen, that I shared with seven other associate consultants. Two of my office mates were women who had been interviewed on the same day I was. The office contained six desks, but there were never more than three or four people in the office, so the numerical discrepancy between the number of people and the number of desks was not a problem. After a while I recognized the informal hierarchy in the bull pen: the people who occupied the desks toward the front of the office near the door had been around longer, hence had seniority over, the people who had desks toward the back of the office.

Marriage

At Touche, my desk was well toward the back of the bull pen. It took several months for me to get to know the names of my office colleagues because most of us were not in town simultaneously. There was one exception. One of the front desks was regularly occupied by a youngish-looking, bespectacled, not short, not tall, redheaded man. He had facial scars that remained from a bad case of adolescent acne. His hair, which showed no sign of a part, might have been described as an Afro in 1974, except for the fact that he was white. He wore the most dreadful shirts I had ever seen. He did not look like the men I had met at the interviews.

When I first met him, he was separating stacks of multipart computer printouts that had three or four carbon sheets between the copies. One by one he separated the carbons from the paper copies by unfolding a foot-high pile into stacks of paper on his desk and rumpled carbons into a neighboring trash can. At NASA, machines called decollators performed that function. He seemed to catch the humor when I offhandedly commented that what he was doing could be more efficiently done by a machine. His name was Thomas Peter Gallagher.

It was my custom to arrive at the office early—at 6:30 or 7:00. In graduate school I adopted an abused, unhealthy, two-month-old Pekingese puppy. I named her Lucile Aurore Dupin Dudevant, George Sand. George taught me that I could avoid messes in my apartment by walking her around the Bloomington town square before 6:00 in the morning. When George and I moved east, I eventually gave the dog to my sister in Boston, but I never got over the habit of getting up very early.

29

Thomas Peter seldom showed up before 9:30 or 10:00. By 6:30 in the evening, when I was ready to quit after a long day, he was ready to break for dinner. He and I had dinner together twenty-seven consecutive nights.

He was the youngest child and only son of Catholic parents. His grandparents emigrated from Ireland to Missouri and Illinois. One sister was a Dominican nun at a convent in Springfield; the other worked in Philadelphia where his mother lived. He was born and grew up in Michigan. His father, deceased, had retired as a regional sales manager for Burroughs (now Unisys) in Philadelphia. He had gone to high school under the watchful eyes of the Jesuits. He majored in English at the University of Pennsylvania and toured the British Isles on a Triumph motorcycle with a sidecar while he earned a master's degree at Edinburgh. He had worked for a low-income housing developer in Philadelphia, where he married a librarian named Rachel. He had been separated for the six or eight months since he had come to Washington to work for Touche. He drove a beat-up Plymouth station wagon referred to as the "Beige Eminence."

In April, a little more than a month after we met, we went to visit my old Hollins College teacher Julie Randall at her home in Hartford County, just outside of Baltimore. While driving through the Baltimore tunnel on our way back, we decided to get married. We were unable to schedule the wedding until he formally divorced Rachel. In the District of Columbia, that would take at least six months.

We were a little nervous about policy implications of being married staff in the same office so we kept our intentions to ourselves. I was more than a little nervous about telling my mother and stepfather. Thomas Peter was the wrong religion and did not fit Mom's image of the man to marry—a socially prominent, educated professional. I was happy to keep the matter a private affair.

In the meanwhile, I was assigned to a project to develop a management information system for the Chicago mayor's Office of Manpower, aptly named MOM. Thomas Peter was working on a national survey of housing projects for the Department of Housing and Urban Development. While I commuted to Chicago, he wandered around the country.

Most weekends we worked in the garden at my house in Chevy Chase, D.C., but occasionally we took advantage of our travel schedules and spent a weekend out West. On one such occasion we went to the Frontier Days rodeo. Representatives of tribes of the Indian nations sold their wares in ramshackle booths around the fairgrounds. The bright sun in cloudless sky gave the still day a sparkle. We exchanged silver-and-turquoise bands made by the Indians and called them engagement rings.

There were no women on the consulting staff above the rank of associate, and I recall no unmarried women among the associates. Needless to say, marriages between members of the consulting staff were unusual. When we returned to the bull pen with our Indian "engagement rings" our intentions became obvious. It was great fun to watch the shocked, surprised, or excited expressions on people's faces when they heard the news or came to us to confirm the rumors. The overall excitement was enhanced when Tom and I were both promoted to senior associate consultants, along with several others from the bull pen.

Bob Woodward had entitled his book about the justices of the U.S. Supreme Court *The Brethren*. The title was apt at the time. My mother must have read it because it was on my bedside table at the cottage on Cape Cod where she and Gil were staying for a vacation. Thomas Peter and I had gone up to spend the long holiday weekend with them.

The purpose of our visit, as I saw it, was for Thomas Peter to ask Gil's permission to marry me. That was the southern protocol, and I was a Texan, which made me at least part southern. Thomas Peter, not well versed in matters southern, chose instead to tell Gil that we would be married and that the wedding would take place the day after Thanksgiving in Washington, where it would be most convenient for us and our friends. Mom and Gil would have much preferred that we be married at home, either in Nyack, New York, where they lived summers or Winter Park, Florida, where they wintered. When I went to bed, I tossed sleeplessly. I was upset by my mother's polite but less than enthusiastic reaction to the wedding. Reading about Justices White, Brennan, Marshall, and the workings of the Supreme Court kept my mind off my worries for most of the two nights we spent on the Cape.

That fall Thomas Peter and I each had two projects to manage: one for the client and one for the wedding. Half the ushers were former occupants of the bull pen. The other half were Brother John, Jeff Baldwin, the partner Thomas Peter worked for, and Mike Curzan, a senior partner at Arnold and Porter, a prominent Washington law firm. Thomas Peter's wedding project included whatever it took to deal with ushers, the rehearsal dinner, the wedding trip, and the budget. My project was anything to do with bridesmaids, out-of-towners, flowers, transportation to and from the church, and my mother.

Mom and Gil were stuck with handling a church wedding and a reception long distance. Washington was not, however, unfamiliar to them. Both Gil and my father had spent time in Washington. My family had lived in Washington for most of the time I was in college. It was reasonably convenient to arrange for the wedding at the chapel at Fort Meyer, the army post that surrounds Arlington Cemetery. They chose the officer's club for the reception.

I had never been either a bridesmaid or a bride before, so I delegated most of my work to my only in-town bridesmaid, Sally Keene Craig. She and I had been classmates at Hollins. She seemed to know a lot more about what to do than I did. For decisions like the price range for the bridesmaids' dresses, she asked me to decide. Once the decisions were made, however, she told me and the rest of the female component of the wedding party what we had to do and when we had to do it. I never even knew, let alone worried about, how the bridesmaids had their dresses fitted, or which florist was supposed to deliver the flowers to what location, or what made the limousine appear in front of the house at the right time. Sally Keene just handled it, calmly, patiently, gracefully, and always with a sense of humor.

I managed my project. Thomas Peter managed his. Neither of us meddled in the other's area of responsibility. I was unaware of where we were going on our wedding trip until just before we left for the Virgin Islands. He won the prize for budgetary management—he estimated the rehearsal dinner at $900, and although the number of people who were going to be there changed daily until the night of the dinner, the final bill was $900.01.

With few exceptions, the wedding was a very successful project. Mike Curzan had a head cold that made his nose look like that of a circus clown. He almost missed the wedding. The Owner and his wife were delayed coming back from Mexico and arrived late at the reception. The car keys, Thomas Peter's tuxedo, and the wedding rings were locked in the Beige Eminence at the rehearsal dinner. Bini Herrmann, another college classmate of mine, did not flinch at being assigned the task of solving the problem. The next day Thomas Peter was wearing his tuxedo at the altar where I gave him the wedding ring with "Fuzzy Redhead" engraved on the inside. The Beige Eminence was parked in front of the house when we got back from the Virgin Islands. It was months before Bini told me all that she had to do to make that happen.

Miners

The United Mine Workers of America (UMWA), the miners' union, was the subject of scandal and litigation in the early 1970s, part of which related to mishandling of the trust funds that paid medical, pension, and other benefits to miners and their dependents. The manager of the trust funds was the United Mine Workers Health and Retirement Funds, an organization independent of the union.

At the end of the litigation, the Funds brought in a brand new director. He had to replace many obsolete manual and computer systems that were key to the operation of the Funds. Touche was engaged to replace the systems that kept records for eligible beneficiaries and paid the medical and pension benefits for those who were eligible. Price Waterhouse, another of the Big Eight accounting firms, was the auditor for the Funds.

With my senior associate consultant stripes barely attached and with marginal mastery of the vocabulary of the Big Eight, I became the project manager for one of two projects for the Funds. My project, to build a medical claims processing system, was named Mines—the term stood for something like medical information and evaluation system. (Computer systems always have to have apt names.) Another senior associate, Dennis Fennessey, was project manager in charge of building a system, aptly named Benefits, to maintain the eligibility records and pay pension benefits. Dennis's system and mine were completely independent except for one point: before Mines could cut a check to pay a medical claim, it had to check with Benefits to make sure that the claim was made by an eligible beneficiary. Dennis and I reported to a consulting manager named Jim McCoy. We all reported to Bill Atkins, "the Owner."

Until I started working on Mines, I believed that Bill Atkins got that nickname by virtue of his remarkable presence, ability to focus, and general brainpower. On Mines, I learned that he, along with a couple of other Touche partners had written a book that described a way of managing projects to build computer systems. At IBM it would have been called a project management methodology. At Touche it was called "the Book." I never knew how projects to build computer systems were managed in the hinterlands of Touche, but in Washington such projects were managed by the Book, especially if the Owner was the partner on the project.

There were, however, *two* books that were mandatory reading requirements on Mines and Benefits: The Book and a remarkable history, *John L. Lewis and the International Union, United Mine Workers of America: The Story from 1917 to 1952.* The Book influenced how I did what I did. The history gave me the reason for doing it. The Book I assimilated and internalized, and to this day it is a part of how I do business. Although it is out of print, I have a copy of it on the bookshelf in my office and still refer to it. The history remains with me in my soul and spirit and sensitivities. It told of crippled, disabled, sick miners, all over Appalachia being carried out of shacks with nothing but outhouses to the Appalachian regional medical system that the UMWA and the Funds established. There were major clinics and hospitals in the coal mining areas of this country where miners and their dependents were a huge part of the population served. (Coincidentally I had my appendix removed on my twenty-first birthday in a hospital that was originally one of the Appalachian regional hospitals.)

The Owner had a speech that he gave to green staff, in which he explained the five criteria by which he defined a successful engagement: you had to make money, learn some things, teach people some things, do a quality job that was perceived as a quality job, and you had to have fun. He usually went on to say that these five criteria were listed in descending order of importance—first you had to have fun!

I loved the job. It was fun. A lot of the fun was introduced into what I did by the crazy man who was the client and the director of the UMWA Health and Retirement Funds, Martin B. Danziger. Marty, as he was called, was an attorney. He had worked for Attorney General Elliot

Richardson and resigned when Mr. Richardson and a number of his top staff left the Justice Department over an integrity issue. Marty had a Mr. Clean reputation, which was probably one of the reasons that he was made director of the Funds.

Marty was, however, a bit eccentric. He rode his bicycle down the Rock Creek Parkway to work, usually before seven in the morning, and parked it in the boiler room at the Funds' office building downtown. In the summer, he wore shorts to ride his bicycle and changed into a business suit in his office. Like many attorneys, he maintained an adversarial relationship with the firms that the Funds engaged or retained. He basically did not trust outsiders. Partly for that reason and partly because of a shortage of office space, I had an office in an open bay outside of Marty's office. There could never be any question about the number of hours that Touche billed the Funds for my services—Marty could see me when he came in and when he went out. I was known as "Danziger's dog"; I guarded his office door.

I adored the man. He was smart, aggressive, had a clear sense of where he was going, and he would tell you exactly what he thought about any issue. He was not always right, but he spoke his mind—and he was unbothered by being wrong.

I was one of the few people who dealt with Marty personally. He almost always kept people at arm's length. Marty and his wife, Joan, who was and is a prominent Washington artist, bought the oldest house in Cleveland Park, the next neighborhood uptown from where I live. The house was originally the farmhouse on the land that developed into the neighborhood. The grounds were darkly shaded by old trees, many of them evergreen. At some point, just after they moved in, I surveyed Marty's garden and told him, quite definitively, that he could not grow radishes and that he should not even try. I forgot all about it.

Six or eight weeks later, I was sitting at my desk, concentrating intensely on reviewing some technical document very early in the morning. Marty's arrival in his bicycle shorts went unnoticed until a clump of radishes, complete with greens and dirt bounced off my desk onto the floor as he said, "Don't tell me that you can't grow radishes in Washington." I acknowledged my error by eating the radishes after wiping off most of the dirt and ignoring the greens.

We made lots of errors, as all professionals do. Fortunately, none that I remember was uncorrectable. Also fortunately, both the Owner and Marty expected some level of error—and the consequences of making an error were not bad if you identified the error and proposed a fix or asked for help. Covering up could be career ending.

At the beginning of the project, there was not much chance of making errors. We looked at what other organizations with similar functions did, such as the Medicare and Medicaid processing units in Michigan and Virginia. We went to the Funds' field offices to interview people to find out what they did and what the field office people thought was wrong.

Because we looked at several organizations doing medical claims processing, if we missed something with one, we picked it up with another. Similarly, the field offices were enough alike that if we missed something one place, we picked it up at another. And we went to a lot of places. From Pennsylvania to West Virginia to Colorado, I went to field offices and listened to the people tell me about medical claims payments. But they also talked about the community and the miners and the clinics and the hospitals and the working conditions. They talked about black lung disease and emphysema and cave-ins. They described the consequences to the miners and their dependents of late payments, no payments, and other system errors. It was clear to me that the system we built had to make things better, not just for the accountants back in Washington but for the beneficiaries out in the coal fields.

The real opportunity to make errors came when we finished the fieldwork, got back to Washington, and had to design the system. On one hand, we had to make sure there was enough information required on medical claims forms to pay bills in compliance with federal law and prudent accounting. On the other hand, we did not want to require anything unnecessary or that would put a burden on either the miners or on the medical facilities that provided care to them. If we asked for too little, we risked lawsuits or the horror of going back and fixing a system that served 850,000 people. If we asked for too much, we could lose the cooperation of the medical care providers that were already frustrated by late payments and stacks of paperwork.

We decided to create a unique medical claims form for providers to use to submit bills for medical services to the Funds. In terms of content, that form had to comply with whatever Medicare and Medicaid demanded because the miners were an aging population and many were covered by those programs. The form had to be easy for the medical care providers to use. The providers had to be able to send in computer tapes instead of paper if they wanted to. The form had to be designed so that the providers' computers could print on it like computer paper and the

Funds' computers could read it directly, without keypunching. We negotiated with the skeptical providers. They finally agreed to use the forms in return for assurances from the Funds that their bills would be paid faster.

A year before we were scheduled to put the new Mines into operation, my staff designed the forms that were, in turn, laid out by a design print shop on one side of town and printed by a business form printer on another. We planned to test the forms carefully in the field offices and make whatever changes were needed before we printed the final forms. I spent a month running back and forth between printers by cab. It was summer, hot and humid. I was pregnant: the odor of anything except cool, fresh air made me sick. Print shops and taxicabs made me especially sick.

I hated the technology we had to use for the system. It included some of the latest, state-of-the-art Burroughs hardware and software. I preferred IBM products, partly because I had been trained on Big Blue and partly because it was general purpose, not state-of-the-art. I had worked with state-of-the-art, leading-edge everything at NASA where there was no alternative. But I knew there was a reason why it was referred to as the "bleeding edge"—the first guys who used anything had to work out all the kinks. The guys who came a little later got the benefit of the blood, sweat, and tears that it took to work out those kinks. (The guys who came a lot later were obsolete.) The Funds had several of the first few serial numbers on a lot of types of equipment. We at Touche knew it was going to make building the systems hard.

There was always a controversy about how the Funds picked Burroughs. Marty believed the Owner had recommended it; the Owner believed the Funds had selected it because it was made by a union company. Because they were both men of integrity, I assumed there was some communication misfire that caused the difference between them. But that difference intensified the naturally adversarial relationship that stemmed from Marty's being an attorney.

My team, the Mines team, consisted of several Touche consultants, a few programmers who worked for an organization under subcontract to Touche, and a few analysts and programmers who worked for the Funds. The size of the team varied a lot depending on where we were in the system construction process. The Benefits team that Dennis managed was similar in composition.

Dennis and I had different philosophies of building systems. Dennis liked state-of-the-art. He thought it was neat. Dennis, who had been at Touche longer than I, also took the Book more seriously. I viewed it as a guide; he viewed it as the Bible. I threw it away when it seemed inappropriate. He used it more pedantically, as if doing things by the Book would relieve him of responsibility if things went wrong.

The differences in philosophy between Dennis and me were reflected in the systems we built. He used most of the published capabilities of the Burroughs hardware and software. I made my team justify the use of any capability that was not generally available, not just from Burroughs but from any hardware vendor.

Even when my team convinced me there was no technical choice other than to use some new capability, we tried to estimate how badly something could go wrong if we used it. There was one situation where Mines would be required to check the valid claims that accumulated during the week to create some complicated history files before it could write checks to pay the valid claims. Early in the system design process, I got out the Burroughs speeds and feeds manuals, so named because they quoted all the average speeds at which the equipment operated. A little arithmetic told me that six months into operation it was going to take Mines forty hours of computer time to do the weekly history check. I told Jim McCoy, the managing consultant on the project, that I was worried; this weekly historical check might run weeks. At the time he thought the calculations I used were too simplistic and dismissed them. He told me not to advertise the numbers, lest we elevate the client's hysteria level.

When Dennis and I both had to start constructing and testing our systems in the Burroughs environment, all hell broke loose. Mines, Benefits, and the routine data processing of the Funds all competed for computer time, and all lost. Every defect of the newly installed environment surfaced at the worst possible time. Every published new capability that Benefits used blew up and brought the computers crashing down the first time it was tried.

Mines could not process medical insurance claims until Benefits could identify beneficiaries eligible for medical benefits. As Benefits struggled into operation, the bottleneck on the computer worsened. Only if there was computer time left over, and there frequently was none, could Mines use the machine. To get everything we could out of the computers, my Mines team worked three shifts a day. I usually worked the better part of one evening and one night a week to keep in touch with those of my people who regularly worked the evening or night shifts. I spent a lot of time in the computer room deciding what to do when things blew up, but they were beginning to blow up less frequently.

When we could prove that a problem was due to hardware failure, Burroughs gave the Funds backup support, sometimes graciously and cooperatively, sometimes under the influence of Marty's pointed boot. But no one, not even Burroughs, had a facility like that of the Funds, so we had people flying backup tapes to Detroit and other Burroughs facilities to try to continue what we were doing while the kinks were worked out. It was a nightmare. We were not having fun.

Marty was enraged over the computer situation. About half the time he was enraged with Touche for what he imagined to be bad system design; the other half, with Burroughs for bad technology. Furthermore, he was not satisfied with his own staff's ability to deal with the situation. But he was an attorney, not a computer whiz, and he had the wisdom to recognize that he could not fix the computer mess, no matter who was at fault. He wanted to hire a new team to run the Funds' data processing organization.

The key manager on that team was Dan Maceda, a forty-year-old who looked like a cross between Burl Ives and Santa Claus. He had an unkempt goatee and a jolly figure. He was the only man I ever met who could wear an expensive, imported cashmere overcoat and still look like Columbo. And like Columbo, he was no dummy. He took the job Marty offered him, but he told Marty that he would not start to work until the day after the Mines system went into operation. He wanted to be the guy who saved the day, not the guy who got the rap for creating the mess that he expected. On October 2, 1976, Mines was committed to "go live," as we call it when you cut the umbilical cord on an old system and let the new system operate all by itself. Dan was scheduled to start on October 6.

Late in the summer, Benefits got tested and went into operation. Mines was next. One of the early steps in the going live process was to ship several truckloads of claim forms to the high-volume medical care providers. The system first had to preprint the hospital or clinic number and other identifying information on the forms. Getting the computer time required to run the hundreds of boxes of business forms through the preprinting process was difficult. The timing was also tricky. On one hand, we had to send the forms out early enough that the providers could start using them when Mines went into operation. On the other hand, we had to be sure the system worked and could work with Benefits when the forms arrived back from the providers complete with the billing information. Things looked good though. Hundreds of thousands of pin-feed computer forms had been run through Mines, pre-printed, boxed up, and addressed to the providers. They were sitting on the loading dock waiting for UPS pick up.

UPS went on strike the day after the trucks left the dock. There had been talk of a strike, but we rolled the dice and prayed the strike would not delay delivery. For a couple of days we waited. Then we called providers all over coal country to see if the forms had arrived. Most of them had. Mines went live.

The week Dan Maceda started was the best week he was to have for the next six months. In November, his second month on the job, Benefits bogged down. About 275,000 changes to beneficiary records piled up in computer limbo. The computer program that was supposed to change the official beneficiary information and reduce the backlog ran for days. New changes introduced in the interim merely increased the backlog.

Mines bogged down right behind Benefits. All the medical bills for beneficiaries in the Benefits backlog contributed to a rapidly growing backlog in Mines. More medical bills were going into the backlog than were getting paid.

At the height of the crisis, Dan called together his staff, Touche staff, and Burroughs staff. The Funds' people pointed the finger of blame at Touche; Touche blamed Burroughs; and Burroughs claimed their hardware was being misused. Dan made no effort to identify villains. Instead, he made it clear that blame was irrelevant, and he demanded that everyone focus on identifying problems and related solutions. Through his considerable efforts, everyone involved began to work together as a team.

Dan's team approach contributed to making dramatic progress toward diagnosing the Benefits problems. It took months, however, to solve them, and as the problems on Benefits subsided the problems on Mines became more visible.

The trend was ominous. When Mines first went live, the system paid only a few medical bills, amounting to $100,000 a week. Over the first few months in operation, as the high-volume providers gradually converted to the use of the new forms, the total payments increased dramatically each week. We were expecting the volume to rise to an average of $6 million to $7 million per week.

Mines testing had been managed by the Book, but with all the problems to date everyone was worried that some untested phenomenon would result in making erroneous payments. Consequently, we had elaborate procedures to check the numerical results of many computer programs before checks could be printed. The procedures involved a lot of simple arithmetic that had to be recorded on an official form and signed by an authorized individual. If the arithmetic failed to yield the right numbers, then the authorizing person stopped all the processing. One of my analysts, all of whom worked for the Funds, had to be called in to fix things before the checks were printed. Only if they had proper authorization would the computer operators get the blank check stock out of the vault to print payment checks.

I was one of three or four people authorized to review control reports and sign check releases. I avoided the job because it involved lots of arithmetic and usually had to be done after midnight on a Friday or Saturday. The last time I ever did the job, it was two in the morning some weekend. My arithmetic produced the wrong numbers. I immediately called in one of the analysts, who carefully checked the numbers. When his arithmetic got all the right numbers, he pronounced me an idiot, released the checks, and went back home to bed. The staff laughed about the incident for weeks and never again permitted me to do that job.

The Mines backlog was growing. In fact, it was growing at such a rapid rate, by my estimate, that in about two months the computer would not be able to do anything except store the backlog. Furthermore, the weekly historical check was running forty hours and the system had only been live four or five months. By the end of the year it would probably take twice that. Mines was in trouble.

Marty was justifiably furious. He had been told by his staff that the backlog was growing because of inadequate procedures used by the Funds people who processed the claims. His staff believed that the faulty procedures, which Touche had developed, were a large part of the reason that valid claims were being thrown into the backlog instead of being paid. I told anyone who would listen that I believed the backlog was the result of Mines doing too much checking for irrelevant or immaterial errors. I believed that the overly complicated error checking held up payment of claims that were almost always valid.

Because I was responsible for both the procedures and the error checking, I was prepared to fix whatever the problem was. I did not, however, want to fix an undiagnosed procedural problem if the system had an error-checking problem. To his credit, Marty kept an open mind. To determine if there were procedural problems, he required that his entire executive staff try to pay medical claims according to the procedures manual. And he sat down at a computer terminal with a stack of medical claims and joined the rest of his staff trying to pay the bills. The man had style.

While the executives remained diverted doing claims processing, I did a statistical investigation of the backlog. I was pragmatic—no statistician I ever studied with in college would have declared the sampling technique I used to be statistically valid. I never used a formula more complicated than what it took to compute a mean or a standard deviation. I estimated that if we stopped checking for three or four conditions, the Mines backlog would drop to 20 percent of its current size and less than 1 percent of the individual items would be paid in error.

Dan Maceda was intrigued at my recommendation to stop some of the error checking. At the risk of making less than ten thousand dollars in erroneous payments, he could virtually eliminate the backlog. He listened to me as I told him about all the academic defects of the analysis. He grilled me about what I had done and how I had done it. And then he told me to do what I recommended.

The analysts on my staff, all of whom reported to Dan, were outraged when I told them what we were going to do. They vociferously expressed their reservations to Dan. "How can you accept these recommendations? The woman can't do arithmetic," they said. To which Dan replied, "If she were adding a column of numbers, I would have each of you double-check her work. But none of you can challenge her analytical thinking."

As I had predicted, the backlog all but disappeared when we selectively stopped the error checking. The analysts were impressed. Dan was also impressed and greatly relieved. Had the situation resulted in a disaster, he, not I, would have been held accountable.

The first year in operation, Mines handled an average of one hundred thousand medical claims a week to cut checks to pay $362 million for medical services provided to miners and their beneficiaries.

Children 1

When Thomas Peter and I were married, he was twenty-eight, I was thirty—eight years past the statistical child-bearing prime. At our rehearsal dinner we toasted to many children in few years. There was something about five in four or how to build a baseball team. It seemed like a good idea at the time. Reality, however, tempers plans. With the onset of pregnancy, in mid-Mines, I stopped eating almost everything except the saltines I carried everywhere I went. I knew I would eventually stop vomiting, but plans had to be revised—I was not going to carry nine children.

The chaos at work was easy to contend with compared to the chaos on the home front. The two-bedroom house in which we lived was appropriate for the single woman I was when I bought it several years earlier. It was built in the early 1930s and had been basically unaltered since then. It had only one bathroom, but then I could only use one at a time. The shower poured scalding water when the toilet was flushed, but I never used both simultaneously. Hot water barely trickled in the sink, but then, I never shaved in the sink. The second bedroom was about the size of a large dressing closet and that was what I used it for. The housing situation was out of line with the growing family.

Thomas Peter and I decided to double the size of the house by attaching, to the rear, a two-story addition—master bedroom and bath upstairs, kitchen downstairs. He agreed to run the project: he was, after all, the housing professional, and between the Mines and the developing baby, I had my hands full. He got a contractor to develop plans and make estimates. Then he walked into a bank and with my house, in which he had no ownership interest, pledged as collateral, he borrowed whatever it took to pay for the construction. I was flabbergasted. He had been able to borrow thirty thousand dollars against an asset he did not own and it only took an afternoon.

When I originally bought the house, I had a hell of a time getting a loan. The banker asked how I planned to make the down payment. "What I don't have in cash, I plan to borrow on the margin against IBM stock in my Merrill Lynch account," I replied. He told me to sell the stock, put the cash in a bank account, and bring him a bank statement. Calmly I explained that I would happily bring in the stock certificates and he could sit on them, but I would not sell the stock. After weeks, several meetings with the arrogant banker, and a lot of hassle, I did get a thirty-thousand-dollar mortgage on the house, which was appraised at a lot more.

The construction project, like Mines, started off well enough and then rapidly degenerated into confusion and schedule delays. It rained when it was supposed to be cloudless and sunny. The bricklayers showed up before the bricks did. The floor people delivered the wrong solarian for the kitchen floor. A project that was supposed to end in the second trimester slipped into the third.

At seven months, I had to deal with the humiliation of trying to buy maternity clothes. To this day I remember the pregnant, professional woman, a little older than I, that Thomas Peter and I met in a changing room somewhere. As she looked in the mirror at some stylistic abomination, she said, "They think because I've lost my shape, I've lost my mind. I didn't wear lambkins across the boobies when I was sixteen; what makes them think I'd wear 'em now."

Worse, however, was the humiliation of transition planning at the Funds. As I saw it, I expected to be away from work for a couple of weeks on a medical matter. That was what I told Marty Danziger. That was what I told Jim McCoy. I was unprepared for what happened. Marty reacted as if I were planning to quit, and Jim seemed to believe that Marty's reaction was reasonable. Marty insisted on detailed transition plans. I was irritated with him for elevating my personal pregnancy to the level of a professional crisis. I was more irritated with Jim for not exercising control over Marty's irrational behavior. For a period of time during the last trimester, I spent less time running the project than I did transition planning and explaining that I was only going to be gone a couple of weeks.

January 10, 1976, the day that the baby was due, was a clear, crisp, sunny Saturday, mild for January. The contractor had finally finished up the week before. He had removed all the dust-covered tools and junk that lay in stacks all over the house. He even did a decent job of cleaning up.

Thomas Peter and I were at Sears picking up odds and ends for the baby's room and the kitchen. At lunch time we looked around for a place to eat. Something cramped. It was no big deal, but I called Mom to ask what she thought and if it was okay to eat lunch. Being in labor on a full stomach was reported to be messy. She laughed merrily at my description of occasional mild cramps, explained that when I was in labor, I would recognize it, and suggested that I enjoy lunch but lay off the french fries. I was in a gay mood when we rang off.

Thomas Peter and I had lunch and finished our shopping. Later that afternoon when the cramping got more persistent I talked to Mom again. By her assessment, it still could not be characterized as labor but she advised that I call the obstetrician, just in case.

Preventing babies, not having them, was my objective when I picked the obstetrical and gynecological practice nearest to my office as a source of birth control pills. I had no sense of attachment to the primary pill dispenser who was the youngest man in the practice. He was a shade pompous for my taste. Inertia was probably at play when I became pregnant and the objective changed, because it never occurred to me to change physicians. In the monthly poking process that accompanied prenatal care, I had met one of his partners, the gray-haired, grizzled old-timer, with very hairy arms, a man about fifty. Although I did not have any particular sense of rapport with him either, he was not pompous.

The Old-Timer called us back at the house a few minutes after we left the message with the answering service. Even though it was the baby's due date, he was unconcerned. First babies were frequently late and the symptoms I was describing were uncharacteristic of labor. Just in case though, I was instructed to go to the hospital to have things checked out.

In the twenty minutes or so that it took Thomas Peter and me to get to the hospital, my level of discomfort escalated noticeably, but there was nothing consistent, periodic, or regular about the pain. The hospital staff laid me out on my back on a tablelike bed and attached devices to my arms and abdomen. They took my blood pressure three times. It was always 80 over 60, I told them.

They observed no dilation, zero. They were about to tell me to go home and take a warm shower when the Old-Timer got involved. He knew me well enough to know that if I said that something was going on, I was doing something other than just whining. He confirmed that I was not in labor, but told someone to admit me.

I was furious at being told by the hospital staff that I had to fill out the hospital admission forms. In a high state of anxiety, I asked why Thomas Peter was unable to take care of it. I was politely told that *unmarried* women had to do their own paperwork. Only I recognized the irony of the situation: to avoid paperwork was the only reason I kept my name when we were married. I would be Ann Gallagher but for the requirements to change the phone listing, my social security and IRS data, bank accounts, credit card accounts. The hospital, however, encountered more unmarried mothers than married people with different names.

The urgency with which I was sent to X ray should have told me something was amiss. When I returned, the Old-Timer told me that the baby was severely hyperextended, appeared to have an abnormal abdominal mass, might be malformed. I was going to have a Caesarean section, immediately. So much for natural childbirth classes. At the nurse's station, a nurse was on the phone trying to contact a pediatric specialist as I was wheeled by on my way to surgery. My last memory before the general anesthetic took over was of the gray hair curling out of the neck of the Old-Timer's surgical gown.

My low blood pressure kept me in a stupor in the recovery room for hours. It was well after midnight before I got an assessment of the baby's condition from the pediatrician. Initially the doctors were concerned that the baby would be stillborn. It was only after she was born that they figured out what happened. At some time during the pregnancy, she must have lifted her nose up off her tummy, out of the usual prenatal position, and gotten stuck. The revised prenatal position that she assumed until she was born consisted of being bent over backward with the back of her head up against her bottom. For months after she was born she retained that backward U shape. It was almost a year before the kink in her spine disappeared.

The next morning one of the hospital's administrative people, looking sheepish, with clipboard in hand, asked me what I planned to name the child. More paperwork, I imagined. I responded Tela Margaret Gallagher, Tela after my mother, Margaret after Thomas Peter's mother, Gallagher after Thomas Peter. The clerk, who was really a very nice person, finally came clean. "Look, Miss Hopkins," she said, "this is a Catholic hospital. We are just not set up to have a baby with one name when the mother has another." Visions of Hopkins showing up as the last name on Tela's birth certificate danced through my head. The records were changed, I became Ann Gallagher, baby Hopkins became Tela Margaret Gallagher.

Ann Branigar Hopkins disappeared. People who called and asked for me were told there was no patient named Hopkins in the maternity ward. The hospital had an integrated computer system—the same computer system spewed birth certificate data, little plastic identification bracelets, bills, names, addresses, and telephone numbers. The same name that went on the bracelets attached to my wrist and Tela's to make sure that I was given the right baby was the only name in the hospital's telephone system.

Our new family was a mess. Tela Margaret turned a mild yellow the day after she was born. To reduce the jaundice, she spent time each day in a light box wearing baby sunglasses. I got over the hangover-like headache that comes with a general anesthetic, only to contend with the painful incision that split my abdomen from navel to hairline. While I was coping with the normal problems on the hospital front, Thomas Peter had worse problems on the home front.

We had hired the perfect housekeeper. She was a licensed practical nurse from West Virginia. The fact that she was a young grandmother indicated that she had lots of relevant experience. She had references. She would live in. She viewed housekeeping positively and she would love to cook for us. She was short on brains and personality, but that, we thought, was irrelevant. After all, we were not hiring a consultant.

The West Virginia grandmother started to work when Tela was a day or two old. She was Thomas Peter's biggest problem. Everything she cooked she cooked for hours. She preferred pork to any other meat. The only two spices she recognized were salt and sugar, and she used one or the other, in great quantities, on everything. Thomas Peter raved about the sugar in the rice. The coffee was unrecognizable. She either did not know what dirt looked like or she suffered from badly failing eyesight.

Thomas Peter was exhausted. He was trying to visit his family in the hospital, keep the house and the West Virginia grandmother under control, and still take care of things at the office. The day before Tela and I were supposed to come home, the refrigerator developed a high temperature problem that proved terminal. He was at his wit's end about the time that I was beginning to feel like a human being. I solved the refrigerator problem from my hospital bed over the phone with a sob story to Sears.

As Tela and I were preparing to check out of the hospital, I asked the Old-Timer when I could go back to work. He gave me the litany of medical considerations that went into such a decision. He would let me know when I came in for a postpartum checkup in a month or six weeks. There was no arguing with him. I rented a wheelchair and planned to return to work in a week. My plans were extended by a week when Thomas Peter, the West Virginia grandmother, and I all came down with a debilitating streptococcus infection. The wheelchair lasted two days.

We fired the West Virginia grandmother and hired another house-keeper. This one had no appropriate credentials. She had come to the States as part of the staff of a Korean diplomat who had returned to Korea. She wanted to stay in the United States. She had no references to speak of. She was twenty-two years old on an oriental scale that sets birth date at conception. She had never seen a baby up close. But she was charming, had a sparkling smile and a wonderful sense of humor. I had never seen a baby up close until very recently, so she was only a little less qualified to take care of Tela than I was. Thomas Peter and I hired Sull Shin on Saturday. She started on Monday and stayed with us for the better part of seven years.

If the West Virginia grandmother was a major short-term disaster, Sully was an equivalent long-term miracle. Although it was not obvious at the time, when we hired her we received, as an added benefit, an extended international family. Sully married a Greek, George Ramakis, who lived with us until the two of them bought their own place. Her Aunt Kayong and three of her children Won Kyung, Hyun Heh, and Won Ju wandered in and out of the house at will and lived with us for various periods of time ranging from a day here and there to months. If Sully wanted or needed to be away from the house, she usually found a family member to fill in for her. George, who was a superb mechanic, disassembled and reassembled Thomas Peter's car in the driveway whenever something mechanical failed. The car usually worked better after George finished with it. While they all began as illegal aliens, each became a "green card" holder and most of them are U.S. citizens today. Kayong, who is older than I am, studied accounting and became a bookkeeper. Her children are all college educated.

"I hope Thomas Peter has the maternal instincts in the family," Joey Biero said at a surprise birthday party that Thomas Peter held for me. She was backhandedly saying that I had none. If maternal instincts are what enable a parent to prepare for and cope with the early stages of parenthood, then she was certainly accurate in her characterization of me. If I had them, I was unaware of their existence until Tela turned five or six months of age. Physical and mental exhaustion contributed mightily to my inability to cope effectively. "How could you leave your newborn and go back to work so soon?" I was often asked. "I go to the office for peace and quiet, rest and relaxation," was the gist of the usual answer. Although working contributed nothing to my opportunities to sleep, it offered relief from the mental and emotional stress and noise.

Ignorance and inexperience also made coping difficult. Tela, Thomas Peter, and I came home from the hospital with a box full of bottles and tubes of baby supplies, most of which were supposed to be helpful but ultimately could only be classified as junk. One evening I watched Thomas Peter with one hand supporting Tela's head while the remainder of her body was partially submerged in a plastic baby bathtub. He read instructions off the label of one of the bottles that he held in the other hand. He discovered that it either required four hands or two people to bathe an infant according to the instructions. With that experience, the baby bathtub went out in the trash. Tela was washed in the shower.

It took me many months to compensate for the exhaustion that I was unable to overcome. During those months, I also became more comfortable with my own inexperience, ignorance, and fear of doing something wrong with catastrophic results. The Book and the history that so influenced my life at the office were supplemented with the Baby Book at home. (The Baby Book was actually a collection of volumes that largely said the same things.) Like the Book at the office, the Baby Book had to be used with care and ignored when the information seemed inappropriate.

Exhaustion, ignorance, and incompetence started to come under control with the passage of time. Logistics and priorities, however, went out of control as Tela grew. Under most circumstances, an infant is easy to care for because it is immobile. When she was tiny, I frequently left Tela wrapped in a receiving blanket on a pile of bed blankets in the middle of the dining room table. She was unable to move, even to roll over, so the three- or four-foot drop to the floor was no threat to her well being. Having her on the table was convenient for me because lifting, even light loads, and especially bending over and lifting, was uncomfortable.

Immobility is, however, short lived and rapidly followed by dramatically increasing ability to get or crash into things. The frequently resulting medical unpleasantness created logistics problems that left Thomas Peter and me in continual states of priority assessment. Sully was terrified at the prospect of Tela coming to harm and tended to panic earlier than I would have. Blood, in any amount, was cause for alarm and a phone call to me at the office. If a telephone assessment of the problem as described by Sully required that Thomas Peter or I go home to assess further or do something, we had to respond instantly.

Depending on whether Thomas Peter was in town, what each of us was doing, who was closest to the house, and what could be rescheduled, one of us might have to race home, whether we were needed or not. I received one call involving blood from a cut over the eye. Even after asking many specific questions about the location and size of the cut and the volume of blood, I was unable to determine the magnitude of the problem. Of necessity, I assumed the worst. I immediately walked out of the office and took the first cab to the house only to find that the crisis was over a drop of blood from a nick caused by one of Tela's own fingernails. I clipped off potentially dangerous fingernails, made sure there were no more rough edges, and returned to work in the same cab.

As time passed and Sully learned what was worth a call, the number of calls decreased dramatically. Both of us, however, had to overcome some of the cultural differences between us. Fear of disease left Sully horrified when I took infant Tela to the grocery store. When I asked Sully's aunt, Kayong, why she completely covered herself with clean receiving blankets from the waist up, including her face, to burp the baby, Kayong replied, "to keep away oriental bacteria." Kayong had apparently been told by an ignorant former employer to guard against transmitting oriental fevers. Kayong, Sully, and I had a comparative discussion of bacteria and bias with the effect that, from that day forward, Kayong used receiving blankets only to protect herself from vomit.

Kayong spent quite a bit of time around the house with us. She frequently substituted for Sully. I learned to like Korean food, which Sully or Kayong cooked all the time. Later, I learned how to pronounce the words that described what I ate. Still later, I learned how to recognize some of the strange ingredients that filled the refrigerator with interesting odors. I even learned how to cook Korean dishes. My favorite was a strong-smelling cabbage concoction called *kim chi*. Tela started using chopsticks at the age most children learn to use forks.

Tela was beginning to talk when I started on my second adventure in motherhood. By then I thought I knew more about what I was doing. The Baby Book was ignored more and more often. Instead, I relied on my own intuition or common sense. As Mom put it, I learned to follow my nose.

I assume that because Tela's birth left business relatively uninterrupted, people at Touche were professionally unconcerned with the second pregnancy. To my great relief, there was no requirement for transition planning with the client. Bloomingdale opened a store in the Washington area complete with a working women's maternity department.

The Owner called Thomas Peter and me to an unusual joint meeting. By then, Bill was the partner in charge of the consolidated audit, tax, and consulting practice in Washington. Thomas Peter had never had frequent business dealings with Bill, and my work with Mines was finished—I was working for Jeff Baldwin on a job for National Public Radio. When the three of us met, Bill conveyed mixed messages. The good news was that Thomas Peter would be promoted to manager at the start of the new fiscal year. The bad news was that, according to firm policy, neither Thomas Peter nor I could be considered for admission to the partnership as long as we were both employed at Touche.

The policy that governed this anachronistic view of spouses was referred to as a nepotism policy. The same policy applied to any close relatives, such as father and son or siblings. The policy, so I was told by one partner, was intended to guard against conflict of interest. A partner who was a close relative of an employee might not be able to review the work of the employee objectively. Another partner told me that years ago the policy was used to eliminate weaker family members in mergers with small, family-owned accounting firms.

Neither of these, nor any other explanation I ever heard, made any sense at all. Thomas Peter and I had nothing in common professionally. I was hard pressed to understand what he did, even at the conceptual level. I was absolutely incompetent to review or analyze his work even though most of it was described in plain English. Much of my work was done in technical terms and diagrams that were uninterpretable to anyone untrained in data processing. Thomas Peter was unable to even understand what I did except when I described it by analogy. Furthermore, it struck me as peculiar, to say the least, that we could sleep together and be admitted to the partnership as long as we were unmarried. There were no policy prohibitions against partners or employees living in sin one with the other.

One of us had to go. Because Thomas Peter had seniority at Touche and outranked me, I went looking for another position. We planned to have the baby in the transition period between jobs. That way, I could do the job search before I was obviously pregnant and start on the new job when I was no longer pregnant—I had no desire to have the pregnancy complicate the job search.

I was uncomfortable, occasionally to the point of anxiety, with the second pregnancy. The Old-Timer's concern over the possibility of a rupture of the uterine wall along the impressive ten-inch, vertical scar on my abdomen ruled out all possibility of natural childbirth. The prospect of another round of major surgery, accompanied by anesthesiological hangover, immobilizing pain, catheters, enemas, and exhaustion to the point of hysteria, left me nervously cold and frequently depressed.

Dennis Fennessey, however, was relieved at this development. The second time around he could avoid the responsibility of saving me from the motorcycle-induced wrath of Thomas Peter. Thomas Peter and I had attended natural childbirth classes in anticipation of Tela's arrival. In the beginning, we went together. As time wore on and his travel schedule picked up, Thomas Peter could not always be with me. Because he disapproved of my riding the motorcycle while pregnant, I usually took a cab when he was in town. Not so when he was out of town. I panicked on those occasions when Thomas Peter returned unexpectedly. Dennis always stopped in the middle of whatever crisis he was dealing with to help me dispose of the illicit motorcycle.

The second Caesarean did have some pluses. It could be scheduled for a decent day of the week and a decent hour of the day. We tried to schedule it for a Monday in hopes that I could rest over the weekend.

However, the Old-Timer's schedule conflicted, so we opted for Friday morning, November 4, 1977, early.

The nature of Tela's arrival left more than just Thomas Peter and me concerned about the birth of our second child. As a consequence of his concern, the Old-Timer decided to monitor development more frequently and with more than just the usual poking and stethoscope monitoring. In addition, he scheduled periodic sonagrams. What a logistical pain: I lived north of downtown; my client was across town; I had job interviews in suburban Maryland and Virginia, obstetrical appointments in one Maryland suburb, and sonagrams and other tests in another Maryland suburb—and Thomas Peter wanted to buy a different house.

"Five people can't watch a football game in the living room," he noted. "When you narrow it down to one or two, let me know," I told him. Buying a house is a major decision to many people. It was low on my list of priorities. I had no interest in spending what little time and energy I had traipsing around the Washington area looking at real estate. In fact when I originally bought the much-improved house that we lived in, I selected it from a field of only three houses that I looked at. My approach to buying a house was to find a good real estate agent, provide clear, comprehensive specifications, and then buy the first house that met the specifications.

We had to spend the late summer and fall finishing a basement fix-up job on this house, a job that had been hastily initiated by Sully's marriage to George. After the wedding, George moved into the basement bedroom with Sully. We had a contractor do the major plumbing work required to add a convenient bathroom. The rest of the work we did ourselves.

Tela followed me around everywhere I went as I carried hammer and nails and construction materials from place to place. She watched with fascination one afternoon as I tried, unassisted, to fit and then nail a four-by-eight-foot sheet of ceiling material with a hole in it in place around a light fixture. On the occasion of the third falling of the panel I uttered an expletive. For a week, she wandered around the house muttering, "Sit. Sit. Sit. Sit." in a singsong refrain. I was more careful with my choice of words after that.

As the scheduled birth date drew near, we were reasonably ready. There was not a whole lot that remained to be done at the house. Sully and George had the basement to themselves, with their own entrance through the side door. My work at Touche was finished. My new employer, American Management Systems, and I had agreed on a start date.

The last week in October, I had a final sonagram as a double check on the size of the baby. The fetus was 42.3 weeks old—so reported the radiologist who interpreted the sonagram. I read his report absentmindedly as I waited for the Old-Timer to show for the final prenatal examination before checking into the hospital. "When I took biology, the gestation period for humans was 40 weeks," I commented when he arrived. "If the Caesarean is scheduled at week 38, how can the 'fetus' be 42.3 weeks old?" (I hate referring to children in medical jargon.)

The Old-Timer responded with a discussion of statistics—fetal age is estimated by measuring the cranial diameter on the sonagram and comparing it to standard tables of cranial diameters as a function of gestation period. The standard tables were based on populations of fetuses in Appalachia, Scotland, and other places. Thomas Peter and I probably had larger cranial diameters than the parents of the fetuses in the tabulated population. The baby was big enough. We could go ahead with the Caesarean. "The radiologist was reporting too many decimals," I remarked. So much for statistics.

We checked me in, under the name "Gallagher," to the same hospital where Tela was born—I had warned everyone that I could be found under Thomas Peter's name. To avoid the anesthesiological hangover, I decided to have a local anesthetic. I would have been less apprehensive but for the fact that a good friend of my mother's became a paraplegic as a consequence of a spinal anesthetic administered with a nonsterile needle.

"It's the extra inch that makes the difference," Mom said about the sex of babies. Boy Gallagher was delivered without mishap. I was not a paraplegic. I knew everything was fine when, late in the afternoon, just after I regained my senses, Mom and Gil arrived to visit. Mom carried a bottle of Canadian whiskey, appropriately wrapped in a receiving blanket and conveyed in a cloth L. L. Bean bag. She had probably been at more deliveries than most of the hospital staff, so the fact that I was under strict orders to eat or drink nothing was irrelevant. We held Happy Hour to celebrate the arrival of Thomas Gilbert Gallagher; Thomas after his paternal grandfather; Gilbert after my stepfather; and Gallagher after his father. We would call him Gilbert.

Like Tela, Gilbert almost instantly turned yellow and was banished to the light box decked out in sunglasses. Also like Tela, when my milk came in, the baby was out. I had tried nursing and pumping, to no avail. I abandoned any notion of breast-feeding after a week or two of futile attempts.

Clearing up Gilbert's jaundice required that he stay in the hospital longer than there was any medical necessity for me to stay. I found myself on the horns of a dilemma when offered alternatives of staying with Gilbert until he turned a normal color or going home and leaving him in the hospital for a couple of extra days. I was reluctant, to say the least, to leave Gilbert.

The hospital was, however, a very unpleasant place. The food was terrible. I was awakened every few hours for a check on my always-normal vital signs. Low blood pressure, the heating system, and the plastic mattress cover conspired to create alternating cycles of heat and soaking perspiration followed by numbing cold. I had encountered these same problems when Tela was born. To no avail, I patiently explained that I wanted someone to get rid of the plastic. The hospital staff was more concerned with protecting the bed from blood stains than it was with protecting me from pneumonia. Only when the hospital staff caught me showering off the salt at two in the morning after I had pulled the perspiration-inducing plastic off the bed, did they get the message. The plastic banished from the bed, I stayed in the hospital until Gilbert and I could leave together.

Tela was about twenty-two months old when I brought Gilbert home. Her bedroom was in the original part of the house and served as a guest room when appropriate. The small room that served as the dressing room next to our bedroom became Gilbert's room. After Mom and Gil left, Thomas Peter's mother and his sister Rose came down from Philadelphia to help out. They stayed with us for five or six weeks, during which time the second floor of the house resembled a small overbooked motel.

It seemed certain that house hunting was more than a passing fancy with Thomas Peter. He was absolutely right about the house—it was too small. The limited capacity of the living room went unnoticed by me before Gilbert's birth. Afterward, even I became claustrophobic. George and Sully lived in the basement with occasional visits from Kayong. Thomas Peter, his mother, Rose, Tela, Gilbert, and I lived upstairs. The only room on the first floor that was large enough for a family gathering was the kitchen.

I called Peggy Smith, the agent who had negotiated the purchase of the house we lived in, and asked her if she could negotiate another one. Peggy had moved into commercial real estate and no longer handled residences. However, she referred us to Hans Lichtenstein, another agent who was prepared to solve the housing problem. Apparently Hans did not believe us when we gave him our specifications. He called Peggy to ask, "Why would a young professional couple with babies want a big, modern townhouse, with no yard, downtown?" Peggy made no attempt to answer that question. Instead, she advised him to meet the specification. "If that's what they said they wanted, show it to them. They won't buy anything else."

The first house Hans showed us was a vintage 1950s rambler with a nice lawn in the Maryland suburb of Rollingwood. It was an instant reject. We bought the second house he showed us, a four-story, brick townhouse, built in 1965, two subway stops from downtown, no front yard, and a tiny patio garden in the back. Hans earned a handsome commission for what had to have been less than two days' work.

Whatever Hans gained financially on our purchase of the new house he lost on the sale of the old one. He held open houses on what seemed like every weekend. He advertised "Snoopy's Dog House" weekly. He brought a steady stream of people through to see the place. I was beginning to feel like we lived in a fishbowl that had to be cleaned all the time when he finally sold it. We managed to close on both houses, within days of each other, when Gilbert was five months old.

Citizens

American Management Systems (AMS) is a modern, high-tech consulting firm that is renowned for building huge financial systems, largely for governments. The company was founded by five men who worked together under Robert S. McNamara when he was Secretary of Defense. When I went to work for AMS in December of 1977, the five founders managed the company.

The accounting community, in the form of Arthur Andersen, had declared the financial records of the District of Columbia to be unauditable. An oversight committee established by Congress was in charge of "fixing the problem," hopefully with the result that the books could be audited and Congress and the public could understand the financial state of the District. AMS was the contractor responsible for building an auditable financial system for the government of the District of Columbia.

One of the founders managed the D.C. financial system project. With regard to government accounting and financial systems, he was probably the most knowledgeable person I ever met. He may also have been the most arrogant and abusive man I dealt with in any professional context. A woman named Mary Procter was responsible for the budgeting piece of the financial system. I worked for Mary.

She had to be about my age—we graduated from college in the same year—but she had white hair. She went to Smith and earned her master's degree in public administration at Princeton in the late sixties.

She had three children, two of them twins. The twins should have been born about the same time as Gilbert, but were two months premature. In an effort to prevent them from being born even earlier, she had conducted her business with her feet up from what was, in concept, a dentist's chair.

I liked and admired Mary. She was unquestionably in charge, not only of the budget team, but also of just about any group discussing an issue in which she had a business interest. She was curious, smart, analytical, objective, only vested in an appropriate answer, and unafraid of expressing her views, even if they conflicted with those who outranked her.

I could not stand the founder-manager. He had all the solutions to his view of the District's problems, with or without the benefit of any observations or insights provided by the client people with whom I dealt. His team leaders' meetings, which, thank God, I only occasionally had to attend in Mary's absence, were opportunities for him to demonstrate his technical brilliance at the expense of everyone in the room. It was offensive. The technical staff that he routinely berated, were, as a group, a remarkably able collection of technology professionals who worked hard and knew what they were doing. They deserved better than the constant onslaught.

It took less than six months for me to figure out that I was in the wrong place. I was learning a lot. I was teaching nothing. I was not having fun. By the Owner's criteria, the engagement was a failure. Thomas Peter and I talked to some of the partners at Touche about the dilemma. "If I couldn't practice at Touche, I'd want to practice at Price Waterhouse," Jeff Baldwin remarked. He made some suggestions and put me in contact with Paul Goodstat, one of the partners at Price Waterhouse.

Stability

The new town house on Cathedral Avenue was as right as the job with AMS was wrong. "With all the furniture in place, you can still play basketball at the other end of the room," Thomas Peter said about our fourth-floor bedroom—and that room was largely furnished. Tela and Gilbert each had individual gymnasiums, one of which, Tela's room, easily accommodated Thomas Peter's mother and Rose when they came to visit. The place had its drawbacks, however. Leftover effervescence of cat permeated the ten-year-old, dirty beige, wall-to-wall carpeting on the first two floors. When Thomas Peter took the twenty-seven-foot span of living room drapery to the dry cleaner, he was cautiously advised, "Mister, this thing has dry rot; I don't think we can clean it." We characterized the wallpaper in the foyer, which had a fourteen-foot ceiling, and up the stairwell to the third floor as "early French whorehouse." The small patio off the living room at the back of the house turned into a mud flat when it rained. Although the place was structurally sound—nothing leaked and everything seemed to work—it needed an interior decorator, a luxury we were unable to afford.

We pulled out the smelly carpet, only to discover that some of the stairs had never been finished and the landing on the first floor was bare cement. Thomas Peter learned more than he ever wanted to know about sanding and finishing floors. We had the stairs and most of the first two floors recarpeted to kill the echo and to prevent injury to Tela who was running around and was into everything. For months I spent all the spare time I had soaking and scraping wallpaper off the walls by hand with a plaster knife, usually while standing on a ladder. Mom and Gil schlepped spare furniture down from their house in New York. Gil cut pressure-treated two-by-sixes and supervised Thomas Peter and me as we covered the mud flat with a deck during one holiday weekend.

Thomas Peter became a principal at Touche the summer of our first year in the house. Among his other accomplishments en route to the partnership, he developed $10 million in business doing drug program reviews. The work was a little far afield from housing programs and real estate, but he was flexible; when work in his area dried up, he changed areas. He eventually wrote a book on programmatic reviews.

Sully and George bought a condominium in Virginia. That took some getting used to. She had to rely on George or the bus to get to and from work, with the consequence that my schedule and Thomas Peter's were less flexible than they had been when she and George lived with us.

Tela and Gilbert, less than two years apart in age, got along famously. I am convinced that, in some respects, it is easier to have two children than only one. Only a child can entertain another child for more than a few minutes. Gilbert was Tela's doll. Until he developed enough to wriggle out of her clutches, she would sit and hold him or, with her arms under his armpits and hands clasped on his chest, drag him around from place to place.

About the time that Thomas Peter and I were getting comfortable enough with parenthood that we thought we knew what we were doing, the children began to exhibit behavior patterns that shook our developing confidence. Tela, who was always glad to see us and hopped into one or the other of our open arms or laps when we got home from work, took to screaming whenever she was on the ground. At night, usually late at night, Gilbert preferred screaming to any other activity. After several sleepless nights of dealing with Gilbert's screaming sessions, Thomas Peter, who was on the verge of once again going downstairs to Gilbert's room, reversed field, uttering, "Either he's going to train us or we're going to train him; I'm going to let the little bastard scream." With that he closed our bedroom door and went back to bed. We all slept better after that.

A conversation with Sully led me to believe that Tela was also engaged in training us and that her training of Sully was nearly complete. During the day, every time Tela whimpered, Sully picked her up and played with her. Only after a couple of days when Tela, unelevated, was left to her toys and her own devices for an hour did we succeed in breaking the developing habit. But Tela needed a wider social circle, so we enrolled her in the Owl School, a little day care center located in the basement of a church, three short blocks from the house.

I took advantage of Jeff Baldwin's advice and contacts with the result that, after a letter, a few phone calls, and interviews, Price Waterhouse offered me a consulting position. In addition to the obvious advantage of returning to client-focused, Big Eight consulting, the work offered the convenience of an office ten minutes from the house and three blocks from Thomas Peter's office at Touche.

A few days before I started to work at Price Waterhouse, I returned from the grocery store. The phone on the elevator rang as I lowered grocery bags to the elevator floor to be transported upstairs to the kitchen. When I answered the call, Paul Goodstat, the partner responsible for federal government consulting, greeted me gravely.

Policy anomaly! How could I be a policy anomaly? Paul explained that he had made an error in hiring me because firm policy prohibited employing spouses of partners in others of the Big Eight. I was close to panic. I had already left AMS and was looking forward to going back to Big Eight consulting after a few days off. Furthermore, I needed a job. Partners at Touche started out at about thirty-five thousand dollars a year, and that would not support the family even though we had always lived well below what our combined incomes would permit. The relief was dizzying when Paul continued the conversation by stating that the firm would honor its commitment to hire me in spite of the policy. "Paul is a nice man," I said to myself as I unloaded the rest of the groceries and rode up with them to the second floor.

That night, over dinner, Thomas Peter and I disparagingly discussed our second brush with what we thought were anachronistic policies in the Big Eight. The morning's brush with unemployment did not bode well for my becoming a partner at PW. That, however, was at least five years away because five year's tenure was normally required for admission to the partnership. We were not thinking long term at the time and brushed off any consideration of possible events that far into the future.

Indians

"Project Integrity" was the name given by the Department of the Interior to the first project I worked on at Price Waterhouse in 1978. The General Accounting Office had written a report critical of some financial practices at Interior related to the Bureau of Indian Affairs and had recommended improvements. Interior asked for proposals from the private sector to help implement the GAO recommendations.

For what seemed like months after I joined the firm in August of 1978, I did nothing, because I was scheduled to be assigned to Integrity if and when the contract was awarded. The fifteen or twenty people in my office were all waiting and hoping the job would be awarded to us.

We had proposed to formulate requirements for an improved financial system in return for two hundred thousand dollars. That was a big deal at a time when, firmwide, fifty thousand dollars was considered to be a large engagement. Like most projects done for government, Integrity was bid at hourly rates that were heavily discounted, typically 40 percent or more. The firm could, however, manage quite profitably, even at 60 percent of standard billing rates.

A tall, lanky, affable fellow named Tom Colberg who had worked for the Office of Management and Budget before he joined Price Waterhouse wrote our proposal for Integrity shortly before I arrived. The responsible partner was Lew Krulwich, who like Tom had worked at OMB.

Lew was quite a bit shorter than I, bald with a neatly groomed, monklike fringe of hair around the sides and back of his head. He was slender to the point of looking frail. The apparent frailty was deceptive, however, for he had a reputation as a wicked tennis player. Lew was a quiet, thoughtful man who seemed to worry a lot, especially about the well-being of his people, the people who worked for him.

Tom and I were ecstatic when we won—he because the sale would look good in his file, and I because the project was my ticket out of boredom. The work required that we interview key managers at Interior and the Bureau of Indian Affairs in Washington and in Albuquerque. We also had to interview representatives of the Indian tribes that the bureau served all over the West. Although I helped Tom with the management interviews in Washington, he and a woman named Pat Bowman did most of the work in town. I had the glorious task of doing the work out West.

"You need a good out-of-town assignment so you can get some rest," Thomas Peter said on more than one occasion. What he meant was that I needed some time when only wake-up calls interrupted my sleep and getting dinner meant going out or calling room service, not cooking. An assignment that required traveling, on a less than hectic schedule, to one or more interesting places was, by definition, a good out-of-town assignment. Nothing fit the bill like a few trips to Indian reservations out West.

I spent several weeks in the late fall and into the winter of 1979 interviewing bureau representatives and tribal officials at field offices and on reservations in Oklahoma, New Mexico, Colorado, and Montana. It was hard to believe that I was being paid while having the opportunity to observe the cultures of the Navaho, the Hopi, a number of the Pueblos, and others in or around Billings, Santa Fe, Taos, and smaller western towns, some of which were identifiable only by the intersection of a couple of county roads. Western cuisine—burritos, blue tortillas, enchiladas with red and green sauce, salsas in varying temperatures—has been my favorite, practically since birth.

The people, in and out of professional context, were a fascinating diversion from the consultants, accountants, attorneys, and bureaucrats who represented most of the population with whom I typically dealt in Washington. The response to a simple question, "How did you wind up on this reservation?" was "I slugged the tribal representative," followed by a discussion of a conflict between two Indian nations that had been going on for hundreds of years.

I finished my work out West on a cold, snowy winter night in Billings, Montana. I struck up a conversation with a man standing in line with me as we tried to get the last flight out, he going south, I going east. He entertained me for an hour discussing bull semen management. As a manager with W. R. Grace, a Price Waterhouse audit client, he was responsible for collecting, storing, and managing the inventory of prize bull semen used for cattle breeding. He ran a high-tech operation: the asset was stored in containers cooled by liquified gas. He described the federal regulations governing the life of the asset and the accounting issues related to depreciation of bull semen.

Upon my return to Washington, Thomas Peter, Tela, Gilbert, and I went to Bloomingdale's to do some Saturday morning Christmas shopping. I nearly passed out in the parking lot. I got over the dizziness in a matter of seconds, but it scared the hell out of me. We went on about our holiday business, but I concluded that I was either real sick or pregnant again. I made an appointment first thing Monday to see the Old-Timer. Sure enough, I was pregnant, not ill. Thomas Peter was startled when I told him. Mom was terrified at the prospect of my having a third Caesarean.

Tom, Pat, and I wrote the final report for Project Integrity during February and March of 1979. During the client review process, Tom and I worked with a number of managers at Interior and the bureau, most of whom had other problems they wanted us to solve. As Integrity wound down, Tom and I wrote proposals to help them. When Integrity ended, in the spring of 1979, Tom sold a fifty-thousand-dollar follow-on project to keep Pat and him busy. I sold and planned to manage a two-hundred-thousand-dollar project to help the bureau convert its computer operations from one manufacturer's hardware to that of another. The new project was scheduled to start four days after the Caesarian.

I also helped Karen Nold with the fifty-thousand-dollar sale of another project to prepare a data processing plan. Karen had joined the firm from the Federal Reserve. She and I were both part of a group of experienced data processing professionals who were hired during my early days in OGS (Office of Government Services) as part of a strategy to expand the business in the area of computer systems. Once Karen's project got started, she and I bumped into each other around town and occasionally out West. Both of our projects were slated to end in the fall.

Interior made changes to the Integrity contract to authorize us to do the follow-on projects, all of which were subject to the same billing rates as Integrity. Although the firm could be profitable at discounted government rates, my office had to be extremely careful if we used staff from other offices because we normally lost a little money on every hour charged to a job by other office staff. The firm's accounting system was the villain. Even though my office could only bill the government at 60 percent of rates, the accounting system automatically charged it for all other office staff at 70 percent of the standard rate. It then transferred the money to the other office.

Under the best of circumstances, the overall effect of the variance between rates was to export profits, amounting to about 10 percent, from my office to the other office. Furthermore, the accounting system was unconcerned if my office was unable to bill the government for the time other office staff charged to the job. It automatically exported 70 percent of the full billing rate for unbilled or unbillable hours. Under those circumstances, my office could lose more than a little money; it could lose a lot of money.

The villainous accounting system was no problem on Integrity or on Tom's follow-on project. Other than an occasional expert brought in from another office for a few hours, those projects were done entirely with OGS staff and mostly in Washington. All the work on my follow-on project, however, had to be done at a data processing center in Albuquerque, New Mexico. The project budget could ill afford the travel costs of two or three consultants from OGS working full time in Albuquerque. Furthermore, OGS's small staff was booked solid on other jobs. My project had to be done with staff from other offices.

Lew selected a senior manager named John Lawrence (John L) McClure to start up and run the job until I had recovered from Peter's birth. He also negotiated with the partners in Houston and Denver for a consultant from each office to do the staff work. Bill Devaney, the partner in charge of the Houston consulting practice, assigned a consultant named Linda Pegues to work for John L on the project. Denver assigned a manager named Al Liljekrans. Lew, John L, Al, and Linda got the project set up and started work while I was in the hospital.

A couple of weeks after I was released, I went back to my desk in Washington. Two or three weeks after that, I began commuting to Albuquerque two, occasionally three, days each week to manage the job. I usually flew out early Thursday morning and took a late afternoon flight back on Friday. Time-recording policies and practices were set up and running by the time I made the transition and replaced John L.

We only billed Interior for eight hours per day, so by established project policy we only charged eight hours per day to the project accounting code. That minimized the amount of profits exported to Houston and Denver. It was a fairly common policy in OGS. Staff on out-of-town assignments, however, frequently, if not usually, worked way in excess of eight hours per day; ten or more was typical. There were two reasons for the long hours. First, there were few diversions. Second, the quicker the job got down, the faster the staff got home.

The staff work on the job was done by Linda Pegues. She was tall, a lot taller than my five feet, seven inches. A slender woman in her early twenties with flaming red hair, she had a southern accent that announced she was from Texas. She was always in a good mood. When I first arrived in Albuquerque, Linda and John L were up to their ears in technical alligators, in this case operational computer flow diagrams. John L was supposed to have developed a work plan and Linda was supposed to be executing it. But when I arrived, several weeks into the job, all I could see was John L and Linda with their heads down, buried in piles of diagrams, working like mad from early in the morning until late at night. There was no evidence of a plan and no indication of where we were in terms of the overall project timetable. When I asked Linda when she was going to finish whatever she was doing, I was greeted with a vacant stare and an enthusiastic statement that she was going to do whatever it took to get done according to the schedule.

Linda and I had a conversation about management. I told her that all she could manage was what was under her control and that in her position all she had under her control was her own time. She and I agreed that she would count the number of diagrams that she produced in a day and determine the average number per day. After a few days we were able to estimate, based on the number of diagrams left to do, how we were doing compared to the project schedule. It turned out that we were not doing very well. To catch up to the schedule, I joined John L and Linda down in the pile of diagrams.

And so it went through the summer, one pile of diagrams after another. John L returned to Washington, to be replaced by Al Liljekrans when he became available after completing some other assignment in Denver. Lew flew out from Washington to check up on us every now and then. Jack Adams, a partner from California and former IBMer also flew in to check up on both us and Lew. Norm Statland, the firm's data processing guru checked up on everyone. Norm was negatively impressed by what he reviewed, but Jack and Lew seemed unimpressed by Norm's negativism.

Late in the project Al Liljekrans left the project. An OGS consultant named Bob Caplan who was not billable to a client, was assigned to Albuquerque. It was wrong. The reason Bob was not billable was because his experience was in health care and related services, and there was a major slump in the firm's practice in that area. He was about as appropriate for Albuquerque as a medical technician was to run a computer room. His performance ratings were mediocre to bad. I had objected to his assignment, to no avail. Less than a week passed before the phone rang on my desk in Washington and an irate Linda explained that Bob was only in the office from nine to five, and it was not clear that he did anything when he was there. Linda was putting in long hours. She expected Bob to do the same and she was not reluctant to tell me so. I called Bob to find out what he was doing. When he explained that he did not like the job and had no intention of exerting himself, I gave him hell. He eventually left the firm, one step ahead of the ax.

I was sorry to see the job end. I enjoyed working out West and with the people in Albuquerque. Linda, however, was far sadder than I. She was devoted to the people, largely Indians, with whom she worked at the Bureau of Indian Affairs, and she loved Albuquerque. Over a period of six months after the project ended she worked on a couple of small jobs, one in New Orleans and another in Dallas. She continued to be drawn to Albuquerque, however, and decided to leave the firm to take a job there. Bill Devaney helped her by giving her time off to travel for interviews.

Before Linda left, she recognized the cash value of the overtime that she had invested in the Albuquerque project and sought to be paid for it. When she discussed the matter with Bill Devaney, who was unaware that she had been working but not recording a lot of overtime, he hit the roof, with some justification. Bill fired off a nasty memo to Lew in which he expressed his displeasure over not having been credited with Linda's overtime hours (at 70 percent of her rate). Bill demanded that Lew transfer the money to the Houston office to cover the overtime hours.

Lew discussed the memo with me. I was more than a little surprised because I was unaware that Linda was even entitled to be paid for overtime. However, the four or five hundred overtime hours in question seemed in line with what I had observed and I recommended that we pay the Houston office for them. I also advised Lew that there was no chance of recovering the costs from Interior. I thought that was the end of the matter.

Children 2

Although I had not reached an age where having a baby was medically dangerous, at thirty-seven I was no spring chicken. Mom did not discuss my third pregnancy until after the birth of my youngest child. Her anxiety, together with my still-fresh recollections of the medical profession caused me to reassess the situation.

It was time to change obstetricians and hospitals. I wanted an obstetrician who dealt with high-risk pregnancies and practiced at a hospital with a neonatal care unit. Furthermore, it would be pleasant if the replacement for the Old-Timer had a sense of humor and the hospital had some regard for the people who were its patients. It would also be helpful if the doctors, laboratories, and hospital were all conveniently near home and office.

Thomas Peter and I were able to find an ideal situation without an awful lot of work. A high-risk obstetrician, Joseph M. Giere, practiced fifteen minutes from the house or office, in the same building where the children's pediatrician was located. When we interviewed him, he suggested we call him Joe.

Dr. Giere (I never could call him Joe) used Sibley and Georgetown University Hospitals, both reasonably regarded for humane treatment of patients, for deliveries. Georgetown was a teaching hospital, had a neonatal care unit, and was the location of the specialist where I could have sonagrams and amniocentesis.

Dr. Giere was a pragmatist. Instead of a standard litany of prohibitions on my actions or a long list of the medical risks associated therewith, I got explanations for his recommendations. His initial guidance for my third pregnancy was, "If you could play the piano before you were pregnant, you can play it now. I would prefer that you not ride horseback during the third trimester." I was more confident when I left his office that wintery morning than I had been when I carried either Tela or Gilbert.

Washington goes into cardiac arrest shortly after the first inch of snow accumulates. When Thomas Peter and I dragged out of bed that morning the snow was falling fast and predictions were for six inches. I did not believe the predictions.

It was bone-chilling cold, like only February can be when a great, dry, and bitter jet stream descends from Canada. A big, warm, wet air mass was slowly boiling into town from the southeast. I knew when that mess encountered the Canadian air and got stuck, it would dump a foot or more of dry powder on the already frozen ground.

Sully could not get in from Virginia to take care of the children. I dropped Tela off at the Owl School for the day. Thomas Peter drove Gilbert out to stay with a former neighbor near Chevy Chase Circle because the Owl School did not take children under the age of eighteen months.

Going in to the office had not been worth the small effort it took to make the trip ten blocks downtown. Revised predictions of twelve to fifteen inches of snow had closed down the government. Most of the twenty or so people who worked in my office went home early.

The situation at Touche was pretty much the same. Late in the afternoon Thomas Peter and I picked up Tela. I kept an eye on her at home while he drove out to Chevy Chase to pick up Gilbert. It got dark as the snow passed the six-inch mark and showed no signs of letting up.

I felt cooped up in the house and was anxious for Thomas Peter and Gilbert to get home. It snows so infrequently in Washington and there usually is so little accumulation that neither the cars nor the people are ever prepared for it.

As time passed, I worried that even if Thomas Peter maneuvered the inevitable dozens of stranded cars on Connecticut Avenue uneventfully, he might not be able to get the Plymouth up the steep incline at the bottom of the driveway. I put on my leather motorcycle/gardening boots, took a shovel from the garage, and absentmindedly moved snow around the driveway.

I knew my right arm was broken the instant I hit the ground. After rolling off the arm that had been pinned under me behind my back, I crawled to the top of the driveway and supported myself on the neighbors' cars as I groped my way to the front door of the nearest house.

Although I had lived in the house on Cathedral Avenue for almost a year, I did not know any of the people who lived in the five other townhouses on the cul-de-sac. I recognized most of them, knew the names of a few of them, and did not know the phone numbers of any of them. The door was opened by two of the people who rented the house two doors down from me.

They were gentle people and gave the impression that they might have been flower children ten years ago, but all they could do was help me back to my house. They did not know anything about even the basics of first aid. Relying on my Girl Scout training of twenty-five years ago, I directed them as they got newspapers from the garage, ripped up an old sheet for ties, wrapped the arm in a makeshift splint of newspaper, and tied it on. They did not drive and were unaware of the location of the nearest hospital.

Calling an ambulance was out of the question—under the best of conditions the D.C. ambulance service was overtaxed. I hardly considered myself to be an emergency, and the snowstorm was almost certainly creating plenty of crises more significant than mine. Besides, what would I do with Tela?

I called for Sally Keene who lived in the neighborhood. Thomas Peter had still not returned with Gilbert when she arrived. While she kept an eye on Tela, I went next door to meet my neighbors.

Although David and Ruth Hopper had moved into their house about the same time Thomas Peter, the children, and I had moved into ours, I did not know them other than to say hello. David and Ruth were private people. Both worked, he for the World Bank and she for the Agency for International Development. Both of them frequently traveled internationally. I hated to bother them, but I was lucky they were at home.

Ruth opened the door. Perceptively, she made no attempt to shake hands. I asked if perhaps she or David could take me to the nearest emergency room. Ruth needed no explanation. On her call, David stopped writing a speech, already way behind schedule, to the international organization of something or other.

In what was by then the closest thing to a blizzard that Washington had experienced in ten years, he drove us through Rock Creek Park to the George Washington Hospital. He gaily told stories about driving in the winter in his native Canada as he smoothly avoided the sliding traffic. When he deposited Ruth and me at the emergency entrance, Ruth told him we would call a cab to get home and he turned around and went back to his speech.

We checked me in along with what we were later told were the twelve other coleus fractures for the evening. I was on the verge of dizzily keeling over when I sank into one of the few remaining chairs in a small waiting room. For maybe twenty minutes, Ruth sat across the room reading and looking up watchfully at me as I hung on the edge of consciousness. She then decided that I was not in control of my senses and took charge.

Ruth proceeded calmly to the desk where the harried emergency room attendant was reviewing a growing pile of patient paperwork. She politely addressed him and in a quiet, dignified voice told him that I was five months pregnant and about to pass out from pain.

It was unnecessary for Ruth to ask how long it would be before a doctor saw me. The emergency room swung into action like something out of a hospital television series. Two medics put me in a wheelchair and rolled me out of the waiting room where one doctor looked at my swollen arm while someone started trying to locate the orthopaedic surgeon. The medics then whisked me off to radiology with instructions to give due regard to my delicate condition.

X rays completed, I was delivered into the waiting hands of a tiny young woman with a sparkling sense of humor and two big men in hospital garb. She was the orthopaedic surgeon, she told me, and while the two men immobilized various parts of me, she was going to set my arm by pulling it around until she thought the bones were in the right place. She finished by installing the first of what became a series of four casts that I would have to wear over the next two months.

Ruth overestimated the capabilities of the D.C. taxi system. When the cab failed to arrive after fifteen or twenty minutes, and it became evident that none was coming, she interrupted David's speechwriting efforts again. It was still snowing when David and Ruth delivered me back to my family. I never heard how the speech went.

The odds were heavily in favor of my third child being a boy, so the radiologist who administered and interpreted the sonagram said. On the blackboard that was barely noticeable in the background over his shoulder, I could see his scoresheet. The hashmarks that counted the children, by sex, guessed and actual indicated that he usually predicted sex correctly.

He made no effort to discuss cranial diameters, merely stated that the baby was well enough developed that Dr. Giere could proceed with the scheduled Caesarean. He also explained amniocentesis. One component of amniocentesis was a test to determine the ratio of two proteins in the amniotic fluid. That ratio indicated whether the baby's lungs were well enough developed to proceed. While the lab was running tests of the proteins, it could also do other checks to determine the sex of the baby. In my case, it was all moot, I had too little amniotic fluid for amniocentesis.

Sister Thomas Margaret, as Thomas Peter's sister Sheila was known in the order, had a habit of dropping in unannounced. She just showed up one day about the time that Peter was born—moved in with us. She had taken a leave of absence from the Dominican convent that she had entered at the age of eighteen. The technical term for the leave was "indult of exclaustration." I referred to it as "an adulterous excloseture," partly because I was unable to pronounce or understand the words, which were meaningless to me, and partly because she was so sensitive to and unsettled by her state, that a little humor was welcome.

Although I had very little acquaintance with Sheila, I always liked her. She was the younger of Thomas Peter's two sisters. I first met her the summer before we were married, when he, his family, and I spent a summer vacation in a Victorian barn of a house on Cape May. Although I was unaware of it at the time, the feeling was not mutual. On her return to the convent, she apparently wrote Thomas Peter to tell him that he "was out of his mind" if he married me.

She did not come to our wedding—she was denied permission to leave the convent, or so she said. Thomas Peter and I took Tela Margaret to Springfield to visit her and the other nuns when Tela was six weeks old. Tela pooped on the front of the white habit of at least one nun who graciously reacted as if that sort of thing happened every day and she had a closet full of clean habits just for the occasion.

Sheila came for Christmas a month after Gilbert was born. She was instrumental in selecting Tela's gift, something called a Toonerville Tootie, a plastic train that ran around in circles and played a variety of offensive and very loud tunes. Somehow she knew I hated noise. As I expectantly descended the stairs on Christmas morning, gingerly because I was still wary of Caesarean pain, she unleashed the tooting train. In feigned terror over the noise, I receded back up the stairs. We laughed, a lot.

She also arrived unexpectedly the day of the move into the house on Cathedral. She had been able to escape the convent, briefly, because she was in a graduate program at Notre Dame and it was spring break. I was on my hands and knees with a toothbrush and a bottle of ammonia scrubbing the black stuff that infested the depressions that separated the raised marbled pattern in the linoleum floor on the kitchen.

When we contracted for the house, I had mistaken the dirt for part of the pattern and thought I could simply wax over it periodically. With all the other more pressing household chores, I had failed to notice that the pattern was dirt until a spill acted like a solvent and exposed it for what it was. I gave her a toothbrush and she scrubbed along with me.

To the relief of Thomas Peter, Sully, Sheila, the Owl School, and me, Tela gave up diapers on Thursday, June 7, 1979. Thomas Peter, who had always done his share of the diaper changing, was particularly relieved. I had difficulty bending over and lifting in the last trimester, with the consequence that he had been changing both his share and mine.

Thomas Peter expressed his frustration over the situation one evening by getting a clean diaper from one of the several boxes of different-size Pampers in the kitchen, wrapping it around a few stalks of celery readily available from the refrigerator, and throwing the resulting package into the trash container under the sink. "There," he said. "Now we can cut out the middle man." Had Tela persisted, we might have had three children in diapers simultaneously. My son would be born the following Thursday.

Thomas Peter and Dr. Giere were both in lighthearted moods. This was the first delivery in which Thomas Peter could participate. Although he was not allowed in the operating room, he and Dr. Giere were in voice contact throughout the surgery. The field of vision that would have allowed me to see what was going on was obscured by a lot of green sheets.

I was perfectly comfortable, but the steady stream of sarcastic humor that was bouncing back and forth between the two of them on the other side of the green wall threatened to send me into gales of laughter. "I would appreciate it if you two clowns would cut it out," I said. They settled down.

Thomas Peter Gallagher Jr. was named after his father, mostly. He was also named after his brother, Thomas Gilbert, whom my mother-in-law had taken to calling Tommy, a name she had apparently used for Thomas Peter's father when he was alive and for Thomas Peter when he was younger.

I could ignore it when by an occasional slip of the tongue, Gilbert was inadvertently called Tommy, but recently Sully had picked up the habit. Having two sons named Thomas would ensure that neither of them was called Tommy. As I was to learn later, it also lengthened the period of time required by insurance companies to pay medical claims as they sorted out all the Thomases in the family.

Peter escaped whatever the mild blood type incompatibility was that sent Tela and Gilbert to the light box after birth. He remained that peculiar reddish color characteristic of most babies. There were no plastic sheets. My vital signs were only checked when I was awake. Other than a horrendous breast infection that surfaced shortly after I left the hospital and had to be treated with an antibiotic that cost $2.40 per tablet, Peter's birth was uneventful.

Transition

While I commuted to Albuquerque, paperwork that stacked up during the week was reserved for consideration on the plane trip between there and Washington. Late in the summer, one of the items in the stack was a request for proposals from the U.S. Department of State. The request had been circulated to most of the partners and managers in the office, none of whom had expressed any interest in it.

Writing proposals is dog work and was something that I had generally avoided except when it was necessary to develop my next assignment. This one, however, showed promise: the department wanted an analysis leading to design recommendations for a worldwide financial management system. It planned to contract initially with two companies, each of which would independently do the analysis and design. The department would then select a design and require the two companies to compete in a procurement for a contract to implement the design. This type of contract was called a "fly-off," based on a type of aircraft procurement whereby two competing contractors would each build one aircraft. After flying both of them, the government would award a contract to build the better aircraft in volume.

Because of its fly-off nature, the odds of winning an initial contract were twice as good as they were on most contracts. The initial work was to be done by a small number of people, so my office could credibly propose. The time frame for the analysis covered more than a year, so we could be assured that a core of people would be billable full time. The work looked like it would be fun to do; the travel prospects looked interesting; and if we did a good job, the firm would have the opportunity to develop and install the resulting system at State Department facilities all over the world. That would be a huge job. By the time I got back to Washington, I had worked up a lot of enthusiasm for writing the proposal.

Thomas O. Beyer, the partner in charge of Federal Management Advisory Services in OGS, was not someone I knew very well. His father had been the managing partner at Touche Ross. Tom transferred from Boston the summer Peter was born. He was a lean man, not tall, fierce steel-blue eyes, bald on top with very curly, close-cropped gray hair on the sides. Decisive, direct, his demeanor scared some, offended others. When he took over the consulting function, OGS was a cost center of the firm's national office—it was not required to make a profit. He either had been given or had taken on a new charter and an aggressive posture for OGS. It was going to be a profit center and he was going to make it grow, exponentially. He gave no indication that he had a plan of action, but everyone in the office knew what the objective was.

Some of the managers characterized Tom's approach to growth as "fly it up the flag pole and see if anyone salutes." Tom was willing to support almost any manager with almost any scheme, for a while. If the scheme and the manager contributed to his growth objective, then the manager got more and more opportunities to try more and more schemes. Managers who produced failures, and there had to be more than one, were assigned to harmless efforts. For all Tom's apparent fierceness, I am unable to identify a single person that he ever fired.

When Tom and I met to discuss the proposal effort, I told him it would be difficult. The firm was required by the request for proposals to have a facility cleared for security by the Department of Defense, a clearance that the office had never applied for. The request required that people proposed also have security clearances, a relatively uncommon credential among professionals who did little work for the federal government. The firm was required to have a methodology, and although there were various components available in various parts of the firm there was no single stack of volumes entitled "Methodology" that we could point to. Furthermore, even a blind man could see the potential for business growth that the job offered—the competition, therefore, was going to be fierce. Tom wanted to go for it and told me I could have whatever I needed to get it done.

True to his word, Tom committed all the staff time he had and whatever money it took to getting it done. The staff in OGS did anything it could. Anyone we needed from other offices, we flew in from wherever they were to write parts of the proposal, to fill out clearance forms, to do whatever it took—and it took weeks of twelve- to sixteen-hour days to draft and tailor each component of the proposal to meet the detailed terms and conditions specified in the request for proposals.

The largest proposal that OGS had ever written was in the final, chaotic stages of preparation when the phone rang. "Are you busy, Mom?" asked Sully, who had not laid eyes on me in three days. She had my immediate attention. There must be a crisis of immense proportion—the last time she called me at the office was months ago. "No," I lied, "What can I do for you?" "I'm stuck in the elevator, Mom. I can't get out." By asking a few questions I was able to determine that Tela, Gilbert, and Peter were walking or crawling around the house somewhere, that Sully was trapped between the second and third floors, and that the power to the elevator must be off because the light went out when it stopped.

Sheila had taken a job in Washington when she left the convent. She lived in an apartment three blocks from the house. To my great good fortune, she was home and could race to the house. She phoned back to say she had located all of the children, unharmed, but was unable to rescue Sully from the dark three-by-three-by-eight-foot box in which she was incarcerated. I gave Sheila the phone number for the elevator maintenance company. Two hours later the elevator repairman called to say, "Miss Hopkins, you better put a dead bolt on the utility closet door. I think one of the kids pulled the master power switch. There's nothing wrong with the elevator."

For a week or two after the proposal was submitted, I worked from nine to five, organizing the proposal papers and recovering from exhaustion. Then we waited along with the ten or twelve other bidders who submitted proposals while the government's evaluation process plodded along. While we waited, Tom assigned me to a project to do statistical analysis for a law firm. I struggled to write FORTRAN programs to do the analysis. The assignment kept me billable to a client but was not critical to the project. Tom wanted the flexibility to get me off the job quickly if anything requiring my attention developed on State. To finish the job, Tom brought in a woman who had worked for him in Boston.

When I first met Judy Reach she blurted out, "FORTRAN, you're using FORTRAN to do that? I haven't seen anyone use FORTRAN in years!" She stood leaning with one shoulder against the wall, head forward, arms crossed aggressively, as she gazed over my shoulder at the FORTRAN error messages scrolling by on the computer monitor in front of me.

"Who is this woman?" I thought in frustration. I was having a hell of a time getting a statistic of any kind, and FORTRAN, although it may have been inappropriate, was the only language I knew. Judy, who was ten years younger than I, was as outspoken and direct as Tom. Mercifully, developments at the State Department rescued me from the FORTRAN. Judy, who knew what she was doing with computer languages, relieved me of my statistical chores.

On very little notice, State invited us to bring the proposed team and present our proposal to the technical evaluation committee. The short lead time was no problem at all for me—I had been waiting around anxiously hoping for something to happen. It was only a minor inconvenience for the Washington-based people to rearrange their schedules. Whatever scheduling problems there might have been for the proposed out-of-towners, Tom simply eliminated. Everyone showed up with military precision, were briefed, coached, and rehearsed. We were prepared, or so we thought.

In evaluating a contractor, federal clients tend to focus on the project manager because the person in that role is normally the individual with whom the client has the most interaction. The Big Eight firms, on the other hand, tend to focus on the partner responsible for the job, who is rarely the project manager, largely, I believe, out of arrogance or a misplaced sense of confidence in one who has been admitted to the exclusive society that a firm represents. The difference in focus sometimes results in presentations that are at cross-purposes—the partner presents the firm and the proposal, while the client wants to hear the project manager and watch the interactions between the project manager and the team proposed. So it was at State.

We were outnumbered by the members of the State technical evaluation committee who were lined up, in no apparent hierarchical order, along the opposite side of a pair of tables pushed together in a small conference room at the main State Department building. After appropriate introductions, Ben Warder, the partner proposed to be responsible for the job, began our presentation, which, like Ben, was well presented, polished, low key, colorless, humorless, and harmless. The audience responded with nothing—straight faces, perfectly neutral body language, zombielike eye contact. It was unnerving.

More unnerving was one of the questions. "Mr. Warder, it is not evident that the project manager you proposed has ever managed a project anywhere near this size or complexity. How did you select her— next one off the availability list?" asked an attractive man with dark crew cut hair and what, at the time, appeared to be a mildly malevolent expression. Warder waffled. Tactical options flashed through my mind as I realized that only I, as the proposed project manager, could dispose of the question. This client was not a collection of hard-fact scientists and engineers like those I had seen at NASA; it was the agency responsible for the conduct of foreign affairs abroad, a collection of diplomats. Should I counter overt aggressiveness with an equally aggressive response or ignore what appeared to be hostility and deal with the man as I would with a boor at a debutante ball? Visions of the lady or the tiger came to mind. If I made the wrong choice, I could blow us out of the water.

"Follow your nose." My mother's words rose out of my subconscious. "Would you like me to respond to that?" I asked Ben in a calm, dignified, polite tone of voice. When Ben said "please," or "by all means" or something of the like, I verbally decked the apparently antagonistic, hostile creep. I looked him straight in the eyes as I told him, as concisely but specifically as I could, how much I enjoyed managing projects to build computer systems. I went back through my days launching satellites and in the Mines and described what I had done in the terminology of the State Department as I understood it from the request for proposals. He never lost eye contact, never flinched. No body language changed.

When we left the oral presentations, the clear, cool day made me realize how hot it had been in the conference room. As we talked among ourselves, we gave the situation mixed reviews. I had no clue as to whether we had been successful. It was months before I learned that the "why is your project manager an idiot" question was a setup. A different member of the technical committee asked what was referred to as the Question of the project manager proposed by each of the firms that were invited to make oral presentations. The purpose of the question was to test the mettle of the project manager.

Hernia

Thomas Peter and I were convinced that Gilbert was born with a hernia. From birth he had an intermittently appearing abdominal bulge that vanished like the Loch Ness monster every time Thomas Peter or I mentioned it to the pediatrician, who treated us with all the disdain to which most monster-sighters are subjected. We, however, had solid scientific support for our conclusion. Thomas Peter himself was apparently born with a hernia, at least that was what we were informed by the surgeon who repaired it shortly after Tela was born. Until an annual physical revealed ten inches of the colon hanging into the scrotum, Thomas Peter thought he was merely well hung. Long after the problem had been corrected, Thomas Peter's sister Sheila was horrified at my casual reference to the matter in conjunction with a discussion of Gilbert's problem.

Neither Thomas Peter nor I liked the pediatrician. He kept one or the other of us waiting for at least forty-five minutes at regularly scheduled checkups. Emergency visits, for which we had to be slotted into an already unmanaged schedule, were guaranteed to consume at least half a day. Furthermore, the pediatrician had a medically arrogant way of making us feel like child abusers over the damndest issues. Weight was one such issue. Gilbert and Peter were both consistently small, and until Gilbert reached his late preteens, he and Peter were about the same size. At one checkup, the pediatrician expressed concern about Peter's size relative to his age. The questions that the pediatrician asked led me to believe that he had concluded that perhaps Peter was undernourished. "If you think this is bad," I commented, "wait till you see his brother. He's eighteen months older and is about the same weight." My sarcasm went unappreciated by the pediatrician. I was irate with him.

My level of frustration, as well as that of the pediatrician, rose steadily, as I insisted from checkup to checkup that Gilbert had a hernia and the pediatrician insisted that he was unable to diagnose it. Finally, the pediatrician told me to take Gilbert to the Children's National Medical Center, simply known as Children's Hospital, to see if one of the pediatric surgeons there could diagnose it. I liked the idea. Children's had a distinguished reputation for the treatment of children and was ten minutes from the house.

Thomas Peter coped badly with medical situations. Part of his inability was probably related to ignorance. He was, as an example, concerned that he might be sterilized in the process of having a left inguinal hernia surgically repaired. When we discussed the possibility, I commented that "only by one hell of a slip of the scalpel," could it occur. He was not amused.

He pushed the envelope of panic when confronted with medical situations involving the children. While showering with Thomas Peter after a swim at the YMCA, Peter fell on his glass baby bottle. Wrapped in a towel loincloth, Thomas Peter, close to tears and with an absolutely panicked expression on his face, delivered the baby, bleeding from the hands and chest, to me in the lobby. I grabbed Peter, rapidly walked barefooted into the parking lot, stopped the first car trying to exit, and asked the driver to take me to Suburban Hospital, about a mile away. Thomas Peter's tearful panicked state only diminished when he later observed his cheerful younger son in the emergency room, twenty-four stitches and some impressive bandages later.

I waited until Thomas Peter was out of town to take Gilbert to Children's.

Gilbert wandered around the examination room exploring while I sat uncomfortably on the hospital equivalent of a bar stool. Unable to gain access to any of the cabinets, he settled down to play with the blocks and toys that were strewn on the spotlessly clean, shiny waxed floor. The pediatric surgeon and his head resident entered and shook hands as they introduced themselves. I returned to my bar stool where I quickly became uncomfortable because I towered over Gilbert and the doctors who had seated themselves on the floor next to a now-standing Gilbert. I joined them on the floor, still feeling awkward, this time because of my inability to sit properly in the straight skirt of my business suit.

The doctors more or less ignored me as they engaged Gilbert in a cheerful dialogue. After first asking permission to touch him, the pediatric surgeon lightly felt Gilbert's abdomen with two fingers, below and to the left of his navel. "That's one," he said. He repeated the procedure on the other side. "That's two. Gilbert has bilateral inguinal hernias." I was impressed and astonished, less with the diagnosis than with the sensitivity of the doctors in dealing with children.

A month later, Thomas Peter and I stood by while Gilbert had outpatient surgery to repair his hernias. When Gilbert went into surgery, Thomas Peter was almost as gray with concern as Gilbert was from the effect of the general anesthetic. We brought Gilbert home with no bandages over the almost unnoticeable incisions. His abdomen had been sprayed with a clear plastic material that resembled impenetrable nail polish. A week later, there was no evidence that Gilbert had ever had surgery. We changed pediatricians.

Diplomats

Two firms, representing two very different styles of consulting, were awarded contracts for the project to design the worldwide financial management system (FMS) for State. Price Waterhouse, representing a user-oriented, client focus, was one. AMS, my previous employer, representing a technology-oriented, issue focus, was the other.

The staff of the State Department consisted of about five thousand civil service and foreign service officers in the United States and about fifteen thousand people overseas, only one-third of which were U.S. foreign service officers. The remainder of the staff overseas were almost entirely foreign nationals. There were dramatic differences between State's financial operations in the United States and those overseas, the most obvious of which related to the requirement to make payments and keep track of about 150 foreign currencies.

State wanted both of us, PW and AMS, to have an in-depth understanding of domestic and international operations. To meet that objective, we were required to study and analyze activities at departmental facilities in the United States and at several State facilities, mostly embassies or consulates, overseas. State also wanted to be scrupulously fair in dealing with both contractors. Therefore, wherever one contractor went, the other also went, although not usually at the same time. Furthermore, each contractor was always accompanied by a person from State to make sure that questions raised or information gathered by one contractor could be made available to the other.

State planned for me to take my team to Asia while AMS went to Europe and East Africa in the summer of 1980. Shortly thereafter, my team would go to Europe while AMS went to Asia. "Do we really need to go around the world?" I asked Ed Gulli (pronounced ghoulee), and "If we do, couldn't we take a brief trip to somewhere close by, like Canada, to get a feeling for things before we take off around the world?" I had difficulty believing that administrative and financial practices varied so widely from post to post overseas that we needed to go to so many places. Ed was State's contracting officer's technical representative, a long title meaning that he was our duly designated, official client contact. Ed reminded me a lot of Dan Maceda except for the fact that, unlike Ed, Dan was a smoker. Ed had an easygoing manner and a lively sense of humor that were only adversely affected by occasional bouts of chronic back pain for which he carried spine-stretching equipment everywhere he went.

Ed explained that there were political reasons why we had to travel to so many sites overseas: State was regionally, that is geographically, organized into bureaus that served various territorial domains. Any regional bureau might be offended if its posts were left unvisited because the posts of some other regions were assumed to be representative of the department as a whole. It sounded like a variation on the theme of "not invented here" to me. However, I had been a financially conscientious consultant by suggesting that it was absurd to go around the world if we could get away with reviewing operations in Canada. Ed decided that going to Canada as an orientation site was a good idea, but we had to go around the world anyway, for political reasons.

Roger B. Feldman, the comptroller at the State Department was going to Canada with us. He terrified me more than anyone I ever met. In hindsight I guess it was because he could make large components of the bureaucracy at State nervous. The resulting anxiety seemed to be contagiously transferred to us as contractors. He could put Tom Beyer on edge with the slightest bit of quizzical body language or even a sentence that ended in a negative intonation. A criticism from Roger was cause for a lengthy analytical meeting to determine immediate corrective action required, whether the criticism was well founded or not.

The origin of his ability to make otherwise unflappable diplomats nervous was the control that Roger had over State's budget. On one hand he was the bureaucracy's chief advocate before Congress when State had to justify funding requests on the Hill. On the other hand he had considerable discretion in how funds, once approved on the Hill, were allocated to the bureaucracy. Roger was also the guiding light for the FMS. He had managed the consensus building process, on the Hill and among the high-ranking bureaucrats at State and at the agencies that State served, that was required to get the project approved and funded. We may have been wrong, but we were under the clear impression that if Roger, for any reason, decided that AMS should be the contractor to help him follow the FMS star, then we were dead in the water.

I was happy to see Ben Warder paired with Roger on the trip to Canada. They could go off together and interview high-ranking embassy personnel engaged in the conduct of foreign affairs while I worked with the people who did the mundane paperwork. To me Roger and Ben seemed like two of a kind, both unknowable, formal, reserved, more than a little arrogant. It seemed perfect.

I was not there. I never knew what happened but somehow, in Roger's presence, Ben irrevocably breached an unspoken protocol in an inter- view with an economic or political officer. I have no recollection of Roger saying anything at the time, but his relation with Ben instantly turned cold. When we returned to Washington from Canada, Ed Gulli told me there was a problem, that there was nothing that I, or anyone else at Price Waterhouse, could do, and that we should just keep our heads down, work like hell, and hope the impact of the problem would diminish over time.

The core team of five people we proposed was not the team that I wanted to do the job with. One of them was unacceptable anyway—he had flunked State's reference check and had to be replaced even before the contract was awarded. There were no great, glaring defects in the credentials of the others, but they were all strangers from other offices. The devil you know beats the devil you don't, every time, and I knew whom I wanted from the staff in OGS. Furthermore, I could get them: Ben Warder may have been the partner designated as the one in charge of the project, but my project was Tom Beyer's pet. Within reason, he would assign anyone I asked for. And I asked—for Karen Nold and for Pat Bowman.

"It's one thing to sell a job. It's another to do it," I remarked when I told Ed what I was doing, that I planned to use people different from those proposed, and that I was willing to wait a few weeks for them to become available if he would bear with me. He had no objections.

On her first day on the project, Karen Nold and I got on a plane headed for Asia: Hong Kong, Indonesia, Malaysia, India, Thailand, Singapore, and Japan. Getting off the ground had been a major effort. Although State had picked the itinerary, I was responsible for drafting a cable for State to send to each of the posts advising them of our plans. I was also responsible for all the travel arrangements for Karen, Ben, the State people who were going with us, and myself.

It took me the better part of fifty hours of effort to get the cable out. It had to go through a clearance process whereby it was reviewed and officially signed off, first by Roger and then by authorized people in the regional bureau responsible for the posts we were visiting. Initially, nothing I drafted was right—whatever I wrote and submitted to Ed came back covered with the green felt-tip scribblings that were Roger's trademark. After six drafts I was on the verge of professional hysteria when to my amazement and relief the cable cleared Roger. Everyone else signed off without comment.

Getting the plane tickets was equally time consuming, although I managed to shift most of the burden to the firm's official travel agent. The body of government regulation covering travel of State Department officials abroad was a major obstacle to be overcome. In general, we had to fly an American flag carrier, although there were exceptions. Flying over Viet Nam was prohibited, as was landing or stopping over in certain countries where the United States was at diplomatic odds with the government. Fortunately, John Ferraro, the travel agent, knew what he was doing and patiently put up with a changing itinerary. (Until a week or so before we left, there was considerable uncertainty about Australia. It was in one day and out the next until I finally put my foot down. Including Australia would have added at least a week to a trip that was already approaching five weeks in length.)

I thought we had the trip nailed down.

"Use my travel agent," Ben said as he wrote down the name and phone number. "I can't do that, Ben. Ferraro has hours invested in these arrangements," was my flabbergasted reply—to no avail. I called John and told him that we would use another agent. When the new itinerary came in from Ben's agent, I reviewed it with Ed in anticipation of having the tickets printed. "You can stop over in Taiwan, but we can't," he said with a sarcastic smile. He was referring to the fact that government regulations prohibited people traveling on diplomatic passports from stopping there. He was insistent, not angry. I was embarrassed at the error that I knew John would never have made. "What a pain," I thought as I called Ben's agent and told her to fix the problem and print the tickets.

Mount St. Helen erupted on May 18, 1980, killing sixty people. The event was widely covered by the media. For several weeks after the firestorm, Gilbert slept uneasily. "Mom, are there any volcanoes in Washington?" echoed up the stairwell to wake me one night. Minutes after I groggily explained that there were no volcanoes, active or dormant, within a thousand miles of Washington, he followed up with, "How about earthquakes?" A few nights later he woke me with, "If there were a brontosaurus in the driveway could he see in my window?" Gilbert naturally associated volcanoes with earthquakes and dinosaurs. "No Gilbert, brontosauruses always look up at the tops of the trees." The children were apprehensive about my going to California en route to Asia.

Karen and I were accompanied by Ed Gulli and Howard Renman to San Francisco and on to Hong Kong where she and I were scheduled to interview foreign service officers. We landed a few hours after a major cyclone had blown through and cleaned the air, leaving behind a sparkling sunny day. My first view of Asia was the dark green mountains of the Chinese mainland dropping precipitously into the Pacific. As we taxied in to the terminal I watched the people cooking dinner and hanging laundry on the small boats that crowded the edge of the pavement where the runway met the ocean. That night after dinner Karen and I danced with the client to Viennese waltzes played by an orchestra, largely strings, of oriental musicians more than twenty stories up looking out at the skyline of Hong Kong. It would be a good trip.

Five weeks of togetherness on planes, in hotels, at meals, and in ever-changing offices is an extreme test of a relationship, personal or professional. Karen Nold passed higher than anyone I ever traveled with. She was cheerful, never complained, always showed up on time, never lost anything, worked like a beaver, and played with enthusiasm. All this in spite of the fact that she had what I thought was the more difficult work and travel assignment: she had to be in Delhi and Jakarta, places that I did not want to go, with Ben and Howard, both of whom I avoided. Furthermore, she never missed an interview in spite of the fact that she picked up an intestinal bug in Hong Kong with the result that she lost 10 of her 115 pounds on the trip. She later told me that some of the interviews were better done than others.

My initial impression of Karen, gained on our interactions over proposals and projects for the Bureau of Indian Affairs, had been positive. She was her own woman; you might persuade her with a good argument; short of that, however, she simply stated her position and disagreed—Karen was no chameleon. She and I, for instance initially had entirely different views of Howard Renman.

Somewhere over the Pacific, I said, "I think he's a snake. I just don't trust the guy." Her simple response was "I do and I think you should reconsider." When I thought about it, I realized that the problem was me not Howard. He was Roger's trusted aide and I was, to some extent, transforming my nervousness at dealing with Roger into a distrust of Howard. When I stopped avoiding him and learned to listen to what he had to say, I found him an invaluable source of good counsel.

Howard observed that I had a tendency to take a binary view of everything without much regard for context or culture. He admired that trait when I applied it to personal integrity or technical details. When applied to organizational cultures or without taking context into account, he thought it limited my effectiveness. "You carry only two paint cans—one black, one white," he said. "You have to learn to mix the paint. At the State Department, there is lots of gray." After a contentious meeting or when I would stiffen on some issue, Howard would say, "Mix the paint." I always knew exactly what he meant.

I believe the turning point in our relationship was just after Ben, Howard, and Karen finished their work in Delhi and rejoined me in Thailand. That evening over dinner, Howard, who was over six feet and skinny—I would be surprised if he weighed more than 135 pounds— discussed his interactions with Ben over a clean shirt. It seemed that Ben, who was a little shorter and a lot heavier than Howard had become separated from his luggage when he arrived in Delhi from Washington. With no other obvious alternative, Ben had to borrow a shirt from Howard. (I never could understand why a man absolutely must change shirts every day.) Howard's glee was evident as he described Ben, in the 110-degree subcontinental heat, with the vest of his three-piece suit fully fastened to cover the shirt that was only buttoned up tight at the collar. My discomfort with Howard had blinded me to the fact that the man had a fine sense of humor.

Karen and I did four to six interviews each day in spite of whatever obstacle confronted us. In our spare time, we studied the people and the culture of the American foreign service.

In Bangkok I carried my shoes along with my briefcase and walked the last hundred yards to the embassy through two feet of standing water, dumped the previous night by the monsoon. George Jenkins, the chief administrative officer, rose as we entered his office. As I extended my hand, in anticipation of an introduction, he walked right past me as he addressed Ed Gulli with a string of insults and expletives. He muttered about how he resented the department, as the State people back in Washington were collectively referenced, spending money to send worthless civilians overseas when he needed to improve the security at his post. With an expansive gesture that nearly knocked me over he told Ed that he was insufficiently funded to repair the machine gun bullet holes that were the object of his gesture. As I gazed nervously over my shoulder, George gave Ed a big bear hug that indicated that they were the best of friends. For the duration of the interview, as I sat with the bullet holes in the window behind me over my head, I had to concentrate intensely on my questions about how the post did purchasing and accounting and the like. It never occurred to me that foreign service officers were shot at.

A lot of things never occurred to me. In some contexts, it was Thai culture either to revere or to ignore women. As a cultural consequence, I was usually not served when I arrived alone for meals and, in mixed company, I was unable to pay a bill at a restaurant. To overcome the situation, I ate breakfast when one of the men could join me, and let one of them pay. When Karen and the others finished in Delhi, she rejoined me in Bangkok. Early the next morning, we met to discuss the events in Delhi over breakfast. We were the only customers in the restaurant served by five waiters. After about ten minutes Karen, who was suffering from coffee deprivation, commented on the apparently bad service. "Don't worry," I remarked "it'll pick up when one of the men gets here." Karen laughed.

In Kuala Lumpur, we hiked up several flights of stairs to find access to the embassy guarded by a marine standing at attention behind several layers of bulletproof plastic. After carefully scrutinizing the credentials we presented, he cautiously admitted us through a couple of steel doors that reminded me of a bank vault I had seen somewhere. In response to my ignorant question about the need for all the security, I was told, "Malaysia is a Moslem country. When Teheran hiccups, Kuala Lumpur covers its mouth." The embassy had been under siege in the recent past.

Singapore was as spectacular as Ruth and David Hopper had told me it would be when I talked to them about where I was going before I left Washington. The sun rose and set in twelve-hour cycles. The temperature never varied by more than a few degrees from seventy. The humidity was ideal. We stayed in the old, expansive, Victorian Raffles Hotel that Somerset Maugham had written about. It was indeed scenic, but I had to ask Ed to check me out of the place and into someplace else after getting up one night and, in the dark, stepping on what, with the lights on, looked like a roach that was more than three inches long. Ed laughed, almost convulsively, when he ran into me in the lobby the next morning, clearly distressed, with my packed hanging bag over my shoulder making preparations to check out of the hotel. I explained, "This is not a rational matter. It is a psychological matter. I cannot stay in this place one more night." At Ed's request, the embassy staff moved all of us to a modern hotel for the remainder of our stay.

All I said was, "My name is Ann Hopkins and I have an appointment with Miss Anderson." The reaction of the marine guard was visceral. Already at attention, eyes forward, he straightened up even more and I could feel his heels click mentally. His reaction left me unprepared for the white-haired woman wearing a pastel patterned shirtdress and an elegant double strand of natural pearls. Lea Anderson, counselor for administration at the American embassy in Tokyo, had the quiet confidence, apparent competence, and dominating presence that I remembered seeing in my grandmother and some of her contemporaries. She was the most prominent foreign service officer I had met overseas to date. I had the privilege of being invited to her home for dinner while we were in Tokyo and the even greater privilege of listening to her tell of her career. She had started with State as a foreign service secretary about the time of World War II, served in Africa where she earned a position as an administrative officer, and worked her way to her current post, which was probably one of the four or five most prestigious assignments available.

Karen and I returned from Asia with a pile of paperwork to do. We had to have typed, reviewed, indexed, and filed all our interview documentation and the dozens of financial and administrative forms that represented the existing financial management system overseas. We had to do it quickly because it would be only about a month before we hit the road again, this time for South America, Africa, and Europe. Ben would not be going with us. The State Department had asked Tom Beyer to take him off the job. Tom became the partner on the project.

Karen and I expected this trip to be easier for several reasons. First, we were getting pretty familiar with administrative and financial operations at posts overseas. Although the adage "if you've seen one, you've seen them all" certainly was inapplicable, we had overcome the bulk of the learning curve and could focus on deviations from general practice. Second, Karen and I would have staff to help share the load on this trip. Pat Bowman had finished up at the Bureau of Indian Affairs and started some of the interviews and related analysis in Washington. Her area would be budgeting system requirements. She had worked on such systems on a previous project for the Commonwealth of Virginia. Mark Jones, who had volunteered for assignment to the project, could also help out in the accounting area. I had little acquaintance with Mark, but he was a CPA and had lots of enthusiasm.

Caracas, Dakar, Abidjan, Bucharest, Vienna, Paris, Bonn, Moscow, Geneva, and Brussels were the posts that Karen, Pat, Mark, and I had to cover in the month before Halloween. Putting the trip together was like staging an assault on Europe. Karen would start out a week or so earlier than the rest of the team and take Caracas, Dakar, and Abidjan by herself. I would take Mark to Bucharest and Vienna where we would meet Pat. All four of us would meet in Paris, a big post where we needed lots of coverage. Karen would return to the States from Paris, leaving the rest of us to go on to Bonn. After Bonn, Pat would go on to Geneva and Brussels. Mark would stick with me and go to Moscow—I was reluctant to have him work by himself, only because we had never worked together.

The size of the team was actually much larger than just the four of us because we were each accompanied everywhere we went by someone from State. We affectionately referred to our companions as shadows, from the nursery rhyme "I have a little shadow that goes in and out with me. . . ."

With all the cables, clearances, and advance notice, it was hard to understand how an itinerary could be changed on the first day. However, when Will Robinson, my shadow throughout Europe, checked in with Washington from the London airport, we were advised that Vienna and Bucharest had been flipped. Will and I changed what we had to and the team went on to Vienna. Will was a very decent man who said little, did his job, and avoided crowds—other than official functions, he infrequently went out for dinner with the group. He was direct: In Vienna, our first stop, I referred to some triviality as a "gnat's ass" only to have him correct me immediately. "Gnat's eyebrow," he said. "In the foreign service, we have gnats' eyebrows."

A cold, heavy, relentless rain poured down on us while we were in Vienna and dampened our initially high spirits as we started to work. I had been to Vienna years before as a kid. The part of town in which we worked had changed little since then, in fact it had changed little in the last couple of centuries. The historic old buildings that appeared quaint, charming, or interesting to any tourist, represented a hardship, administratively, financially, and personally to the foreign service.

Much of Vienna is the U.S. equivalent of a "historic district." To change, even to repair, the facade of the older buildings required government authorization comparable to an act of Congress. Once authorized, construction was prohibitively expensive, partly because of the local economy and partly because of the level of skill required to work with materials and techniques appropriate for buildings of that vintage. In some instances, foreign service officers and their families actually had to live in these gothic relics. I received a guided tour, from basement to attic, of one such house.

The tour was conducted by a woman who had two children, an infant and a toddler. It was initiated when I struck up a conversation with her after dinner, which she had prepared for us visitors. What began on the subject of children led to a discussion of living conditions for foreign service families. She would have much preferred a manageably sized, modern apartment with conventional heating and plumbing to the multistoried, unheatably cold, damp, stone monstrosity, with high ceilings and unsealable windows and doors. She viewed living in a castle as a threat to the health of her children, but perceived that she had no alternative because the house was automatically assigned to the position occupied by her foreign service officer husband. I remember that woman every time I read about the supposed financial advantages and high living conditions of government employees living abroad.

Mark and I were a little concerned about going into Bucharest. Because of a mix-up in Washington, we were unaware, until it was too late, that we were required to have official visas to enter the country.

When the Romanian embassy described the elaborate, time-consuming process of sending cables back and forth between D.C. and Bucharest to get authorization for the visa, it was clear that we would never meet the travel schedule if we had to wait for the visa. We left Washington hoping we would be admitted as tourists. Will had cabled ahead to the embassy to let them know that Mark and I would be arriving "unofficially."

I could see machine guns atop embankments as we landed at the airport in Bucharest. They looked like something out of a World War II movie. The chief administrative officer from the embassy was standing by with all kinds of official forms when we arrived. We "tourists" had no trouble; Mark and I were waved through with our bags unopened, virtually untouched. Will, however, who was traveling on a diplomatic passport, was subjected to different treatment. He was frisked and his bags were opened and meticulously searched.

Mark's propensity for brushes with trouble justified my decision to avoid having him travel alone until I was more comfortable that he could handle it. He looked like innocence abroad: on the near side of thirty, he had a shock of blondish hair and good looks that were intensified by good teeth and a broad smile. Mark was single, no wedding band, and dressed with an understated elegance, but his clothes were obviously American in origin. From the first moment that we arrived at the hotel in Bucharest, people followed him around. He was offered currency at black market rates. People stopped him walking on the street to ask if he had Levi's for sale. A mournful looking, cow-eyed maiden followed him around the hotel restaurant for a couple of days. A friend whom he visited gave him a bottle of an exotic, home-made, fruit-flavored cognac that he was seriously considering trying to take out of the country in his suitcase.

Karen Nold was as glad to see me as I was to see her when we finally met up in Paris. South America and Africa had been "difficult" she said as she sat cross-legged on the bed in her tiny, dark hotel room, where I sought her out on my arrival. The one word said it all, but she elaborated. One of the hotels had charged her more than a hundred dollars for a brief phone call home. Her shadow was xenophobic—the street merchants in Africa terrified him when they put bracelets on his arms as part of their normal sales pitch. He hated to go anywhere or do anything. He had no sense of humor. (When I traveled with him in Asia, he spent his idle moments reading a book entitled *On Death and Dying*.)

Unlike Mark and me, who could occasionally be alone by leaving the rest of the group to entertain each other, Karen was diplomatically unable to escape for more than a few minutes during any given day. Upon arrival in Paris, her hotel reservations had been screwed up, leaving her and her shadow wandering between hotels trying to find a place to stay. Karen, unlike her shadow, spoke French. She managed to talk her way into a hotel by pleading, in French, that she was desperate to get away from her traveling companion and putting herself at the mercy of a sympathetic French woman. The French hotel keeper put them in rooms at opposite ends of the hotel. Karen needed relief from being center stage entertainment. I promised her the whole team would work to entertain her shadow while we were in Paris. Everyone was in great spirits by the time we met for dinner.

Karen and I met for an early breakfast the next morning. "Open-toed shoes are inappropriate professional attire," I cracked sarcastically to Karen who was wearing heels higher than mine, but with open toes. "Just because you don't wear them doesn't make them unprofessional," she retorted. Karen was on her way to interview the project manager responsible for the renovation of the Talleyrand building, which offsets the American embassy at the other end of the Place de la Concorde. It had been acquired just after World War II and, as property owned by the U.S. government, was the responsibility of State. We had to determine the financial and administrative requirements of State construction project managers all over the world. The Talleyrand project had been selected as representative of State's general requirements.

Karen became something of a legend that day. After she interviewed the project manager, he asked her if she wanted to tour the construction site. The way he asked the question made the offer seem more like a professional challenge than an invitation. When Karen accepted, he handed her a hard hat and escorted her, dressed in high heels and a business suit, to the roof, up and around the scaffolding that stood several stories high around most of the building.

We also had to interview State managers at the Regional Administrative Management Center (RAMC) in Paris. It was one of three large, centralized data processing centers operated by State overseas; the other two were in Mexico City and Bangkok. Budgetary accounting, check preparation and disbursing, timekeeping, and payroll for posts all over Europe, Africa, and parts of western Asia were handled by the

RAMC in Paris. Austin McHale, the foreign service officer who ran the facility, was a short, wiry, animated, enthusiastic man with an open face covered with freckles. Mac, as he was called, brought me face-to-face with the magnitude of the problem that confronted State in building a worldwide financial management system. I had just picked up a few punched card stock checks that had slipped into the crack between the wall and the cabinet where checks were sorted for distribution to the posts. Mac came into the room, carefully sidestepping piles of punched paper tape that recorded the time and expense records of people at the posts served by his RAMC. Knee-deep in punched paper tape, Mac spoke dramatically of a future with paperless input for information and electronic transfer of funds. As I saw it, State had a long way to go.

On the first work day in Paris, Mark succumbed to the effects of the bad weather in Vienna, something in the food, or a latent bug. Whatever it was went to his ears with the effect that he was unable to stand. He was confined to his hotel bed. I reallocated his work in Paris to the rest of the team. He was still unable to stand as the time for us to go to Bonn neared. I spent two hours walking around the Place de la Concorde trying to persuade Karen to extend her trip and go on to Bonn with us to fill in for Mark. She did not want to go and it was unreasonable of me to ask, but she agreed. We left Mark in Paris under the care of the embassy physician. He would have to catch up later.

"Receiving line?" I asked Toni Gibbons. "We're supposed to be in a receiving line?" I had been in lots of receiving lines, but never in a professional context. Toni and I grinned at each other. Elizabeth Antoinette Gibbons was the highest ranking of the shadows on the trip. She and Pat Bowman traveled together. Bob Lamb, the counselor for administration at the embassy, planned a reception for the shadows and my team. The embassy staff, both American and German, including spouses were invited. Toni and I were to represent our respective groups in the receiving line at the reception.

Bob, Toni, and Roger Feldman had great respect each for the other, and personal relationships that went back many years. Bob was a career foreign service officer, probably five years older than I, who looked like the grown-up version of a redheaded Norman Rockwell kid. He had a smile that would break hearts and a frown that would scare the devil himself. He had long been a proponent of automation at State and had designed some of the domestic systems before he was assigned to Bonn.

Toni was a contemporary of Bob's and, like Roger, a member of the Senior Executive Service. She was the highest-ranking line manager who reported to him. She began her career, straight out of college, in data processing with State, had been responsible for the development of State's U.S. payroll system, and had worked her way up to become the director of financial operations in Washington. The reception was one way for Bob to publicly show his support for Roger's project and his regard for Toni. It was also a means of thanking the people at the embassy for the time they took to participate in the interviews conducted by the PW team.

"That's okay, he and I will share a room," I said gesturing to Mark, when the Soviet clerk at the Hotel Rossiya advised us that we had fewer reservations than people. The general services officer from the embassy could only stand helplessly by. He could hardly start an international incident over a room reservation. I was beginning to get an impression that Soviets who worked in places that dealt frequently with people from an American embassy sometimes made an all-out effort to inconvenience or irritate them. Mark handled the situation like the capitalist that he was, "If we pay more, can we get another room?" Sure enough, the clerk gave us four keys and four hotel access passes, one each for Mark, me, and the two shadows.

Moscow was a hostile town for foreign affairs in 1981. Although not particularly well publicized outside of State at the time, within the agency, the newly constructed American compound was a well-known debacle: the place was bugged—there were apparently listening devices all over the new compound wired straight into the KGB. The situation was so bad that the facility could not be occupied. With good reason, people were generally concerned about bugs, but it seemed a little extreme to me to assume that the hotel rooms were bugged or that we were being followed. That, however, was what our shadows assumed or suspected, and it dampened any enthusiasm they might have had for the city and its people.

I found the notion that anyone in the Soviet Union might find anything I did or said to be of interest almost unimaginable, with the result that I was prepared to wander unsuspiciously around Moscow with the fascination of a tourist in a remarkable city. One night after a visit to the "New Circus," which was more an exhibition of gymnastics than an animal and clown show, Mark, the shadows, and I were confronted with the problem of getting back to the hotel, the location of which was a mystery to us. The general services officer at the embassy had told us he would send a car to pick us up if we called, but that seemed to be an abuse of courtesy. Cabs were scarce and how we might communicate with a cab driver was less than obvious, even if we found one. I thought it might be fun to take the subway back to the hotel.

It should be easy; after all we were going to Red Square. We bumbled into a convenient metro station, where for ten kopecks each, about fifteen cents at the official exchange rate, we managed to get tokens. We also received directions of a sort, in broken German, from the woman who sold the tokens. As we approached the turnstile to descend to the platform, we were confronted with a conventionally laid out subway map with all the lines and stops described in groups of Cyrillic characters. I hoped our directions were good.

After an unplanned tour, which was entirely too long, of a neat, clean, orderly, and apparently well laid out subway system, we concluded that we were lost. It was inconceivable that we should need forty-five minutes to get to Red Square. Next to me stood a tiny, plump woman, with a dull-colored scarf over her head tied under her chin and an equally dull-colored shawl over her shoulders. As I removed my hotel access pass, which I hoped contained the address somewhere in the sea of Cyrillic letters, I gingerly tapped her on the shoulder. She turned and greeted me with an unexpectedly charming but quizzical smile. With a palms up, shrugged shoulders gesture intended to say "I'm lost, can you help?" I displayed the hotel access card. She apparently got the message because she pointed to the ground and gave me a "don't move" sign. Two stops later she waved "follow me" as clearly as any army officer in any John Wayne movie I ever saw. Like overgrown ducklings imprinted on a miniature mother, the four of us followed her off the train. I must have looked panicked when she prepared to reenter the train because she let it go and led us around a corner and up a long flight of stairs. At the top she took my hand and with her other hand pointed straight up. We were standing under the Kremlin. She laughed, waved, and disappeared back down the stairs.

"Damn," I thought. "I never oversleep." But I did that morning. An embassy car was supposed to pick me and some army officers up at the hotel at 5:30 for the trip to the airport. It was 5:35. I grabbed my bag and rushed to the appointed place on the off chance that the embassy car might have waited. No luck.

Halloween is second in importance only to Christmas for small children. I had violated the "fly American" clause of our contract with the State Department by making a reservation on SwissAir because it was the only airline that could get me out of Moscow and back to Washington in time to go trick-or-treating with the children. Somehow I had to get to the airport to make the eight o'clock flight.

A few trial words in English and German were all that were required to convince me that the clerk spoke neither English nor German. A little French worked just well enough for me to determine that there was another clerk who spoke German diagonally across the hotel from my current position. To get there required that I circumnavigate the hotel, which was a long city block square, on the outside because internal security blocked access between the wings inside the building. It was bitter cold and snowing.

Huffing and puffing, I dragged my bag to the counter in front of the sleepy clerk who must have been awakened by the echoing clatter of my heels in the cavernous, empty hall. Terrific. Her German was about as good as mine. Did I have any rubles she asked in response to my urgent, but extremely polite, inquiry about how to get to the airport. No, will dollars work, I replied in German. Rubles, I was told, were required and available from the clerk across the hall, but when I looked across the hall there was no one there. I went to the empty exchange desk and interrupted the sleep of another clerk, who was lying out of sight behind the desk on two chairs.

Rubles in hand, I returned to the first clerk. Had I made arrangements with Intouriste? No. Why not? I had not planned to oversleep, I explained in frustration. Government regulations require that all in-country travel arrangements be made through Intouriste, she chastised. Upon further inquiry I was directed to the apparently closed Intouriste office. This time, however, I knew where to look for the sleeping clerk.

She too spoke enough German that we could communicate and although, she said, my request was unusual, she was prepared to help me get to the airport in a taxi. My watch said 6:25. As she fiddled with paperwork and I caught my breath, I tried to remember how long the ride from the airport to the hotel had taken when we arrived. Without looking up she asked a question about which airport. Her response to my bewildered expression was, "In Moskau gibt es viele Flughafen!" I should have known that. Moscow is a lot bigger than Washington, which has several airports.

My ticket said Moscow SVO; my itinerary said Moscow SVO. Nothing in my possession gave the name of an airport. A month ago, when John Ferraro and I had discussed the final travel arrangements, he mentioned the name of the airport. "What was it?" I thought but there was no reply. "Please—name a few airports for me, slowly," I requested, again in German. I selected the first one that sounded familiar, something like Sri Lanka.

It was 6:40 when the driver maneuvered the cab out of the parking lot. He smiled as he said something incomprehensible to me. I smiled back and offered him a cigarette, which he accepted. We rode in silence for a long time before I thought I recognized the surroundings. Once again he said something, which from the intonation had to be a question. I offered him another cigarette. He declined the cigarette, and in apparent frustration said "Sri Lanka," raised his index finger defiantly, repeated "Sri Lanka," raised two fingers and then gave me a glance that said he was waiting for an answer. I finally realized that he wanted me to identify one of two same-named airports. "Zurich" I said. Based on that guidance, he got me to SwissAir where I made the flight with ten minutes to spare. I was more fortunate than I knew at the time—Zurich is pronounced the same in English and Russian. Many European cities are not.

Therapy

Christ, Thomas Peter had a bad sense of timing. My return from Moscow took thirty-one hours. What started in the snowstorm was unexpectedly interrupted by a stop in Warsaw where all of us were escorted off the plane by brown-uniformed men pointing machine guns at us. A pleasant man who worked for *National Geographic*, spoke English like a native, and seemed to speak Russian equally well, offered to buy me a warm Coke or a warm beer while we waited out the siege. Under the circumstances, I had a Coke. After a planned stop in Zurich and a long flight to Dulles, I managed to get home by seven o'clock, just in time to take the excited children trick-or-treating. Later that night Thomas Peter decided to tell me that he was disturbed and planned to start seeing a psychiatrist. We would discuss it in the morning.

Maybe seeing a psychiatrist would make him feel better. Thomas Peter had always been inclined to introspection and self-study. At Touche he had signed up and attended an occasional Erhard something or other session, EST it was called. There were a couple of partners at Touche, Jeff Baldwin being one of them, who seemed to benefit from what was referred to as training but what sounded to me like expensive, sensory deprivation sessions involving a great deal of omphaloskepsis to no apparently useful end. One of the partners actually left Touche and became an EST "trainer," at least for a while. I thought he was a nut.

Thomas Peter tried a couple of times to talk me into going to "training" with him. I actually went to one free "try it you'll like it" session as his guest. For his sake I tolerated it to completion, but I was absolutely turned off, especially at the end when a dozen or more enthusiastic participants tried to convert me to a regular customer.

The training seemed harmless enough though, and I was occasionally amused by its effect on Thomas Peter. Gilbert must have been nine months or a year old at the time Thomas Peter attended a session that included training on the subject of "intending," apparently an active process that, when Thomas Peter described it to me, sounded like an attempt at controlling the behavior of others by mental telepathy. One evening Gilbert was hollering up a storm, as he was inclined to do when he was tired. I went into his room to check on him and found Thomas Peter sitting calmly near the crib. When I asked what was going on, Thomas Peter told me that he was trying to "intend" Gilbert to stop screaming. The noise did eventually stop.

Journeyman

"The hard part about playing chicken is knowing when to flinch," Bert Mancusa said as he steered the submarine under his command on a collision course with disaster in *The Hunt for Red October*. My team became intensely aware of the competitive game that would eliminate us or AMS almost immediately after the return from Europe. It was less evident while we were overseas, because the AMS people were half a world away. We were occasionally unnerved or irritated when State people confused the system (FMS) with the other contractor (AMS) or referred to us as Price instead of the more familiar PW or Price Waterhouse. Those situations left us with nagging concern that perhaps the other contractor was associated with the system and we were associated with high prices.

The competition began for real when we started bumping into each other in meetings or in the halls at Main State, as the largest of the several buildings occupied by State people was called. Everywhere we went and in everything we did we were being compared to AMS. The competition intensified to a nervous pitch after we negotiated common contents for the requirements document and began writing.

Then they flinched. "AMS asked for a one-week extension of the due date," Will Robinson said over the phone about a week before the requirements were due to be delivered. By then, Will was the acting contracting officer's technical representative. He had replaced Ed Gulli, who had retired. Will continued in a monotone, "The purpose of my call is to offer you the same extension." In the brief conversation that followed he gave me the option to deliver according to the current schedule or a week later and I told him that I would call him back when I decided what my team would do.

I convened a meeting of the team to discuss our situation. Any honest, reasonable assessment of the status of our work would indicate that we could surely use an extra week. We were already working bad hours. We were behind schedule and tired. Pat Bowman was at most less than a month away from the birth of her first child. All these factors suggested that we extend the delivery schedule.

Karen, Pat, and Mark had a different view. As they saw it, there was a glimmer of hope for a competitive edge. We had been working on the requirements document for the better part of three months. It would only be marginally better after an extra week's work. Knowing that AMS was in trouble created a spark of excitement that raised adrenalin levels so that they might all be able to add a little extra to the already superhuman effort. They all wanted to go for it—and so did I. "It's going to be rough," I said as I closed the meeting.

I relayed the team's message to Will: "We will deliver according to schedule."

Tom Beyer wanted to help. He called me aside to let me know how much he appreciated all the effort that we had expended and would have to expend to get the document delivered. He wanted, to do something to ease the pain. Over the last couple of weekends, he had been in the office, ordering pizza for my people and the word processing people who were working pretty much around the clock. Dressed in Bermudas, he sat in the staff lounge and chatted cheerfully with all who passed through, paused for a cup of coffee, or stopped for a snack. For Tom it was unusual behavior. He infrequently worked weekends. It was not that he worked banker's hours—he was usually in the office at seven and frequently left after six—rather that he planned and organized his life to avoid weekend work. In general, he socialized very little with the staff. He was a master of one-on-one interactions but handled himself poorly in mixed groups. I believe small talk made him nervous. He was really making an effort. He could be an awfully sweet man.

On the other hand, the guy could make the damndest, most inappropriate, badly timed statements. Policy required that Norm Statland, who was designated the firm's national data processing expert, review and comment on a draft of the requirements. He had performed similar functions related to other work for which I had been responsible. If Norm ever had a positive thought about anything I ever did, I was unaware of it. During the week in which the final requirements document was prepared, I commented on Norm's review of a draft, "If he has anything to do with it, I'll never make partner." Tom responded to the effect that Thomas Peter's status as a partner at Touche was a far more serious problem than Norm's disregard for my technical ability.

The frustration, irritation, animosity, and anxiety, latent since I started with the firm as a policy anomaly and possibly since I left Touche as a policy anomaly, blasted to the surface of my consciousness. It must have been exhaustion or shock that prevented me from lashing out in response at the time.

"Whom the gods would destroy, they first make angry," my father had said on more than one occasion. It was a backhanded way of telling me to control my emotions. I believe mental health is better preserved by emotions expressed than by those controlled. Philosophical views aside, however, I had to express or control myself, immediately, lest I lose the required focus on delivering the requirements document. My resignation, handwritten on formal notepaper engraved with my full name, was in a sealed envelope on Tom's desk in the morning. It was effective on delivery of the requirements document.

The OGS boardroom was the business equivalent of a large, formal, Victorian living room: elegant, expensive, dark, and uncomfortable. Its most prominent feature was a roughly rectangular conference table that would seat twenty, with lots of elbow room; it was so wide that a person had to stand and lean in order to pass a pencil to someone on the other side. The partners regularly held breakfast meetings in the boardroom before the start of the work day on Friday mornings.

Tom canceled breakfasts and gave us the boardroom as a staging area for the accumulation and assembly of the parts of the requirements document. We were contractually required to deliver only fifteen copies, but each copy comprised eighteen volumes and almost filled a box the size of that in which Xerox paper is normally shipped. The document contained dozens of oversize, fold-out diagrams to illustrate the flow of paper and information from process to process within organizations of State, domestic and overseas. More dozens of tables displayed volumes of transactions and other numerical information. Hundreds of illustrations showed the types of financial and administrative information that State people needed from the new FMS.

Early in the production process, I dismissed all thoughts of copying and binding the document in the office and retained Balmar, a local printer, to produce the magnum opus. At the time, my decision was based on what I expected to be the complexity of the document, not its size. Only when the camera-ready copy began to roll out of word processing and stack up, section by section, in volumes on the board-room conference table, did any of us realize what we had committed to when we decided to deliver on schedule. It was going to be close.

We shuttled back and forth to Balmar, dropping off sections to be printed and pausing for a beer and tacos at a nearby Mexican joint before returning to the office to write or proofread or double-check assembled components. Balmar printed all one night and all the next day. They were getting concerned after midnight on the delivery date, by which time the document was already twice the size I had originally estimated, with two volumes left to print. They were up all night; we were up all night.

The pain stopped. We delivered.

Pat Bowman's firstborn child, David Louis Otanazio, was born on January 23, 1980. Because she decided to take some time off, she was unable to participate in the formal review process required to go over the requirements with the people at State. Tom Colberg eventually replaced her. After a few months, she returned part-time, but Karen and I sorely missed her during the reviews.

I wondered why State wanted one hundred additional copies of the requirements document. More than that, I wondered what the AMS people were doing while Karen and I spent the better part of six weeks, all day, every day in review meetings. State brought people, many of them from posts we had visited, in from everywhere. Their job was to pore over the document, ask questions, and find errors, which we were then obliged to fix. Most days, after a full schedule of meetings, Karen and I returned to the office to record problems or fix errors.

Roger Feldman kicked off the initial review meetings. Later on, when he was not shepherding State's budget through staff and committees on the Hill, he attended many of them. My God, the man was smart. He never forgot anything. He could attend two meetings, several weeks apart, on different subjects and identify inconsistencies or discrepancies in material presented. His staff universally acknowledged that he had an unerring eye for numbers, something I did not fully appreciate until I watched him study a sixteen-column spreadsheet of fifty or sixty lines, frown, then circle a few numbers with his green felt-tip pen, and write a terse note in the margin. Someone later told me the green circled numbers were in fact wrong. I found myself overcoming my nervousness in his presence and actually beginning to like the man.

In spite of all the work, the review sessions were fun, largely because of the remarkably able and entertaining group of State people involved. Bob Lamb was in from Bonn. In my experience, he was the consummate diplomat and a most sensitive and gentle fellow. Thomas Peter and I invited him, a couple of other foreign service officers and their wives, and Ruth and David Hopper for dinner. Our intention was purely personal—to return the kindness and hospitality that had been extended to me while I was overseas—so we cooked, business was not discussed, and there were no Price Waterhouse people invited. When I escorted Bob to the front door at the end of the evening he remarked to the effect that I had his confidence, I should relax and not take matters too seriously. I was close to tears as I returned to the other guests upstairs. It dawned on me that I had been working too hard.

As the review process ended, State changed the contracting officer's technical representative. Austin McHale, from Paris, replaced Will Robinson. I arrived at the main State Department building a little early for a meeting at which the ground rules for preparation of the next deliverable report, the design concept, were to be discussed. I recognized a number of AMS faces from my days working with the D.C. financial system. That's what they had been doing, I realized, reorganizing and bringing in the guns. Bob Freeman, the AMS project manager, was not there to introduce his new staff, so I summarized the credentials of each new member of the AMS team and introduced them one by one, to the already assembled State people. Body language said that the State people were impressed at the polite use of appropriate protocol and my ability to remember the names of the competition's staff. When Bob arrived on time, but too late, he was embarrassed.

I later learned that after we delivered, State apparently decided to review only our requirements document, leaving the AMS team free of the time-consuming review process. While Karen and I were tied up in review sessions, Bob Freeman persuaded upper management, in the person of Ivan Selin, the president of AMS, to assign more, and more technically expert, people to his team. The new guys were good, and they had a head start on us. We were in for trouble on the next report, the design concept, which was due in just a few months.

Tom, Karen, and I could not go up against AMS's technical gurus without some help. Tom was at least as knowledgeable about federal government budgeting as anyone at AMS, and Karen and I knew more about State's operations and had probably been to more posts overseas than all but the most senior of foreign service officers. If, however, the topic of concept turned to telecommunications protocols, a comparative technical analysis of data base management system operations, operating systems internals, or encryption methodologies, then our understanding of State's operating activities would be of little use. We had to bring in some technical guns to counter those of the competition to write the design concept and, more importantly, the final technical report, the detailed design.

Norm Statland selected the top guns for our team. Gun number one, Steve Higgins, was a displaced southerner who commuted to Washington from New York for a while before he moved down permanently. Number two was a tanned Adonis from Newport Beach, California, named Nick Homer. Nick left Arthur Andersen to join PW, at least partly because he wanted to stay in Newport Beach. Both were senior managers like Karen, Tom, and me. My beefed-up team spent two months writing our design concept.

The finished report consisted of two fairly skinny volumes. We made the required copies on the Xerox machine in the office. While we packed them up in three Xerox paper shipping boxes, Gilbert and Peter practiced making copies of their hands and faces. Nick and I put Gilbert, Peter, and the boxes into the car and drove the eight blocks to the main State Department building. Nick wheeled Gilbert and Peter, sitting atop the boxes of reports waving their cowboy pistols, through security. Delivering the design concept was easy compared to the requirements report.

When the boxes of competitive design concepts were opened, both on the same date this time, I needed my memories of Bob Lamb's comforting thoughts. To State, the AMS design concept looked like the winner.

In hindsight I was never convinced that theirs was a better report than ours; there were too many problems lying just beneath the beautifully presented surface. For a few days, however, until I carefully read their document, I was on the edge of panic at the prospect of losing whatever advantage we gained with more than a year of backbreaking work, including the successful game of chicken in the early summer. Worse still was the prospect of losing the opportunity to work with State to build and install the new FMS.

"Panic of error is the destruction of progress," said Alfred North Whitehead, probably referring to fear of failure. I had to get over mine. The situation was not as bad for us as it had been for AMS the first round: at least we would have joint review sessions. That would give us the opportunity to expose our strengths and AMS's weaknesses in a public forum that was positively inclined toward Price Waterhouse as a result of our requirements report. Our cause was not helped, however, by Norm Statland's intermittent snoozing during the first joint session. Matters might have been better had his sonorous state escaped Roger's attention.

AMS and PW fought it out through the design concept review sessions. My team managed to turn what had initially appeared to State to be an AMS victory into an ambiguous tie. We were not losing, might have been winning, but were frustrated by the fact that the client, the State Department, was making only marginal progress, at considerable cost, toward building and installing a new financial management system.

We started work on the next report, the functional requirements, with a larger staff and a new project organization. Tom headed a team dealing with budget functions. Karen was responsible for disbursing, accounting, and financial reporting functions. Steve and Nick worked on technical considerations.

For the third time, the contracting officer's technical representative changed. Austin McHale took a job with the Multinational Force and Observers in Rome. He and his replacement, Joe Linnemann, had little in common. Joe was renowned for his political savvy. He was described by some at State as devious, but I never had any experience with him to support the description. To the contrary, he had plenty of opportunity to be devious in his treatment of me, but he was not; I have always assumed that he was merely misunderstood.

If a manager is measured by the decisions he makes, then based on the only decision I know Joe made, he was a gifted manager. He stopped the war between PW and AMS that was so detrimental to the interests of the State Department. On his instruction, the contracting people issued a "stop work order" on both of our contracts. We were each told to skip the final competitive product. We would be instructed to write the proposals to build and install the FMS. After the instructions were issued, we would be required to deliver the proposals in a month.

Although a month may seem like a short period in which to write a proposal that we were not expecting to write so soon, in reality we had more time. Before Joe started the official process in the contracting office, he told both contractors what he planned to do. For more than a month after the technical work stopped, while the contracting people were preparing the paperwork to specify the terms, conditions, and specifications for our proposals, we worked half-heartedly. Christmas came and went, as did the New Year. We all spent anxiously relaxed holidays with our families.

David and Ruth Hopper's grandchildren, Debbie and Karl Zagorin, had visited their grandparents before Christmas. They were in the same age range as Tela, Gilbert, and Peter and had played together happily, just being children at holiday time.

Sometime around New Year Ruth called. "Have your children had the chicken pox?" Karl and Debbie both had it, she explained. We discussed the incubation period of the disease and estimated that my children should come down with it shortly. They did, right on schedule. Tela developed spots one day and the boys followed right behind. They were actually fortunate to have the disease so young. Each child had poxes that numbered about three times the child's age. Tela was pretty scratchy and uncomfortable, even with only forty or fifty poxes. Peter barely noticed his, and Gilbert was in between. Three sick children confined to the house, however, kept Sully, Thomas Peter, and me on our toes for the week or two it took to get over the symptoms.

I was surprised by the short schedule, when I finally received the long-awaited request for proposals, even though I had every reason to expect it. It came like a sudden, massive spray of cold water to wake us from a restless, professional slumber.

Price Waterhouse employed no programmers, a large number of which would be required to build the FMS for State. To compensate for the skill deficiency, I had to find a programming firm willing to subcontract to us. That firm had to be acceptable to State and cost competitive, for obvious reasons. It also had to have depth in staff experienced on both Wang and IBM computer systems because State wanted to build the FMS overseas on Wang computers and in the United States on Big Blue.

There were four programming contractors doing business at State, all of which had decent reputations working on State's Wang and IBM systems, only two of which, however, were big enough for me to consider as possible subcontractors. Unfortunately, PW would have to compete with AMS for the better of the two subcontractors because although AMS employed many skilled professional programmers, few knew Wang systems.

"Would the competition never end?" I asked myself. I scheduled meetings to speak with people from each of the two potential subcontractors. I had two objectives: the first was to figure out if I wanted them, the second was to make sure that they preferred PW to AMS. The man who spoke for the first firm impressed me as an arrogant, pompous, pontificator, but one of his lieutenants, a woman named Anne Spanos, who seemed to have actually gotten her hands dirty and done some work at State, impressed me positively.

The head man from the second firm came alone. Jim Craig represented Pinkerton Computer Consultants. He vaguely reminded me of Alfred E. Neuman and had a Kentucky twang. After a brief interruption while Jim took a phone call, we talked at length about how Pinkerton and PW might work together. He impressed me as down-to-earth, sincere, hardworking, honest, and reasonable. I liked him, but would Pinkerton select us over AMS? When I asked him, he quite candidly told me that he would explore all options and make his decision based on who he thought would win the competition. Although the candor was refreshing, I would have preferred an immediate, positive response.

A lot later I learned that Jim's decision was basically made before he and I met. He had checked around with people at State to see who the perceived winner was. Apparently his informal poll indicated that PW was most likely to succeed. His decision was clinched when a call from Ivan Selin interrupted our initial meeting. Ivan irritated Jim by telling him that it would be a mistake for Pinkerton to join with PW.

Jim called to tell me that Pinkerton would join us and to ask what his firm could do to help. He brought some of his staff by the office for an organizational meeting. The Pinks, as the people from Pinkerton were affectionately nicknamed, joined the proposal team. They all seemed very uncomfortable in their suits. I had the impression they would have been more at ease around a campfire somewhere wearing blue jeans and boots.

Jim's decision was a positive sign but did little to relieve the mounting pressure associated with putting together a winning proposal for six years of work to be done by an average of forty or fifty consultants. With a little simple arithmetic, that translated into $25 to $50 million, which, if won, would be the largest single consulting engagement in the history of the firm.

Somehow Karen, Tom, Steve, Nick, and I, with a lot of help from the Pinks and others at PW, put together a technical proposal. At two o'clock in the morning on the day the proposal was due, Tom Colberg, cheerful but with bloodshot eyes and looking a little faded, leaned on one arm against the door jam of my office and said, "Well, it looks like it's time for the captain to go down with the ship. Unless you need me for something else, I'm going home." Tom, who was certainly the least technical of the crew of senior managers who wrote the proposal, was also the best writer. His departure signified that the technical proposal was finished.

The cost proposal was still unfinished, largely because the level of effort required to do the job could not be reasonably estimated until the technical proposal was nearly complete. Steve and Nick had prepared the work plan to do the job. They were responsible for getting the staffing estimates through Norm Statland's review, a task that was no problem for them but would have been contentious for me. The revised (upward) estimates had only been finished a few hours earlier.

Finishing the cost proposal was my job. Ick. At its best, my facility with arithmetic was bad. In the early hours of the morning after long hours of work for the preceding several weeks, it was awful. I would never have finished without the careful, patient assistance of John L. McClure, who had filled in for me at the Bureau of Indian Affairs when Peter was born. I laid out all the cost estimates and John L made them right. By noon the day of delivery, we had a $32-million cost proposal.

Steve was upset when he came into the office. He had found an error in the work plan, he told me. How big, I asked. A quick conversation and a little mental arithmetic indicated that the error was on the order of a million dollars. Should we change the technical proposal? Forget it! was the gist of my remarks to Steve. I told him that I believed the cost numbers were so far beyond anything that State wanted to see that a million dollars, more or less, would hardly make a difference. If we survived the technical evaluation, then State would pursue us aggressively on cost and all the numbers would change. We could fix the error later. He was shocked—relieved but shocked.

"That's rude, just plain rude," I said to Howard when he called to tell me that oral presentations related to our proposal would begin at nine the next morning. His phone call caught me at the Xerox machine copying the last few pages of the cost proposal. The technical proposal was at Balmar being printed. The proposal team was exhausted—and State wanted us to make an oral presentation and answer questions tomorrow? I asked him to change it. He was apologetic and sympathetic but not optimistic that the schedule would change.

Balmar had only produced half the number of copies required by the department. There was some hang-up related to an inadequate supply of three-ring binders or some other absurdity. Deliver what we have now, was all I could say. I went to the department to deliver the cost proposal and to watch the first half of the copies of the technical proposal arrive. The contracting officer signed for the sealed boxes—the number of copies unverified. I was mentally prepared to deal with the remainder of the copies being late. Ten minutes before close of business, the delivery cutoff time, Bob Freeman arrived to deliver the AMS proposals. We shook hands and chatted amicably—I liked Bob, he was a nice human being. Each of us mentally compared the sizes of the stacks of boxes of proposals; they were about equal, for whatever that was worth. Shortly after Bob left, and barely before the cutoff, the other half of the copies of our technical proposal arrived.

At the oral presentation the next morning, I was so tired that I was having trouble finishing my sentences. Fortunately, my role was only to introduce people and coordinate my team's efforts to answer questions. I was not proposed as project manager. State wanted a project manager with organizational clout comparable to that of a partner running one of the four or five largest consulting practices in the firm, which was what the FMS project, by itself, would represent. State had learned that the real value of partner involvement in a project came from a partner's ability to control allocation of resources—people and money. The department wanted every assurance obtainable that its FMS project would win any competition for resources with other projects.

Don Epelbaum, the proposed project manager, introduced himself.

He said that he was new, knew nothing, had been hand-picked by Joe Connor, the senior partner of the firm, would transfer in from St. Louis, and be the partner to run the job. His mild arrogance was offset by Nick Homer's outrageous humor. In response to a very dull, complicated technical question, he had various members of the project team standing and waving different greetings to each other to demonstrate variations in communications protocols. The technical committee cracked up and the proposal team waked up at the lively interchange.

It was not long before we found out that there was a single fundamental difference between our proposal and that of AMS: while we proposed to build the new FMS from scratch—write all the computer programs—AMS proposed to modify one of its own proprietary financial systems to meet the requirements of the FMS. Technically, we would win or lose based on whether State believed its interests would be better served by building (with PW) or buying (from AMS) the new system.

Then there was a matter of price. Our original proposal estimated the cost over a six-year period with reasonable discounts from full billing rates and with conservative inflation cost escalators from year to year. After State restricted the period of the initial contract to fewer years and applied a little pressure, we raised the discounts and lowered the inflation factors with the result that the cost estimate dropped dramatically. As Tom Beyer and I walked hurriedly down the hall one afternoon, he told me that the contracting officer called to ask if that was the best we could do. In a mild state of irritation he told me to whack a third off an already discounted general and administrative expense rate, recompute the numbers, and submit it as final. That was it: this was poker not rocket science.

Fidelity

State called late one April morning to tell us we won. The Office of Government Services was euphoric. I celebrated with my team, half the office, client people, and just about anyone else who wanted to join in the merriment, first at lunch, later in one of the bars near the office, and finally at dinner where Thomas Peter joined us.

We were in bed at two in the morning when he told me, out of the blue, that he was having an affair. I wondered how the hell he picked the timing. The day's relief, excitement, fun, and the gleeful anticipation of future work and fun all vaporized. I was suddenly exhausted. We would have to discuss it in the morning.

Thomas Peter was such a sad little fuzzy redhead. I loved him terribly. He had been adorable when, without benefit of his counsel, I submitted my resignation note to Tom Beyer. He had calmed me down and told me that there should be no problem, that he was planning to leave Touche anyway. He would discuss the policy anomaly with Tom and work things out, he promised. And he did.

They met over breakfast. They liked each other. I never heard what happened, but Tom told me it was a good meeting and I took him at his word. Both men handled the situation admirably. Tom never let the note get into any personnel files where it might have been an indication of lack of commitment to the firm, hence a possible blight on the record.

It had been hard for us when Thomas Peter went into partnership with Jim Edmondson, one of the men from the bull pen who had been an usher in our wedding. Jim had left Touche to start his own real estate firm and had been after Thomas Peter to join him practically since the start. When Thomas Peter joined him, however, Jim had a struggling little business.

The two of them had to work hard just to pay the expenses. Thomas Peter's income was unpredictable. Although I had a sense that business conditions were tough for him, his usual response to my questions about how work was going was an optimistic, but uninformative, "Fine."

In retrospect, I probably should have thrown him out when he confessed to his affair, but I was given to believe that the affair was over. I stated my position, one that over time I almost believed: "If you want fidelity, get a dog."

The next morning Ivan Selin and Bob Freeman were among the first to call to offer congratulations. Ivan asked me to set up a meeting, the subject of which was unspecified, with Don Epelbaum. I had lunch that day with Bob to celebrate the end of what both of us agreed had been a hell of a war waged with dignity. Thomas Peter and I were later invited to dinner in Bob's home with his family. Bob eventually went to work for Price Waterhouse as did Harry Barschdorf and Steve Welner, both of whom worked for him through much of the competitive process. Anne Spanos also joined Price Waterhouse shortly after the contract was awarded.

I was apprehensive when Don started commuting to Washington from St. Louis in anticipation of relocating to Washington. It signified the beginning of the end of a set of close relationships with people at the State Department and the breakup of my FMS team. Don took me and my project team to lunch at Germaine's, a very good Southeast Asian restaurant, north of Georgetown. I was sad. Through most of lunch I fought to control my emotions. To me Don was an interloper on what had been a difficult but happy preserve for years. When he asked me what I thought, I told him how I felt.

I arranged the meeting between Ivan and Don at Ivan's office atop the AMS building in Rosslyn. As we strolled toward the building on the way to the meeting, Don asked what he should discuss with Ivan; I suggested he say nothing and listen. "Give the man all the attention you would give a cobra in a dark room," was my advice.

Ivan was smart and a fierce competitor. I never met a person in a business situation who could use less information to better advantage than Ivan could. Other than to exchange pleasantries, Don said nothing—he too was smart.

Ivan explained that PW would probably be unable to complete the work on FMS and proposed that the firm subcontract with AMS to do a big part of job. Don took the suggestion under advisement. When we left the meeting, Don and I discussed with amusement Ivan's tenacity. We had beaten AMS fair and square, but Ivan would not accept defeat. Nothing came of the proposed subcontract.

Although I helped with recruiting new people to join the firm and work on FMS, I never really worked on the job after the contract was awarded. One of my last tasks was to arrange an afternoon affair in the Diplomatic Reception Room at the main State Department building to announce the long-awaited award of the contract.

Roger Feldman wanted to invite State executives and staff together with others from the General Accounting Office and many of the agencies that State served overseas, all of whom had participated in the fly-off process to date. There was to be a formal ceremony in which the undersecretary for management, on behalf of State, would announce the award and the senior partner of the firm, Joe Connor, on behalf of Price Waterhouse, would accept it.

The job clearly required a caterer—not just any caterer, but one that had a security clearance acceptable to the department and that knew the appropriate protocols. I selected Ridgewell's, one of the caterers that State used for such events. The nice thing about Ridgewell's is that once you select them, you are relieved of the burden of doing anything other than making an occasional decision.

I did, however, have to give Ridgewell's a date. That simple task was complicated by scheduling conflicts for the Diplomatic Reception Room and previous commitments of some of the key players.

I was surprised to find myself speaking directly with Joe Connor after the second ring, when I called his office to see when he was available. I am always impressed when a man of his prominence answers his own phone. It dispels any impression of arrogance and somehow contributes to an aura of humanness that I find appealing.

He told me when he was available to be in Washington and we rang off. By the time all the scheduling constraints were considered, there were few options. The reception was scheduled for May 5, 1982.

June marks the end of PW's fiscal year and introduces a sort of holiday season. A host of social events are scheduled to celebrate the end of one year and the beginning of the next. It is the season to honor people being promoted or retiring or to get together on a purely social basis, to foster organizational bonding over golf or tennis followed by dinner. Each social event includes a measure of speeches, some of which are intended to be informative, all of which are intended to be entertaining.

Probably because I was Tom Beyer's most ardent admirer and generally unafraid of disagreeing with or offending him, I was asked to give a speech in Tom's honor at the annual promotion party that year. On a good day, with very little effort, I can be a very entertaining extemporaneous speaker. Even on a bad day I can keep people laughing with a short speech. As the date of the promotion party approached, however, I realized that preparing a funny, fifteen-minute presentation for a large, mixed audience would take more time than I had to spare.

Necessity dictated that I find a canned speech. I decided to select an essay the right length on an appropriate subject and read it. The shelf over my bedside table contained the best selected works of my favorite management theorist and philosopher, Dr. Seuss. I eliminated "Horton Hears a Who" as being too long and off the subject. "Gertrude McFuzz" was too controversial, as were "The Sneetches" and "The Jax." I read "Yertle the Turtle." Yertle and Tom had a lot in common.

I learned that the partners had decided to propose me for the partnership about the time that Thomas Peter, the children, and I took off for Florida for a family reunion to celebrate Gil's seventy-fifth birthday. We were on a high.

The reunion was a smashing success. Thomas Peter and Brother's wife, Cathy, who was the product of a huge Catholic family, hit it off famously. They teased Brother for being a convert to Catholicism and, as such, inadequately imbued with a proper sense of guilt and blame. They gave Gil a toy plastic fishing pole with complete instructions for snatching mackerels.

Peter insisted on going jogging with my sister, his Aunt Susan, who was accustomed to doing a mile or more each day before breakfast. She got more exercise laughing at the image of the redheaded three-year-old trailing gamely along behind her than she did from running around Mom and Gil's neighborhood.

An age-based hierarchy of adoration and responsibility developed in the children of the different families. Susan's children, Bo and Ami, were the oldest. They were viewed with awe, admiration, and affection by mine. Tela, Gilbert, and Peter obeyed their older cousins more reliably than they did their parents. Katy, Brother and Cathy's only child and an infant, was everybody's responsibility. The poor child was constantly beset by bottle-carrying cousins trying to force-feed her.

When she was not cooking or helping children gain access to the contents of the refrigerator, Mom sat and chatted with me at the edge of the swimming pool where I kept a watchful eye on my sons. In spite of my constant harping about staying in the shallow end or along the edge of the pool, they all too often ventured into the middle. I practiced my American Red Cross life-saving skills an average of once every other day, frequently fully clad.

Gil's sons, both of whom lived nearby, were in and out, usually for supper. As usual Gil burned the barbecue ribs and chicken for the reunion dinner, but everyone ate happily anyway.

Master

On our return to Washington, in June 1982, I started into the candidate evaluation process along with Steve Higgins and two other senior managers from OGS. In the early 1980s, the process began each year with a series of exercises that bore a remarkable resemblance to beauty pageants—week-long quality control reviews, usually referred to only by the initials, QCR.

Each beauty pageant was a chance for a candidate to pick up a few votes. In the evaluation process any partner who had worked with a candidate for more than one hundred hours was required to record a vote, comments, and other information on a lengthy form, referred to simply as a long form. Any partner with any exposure at all to a candidate could comment and vote or abstain on a much-abbreviated short form. Although pageants were not long enough to afford an opportunity for long-form votes, they did offer enough exposure to pick up a short-form vote or two.

The pageant season typically ran through July and August. Separate pageants were held in each of several of the larger offices of the firm. The judges included the pageant office partners. The contestants were senior managers likely to be proposed for the partnership in the next year. Each contestant received an all-expense-paid trip to one of the offices under review. Groups of contestants arrived at a hotel on Sunday night where they had the opportunity to size up the competition before the work began on Monday morning.

The several contestants in each pageant were supervised, only for the last day or two of the pageant, by an out-of-town partner, also a judge. When not on display before the pageant partners, each contestant was charged with reviewing files and working papers for one or more projects managed by the office. At midday and after usual and customary business hours, the supervising partner or the pageant partners entertained the contestants, sometimes into the wee hours of the morning.

In spite of a grueling social schedule, contestants were expected to arrive early each morning, looking well groomed and refreshed, and to keep noses in files and sharpened pencils on notes or checklists for the first three or four days of the week. The final day or so of the week was reserved for writing a report and reviewing it with the manager responsible for the files. The pageant finale was a meeting to tell the partner in charge of the pageant office what was wrong with the files and what the contestants recommended in the way of corrective action.

The criteria by which beauty was assessed conflicted. On one hand, a contestant was expected to find something wrong with the files, otherwise it might seem that he or she was stupid, chickenhearted, or a panderer. On the other hand, the contestant should not find too much that would embarrass or otherwise disturb a partner who might find him or her offensive or irritating or otherwise inappropriate as a future partner. A social indiscretion could be as damning as a technical one. It was a high-wire act. Unlike beauty pageants, it was a long time before the winner was announced, and there could be several winners or none at all.

I had been scheduled to do a QCR the previous summer, but was unable to go because of my work schedule. With the hoopla over and Don in charge of the new FMS project, the only real demands on my time were related to recruiting. There were other people who could do that. I was scheduled to go to Houston to participate in a review of that office.

I looked forward to going to Houston because the trip gave me an opportunity to get down to Galveston. I had not been back there since my father's funeral. Furthermore, my father's second wife, who was the life income beneficiary of his estate, had died recently and the estate was being distributed to my sister, brother, and me by my bank in Galveston. I took a side trip back to my home town to renew a few old friendships. While there, I checked up on estate matters.

All I knew about the Houston office was that it was small and that Lew

Krulwich and Bill Devaney, the partner in charge of consulting, were other than the best of friends. I expected the office to be a little stuffy based on a story that Linda Pegues once recounted about what took place at a dinner held at a posh country club in Houston on one of the weekends that she had gone home. Dinner was nicely served, complete with appropriate speeches. After dinner, the partners, led by Bill Devaney and followed by most of the male staff, which was almost all of the staff, retired to a men's bar for cognac. Linda was left high, dry, and out of the men's bar. Although she wanted to join the group, she thought better of it and went home.

The review went well enough. There were no problematical projects. The social schedule was hectic but manageable. In fact, all things considered, I had fun, largely because we were shepherded around by a new partner, Peter Powell, who had been in our shoes the year before and could deal with us sympathetically.

"Bill, I would appreciate it if you would stop doing that because it makes me nervous," I said, as politely as I could. I had been assigned the job of presenting the findings of our review to Bill Devaney. As I began my comments he started sliding a very long, stiletto-like letter opener through his fingers, letting it fall to the desk, flipping it around, and repeating the process with the other end, over and over. It was probably the most hostile body language I had seen to date.

"Well, how does this make you feel?" he said in jest, as he retrieved a pistol from a drawer and pointed it toward the ceiling. Bill had a wild sense of humor. We spent a few minutes discussing gun laws in Texas and the fact that there had been some criminal activity in or around the office building. Presenting the QCR findings was anticlimactic.

On my return from Houston, Tom Beyer called Bob Freeman and me to a meeting to discuss the possibility of more work for State. Because State is responsible for financial management and administration of all buildings and land used by the U.S. government for nonmilitary purposes overseas, property management was one of the functions of the new FMS. When we were awarded the contract, the part of the system required to manage property was one of State's lower priorities and was scheduled to be built several years in the future. For a number of reasons, one of which was an increased level of interest on the part of a new undersecretary for management, State changed its priorities in the summer of 1982 and decided to authorize a separate project to accelerate the process required to build and install the real estate management component of FMS. Roger Feldman had called Tom and asked for a proposal.

Tom wanted Bob and me to write a discussion of what we would do, including a work plan and cost estimates to build and install such a system. We named it the real estate management system—REMS (pronounced reams). The $6-million proposal, a few dozen pages long, was submitted in July, at about the same time as the OGS partners were meeting to consider candidates to be proposed for admission to the partnership a year hence.

As long as the proposal for REMS was still under consideration by State, I was unassigned and available for short-term assignment. Lew Krulwich, in Washington, and the consulting partners in St. Louis were simultaneously considering a request for proposals that had been issued by the Washington staff of a federal agency with major field operations in St. Louis.

The field office wanted a contractor to support a big system design and development effort, with most of the early work to be done in St. Louis. The contractor would be paid on a cost-plus incentive fee basis. That meant that the contractor could recover its allowable costs plus a variable profit, expressed as a percentage of costs. The variability of the profit would be a function of how the federal agency evaluated the performance of the contractor—good performance would result in higher profit, bad performance could result in no profit at all.

Of all the managers in OGS, I best understood the federal rules and regulations, knew how to fill out most of the federally required forms, and understood the firm's government cost structure. I knew how to manage the logistics required to get the required volumes, in the required numbers, to the right places by the prescribed time. I knew the strengths and weaknesses of the optional bidding strategies that could be used by the firm or, for that matter, by the competition.

When he asked me to go to St. Louis to manage the proposal effort, Lew told me that working in St. Louis would be an opportunity for exposure to partners outside of OGS. St. Louis had three consulting partners, Tim Coffey, the partner in charge of consulting, John Fridley, and Tom Blythe. None of them knew me well enough, or so Lew thought, to cast a vote in the partnership evaluation process.

Washington, D.C., is close to unbearable in the summer. Whole neighborhoods that cling to the hills that drop into the Potomac River were originally built as summer cottages where residents of the city could go to escape the heat. The city all but closes down in August. The reason sometimes given for the close down is that Congress is in recess, but I believe the real reason is related to the unbearable heat and humidity. Not having been in St. Louis at any time in my adult life, I was naively looking forward to spending some time in St. Louis as a means to escape the D.C. heat.

As I commuted between Washington and St. Louis in July and August of 1982, I realized that St. Louis had weather far more disgusting than Washington. But the weather was the least of my problems. Although I understood what had to be done, the partners in St. Louis had to be educated. Their public sector experience had been gained working exclusively with state or local government projects under fixed-price contracts. Fixed-price work, where the amount to be paid is contractually established and the contractor bears the risk of an overrun, is financially much riskier than cost-based work where payments at least cover costs. State or local agencies frequently allow access to their personnel to ensure that bidders have a complete understanding of the technical problem to be solved. This federal agency prohibited its staff from interacting with potential contractors.

When the proposal effort began, and six weeks later when the proposal was signed, Tim Coffey was in charge. In the intervening six weeks, Tom Blythe, John Fridley, and Tom Green, a partner from the National Administrative Center, one after another, were in charge of my efforts. With each transition from one partner to the next, I had to explain and justify why this proposal effort was unlike preparing a proposal for a fixed-price contract with a state or local government entity. Transition management consumed a great deal of time.

Arthur Andersen was another serious problem. Andersen did not develop the most profitable consulting practice in the world by working from nine to five and waiting for the work to roll in. The people in St. Louis believed that Andersen was the competition to beat. Some of the St. Louis staff believed that Andersen had done work for this agency related to the proposed project and that Price Waterhouse probably would lose the job. Getting them jacked up to work on a proposal that they believed they would lose further diverted my efforts.

Although I was convinced that Andersen was beatable, the only reasonable assumption for me to make was that we were the underdog. We would have to work harder and smarter to win. To me that meant that every résumé, every citation of firm experience, everything, would have to be carefully written to address the specific requirements stated by the requesting agency. This was not a proposal that could be put together by pulling prefabricated parts off a shelf full of old proposals.

This was also going to be the biggest proposal ever written by the consulting staff in St. Louis. To respond to the requirements outlined in the agency's request for proposals, we were going to have to bid almost the entire consulting staff of the St. Louis office together with a few key people, including Nick Homer and me, from other offices. The St. Louis staff, however, rose to the occasion, although I was later to learn that they believed their rise had been initiated by my pointed boot in their derrieres.

I asked someone to bring in the beer and order pizza, something that had apparently never been done before. We billed the résumé-writing sessions as pizza parties. Approximately twenty consultants, most of whom spent little time in the office after normal working hours, worked until eight or nine at night drafting their résumés to describe their experience in the specific terms and formats required.

The twenty-eight-hundred-page proposal that was developing from this effort was getting to be so large that the word processing staff in St. Louis was overwhelmed by the volume and was having trouble keeping all the components of the documents under control. I called Washington to ask for help from my office. Hunter Jones, the partner who had administrative responsibility for the word processing group in OGS, responded instantly by sending the best person on the staff to St. Louis and leaving her there for two weeks until the proposal was finished.

As the proposal process was bumping and grinding along in St. Louis, Tom Beyer was managing a different proposal process back in Washington. During the early stages of the St. Louis proposal, Tom called me to say that Ben Warder was writing the documents required to propose me to be a partner. That seemed strange: I was no fan of Ben's and I had the impression that he disliked me. But Tom was my mentor so I assumed that he was trying to force Ben into a position where he had to support the proposal.

A few weeks later, Tom called again, this time to let me know that Don Epelbaum was redrafting the documents. I was reminded of Alice's comment—"curiouser and curiouser." Before I left St. Louis, Tom called one final time to say he had polished the final draft and submitted it. He also told me that the State Department had approved our proposal to develop REMS.

On a Friday morning in late August I flew out of St. Louis with several boxes of proposals to be delivered in Washington. We had been up until two in the morning putting things into deliverable form. We had done a terrific job and I was proud of the team. The St. Louis staff was exhausted and so was I.

After I saw the receipt that proved that the proposal had been delivered on time, I went home to relax for the weekend. Monday would bring the start of the project to develop the real estate management system for the State Department.

Shortly after I returned to Washington from St. Louis, Lew Krulwich showed me the performance appraisal that Tim Coffey had prepared and sent to him. The appraisal carried the comment "just plain rough on staff." Sympathetically, Lew sighed and said, "Well, we knew you were going to be controversial."

It took most of the fall of 1982 to get the REMS team recruited, organized, and ready to get to work. The State contract for the financial management system had to be modified to include the budget for REMS. Office space had to be leased in Rosslyn, across the river in Virginia near the State Department offices. The State Department had to find, assign, and free up a technical officer to run the project. It was hard to find Price Waterhouse staff for the project because OGS was growing in leaps and bounds. It took a lot of recruiting to support the staffing needs of the State Department and other new projects that fueled the growth.

I needed two managers, four or five less-experienced consultants, an administrative assistant, and a dedicated word processor to do the job. I recruited the administrative assistant. Tim Scheve asked if he could be one of the consultants on the project. "Tiny Tim," as he was called because of his towering height, was not an ideal fit in terms of his experience; he was a financial analyst, not a systems analyst, but he was smart and had a history of good performance evaluations. He also had a wonderful, sarcastic wit that made him fun to work with. He joined the team that fall.

I was lucky to get Harry Barschdorf as one of the managers. Harry had worked for American Management Systems when AMS was the competition that we had to beat to win the original FMS contract. I liked him even when he worked for the competition. He was thirtyish and good looking, the classic Nordic type: reasonably tall, well built, blond. The blond hair thinning toward baldness was barely noticeable because of a movie star smile with teeth to go with it. To make matters better, everything about Harry was real. When he smiled, it was to make a sincere statement about how he felt. He was honest, confident, and competent. Tiny Tim was assigned to Harry's team.

Bob Lam, the second manager, was imposed on me. I had worked with him enough to know that he was not what I wanted or needed. He was good looking and loveable, but had not been around long enough or worked on hard enough problems to have the poise and self-confidence to take charge. He had somehow never developed the intellectual or professional stature that was necessary to attract people and have them want to follow. Although I strongly expressed my objections to his being assigned to REMS, I was told that I could do my bit for staff development and that I had no say in the decision.

I got a call from the office downtown about a possible word processor—the only expressed reservation about the candidate was that he appeared to be gay. I told the office that it might make a difference if I were planning to sleep with him, but I needed a word processor and the fact that he might be gay was irrelevant if he could type. He was hired. Actually he only lasted a short while on the project, but his sexual orientation had nothing to do with his departure.

Recruiting for REMS was interrupted in November when the St. Louis proposal resurfaced after being buried for several months in the government's proposal evaluation process. We were invited to make oral presentations to respond to the government's questions and to support and defend the proposal. The key members of the proposal team from St. Louis, Tom Green, the partner proposed to run the job, Tim Coffey, and my old State Department buddy, Nick Homer, convened in Washington to get ready to be grilled by the government.

We were all very happy about being invited to orals, as the grilling sessions were called, because it meant that we had probably made it past some cut of the competition. Some of us, myself included, were more than a little nervous about how we were going to perform because most of the team had never been to orals before. For our team, the technical orals were conducted by Tom Green. He had to be bailed out of trouble every now and then—at one point, Nick leaned over and whispered, "Make him be quiet!" to me—but on the whole, the technical orals went pretty well.

For our team, the cost orals were conducted by Tim Coffey. As is frequently the case, the government man in charge aggressively questioned the proposed level of effort and the related costs. Throughout the proceedings, he was advised by an obnoxious consultant from Mitre who sat next to him and whispered questions and comments in his ear, sometimes audibly. It was disruptive and irritating. When the discussion turned to the cost of a critical component of the work we had proposed, the man from Mitre whispered, "We're really going to hang their ass on this one," in response to which I quipped "every consultant 'hangs his ass' on this one." Thereafter, Tim decided to let me take an active role in the cost negotiations. It went very well. What happened at the cost orals caused Tim to change his partnership vote from hold to yes. He told me so and thanked me graciously. Price Waterhouse won the $3.1-million contract in December of 1982.

Recruiting for the REMS team continued. We hired one consultant, a woman named Pat O'Hern, for Harry's team. Then the State Department decided that fieldwork for the project would begin in late January 1983. Recruiting for Bob's team accelerated. The project, as well as the office, was desperate for staff.

We made offers to three more consultants, Sam Seetheram, Robin Myiang, and Leslie Alton as fast as we found them. As the new staff were arriving or being scheduled to arrive, the State Department decided we would do the initial fieldwork in Africa because the original FMS teams had been to few African posts and there was concern that management of the African Bureau might conclude that its needs were being neglected. Other fieldwork would have to be done in Germany and France because of the large property holdings and the complexity of the property management problems in these countries.

I believed it was a bad business practice to take green staff in large numbers overseas, so we had a project practice that staff only went overseas after first making some kind of an orientation trip to a site where they could not get into too much trouble. (Trouble was measured in terms of things like getting sick, committing protocol blunders, not understanding the functions of the various components of an embassy.) I sent Harry and his team to the American embassy in Panama for orientation because it was not too far away.

When the State Department selected Nigeria and Zaire as the African posts where we were going to do some of our fact-finding, there were only two staff members who had been around long enough to go. Harry, Bob, and I decided that Harry would take Pat O'Hern on one leg of the African trip and I would simultaneously take Tim Scheve on the other leg. Because Harry spoke pretty good French and we understood that Zaire was French speaking, Harry was to go to Zaire and I would go to Nigeria. Fred Cook, the State Department's project manager, would go with Harry. When we finished in Africa, we would meet Bob and the new staff in Germany and proceed to the American embassy in Bonn. Bonn would be the orientation site for Bob's team. Harry's team could continue the fact-finding and analysis. We scheduled the trip to the American facilities in Paris immediately after Bonn.

That Africa trip was the worst trip I ever experienced. Although it had its lighter moments, just about everything went wrong. The trip began uneventfully enough. Fred, Harry, and I, along with our teams, got on the same plane and flew to Frankfurt where we spent the night. We left the next morning for our respective destinations in Africa.

The first sign of trouble appeared to me on the plane to Lagos. I was glancing vacantly at the *International Herald Tribune,* while chatting with Tim as the plane went into the landing pattern to the airport, when I noticed that Vice President Bush was scheduled to visit the American embassy in Bonn at the same time that the REMS project team was due to be there. That would be a disaster. When a high-ranking government official visits an embassy, the entire administrative staff of the embassy is consumed with work for a number of reasons, not the least of which is security and the related logistics. Even if it were not terribly rude to arrive at the embassy during a vice presidential visit, we would be unable to schedule an appointment to talk to anyone. We could not go to Bonn, and I was going to have to make sure that Bob Lam kept his team in Washington.

I failed to understand how the schedule conflict had happened. There were elaborate clearance procedures back in Washington to prevent such conflicts. Tim and I discussed the fact that we were going to have to get in touch with Fred in Kinshasa as soon as we could get to a phone.

That, however, was never to be. The day we landed in Lagos, there was a coup. The building that housed the central communications system for Nigeria was burning when we landed. For our entire stay in the country, the telephones were inoperable. The diplomatic communications system at the embassy was not handling administrative messages. We were unable to contact Fred or, for that matter, Washington.

We landed. The airport was filthy. It smelled of the urine men publicly disposed of in the ashcans. We were met by a foreign service officer from the embassy and a Nigerian employee who was referred to as an "expediter." I had heard the term around the department back in Washington, but it had no meaning to me. After introductions, the expediter asked Tim and me for our passports and travel papers and told us to stand still. He disappeared. He returned a few minutes later, told us to follow him to another spot in the airport, and then to stand still again. He disappeared again. We did this following, stopping, disappearing dance all the way through the airport and out to the embassy van that was waiting to take us to our hotel. It was the dry season and it was hotter than Hades. The air smelled of smoke and dirt. We could see burning tires in piles along the side of the road as we were driven from the airport to our hotel.

At one point, we were stopped at a roadblock guarded by two very big men with sour frowns on their faces and machine guns in their hands. One of the guards waved his machine gun around as he inspected the inside of the vehicle while the foreign service officer politely held out a plastic-covered badge that I assumed was some sort of diplomatic pass. During the entire trip, which was a terrifying experience to Tim and me, the foreign service officer carried on an even-toned, steady conversation explaining the coup. The new regime had decided that the economy of Nigeria could not support the Benins, Togolese, and Ghanaians which, as a group, represented 30 percent of the population. It had ordered them to get out of the country and given them two weeks to do so. We were advised not to leave the hotel, something that had never occurred to us, and to wait for the embassy van to pick us up to go to work in the morning. On that note Tim and I decided to have a drink and dinner after dropping our bags in the rooms.

First, a drink. The State Department was always very careful about advising us what to do and not to do when visiting posts overseas. In preparation for our Nigerian visit, we had been shot for various varieties of fevers, hepatitis, typhoid, and cholera. We were given malaria tablets to take for the period from thirty days before we left until thirty days after we got back. We were supplied with tablets to take if we picked up gastroenteritis. We were told not to drink the water in the hotel unless it came from a bottle with an unbroken seal. The advice about the water included ice cubes, but we chose to ignore it. After asking three times and carefully determining that the hotel served bourbon, we ordered bourbon on the rocks. We should have known that the sun never sets on the British empire—we got scotch, ordered another and somehow avoided getting sick from the water. I do not remember willingly drinking scotch on any other occasion.

On to dinner. Naturally we ate in the hotel. We ordered chicken and rice. You can eat chicken and boiled rice almost anywhere in the world without fear of intestinal repercussions. Nigeria is no exception, although we did accumulate and stack in a pile on a napkin on the table a couple of tablespoons full of small stones that came in the cooked rice. As we were leaving the hotel restaurant to go back to our rooms, Tim asked if I would do him a favor and escort him back to his room. I thought that was a little strange until he explained that he was uncomfortable walking past the hookers and would appreciate the company.

With Tim safely tucked in so to speak, I looked forward to a shower. No such luck. Because of the drought, the water was turned off at night. I brushed my teeth with a bottle of soda that I found in the room and retired. Except for two or three occasions when someone banged on the door and shouted something inarticulate, I slept soundly.

It was hard to believe it was only Monday. I woke up with a congested cold. My head was clogged up with rubber cement. Tim gave me a brand new bottle of Sudafed. I downed a couple of little red tablets while we waited for our ride. An embassy car picked us up and took us to the embassy where we were greeted hospitably, but with a measure of reserve, by Bert Moore, counselor for administration, at the American embassy to Nigeria in Lagos. He introduced the embassy staff with whom we would be working and took us on a tour of the facility to show us his real estate management problems.

The chancery was a relatively new building. Its predecessor had burned down. There seemed to be a problem with fires in Nigeria. They had had a fire in the building a week or so ago, Bert explained. The fire had done some damage, but the fire department had done more. Lagos is built on some islands at the mouth of a river. The city is chopped up by a lot of saltwater canals. Fresh water is scarce. To extinguish the fire in the embassy, the fire department pumped saltwater out of a nearby canal onto the fire. The saltwater apparently did more damage than the fire did.

As Tim and I were taking a walking tour of the communications facilities on the roof and discussing our inability to get a message out of the country, he marveled at my ability to avoid tripping in high-heeled shoes. We laughed a lot when I told him the story of Karen Nold climbing the scaffolding in spikes when she jauntily did the roof tour of the Talleyrand building in Paris. "Just part of the job," I told him.

Foreign service officers have no general obligation to invite out-of-towners, especially nonforeign service people, into their homes. More specifically, Bert Moore and his wife, Marjorie, had no obligation whatever to invite Tim and me to dinner. They did, however; with the exception of the night that we arrived, they invited us for dinner every night we were in Lagos. Dinners, by the way, were not diplomatic receptions. It was the Moores, Tim, and me. We puttered around the kitchen cooking and sat in the living room drinking coffee after dinner as we might have had we been four friends in any town back home. Only I had no friends back home who a had python (or was it boa constrictor) skin hanging on the wall.

Tim asked what it was. Marjorie named the species. She then explained that when she and Bert had been posted to Kinshasa on an earlier assignment, the snake had, unbeknownst to anyone, been hanging around the garden. Apparently the snake ate the family cat and then got hung up by the cat in the iron rail fence that surrounded the house. Some of the foreign national staff from the embassy discovered the snake, did him in, extracted the deceased cat, and converted the snake into snake steaks. All of this accomplished, the staff knocked on the door of the house, described their accomplishments, and asked Marjorie if she wanted any of the meat. When she responded in the negative, they asked her if she wanted the cat back. She declined the cat and asked for the skin instead. I had read somewhere, probably in *National Geographic,* that even the largest of these snakes were unable to swallow an animal much larger than a dog. I made a remark to that effect and Marjorie brought the conversation around to a more serious note by stating that, at the time, they had a child, aged two, who frequently played in the garden.

In one of our early coffee conversations, Bert was describing the difficulties of maintaining vehicles in Africa. He talked about the weather, the absence of roads, and the deplorable driving conditions. As an example he discussed a drive that a group of people from the embassy had made across the Sahara to Tunis. Tim was fascinated. He could not understand how you navigated across the desert without roads or road signs. When he asked, Bert responded, with a perfectly straight "You follow the telephone poles." Tim is from Baltimore and other than a college camping trip to France and the orientation trip to Panama, he had never been out of the States. It took him a while to realize that he was playing straight man to a masterful comedian: there are no telephone poles in the Sahara.

We had serious conversations too. Bert had been the administrative officer at the embassy in Teheran and spent twenty-two months as a hostage while Marjorie waited it out in the Midwest. What Tim and I watched fifteen minutes a week on television, they lived through minute by minute. They had a European post after Iran, but wanted to get back to Africa. Although Nigeria was a hardship post and they were entitled to reassignment after one tour, they asked for another tour there. They loved the foreign service. Their hospitality was remarkable. They will probably never know the extent to which Tim and I appreciated it.

By the end of the week, we had finished our work at the embassy. Although we tried daily to get messages out, we were unsuccessful. I doubted that we were going to proceed to Bonn, but our airline reservations out of Nigeria were unchangeable and it seemed unlikely that the Kinshasa team would be able to change theirs. We had no alternative but to proceed on our original plan out of Nigeria and on to Frankfurt to link up with the team from Kinshasa. We were driven to the airport where, in spite of the best efforts of the expediter, we were searched on our way out of the country.

Both teams were glad to see each other when we met in Frankfurt. Fred and I waited long enough to overcome the time zone difference between Europe and the United States, then contacted our respective home offices. The State Department had canceled our onward leg to Bonn. Bob Lam was holding his team in Washington. Fred and I were told to bring the teams home on the next available flight.

It was late morning. The next flight for Washington was on TWA and left just after one o'clock. We gathered up all of our bags and presented ourselves to the ticket agent at TWA, where we were advised that we had three different groups of nonrefundable tickets, none of them issued by TWA. Each group would have to be changed by a different airline. The three airlines were at opposite ends of the airport. We probably would be unable to get the tickets changed in time to make the TWA flight that day. "Would you like to leave tomorrow?" the ticket agent asked. I had had enough of this trip. I put my beat-up green American Express card on the counter and asked the agent if he could start from scratch and get tickets on the one o'clock flight. Someone in Washington was just going to have to sort out the paperwork later. I was the last person on the plane as the door closed behind us.

A week later, we had barely recovered from jet lag when we had to pack up and leave for a week in Bonn followed by another in Paris. This would be the first time that the entire team would be together. I liked Germany. I had happy times when I lived there as a child. The near-perfect German that I spoke as a child was gone, but I still spoke the language decently. I was always comfortable working in Bonn. It was a good orientation post. Nothing ever went wrong.

We did have a little trouble with one of the government people who was traveling with us. Although he was always well intentioned in his actions and remarks, he had an uncanny propensity for saying and doing exactly the wrong things. It was so bad that one of the State people called me into his office, closed the door, and asked lightly: "Is he one of yours or one of ours?" I was relieved to be able to say, "Sorry, but he's one of yours." He chuckled. "I was afraid you were going to tell me that." I knew that no harm would come of it. The foreign service takes care of its own.

My team had to do its bit though. We were invited to a fairly formal reception that night with all the shadows and a lot of the American and foreign service national staff from the embassy. I called the managers aside and told them that it was our job to keep our blundering buddy out of trouble. Harry, Bob, and I agreed on a schedule whereby each of us would engage in an intense one-on-one conversation with the blunderer all evening. The plan was perfectly executed. We managed to prevent him from offending anyone because he had no time to talk to anyone except for one of the managers or me.

I hated Paris. The weather was cold—the hotel was barely heated. I had to swap rooms with Tiny Tim because he continually banged his forehead on the eaves in his room. I barely spoke the language. I was reluctant to use the subway system—I was afraid of leading my team into the bowels of the system, getting lost, and being horribly embarrassed.

Harry changed some of that. He had a guidebook for the city and the subway system. He laughed at my anxieties and dragged me into the underground. He led and we followed. We got around a lot faster and a lot cheaper. Harry taught me enough French to order ice in my Coca-Cola and later to order more than one ice cube.

The team bonded in Paris. I recognized it when I was invited to a birthday party in one of our rooms. The party was for Leslie Alton, who was on Bob's staff. I arrived to find the entire team all in the same bed, fully clothed but covered to their chins, with roses clenched in their teeth. The purpose of the roses was partly to celebrate Leslie's birthday and partly in anticipation of what they perceived to be their ultimate demise from hypothermia.

By the time we got back to the States it was the last week in February. We had gathered a lot of information and we had our work cut out for us. We had to analyze what we had and pull it together into an organized, coherent description of system requirements. In mid-April we were scheduled to present the requirements to a review group in Bonn.

Disaster struck. After seven years, Sully decided to leave. Her husband viewed her work as a care provider with disfavor. Furthermore, they were considering a move to Georgia. "Tela will be devastated," I thought. Sully was as much a part of the family as Thomas Peter and I were.

Sully made it as easy as she could for everyone. She replaced herself with her cousin, Won Kyung, who was Kayong's oldest daughter. She also continued to call and drop in regularly. When Won Kyung's school and work schedule conflicted, Sully tried to fill in for her.

For months, however, Thomas Peter and I fairly frequently had child-coverage problems. I brought the children to work. They actually liked the office. Gilbert and Peter especially liked to play with Robin and Tim, who made cardboard swords and watched them destroyed as the boys dueled noisily down the halls.

The entire team was inexperienced and having a difficult time using the methodology that I had selected to do the analysis. Bob was having a tough time managing. He missed the schedules that he set, and his team was not getting appropriate technical results. I was spending most of my time in review sessions with the staff trying to help them get it right.

I decided I needed help. Judy Reach was the only manager I knew who had really used the technical methodology that we were struggling with, so on one of those fairly regular occasions when she and I got together for a drink at Mel Krupin's, I asked her to take a look at the team's technical work and give me some advice about what to do to get things on track. She took time out of her very hectic schedule to do a review. Other than to confirm the fact that what we were doing was not easy, however, she was unable to come up with any useful recommendations. The teams continued to slug it out and I continued the review sessions.

Message

An urgent telephone message from Lew Krulwich was impaled on a message spike prominently positioned front and center on my desk when I returned to my office in Rosslyn from a meeting with client staff. Lew wanted to meet me in his office downtown, immediately. Ominous. In the three years since I started working with the Department of State, Lew and I had had little business in common. Furthermore, I had never known anything to be urgent to Lew. My stomach queezed irregularly in the cab ride from Rosslyn to downtown. When I got to Lew's office he gravely escorted me to his small, round conference table, closed the door, and sat down beside me.

My anxiety was well founded. I was on hold. Partnership was out of the question this year. I was in shock. Although the cab trip from Rosslyn had given me a few minutes to prepare for the worst, I still fought back a tearful break-down. Lew was only slightly less upset about the decision than I was. The firm's senior partner, Joe Connor, had called Tom Beyer in the Cayman Islands where he was on vacation. All Lew knew was what Tom Beyer had relayed to him: apparently I had consistently irritated senior partners of the firm.

Together, Lew and I tried to identify partners that I had irritated. We were unable to list any senior partners that I ever remembered meeting. Lew told me that Joe Connor wanted to explain the situation to me personally. I should schedule a trip to New York to discuss the details with Joe. Dejected, I went home. I was horrified at the prospect of telling Thomas Peter what little I knew.

He reacted entirely differently from what I expected. Instead of being sympathetic or miserable or hurt, he was furious and outraged. In the absence of a more satisfactory answer, I should sue the bastards. In my psychologically rattled state, I sought to identify the heinous defect in me that had prevented my making the grade required of a partner. Less rattled than I, he wanted to know what was wrong with the process by which Price Waterhouse had come to such a remarkably bad business decision. I felt a little better. My husband, Thomas Peter Gallagher, was a fierce, fuzzy redhead when he was angry.

On the last Friday in April of 1983, promotion day, Ann B. Hopkins would be among the missing on the list of new partners. To make matters worse, I could offer no explanation. My normally unshakable confidence had been destroyed. I wondered how I would tell my staff, friends, and colleagues. Five years of long hours, hard work, and remarkable results were down the tubes. I was humiliated and embarrassed at the prospect of telling anyone what had happened.

Mel Krupin's seemed gloomier than usual the day after I got the bad news, when Judy Reach and Karen Nold met me there for a drink. We had met at Mel's regularly for years. It was a block from the office. All things considered it was a little sleazy. Bad ventilation permanently trapped the odor of stale cigarette smoke in the all-too-low, too-soft, box-shaped settees. The menu of mediocre food was unreadable in the dim light in the bar. We infrequently ate in the restaurant downstairs. The place was quiet though. Bad recordings of classical music that played softly in the background ensured that the younger, more boisterous crowds hung out somewhere else. An exception to the menu, the freshly steamed shrimp and raw clams and oysters that we frequently ordered with drinks were as good as any I had ever eaten.

Judy and Karen were thunderstruck. Grim-faced, they sat in stunned silence as I gave them the facts of my temporarily derailed partnership bid. I told them I had discussed my problems with the two other OGS partner candidates and with Steve Higgins who had been proposed by his home office, not OGS. The three guys must be okay, I commented. After all, they had no word to the contrary and it was getting close to the end of the process—the ballots were due to be printed and circulated soon.

I wondered why Judy, not Karen, raised the discrimination question. Judy was only a manager, therefore unlikely to be nominated for partner for at least three years. Karen, however, was a senior manager and likely to enter the process in the next year or so. In deadly serious tones we discussed the possibility that sex had been a consideration in the decision to hold me. We found unimaginable any notion that gender influenced business decisions, except in the case of a very selective set of generally illicit professions. There had to be some problem, other than sex, that I could start to work on, especially given that changing sex was not an option. I was sad when we parted company and went our separate ways that night.

Failure

Tom Beyer returned from vacation the following Monday. All he seemed to know was that I had consistently irritated strong partners of the firm. We could identify a few strong partners, but were unable to figure out how the ones I might have met could have been so irritated. We went over all the same ground that Lew and I had covered the previous week. Nothing had changed. I was held for reasons unknown. I had no notion of what to do to fix problems we were unable to pinpoint. Joe Connor had asked that I come to New York to discuss my status—he must know the answers.

The shuttle flight to New York was normally an unpleasant experience. That gloomy morning in early April it was downright depressing. I took an equally depressing cab ride to the national office on the Avenue of the Americas. While the elevator ascended into the heights, I concentrated on holding my head up and standing straight. I was the prince who had been turned into a frog. As I was escorted to the office of the senior partner of one of the most prominent partnerships in the world, I hoped I could avoid meeting anyone I knew.

The office was much smaller than I expected. A stand-alone, structural pillar cut off access to the window around one side of his desk. A water stain streaked down the pillar. I wondered what maintenance malfunction had prevented it from being repainted. He was pleasant, but there was no warmth about him as he summed up the paperwork. I had six votes recorded on long forms: three yes votes, two hold votes, and one no vote. I was having trouble counting. I knew that Tom Beyer and Lew Krulwich had voted for me. I believed Tim Coffey and Don Epelbaum had voted for me. That made four.

Joe neglected to offer who voted how and I refrained from asking. The long-form no vote, he said, had been discounted because that vote had been cast by a partner who almost always voted no. That had to be Norm Statland, I concluded. By Joe's analysis, three yes votes represented strong support.

My downfall had been the result of negative votes and comments on the twenty-six short forms, where the score was ten yes, seven no, one hold, and eight insufficient information. Without comment or attribution, he read the remarks made by partners on the short forms. The august circumstances and my general state of depression prevented me from reaching into my briefcase, whipping out a pad and pencil and taking notes. That seemed impolitic. I listened in horror as I heard my social skills, leadership, technical ability, and even my integrity assaulted.

Fortunately, my mind usually sorts through information and organizes it into categories ranked from most to least important. The integrity question instantly registered as an elephant among gnats. In context, I recognized the author as John Fridley, one of the St. Louis partners. Unfortunately, Fridley's no vote supported by his comments questioning my integrity was one of the last on the list of twenty-six sets of short-form comments. I instantly forgot most of the comments that preceded it.

There was no point in debating various partners' views of my personality or social skills. Integrity questions, however, had to be dealt with. I told Joe that Fridley had a distorted view of the facts. Lew Krulwich, not I, had set the time-recording and billing practices that were at the heart of the integrity issue on that ancient Bureau of Indian Affairs engagement. Furthermore, Lew had straightened out whatever problems he had created, and I was certain that he would assume the responsibility for his actions. Joe said that my integrity was not in question. I was left with the impression that Lew had somehow dealt with it when someone named Roger Marcellin was in Washington interviewing the OGS partners about their candidates.

Joe wanted to know what had happened in St. Louis. He seemed genuinely interested when I summarized the events of the previous July and August in a few sentences. We wrote a proposal; it was hard; we won. He said nothing.

He asked for my views on how I related to my staff. He again showed interest but made no comment when I explained that I saw no problems: bad staff management usually had some adverse effect on performance which, in turn, resulted in client dissatisfaction. There were no indications of client dissatisfaction now, nor had there ever been any.

To preserve my sanity, I needed a plan of action to fix whatever problems there were. I asked Joe what I had to do to make partner in the next year. The answer I got sounded like: keep up the good work, do another quality control review, and avoid getting any negative comments. The meeting was over. It lasted a little more than an hour. Joe had provided no answers or explanations, or if he had, I had failed to hear them.

Back in Washington, I later reviewed my recollections of the Connor meeting with both Tom and Lew. Most of the details, however, were lost, suppressed by my concern with the integrity question. "When you stand naked under the shower, Gilbert, all you have on is your integrity," I once said to my son as part of an effort to persuade him that it was more important to tell the truth than it was to look like a hero in the eyes of his peers. To the extent that I was ever successful in dealing with clients, staff or, for that matter children, it was attributable to integrity more than to infallibility. I told Lew that if Fridley's concerns were still a problem, then I would like to know about it, and I wanted to be sure that Lew either had fixed it or would fix it. Lew assured me that at least my integrity was intact.

I had to force myself to get back to work. The project team was preparing the user requirements document for presentation to the State Department review group. We had a week or so to get everything together and get to Bonn for a week of review sessions. The State Department was bringing foreign service staff in from Africa and other parts of Europe. They expected to see a substantive, useful, helpful product untarnished by my personal problems.

Before we made the travel plans for Bonn, I had to deal with some project staffing problems. Poor Bob Lam was not working out. Harry and his team had to do their own work and then bail out Bob's team in spare time or overtime. I could not determine whether the performance problems of Bob's staff were due to bad direction from Bob, the difficulty of the technical methodology we were using, or simple inability to perform. Bob had to go—we could analyze the performance problems with his team later.

As a manager, Bob had what was known as an employment contract with the firm. In concept, the only real benefit of the contract was that Bob had to be given two months' severance pay or two months' notice before termination. Employment contracts for managers were renewed on July 1, the first day of the firm's fiscal year. March was the time when decisions about promotions and terminations were made. I met with Tom Beyer and told him that based on my past experience and my current formal evaluation of Bob's performance, he had to be taken off my project and we should probably help him find a new job. Tom called Ben Warder into his office and told Ben to tell Bob immediately that his contract would not be renewed.

That left a replacement for Bob as an open issue. I needed another manager—fast. Tom told me about a woman named Sandy Kinsey. She was not a technical person, but she was supposed to be a first-rate organizer and manager, and she was reputed to be smart. Tom described her as an empty beer can (empty of technical substance) that merely needed to be filled. I knew I had management problems on Bob's team and technical problems on the project as a whole. I opted to solve the management problems first—Sandy Kinsey replaced Bob Lam within days. The transition was not smooth. Bob was gone one day and Sandy was working on the project the following Monday.

We had to get our act together for Bonn. Whatever bothered me was set aside as the whole team went into product preparation mode. Sandy did not have the foggiest notion of the details of the material that we were putting together, but she could put together an effective presentation on anything. I refused to let her contribute substantively to the efforts in Bonn—I was afraid of a screwup. But we all used presentation materials that she had either prepared or orchestrated. Furthermore, she kept bumblers out of the project team's hair by exercising her considerable diplomatic skills and diverting them elsewhere whenever they might have gotten in the way. The bumblers got the tour of the bridge at Remagen or obscure restaurants on the other side of town while the rest of the team focused on the requirements review.

Thomas Peter went along on the trip to Bonn. It should have been a lot more fun than it was. He and I planned a partial boondoggle to Bonn by way of London. It should have been followed by a triumphant return to

Washington and an announcement that I would soon be a partner. Instead, every minor irritation was exaggerated by underlying unspoken anxiety. When a gypsy cab driver ripped us off for the trip from Gatwick to our hotel in London, I worried about money instead of chalking it up to experience. When Thomas Peter wanted to take side trips all over Germany as if it were Rhode Island, I suppressed rage at his naïveté about distances and the cost of travel. I was shocked when he gave me a Seiko watch as a memento of Germany. I was irritated and frustrated when, at his insistence, we boarded the train in Frankfurt headed for Munich instead of Cologne and an hour later had to pay the additional fare to get turned around and headed back in the right direction. When we finally got home, promotion day was upon us.

Ipecac

The arrival of *Return of the Jedi* had been heralded by advertisements for months before it opened in local movie theaters the summer I was held. Tela, Gilbert, and Peter had been counting down the days remaining until opening day like retailers before Christmas. It promised to be a marvelous diversion from the tensions at work. Thomas Peter and I had seen, and enjoyed, the predecessors, *Star Wars* and *The Empire Strikes Back,* at least five times each with the children individually or in groups.

I promised the children that I would take them to the first available showing of the opening-day performance. Accordingly, I left work early enough to pick them up at the house and get to the movie about noon. I was wearing a pink linen suit that I had bought in response, partly cynical, to a counseling comment made the year before by one of the partners. He had told me to "soften my image." The children wanted to sit on the front row or the floor under the screen. Sitting on the floor in a pink suit with a straight skirt was not an option. My normal aversion to sitting in the front row prevented me from sitting with the children.

After the movie we regrouped and hopped in the car for the fifteen-minute ride home. About half way to the house, Peter turned a little green behind the gills and told me he was about to vomit. After I stopped the car, he proceeded to do so under one of the big oak trees that line both sides of Albemarle Street. When we got home we sat down in the kitchen with a snack. Peter was still nauseated. He was not tall enough to reach the kitchen sink, so I got him a stool to stand on and held him gently around the pants' pockets as he vomited again.

"Say, Pete, how many of these tablets did you swallow?" I asked calmly when I encountered a bulge in one of his pockets and on follow-up discovered Tim Scheve's Nigerian Sudafed bottle, half full of little red tablets. Full, the bottle should have contained one hundred tablets. "I don't know, Mom," was the sheepish reply. "He knows damn well," I thought. The situation looked like it might require ipecac.

Tela's pediatrician told me to buy syrup of ipecac when she was less than three months old. He also gave me instructions for its use and a telephone number for poison control. I never used ipecac or poison control for Tela. I used both once when Gilbert, at age two, decided to take his antibiotics unassisted. He thought, quite considerately, that it was unnecessary to wake Thomas Peter or me early that Sunday morning. He removed the childproof top and drank roughly half a bottle of Erythromycin. (Because he spilled a lot on the floor, it was hard to determine how much he drank.) When I encountered the resulting mess I called poison control to confirm my worst suspicions. I told Gilbert that he had to take the ipecac, why he had to take it, and that vomiting would ensue. An hour later, after a brief but messy projectile vomiting session, he was cheerfully eating pizza for lunch. He never took medicine by mouth without measuring it again.

I told Peter that he was more than likely in for a dose of ipecac as I dialed poison control. Gilbert was solemnly explaining the situation to his brother when poison control contradicted my hypothesis. This situation required an emergency room visit. I greeted Thomas Peter, who was on his way into the house, as I packed Peter into the car for the trip to Sibley Hospital.

Under the supervision of the emergency room staff, I persuaded Peter to drink an elixir of charcoal. Neither Peter nor the pink suit suffered any immediate ill effects. The ginger ale chaser, however, was a different matter. After Peter swallowed a couple of mouthfuls, the entire contents of his stomach worked their way out. Charcoal elixir–covered popcorn, Smarties, and other movie snacks splattered in a dark-gray Rorschach test pattern across the front of my suit.

Dinner was late that night. I retired the suit. We saw *The Return of the Jedi* twice again before the week was out.

Idiot

The last Friday in April is usually a dead loss from a business perspective. Price Waterhouse offices all over the United States announce promotions on that Friday by posting lists of names of people to be promoted on the following July 1. Staff promotions are posted at 9 A.M. The new partner list is posted later, at 11 A.M., to ensure that the East and West Coasts are simultaneously informed of the exciting news. Celebrations begin almost immediately after the lists are posted.

A miserable, dejected, unhappy failed partner candidate, I stoically and with all the dignity I could muster, attended all celebrations that I would have attended had my name been on the list of partners who would be admitted on July 1, 1983, the first day of the coming fiscal year. They could forget the congratulations, I had told my staff and friends weeks before, at informal meetings after work over drinks. At one party after another, they kindly avoided attempts at verbal condolences. Thoughts unspoken were expressed in sympathetic glances and body language: a hug here, a double-handed handshake there, a gentle pat on the back, a hopeless shrug of the shoulders. They did their best, but I had a hell of a promotion day.

"Buck up," I said to myself; it was time for damage assessment and control. I had to write off my losses and take charge of what I could control. First I would figure out, for myself, if I was on a quixotic quest for the partnership. Over lunch or cocktails I met with some of the partners in OGS. With others I arranged technical meetings or counseling sessions. A peculiar picture emerged; it looked like a personality change operation was required.

Walk more femininely, talk more femininely, dress more femininely, wear make-up and jewelry, have my hair styled. That was the gist of what I was advised by Tom Beyer. For more than three years I had worked almost exclusively for Tom. I knew him very well. If it got results, he could have cared less if a consultant attended a business meeting in Bermudas and tennis shoes. Tom's counsel was nonsense.

If I had a good job offer I should take it, was the advice Don Epelbaum offered. "Dandy Don" he was called by some. He was short, infrequently removed his coat, never had a hair out of place, wore a diamond pinky ring. His office was always immaculate and he disliked other people using it. He owed his very solid business base to my efforts. Sandy Kinsey had warned me that he was not to be trusted. I was deceived; I had never believed her. Don's advice was unpalatable.

Lew Krulwich offered no advice. He was simply sad.

Spend some time working on proposals in his international arena was Pete McVeagh's counsel. A nice man, Pete; he was a father figure. Warm eyes sparkled from under a gray, turning white, marine corps haircut. He had a never-ending smile and an enthusiastic disposition that matched. He spent hours comforting me and bolstering my failed, but recovering, confidence. He was, however, powerless. The international arena consisted of a steady diet of proposal writing interrupted by an occasional small job doing work foreign to me in distant, uncomfortable parts of the world. Undesirable.

Negative in the extreme, unenthusiastic, untrustworthy was how Ben Warder characterized me. When we returned from Bonn I had asked Ben to review my team's work as I tried to address my continuing technical concerns. He was Judy Reach's boss. I thought he had been helpful. He, however, attributed financial losses and diminished professional stature that he associated with being removed from the early work for the State Department to me. He looked fifteen years older than he was and had sad eyes. My relationship with him was irreparable.

That I was dead in the water should have been obvious to a person of my brain power and business acumen. Oblivious to reality, however, I persisted in fixing the unfixable until shortly after the onslaught of technical reviews that began in June.

The situation seemed harmless enough at the start. Paragraph 766 of some policy manual required that, under certain circumstances, a job managed by one partner be reviewed by a second partner. Par 766 reviews, as they were called, were intended to reduce the risks of shoddy, unprofitable, or other inappropriate work. In theory, the interests of the partners as a whole were protected to some extent by having the work of one autonomous partner reviewed with deficiencies recorded by another. My experience had been that Par 766 reviews were sometimes done on proposals, usually on big or risky proposals, but in OGS such reviews were usually a file-papering exercise.

None of the work for the State Department had been subjected to Par 776 review in recent time, so I thought it unusual when Tom Beyer told me to make arrangements for Ben Warder to do a Par 766 review of my project. On June 8 and 9, Ben Warder spent about eight hours reviewing the user requirements report and the supporting papers and files. From then until the last week in July, not a day passed that I or some member of the project staff was free of tasks related to responding to the criticisms of the review.

The project was dinged because certain time-recording and billing documents had not been reconciled to accounting reports. We were told to do the reconciliation. The criticism and related recommendation implied that the project was financially out of control. It was a fact that the records had not been reconciled. It was patently ridiculous to conclude that the project was financially out of control.

When my checkbook was a couple of dollars out of balance from my bank statement, I posted the reconciling two-dollar entry and moved on. Finding the origin of the error was not worth the time it took to reconcile the details. I managed the project the same way. With the implication that money was somehow pouring through the cracks, however, I had no choice but to make the project team reconcile the records. Sandy Kinsey spent forty hours doing the reconciliation. She discovered errors totaling thirty-nine hours out of about twenty-one thousand hours recorded on the job. We posted the reconciling entry and moved on.

Other criticisms of the project were equally picky and misleading. A criticism that the client had not approved the work plan implied that the client was clueless about what we were doing. Outrageous. We had formally transmitted the plan to the client months ago. We reported progress weekly to the client against the plan. We shared offices with the client. Nevertheless, we asked the client to write a letter formally approving the plan.

The entire project team cheerfully pitched in to help out but they were embarrassed to be involved in the useless fire drill. Eventually, the client project manager got fed up with the diversion of project staff to unproductive tasks required to respond to meaningless criticisms. When I billed for the time Ben Warder spent on the job, he tried to reject the charges. I told him that he was overstepping his authority, but he eventually found a way to avoid paying for the time.

As the elephant was about to stomp on my head, I finally saw it coming. The partners met on and off in mid-July. It was general knowledge among the managers that partner candidates for the next fiscal year were under discussion. The final meeting on the subject consumed the entirety of July 22, 1983, a Friday. Partners who before that meeting had at least tried to maintain a cheerful facade, failed to make eye contact with me after that meeting. In response to my questions about what had happened, I was told to talk to Tom Beyer.

Tom Beyer, however, left for the day immediately after the meeting. Over the weekend, I left for Denver to do a quality control review, my second. It was part of Joe Connor's April plan to go on another quality control review and avoid getting negative comments. Although I had not discussed my status with Tom, I knew that Joe's plan and whatever I did at the Denver review were irrelevant.

In Denver I reviewed the files on a thirty-two-thousand-hour project where Price Waterhouse was subcontractor to my previous employer, American Management Systems. I was reasonably well acquainted with the woman who was the AMS project manager. She managed the site where a lot of the files that I reviewed were located. I had always liked her; we had lunch together. The files were clean.

The supervising partner graded my efforts in a performance evaluation based on his four hours of contact with me in Denver: seven A's, 12 B's, and a C. There were no negative comments. I returned to Washington, still waiting to find Tom and to find out what was going on.

Tom was on vacation when I got back in the office. In fact, he was on vacation the entire week. In his absence, Ben Warder was the partner in charge of OGS. The QCR team arrived to review my project files. I was frustrated at my inability to talk to Tom and worried about what I believed to be my rejection by the partners of OGS. I was, however, unconcerned at the prospect of a review of my project files. The job was moving along. The client was happy, and Sandy Kinsey and Harry Barschdorf, my two managers, had put the normally tidy project papers and files into condition appropriate for a spit-and-polish review. After weeks of jumping through hoops related to the Par 766 review, no one expected any problems. We assumed that any defects, real or imaginary, had been cleaned up in response to the first review. We were unworried.

After the second day of the review, Sandy, Harry, and I were downtown reviewing the project plans. The reviewing manager, who was from Denver, gave us his current draft of his report on our project. Sandy made copies for us. We read and discussed the report. Everything was fine. The reviewing manager had lunch the next day with Ben Warder and Don Epelbaum. I turned a little suspicious when he came back for another look at the files, so I fished copies of drafts of his findings out of the trash can. When he kept returning, I kept fishing. The review was going belly up and all I could do was watch in amazement.

It was hard to believe that my job was going to be declared "technically not in conformance with the firm's high standards for quality." I called Don Epelbaum at home at 8:30 in the evening on Thursday to ask him if I should be getting a message. He repeated his suggestion that I take another position and further suggested that I develop a headache for the rest of the week.

This was bullshit. Misery turned to rage.

Huron

Although I had long suspected that I needed an attorney, I was revolted at the prospect of searching for one. On the faint hope that my situation might improve, I procrastinated. Thomas Peter, who had worked with attorneys for years, was undaunted. A senior partner at Arnold and Porter (A&P), Mike Curzan, was one of Thomas Peter's best friends. He had been an usher in our wedding. As my attorney, he was out of the question because he was a real estate attorney, a deal maker, but he knew or knew how to find someone appropriate.

When Thomas Peter and I met with Mike over lunch in the A&P cafeteria, Mike had explained that the large, prominent law firms usually represented organizations. What I needed, he had said, was a firm that represented individuals. Most such firms were small. He agreed to find some names and get back to us.

Minutes after I received Arnold and Porter's list of possible attorneys, I called Stein and Huron to schedule an appointment. (I would have called them sooner but they were the second firm on the list. The first was out of town.) I briefly went over the few facts that I had about the plight of my original partnership proposal, told the attorney that things were looking bad for the next round, and stated my belief that I was about to be declared incompetent.

Mild amusement was my reaction to the attorney's suggestion that I wait until I was sure I was incompetent before I came to his office for a face-to-face meeting. We agreed to an early Friday morning appointment on the day that the QCR team reported to Ben Warder that mine was the only project in OGS that failed to meet the firm's technical quality standards.

The offices of Stein and Huron probably occupied less space than the cafeteria at Arnold and Porter. It was hard to tell because the A&P cafeteria was all on one floor while Stein and Huron was located in a lovely, old, three-story townhouse just off Scott Circle. Instead of an elevator, wide, dark, highly polished stairs turned rectangular corners all the way to the top floor where Thomas Peter and I were escorted to a conference room with a high ceiling. It must have been someone's bedroom twenty years ago. It was made bright and airy by two or three windows that covered most of the wall facing south. The room was simply furnished with widely spaced, modern pieces, and my attention was immediately drawn to an elegant old fireplace.

Douglas B. Huron bore no resemblance to an Edward Bennett Williams. He seemed very serious, even a little stuffy as he shook hands firmly and offered coffee. Stepping into the hall but not out of sight, he produced cups from a curtained closet that also contained neat piles of office supplies. He filled the coffee pot with water from a tidy little bathroom that, judging from the style and pattern of the tile, had not been redecorated since the 1930s. His coal black hair and mustache told me he was youngish. He smiled infrequently, spoke with a tone of voice that varied little and within a narrow pitch range on the low end of the scale. He never sat down. Instead, he paced or stood with one elbow on the mantel over the fireplace.

In response to his questions, Thomas Peter and I told him that I had developed quite a lot of business for my firm, that I had been a candidate for the partnership, that I was not made a partner the first time around, and that I was not even going to be proposed for the partnership in the next round. He asked if there had been any overt sexist comments, verbal or written. There were none that I could recall, but then, I infrequently recognized sexist comments. He wanted to know about the statistical composition of the partners. Other than to note that demographically they seemed to be a largely male, largely white population, I had too few facts to be informative.

I, too, had a few questions. The only context I had for discrimination and civil rights was what had taken place in Gadsden, Selma, Birmingham, and the like in my college years. The fact that the Civil Rights Act of 1964 might apply to me had only recently come to the forefront of my conscious thinking. The term "attorney" had no meaning to me other than to describe a quarter of the people at any cocktail party I ever attended in Washington and three-quarters of all the people at real estate closings.

The modifiers that subtly defined the hierarchy in the court systems confused me. Like most sixth-graders, I understood that the Supreme Court was the highest federal court in the land. I recognized the D.C. superior courts as part of the local judicial system, only because the crime rate in the District of Columbia focused media attention on them. I had to consciously invoke mental images of judges on horseback riding the circuits to differentiate between the federal circuit courts and the federal district courts. The district courts are the ones where trials are held. The circuit courts do not try cases. They belong to the U.S. court of appeals system.

In response to my request for a layperson's introduction to the legal process, Doug told me that I could file a complaint with the Equal Employment Opportunity Commission (EEOC) as a first step in a federal lawsuit. In addition or instead, I could file a complaint with the D.C. Human Rights Commission as a first step in a D.C. lawsuit. A complaint to either commission would allege discrimination and ask for the right to sue Price Waterhouse in the appropriate federal or local court. Either commission might investigate, in which case my costs would probably be less than the costs of a litigation. If, however, the commissions did nothing else, I could expect to be granted the right to sue in six months. It was early August, mental arithmetic said that we would have some sense of legal direction by February or March 1984.

I was less than enthusiastic about remaining with Price Waterhouse as a senior manager with no prospects for the partnership as my work was being declared technically incompetent while the EEOC administered an investigative process. I asked Doug if I had to stay with the firm. For legal reasons that we failed to ask about and he declined to go into, he advised that I remain, at least for the time being. I expressed my distaste at the prospect, told him I would take his advice, and asked him to tell me when the time came that I could resign.

We discussed fee arrangements. If I chose to have him represent me, Doug explained, I had two choices: I could send him a check and retain his firm, or we could work out a contingency fee arrangement. If retained, his firm would bill me periodically for services rendered at usual and customary rates. If he worked on contingency, his firm would be paid a part of any money awarded. He told me to think about it. As Thomas Peter and I walked down the stairs and out the front door of the office, I had a sense of relief and anticipation similar to the one I get when I sink into the seat of an airplane on my way to some vacation destination after having rushed to finish up at the office, pack up the children, drop the dog at the vet, and race to the airport.

Litigant

"I have a fourth option," I said to myself, "an option that you may not have considered, Tom—I could sue the brotherhood." Diminishing disappointment had been displaced by intensifying anger. On return from vacation, Tom Beyer called a meeting to discuss my future with me and Pete McVeagh, the partner responsible for the international consulting practice in OGS.

As Tom saw it I had three options. First, I could take a position with another firm. Second, I could go to work for Pete McVeagh, who would try to groom me as a partner candidate in the distant future. Third, I could accept a career manager position that paid well but had no partnership potential. He wanted me to give up the quest for the partnership and stay with the firm as a career manager. Pete was effusively enthusiastic about the prospects of my working for him.

Caution takes control over communication when I become angry. My voice drops to a barely audible level. I say little, if anything. What my mind analyzed, my voice left unsaid. Reject option one. I would refuse to slink out the doors of Price Waterhouse as a failed partner candidate, one more apparent victim of the up or out policy. Reject option two. I would refuse to abandon my client of long standing, the Department of State, and go work with the heretofore unprofitable international consulting practice doing six-week projects in Costa Rica or the like, on the off chance that lightning might strike twice and I would have another chance at the partnership. Reject option three. I would refuse to give up all thoughts of or aspirations to the partnership and agree to work on whatever I was told for as long the work was acceptable and the job paid decently.

Tom and Pete wanted my decision, right then and there. "I'll get back to you," I said coldly. As an attempted compromise, they asked to be the first to know of my decision. Would I refrain from discussing this matter? I would make no promises. Accept option four, I decided. Stein and Huron were retained on August 11, 1983, with a check for three thousand dollars. Whatever Doug's legal reasons were for wanting me to stay with the firm after I decided to sue, I hoped they were good. Having committed to a lawsuit, I wanted out.

The project team was preparing a major design report to be presented to a State Department review group in Paris. The review was scheduled to be a week long, starting in mid-September. The sixteen-volume design had to be shipped out ten days in advance of the arrival of my project team. Sandy, Harry, and I were ducking internal reviews and responses thereto in order to produce the design. On August 30, 1983, Doug filed, on my behalf, a sex discrimination claim with the EEOC alleging that PW had violated Title VII of the Civil Rights Act of 1964, a federal law.

Four days before we shipped the design to Paris, Tom asked for a meeting to discuss the results of the QCR, ostensibly because Joe Connor had asked for an explanation of the shocking technical deficiencies of the project. Although I had copies of the QCR materials that I had obtained on my various fishing trips, I had never seen the report that was issued to the partners of OGS almost a month earlier. Furthermore, I could have cared less about the QCR report, an internal document. Internally, my fate was sealed.

I was far more concerned about the well-being of my client. As soon as Doug gave the word, I was going to leave the firm, hence the project. Tom would need to know a lot more about the project after I left than he needed to know as long as I was there. He had never seen the design report that I was preparing to ship to Paris. In an extreme state of irritation, I suggested that he send me a copy of the QCR report but review the design report. We could meet to discuss the QCR—later. To his credit, he recognized the priorities. Minor changes to the transmittal letter were all that was required by his review of the design report.

The same day the design was shipped, according to schedule, Tom and I met to review the QCR report. Calmly he read aloud each question and the related response on the questionnaire that recorded the negatives that had resulted in my project being declared technically deficient. After each question and response, he ad libbed his view of the appropriate answer, sometimes in agreement with the party line, sometimes in opposition. After each question, response, ad lib, he paused and asked if I agreed or disagreed. Intuition told me to be very careful about agreeing with any of the negatives. When I observed how fastidiously Tom was taking notes, suspicion overwhelmed intuition. I would not have agreed to the correct spelling of my own name.

With a great sense of relief the project team went to Paris in mid-September. The slight chill of the changing season was refreshing after the physical and emotional heat in Washington. The team knew that it was going to be hard work and a lot of fun. We had one week to explain, review, and figure out what was wrong with sixteen volumes of design documents that we had put together. The State Department brought people to Paris from other European posts and from Africa to review the material. This was no time to blow it. Sandy Kinsey had prepared a spectacular set of multicolored flip charts. Each member of the project team knew exactly what to do. Although the hotel that the embassy put us in looked like it should have started major renovations in 1950, the weather was wonderful; we were prepared for the work ahead; and we were up.

On the technical front, the work went well; on the social front we encountered problems starting on Day One. A group of us, including Bert Moore, the counselor for administration from the American embassy in Lagos, met at breakfast on the first morning. Most of us had wet hair and looked peculiar, if not disheveled and unkempt. No one could get the hair dryers to work. This was quite a source of frustration to the project team because we all considered ourselves to be competent international travelers and had come prepared with hair dryers that were either made for European current or were AC/DC convertible.

That evening when we met for a drink after the day's work, Bert Moore, looking quite well groomed, asked with a wry grin, "Do you want to know what the hair dryer problem is?" We laughed heartily when he explained that the hotel in which we were staying used 110 AC current. For that reason all the hair dryers that used conventional European current were inoperable. The convertibles worked fine when set for the United States.

Later in the week, one of the members of the French national staff at the embassy invited us to go to the display of lights at Les Invalides. Because the light show did not start until late at night, she graciously offered to give us a Parisian's (as opposed to a tourist's) tour of Paris in the evening.

Sandy and I decided that conventional business attire, including high-heeled shoes, was appropriate. We met the rest of the project team and most of the out-of-town staff from the State Department and were escorted to dinner and the light show. Dinner was lovely, as was the light show, although the trek across a hundred yards of cobblestones getting into and out of Les Invalides was a strain on my feet. I was hoping that the evening was over when our French guide decided to show us a number of cavelike pubs where musicians sang in a number of languages and played a number of different instruments. Most of the project team used the late hour as an excuse and took a cab back to the hotel.

Although there is a stereotypical view that the French are hostile, I enjoyed the company of every French person with whom I ever spent any time. Still, Sandy and I did not want to test the hypothesis by appearing to be rude if we refused our French hostess's hospitable offer, so we accompanied what was left of the group. I was pretty tired by the time we got to the caves, as the pubs were called. They were located under the streets and buildings of Paris, sometimes in areas that had been dungeons or way stations into the sewers hundreds of years ago. The typical access to a cave was through a stairwell so narrow and with stone steps so uneven that the Occupational Safety and Health Administration in this country would have ordered that the facilities be closed.

By the time we left the caves to go back to the hotel, I was exhausted and my feet were killing me. Although Sandy uttered not a word, she was no better off than I was. And things got worse, not better. The subway was not running and we put our French national escort into the only cab we saw as we walked the mile or so back to the hotel. Bright and early that same morning Sandy and I were back on our feet running the design reviews. To our great relief, Harry handled the afternoon session.

Although the review went well and the design proved fairly solid, we found that we had accumulated quite a pile of "to-do's" by the Friday we were scheduled to return to the United States. Harry, Sandy, and I met early in the morning to consolidate our individual lists and decide on a short-term course of action. The result of that meeting was a decision that

Sandy, Robin Myiang, and I would work over the weekend, meet with individual review group members on Monday, and if possible return to the States late Monday or Tuesday. We spent the morning with the review group summarizing the criticisms of the week and describing our plans to fix the problems we had discovered. Harry and the rest of the team took off on the afternoon flight from Charles de Gaulle.

"It is impossible," she ejaculated in a snooty French accent when Sandy, Robin, and I told her that we needed hotel reservations. The woman who handled travel and hotel arrangements seemed disinclined to help. We had checked out of the Lutetia earlier. It was booked solid through the next week anyway. To hear her tell it, every hotel in Paris was booked solid.

"What do you suggest we do?" I asked politely while trying to appear hopeless and desperate. It was clear that our very presence annoyed her. She was, however, a critical part of the solution to our housing problem. If she refused to cooperate, then we would have to fend for ourselves—not a pleasant prospect.

"Leave!" she said. I explained that leaving was not an option and decided to counter arrogance with humility. When I asked, "Is there a YMCA in Paris?" she seemed to respond. As Sandy, Robin, and I stood silently by, she made a few phone calls. She looked up with a broad grin after a particularly long conversation in French delivered with the verbal impact of a machine gun.

She usually arranged for people working at the embassy to stay within walking distance, or at most a few stops away, she explained. The Hotel Gavarni was near the Passy metro station, more than eight stops from the embassy, depending on the route. It was well out of the usual range of places where people stayed, but it would just have to do, she continued. We thanked her enthusiastically and left quickly.

The Gavarni was owned and run by a crazy Parisian woman and a distinguished provincial from Burgundy. Brigette and Jean Charles Mornand seemed to have little in common except for the obvious affection that they had each for the other. She was ten years younger than I, blond, short, and a tad on the heavy side, a fact that was hardly noticeable because she dressed in well-fitted, elegant Parisian designer clothes and never had a hair out of place. She was constantly in motion and chattered endlessly and dramatically with both hands and her mouth. Without batting an eye she switched instantly from French to Italian to uncolloquial English, depending on the nationality of the person to whom she was speaking.

In contrast, Jean Charles was ten years older than I, more than a foot taller than Brigette, and had a perfect build for his height. He spoke little, always in a quiet, deliberate manner, and he usually stayed in the hotel office minding the books and the Telex. He was a first-class hotelier who had run Hilton hotels all over the world.

I have stayed in larger, more elegant hotels with better facilities, but never with better service. Brigette and Jean Charles took us into the hotel and treated us as if we were treasured members of the family, not merely weekend guests. The dirty laundry that had accumulated during the week at the Lutetia was magically clean on Saturday. The hotel breakfast room was converted into a place for us to work after eleven o'clock in the morning. They made dinner reservations at restaurants that had been full all week. Plane tickets were changed and new reservations made in a flash. Brigette's response to any request was invariably, "It is no problems!" By the time we left Paris to return to the States, my whole opinion of Paris had changed—I loved it.

When I returned, the contents of my office downtown had been packed up and moved out, whereabouts unknown. I called Doug to tell him how irritated I was and to ask what was happening at the EEOC. "Calm down," he said. The EEOC was doing nothing: it was snarled up in jurisdictional disputes. After a little scrounging around, I found my possessions in boxes in the supply room. The loss of the office was of little real consequence. I used it infrequently because the project team had a suite of offices near our client in Rosslyn and I spent most of my time there. Distasteful, that's how it struck me.

Even more distasteful was the prospect of my next meeting with Tom Beyer. He wanted to meet with Ben Warder and me to finish up the Par 766 review of the user requirements report so that Ben could start another Par 766 review, this one on the design report that had been presented in Paris. The first Par 766 review, which had started in June, was officially finished in late September. About the same time, the project team received a letter of commendation from the client for our work on the design.

In anticipation of Ben's second Par 766 review, Tom spent some time reviewing the project plans and the design report. Ben could not schedule his efforts until early November. In the meanwhile, Harry was considering leaving the firm and returning to his previous employer. The position offered was a promotion and had a salary that was a great deal more than Harry was making at the time. Even though he was a first-rate performer, he was unlikely to be promoted to a comparable level or salary for a couple of years if he stayed at Price Waterhouse. It was just too good to turn down.

Harry was unprepared for what happened when he told Tom that he was leaving. With amusement and consternation, he explained to me that at least two partners had met with him to ask him to discuss his "real" reasons for leaving. In each case he patiently explained that he had a better opportunity. When Tim Scheve later transferred to another project, he too was asked for his "real" reasons for leaving the project. His reason was different: the new project gave him a chance to work in his specialty, financial analysis.

On Halloween 1983, Thomas Peter and I took the children trick-or-treating and missed the evening news. Had we watched, we might have noted that the Supreme Court heard arguments on *Hishon v. King and Spalding*. The Hishon case was a reason, if not *the* reason, that the EEOC was crippled with inaction.

In 1978, about the time I joined PW, Elizabeth Anderson Hishon, a real estate attorney, sued King and Spalding, an Atlanta law firm. She claimed that King and Spalding violated Title VII because it permitted the fact that she was a woman to influence its decision not to make her a partner of the firm.

It seemed clear that Title VII applied to any member of a protected group who was being hired or promoted from one level to another. From King and Spalding's point of view, however, admission to the partnership was an invitation, not a promotion. King and Spalding argued that Title VII did not explicitly state that admission to a partnership was covered by the law. Furthermore, they argued that the partners' rights to freedom of association, granted under the Bill of Rights, might be limited if Title VII were applied to invitations to a partnership. In conflicts between the Constitution and a federal law, the Constitution is supposed to prevail.

The U.S. District Court in Atlanta decided that King and Spalding was right—Title VII was inapplicable. In effect, it decided that partnership admission decisions were exempt from the law. It refused to hear Hishon's case.

Hishon appealed to the Court of Appeals for the Eleventh Circuit. The circuit court agreed with the district court. Hishon appealed again, this time to the Supreme Court. Until the Supreme Court resolved *Hishon v. King and Spalding,* any attempt I made to invoke Title VII in any federal forum would be met by protestations from PW's attorneys that Title VII was inapplicable.

When Ben's schedule cleared out enough that he could start his next review, he decided that he was the wrong person for the job. A technically oriented senior manager was brought in. Nothing, he found nothing problematical. At Ben's suggestion, the State Department was asked to have the design reviewed by a third party. The security staff at the State Department and another contractor both reviewed the design.

I was barely hanging on by my psychological fingernails when Doug finally told me that I could leave in December 1983. My two-page letter of resignation, dated December 21, 1983, stated that I found conditions at Price Waterhouse intolerable, that I planned to leave, and that I would do whatever it took to ensure an orderly transition for the client. It was addressed to Joe Connor in New York, drafted and typed by Stein and Huron. It would have been a lot shorter had I written it. I was relieved to be rid of it and more relieved at the prospect of getting away from the reviews.

For what seemed like an eternity, but was in reality only a little over three weeks, I waited for something to happen. Midmorning Tuesday, January 17, 1984, I was called to Tom's office downtown. I signed for my severance check and returned to Rosslyn to clean out my desk, as requested. While I was en route, Tom called Sandy and told her to take care of me. Sandy said nothing to the project team, most of whom had gone to lunch.

Back in Rosslyn, I boxed up the contents of my desk. Then Sandy and whoever was left in the office took me to lunch. I tried to be upbeat as I talked about going into business for myself. I was, however, sad. There was little opportunity to bid farewell to the real estate management system project team that I had led for a year and a half. After lunch, Sandy went downtown to check on Tom.

He was close to tears. "Are you okay?" Sandy asked Tom. "No," was his simple reply. Tom, who infrequently left before six o'clock, went home for the day when Sandy left. Sandy replaced me as project manager on REMS.

Ben Warder's final Par 766 review was delivered a week to the day after I left the firm. The security and third-party review reports, both indicating compliance with all departmental requirements, were also delivered after I left.

On February 14, 1984, about a month after I left PW, Doug filed another claim with the EEOC alleging that PW had harassed me and retaliated after I filed the original discrimination claim. He requested that I be granted the right to sue PW in the U.S. District Court for the District of Columbia.

The filings with the EEOC were necessary prerequisites to initiating a lawsuit in the federal court system. They started an administrative process in the EEOC, the purpose of which was to resolve the dispute. In my case, nothing happened. The overall effect of the commission's doing nothing was to build a time lag of at least six months into the judicial process.

Doug filed questions, the legal term for which is interrogatories. He also asked that PW be required to produce documents related to the partner candidate evaluation process, compensation of partners, and the like—documents that PW was certainly reluctant to produce. PW's attorneys snarled up the process by maintaining that the EEOC did not have jurisdiction over my claim. They maintained that Title VII did not apply to admissions to partnership. After enough time passed, the commission granted me the right to sue. Had the process worked as intended, both parties and the taxpayers might have been spared the costs of a judicial proceeding.

Unemployment

I was uptight and nervous. For the first time since I graduated from college, I was unemployed and scared to death at the prospect of running out of money. PW had given me six months' severance pay, a lot more than was required by my employment contract, but still only twenty-four thousand dollars after taxes.

My father's estate gave me a couple of hundred thousand in assets, some of which were not liquid. What, as an example, could I do with a couple of oil leases in Colorado County, Texas?

Thomas Peter was essentially self-employed. At the time, his take-home pay about covered the mortgage, various insurances, and child care. Although he always said that business was "fine," I had a queasy feeling about it.

For his first two years in business with Jim Edmondson, his cash flow, hence our income, had yo-yoed unpredictably. As long as I was employed, we could manage the house and three children in a private school. Without my salary, however, I predicted that we would shortly be in deep *kim chi*.

I had to get a job. In September of 1983 Thomas Peter, in an endearing gesture, had bought me a personal computer in anticipation of my leaving PW. As an entrepreneur himself, he was an enthusiastic advocate of my starting a business.

I was more than a little nervous at the prospect of our both being self-employed, so I thought I would also look for a full-time job. I cranked up

165

my PC, prepared several résumés in different formats, and set up a system to respond to recruiters and classified ads.

Getting a job was easier said than done, however. I was a pariah in the Big Eight. When I was told about the original hold decision, Thomas Peter or I had checked around with the Owner and others at Touche.

Everyone we talked to had positive personal opinions but left us with the impression that the partnership as a whole would probably balk at the prospect of hiring or admitting someone who had sued the brotherhood. On the assumption that the others of the Big Eight, where I knew no one, were unlikely to hold different views, I chose not to pursue them.

Marty Danziger was personally distressed at the fact that I had filed the lawsuit. "You'll never win, kiddo," he said. (Marty was one of few people who could get away with calling me kiddo.) Then he proceeded to introduce me to anyone he knew who might be looking to hire a former Big Eight consultant.

Marty had long since left the United Mine Workers' Health and Retirement Funds. After stints as the head of the New Jersey Gaming Commission and the Immigration and Naturalization Service, he had joined a law firm and opened an office in Washington. He had an immigration practice. His contacts were a little far afield and nothing developed in the job search, but his support and the fact that he tried cheered me.

He offered me the use of his administrative staff and surplus office space downtown. I accepted his offer and rented office space from him for the better part of a year.

I talked with a couple of executive recruiters and search firms but always got stuck on the question about what I wanted to do. The problem was that I wanted to do Big Eight consulting. I submitted paperwork anyway but nothing came of it. I had similar results when I responded to ads in the *Wall Street Journal* and the local papers.

Thomas Peter's enthusiasm, Marty's support, and my lack of success with recruiters and classified ads led me inexorably on the path toward starting my own business. I took my skills and what I knew about State's operations and scheduled meetings with everyone I had worked with, beginning with Howard Renman.

Howard was the contracting officer's technical representative for the FMS contract. In his spare time, he was trying to write a request for proposals to get a contractor to design, construct, and install FNPay, a worldwide payroll system for State's foreign national staff overseas. He was so busy with FMS that the RFP was just not getting written. He and I had discussed the problem before I left PW. I had more spare time than he did, so I began helping him with the drafting, even before I left the firm. When I became unemployed, I increased my level of effort.

Howard suggested that I identify other people at State who had small projects that I could do. As long as the problems were small enough to keep State's cost under the purchase order threshold of ten thousand dollars, there was no requirement for competition. Furthermore, purchase orders could be processed in a short period of time. That promised to help my cash flow.

Although Howard had the job of drafting the RFP for FNPay, Toni Gibbons was responsible for getting the project done. She, however, went into the hospital to have a hysterectomy shortly after I left PW. No one expected her back at work for quite a while, possibly months.

When she first entered the hospital I was in a foul mood, preoccupied with my career problems. I thought it inappropriate to expose Toni, in her hospital bed, to my personal turmoil, so I initially sent flowers. A day or two later, when I was cheerful enough not to be a burden, I called to schedule a visit. She had checked out of the hospital.

To everyone's surprise, Toni was back at work in a couple of weeks. When she returned she had to contend with the backlog that had accumulated in her Office of Financial Operations and with the FNPay procurement. She was designated contracting officer's technical representative on the project. Howard turned the current version of the request for proposals over to Toni and commented positively on my contribution.

At Howard's suggestion, I met with Toni in her office in Rosslyn. We discussed how I might help her get the RFP finished and accelerate the procurement process so that State could get a contractor started on the job. I was hired to finish writing the technical part of the RFP, fast, and to prepare a work schedule. My objectives related to the schedule were to give bidders the minimum time required by procurement rules and guidelines and to schedule the work that had to be done by Toni and her staff in the shortest possible period of time. She wanted to get the job done without delay.

Beginning in the late spring, I spent about half my time in 1984 working for Toni. Although she delegated the day-to-day supervision of my work to a member of her staff, she told me to check back with her if I had any problems. The delegate and I met with Toni weekly to report progress officially, but Toni and I resolved issues informally, typically over lunch.

If I had something that I needed to discuss with her immediately but was unable to get on her frequently full calendar, then I would catch her in the ladies room making tea, which she did at precisely the same hour every morning. Alternatively, I would check with her secretary to determine which government shuttle buses Toni planned to take to and from meetings downtown at the main State Department building. Then I would get on the bus with her for a five-minute meeting. That was usually all the time it took to get her decision on something.

It seemed to me that all of State was trying to help out. Hal Niebel, who had asked the Question at the original oral presentations to State, became the first in a long series of clients at the department. In addition to drafting the RFP for FNPay for Toni, I started a project for one of Toni's operations managers who needed help systematizing various accounting functions. Bob Lamb, who by then was the assistant secretary for administration, hired me to do a planning project.

I never did a project for Howard, but he introduced me outside of State. In early 1984, the Railroad Retirement Board (RRB) in Chicago was managing a procurement process similar to that used by State for the FMS. The contracting officer's technical representative from the RRB conferred with Howard and asked his advice and counsel from the point of view of one who was a few years ahead of the RRB in the process.

When the RRB people were in Washington, Howard brought us all together to discuss different bidding and costing tactics that vendors used and how the tactics might adversely affect the future of the RRB's system or its cost.

Apparently the RRB found what I had to say intriguing. I was hired under a purchase order for less than ten thousand dollars to help with the procurement process, initially by doing an analysis of the costs proposed by the bidders on the RRB's request for proposals. Price Waterhouse was one of the bidders.

At the request of the RRB, I flew to Chicago to present the numbers and help at cost negotiations if the bids changed. When the local PW consulting partner found out I was involved, I had the impression that he screamed conflict of interest with the intensity of a stuck pig. The RRB was concerned that PW might protest an award to another bidder if I was involved in the process so I was asked to withdraw. I seethed with anger and cringed with embarrassment on the flight home.

I learned later that Price Waterhouse lost.

Hopkins v. Price Waterhouse

To be a good attorney requires mastery over a huge body of rules governing the timetables by which legal events are managed. Blowing a single date can be case ending. In my situation, time was running out in the District of Columbia.

If I failed to file suit in the D.C. Superior Court by March 24, the anniversary date of the allegedly discriminatory decision, then I would be precluded by D.C. law from doing so at a later date. There was no immediate need to file suit in the federal courts. The right to sue there could be exercised any time in the six-month period ending in October 1984.

"We'll file two lawsuits—one now and one later," Doug told me in February 1984. We could file in the D.C. court, alleging violation of the D.C. Human Rights Act, immediately. Later, depending on the outcome of *Hishon v. King and Spalding,* we might be able to file a second suit in the district court, alleging violation of Title VII. If and when we filed in district court, we could hold the D.C. court case in abeyance waiting for the outcome of the district court case.

Under D.C. law, I could request a trial by jury. A jury trial in the D.C. court had a certain amount of appeal. In David versus Goliath situations, David might have a slight advantage. Furthermore, there was no jurisdictional question about the D.C. Human Rights Act.

The D.C. court, however, was clogged up with criminal cases and the priority-setting criteria gave precedence to those cases over civil cases. Doug warned me that when we went into the D.C. court, we would probably have lots of schedule delays. The case could drag on for a long time. On March 21, 1984, Doug filed the first lawsuit in the D.C. court.

Although I knew the lawsuit would be filed, I was unaware of the exact provisions or the date on which it would be filed. Consequently, I was quite taken aback when I ran into one of my clients at State who greeted me with "Howdy. How's the $6-million-woman this morning?" When I asked what on earth he meant, I was referred to a *Washington Times* article that stated I had filed a $6.25-million lawsuit against PW.

I called Doug to ask where the number came from. "The reporter just added up the damages specified in each count of the lawsuit," he explained. "The total he got was $6.25 million. Don't hold your breath waiting for the check." We waited, as nothing happened for a couple of months.

When Doug called on May 22, 1984, he seemed pleased. The Supreme Court had ruled for the first time that decisions concerning advancement to partnership are governed by Title VII, 42 U.S.C. and 2000e, and must therefore be made without regard to race, sex, religion, or national origin.

The decision in *Hishon v. King and Spalding* meant that Title VII applied to my case. I could file suit in district court without worrying about legal squabbles over jurisdiction. The federal court schedules were subject to more rigorous controls than those of the D.C. court, so there was a chance that my case would be less drawn out in the district court. Furthermore, a win in the district court virtually guaranteed a win in the D.C. court, while a loss in district court did not preclude continuing the D.C. case.

I had read an occasional newspaper article about *Hishon v. King and Spalding*. She had always been referred to as the "Atlanta lawyer"; King and Spalding as the "Atlanta law firm." It did not take a rocket scientist to dial information in Atlanta and find her phone number.

After a few referrals from polite people at former phone numbers, I found myself listening to an exuberant voice with a dramatic southern accent. I offered my congratulations and told her that I was next in the legal line behind her. I thanked her for her efforts on my behalf—after all, had she not started her legal battle in 1978, I might have had to fight it. Betsy, as she prefers to be called, laughed. We said our good-byes. She went on to negotiations with the Atlanta law firm. The Hishon matter was settled out of court—her discrimination case was never tried.

By the summer of 1984, Eileen Stein had tired of the practice of law. Doug called to say that he was breaking up his old office and joining another firm. He gave me a new phone number and address. One of the attorneys at the new firm, Jim Heller, would help us out when we went to trial, Doug reported matter-of-factly. I could meet him the next time we got together.

For the latter part of the summer the office move diverted Doug's attention from the second lawsuit. There was, however, little urgency to file. Many of the courts close down in August when most government people abandon the city and its heat. Any action taken in the summer was likely to be put off until fall anyway.

The second lawsuit did, however, have to be filed by the end of September or the right to sue would lapse. Doug dusted off the interrogatories and the request for production of documents that we used in the administrative proceedings with the EEOC. He polished them up to make them appropriate for a federal case. They were filed with the complaint he wrote.

In the complaint Doug made three accusations: discrimination, retaliation and harassment, and subjecting me to constructive discharge. The accusation of discrimination was based on nothing more than the fact that the reasons I had been given for being held were nonsensical by comparison to my business accomplishments.

At the time the complaint was filed, the only information we had was from copies of my performance appraisals. There were no particularly sexist comments in evidence about me or anyone else. The accusation of retaliation and harassment was based largely on the review process to which my work was subjected and on the Railroad Retirement Board incident. The accusation that I was subjected to constructive discharge, as I understood it at the time, was tantamount to an accusation that I was fired, or at least helped out the door.

A complaint under Title VII must specify how the complainer, referred to as the plaintiff, wants the situation remedied. In my complaint, Doug asked that PW make me a partner retroactive to July 1, 1983, compensate me for lost compensation, and pay my attorneys' fees and court costs. He also asked that PW be enjoined from discriminating or retaliating in the future.

This second lawsuit is what really started my legal battles. The related complaint was filed on September 28, 1984. It was signed by James A. Heller. The court's docketing system entitled the case *Hopkins v. Price Waterhouse* and numbered it 84-3040. I never saw the federal lawsuit or the accompanying papers. I was out of the country.

Nepal

My neighbor David Hopper had been appalled when I was held in the spring of 1983. When I left Price Waterhouse in February 1984, he wanted to help out. More than that, however, he made it clear that he viewed me not as a reject from the Big Eight but as a valuable, underused resource. That made me feel good. Within days of my departure from PW, he put me in contact with his staff in the regional vice presidency of the World Bank that served south Asia. It took until September 1984 for a business opportunity to develop.

The World Bank project sent me to Nepal on a mission. The mission leader was another consultant, a Bengali named A. Muhith. Like many people from the Indian subcontinent, he had an unspellable, unpronounceable, hence unused, first name. He was called, quite properly, Mr. Muhith or simply Muhith.

Muhith had been the minister of planning and finance in the government of Bangladesh. His part of the mission was to determine the organizational infrastructure and placement of a planning ministry in the government of His Majesty, the King of Nepal. My part was to figure out what kind of technology and people, in what amounts and numbers, were required to support the needs of the ministry.

The two of us were formally briefed on what we were to do by a number of David's staff at the bank. In addition, each of us was individually and informally briefed by David. David counseled me not to eat or drink anything unless Muhith approved and to follow his lead on matters social or cultural. He told me to take a pocket knife in the likely event that I might have to peel something. Although I did not know it at the time, Muhith later told me that his objective, as set by David, was to keep me from going into culture shock.

As near as I could tell, most of my shots were up to date, thanks to the State Department and my trip to Nigeria. The bank provided me with the inevitable malaria tablets and a set of tickets on British Airways.

In spite of arriving at Dulles the prescribed number of hours in advance, I was bumped. Twenty-four hours later, I successfully boarded a flight. After another thirty or so hours and a midnight stop in the ninety-five-degree heat of the middle eastern desert at Dubai, I found myself in Delhi.

In a sea of largely Eastern humanity, I joined the search for luggage in and around the great piles of boxes and baskets and crates and sacks and suitcases. The hot air circulated less than freely in the huge, noisy open area where the baggage had been dumped. The only traveling bag that Thomas Peter and I owned was nowhere to be found. I left for Kathmandu without it.

The Himalayas, snow tops of the world, stabbed at the sky through the rainy season's thick clouds that extended to the horizon in all directions. The jagged, snow-covered tops looked like miniature mountains plopped in a fluffy cotton plain.

The Royal Nepal airliner dropped rapidly to land on the grassy runway, which had been cleared of cattle for our arrival. I waited until the luggage was unloaded but my bag never arrived at the shack that served as the terminal of Kathmandu International Airport. The wind that blew through my hair on the cab ride into town was noticeably cooler and dryer in spite of the impending rain.

"Did you have your encephalitis shots?" asked Grant Slade, the resident representative of the World Bank, after we introduced ourselves and exchanged pleasantries. When I responded negatively, he followed up with, "I cabled Washington and told them you were going into the Terai and needed the shots."

Christ, you need shots for encephalitis—my children had had every vaccination known to be required in the United States and I had never even heard of one for encephalitis. I knew the infection was deadly, but

I never met anyone who knew anyone who had had it. Lyme's disease was more common.

"Can I take them now?" I asked. The encephalitis shot program was a multishot, multiweek program that had to be completed well in advance of entering an infected area. I would have to live with the risk when I got to the Terai, the tropical region of Nepal.

I was tired. I had been awake since I left Washington. My bag was not at the hotel. I had to buy a change of clothes and Nordstrom's was not an option.

Among the seven to eight hundred thousand people who inhabited Kathmandu, there were few Westerners and only a minuscule number of those were women. It was evident from a scan of the crowded streets that the average height and weight of the population was about a foot shorter and many pounds lighter than mine.

A survey of every shop in the vicinity of the hotel produced only one outfit that vaguely approximated my size. The purple, pink, and green, vertically striped, Indian cotton shirt and pants combination looked funny with my Rockports and white socks.

The foot apparel was all the more noticeable because the pants only extended to mid calf. I looked better in the white levis and cotton shirt I had worn on the plane, but they had to be laundered, if not disinfected, before I could wear them again.

Without comment, Muhith and the representatives of the ministries of His Majesty's government graciously accepted my peculiar attire when we conducted our interviews. I was professionally uncomfortable dressed up like an Indian tourist or a trekker from the States, but those were my only choices during the first week of my work.

I was uncomfortable at the ritual that preceded each interview. After introductions, Muhith and I were always offered coffee. Muhith, for whatever reasons, always accepted. I too accepted, following his social lead. When coffee was served I again followed Muhith's lead and drank, with relish, the foul-tasting, tepid Nescafé.

What initially made me uncomfortable was the fact that Muhith had given strict orders that I not drink water unless I was certain it had been boiled and filtered. What later made me uncomfortable was the prospect of having to use a bathroom. Kathmandu has no sewage system. Once out of the major hotels, the streets or building grounds usually serve as substitutes.

On the one occasion that I asked to use a bathroom, a boy had to be dispatched to determine if the head of the ministry's facility was available for my use. What I found when I used it was comparable only to the crudest of facilities available on the left bank of Paris. My health never suffered from drinking the coffee, but I quickly learned to manage my intake.

Muhith and I ate every meal together. What I ate I selected from his list of acceptable items. He was most tolerant in his dealings with me— never told me what to do, never treated me condescendingly. When I tripped over some cultural difference he patiently explained.

One morning at breakfast, he was far less cheerful than usual, and he seemed exhausted. I asked what the problem was. "A mosquito kept me awake all night," he said. I had been exposed to a lot of mosquitoes, individually and in large groups, but rarely had a single mosquito kept me awake for long and certainly not all night. To me a mosquito was something one swatted or ignored.

In his country, Muhith explained, the incidence of mortality from the many diseases carried by mosquitoes was more than measurable, it was significant. He had more fearful respect for the insects than I did, enough in fact, to keep him awake as long as one buzzed around, or worse, silently disappeared.

I got over the discomfort associated with not having the proper clothes. Frankly I looked equally peculiar in the navy blue business suit I wore toward the end of the first week of interviews when my bag finally arrived. I was relieved, however, that I would have more clothes when Muhith and I hit the road to interview people at some of the development projects funded by the World Bank and other donors and international organizations.

Thomas Peter had talked about joining me in Nepal before I left the States. I had tried to reach him several times since my arrival, but time zone differences and international communications problems made it impossible. By the weekend, I was concerned because I was unable to confirm his plans and I expected to be out of town the next week.

Grant suggested a tour of the two cities that comprise what most people call Kathmandu. He also recommended a tour of the ancient city of Bhaktapur where there were many ongoing restoration projects.

He offered to provide a car and the services of Bakta, a driver who worked for the bank. He explained that renting a car and touring around was not much of an option. In Nepal, when a Westerner rents a car, the rent-a-car company provides a driver and generally prohibits the Westerner from driving. Most Westerners are unaccustomed to the "normal" road conditions.

Bakta was a charming man and a wonderful guide. He was also an accomplished negotiator, as I discovered in the markets of Kathmandu. Negotiation is counter-culture to me.

I am always at risk of making capricious purchasing decisions because I never negotiate. Consequently, my negotiation skills are virtually nonexistent. I do not know how to negotiate. Unlike the United States, there are many countries where everything is negotiable. Nepal is one of them.

Bakta negotiated for me when I purchased two Nepali rugs. They are worth little, less than four hundred dollars in total. Without his help, however, I would have gladly paid twice that. I bought a lovely, soft goat-hair shawl, called a pashmina, for Mom.

For each of the children I bought a Nepalese mask, colorfully painted papier-mâché renditions of the gods Hanuman (the monkey), Ganesh (the elephant), and Kali (vengeance). Although the starting price was only $10.00 per mask, by the time Bakta finished, each cost $4.50. I felt a little guilty, but Bakta was terribly proud of himself.

After my tours with Bakta, I wrote Thomas Peter a letter.

Just a note from the subcontinent as they refer to this part of the world. I miss you a whole lot. When you think about it, there really is not a great deal to do with your leisure time. It has poured rain daily. Yesterday I took the car and driver and went to Bhaktapur. I learned how rice was grown, how brick are made, how pottery is made. I had many temples, vintage 1200-1700, explained to me: Buddhist and Hindu; Nepalese architecture and Indian.

Many of the old temples have weathered better than buildings built more recently. It seems the brick were treated with mustard oil in the old (ancient) days. Now the oil is too expensive and is used mostly for cooking. As a result, the buildings deteriorate rapidly.

There are many projects, German, Chinese, Japanese, going on to restore buildings, build roads, implement transportation systems. But there is so much to be done. Everything is falling down and is incredibly dirty. The average life expectancy is now 47. In 1953 it was 26. Looking at things now, I wonder what it was like in 1953.

Tomorrow I leave for the "country." I've been told not to worry: if I get stuck I can fly back. I don't know quite what that means but there are tales of landslides and impassible roads. I will be back on Friday, Sept 14.

If you come, don't stop in Delhi—just keep going. Kathmandu is better than Delhi. The hotel is very nice. There are plenty of things to do by day and you can rent a car w/ driver for 20$/day.

I love you and miss you. I look forward to coming home. I am, however, having a wonderful time.

Bakta picked Muhith and me up in the four-wheel-drive Toyota early the next morning. Our destination that day was the village of Gorkha, he told us, in the hill country. He told us how far it was and how long it would take. My bad arithmetic concluded we would average fifteen kilometers, a little under ten miles, per hour. I prepared myself for a rough ride.

In the middle of a village consisting of a few shacks, Bakta pulled off the road and parked the car. The first project site that we were to visit was a biological gas project sponsored by the Asian Development Bank. Project funding helped a group of farmers build a facility to collect and process cattle dung to produce methane, which could in turn be used for cooking fuel. Muhith explained the process in considerable detail as we turned away from the road and headed down a trail into the scrubby forest.

"Have you ever seen a suspension bridge?" asked Muhith casually. "You mean like the Golden Gate?" I replied to what seemed to me to be a strange question.

As we abruptly left the forest behind, I saw before me a bridge of hand-finished wooden planks, swinging from cables, supported by steel beams. "Not exactly," said Muhith.

I could only see his back as he plodded in front of me toward the bridge, but he must have had an incredible smirk of amusement on his face. Tentatively, I followed Bakta and Muhith as they stepped from plank to plank, hanging on to the vertical cables to keep their balance as the bridge bounced up and down with every step and swayed from side to side under the influence of a light wind.

An inadvertent glance downward exposed a gorge several hundred feet deep. I fought panic by focusing on the pylons to which the cables were fastened on the other side.

As we walked back into the woods, Muhith told me that the various donor organizations had funded hundreds of projects to build bridges like that one all over Nepal. Preoccupied with concerns over whether I would have the courage to go back over the bridge on our return, I failed to hear a lot of the details.

After a short, but calming, walk we arrived at a neat little cinder block building that housed the offices of the Asian Development Bank people who monitored several projects in the area, including the one we were visiting. As the charming, clearly committed bank staff, Muhith, and I sipped hot tea and ate bananas right off a neighboring tree, I thought about the arrogant bankers with whom I had dealt back in Washington. The wonderful bananas were only about six inches long and tasted nothing like any banana I have ever eaten in the States.

After seeing the project, I managed to get back over the bridge. I never looked down.

We stopped for lunch somewhere. Flies swarmed under the thatched roof supported by six or eight timbers. The day's special was a thick, dark, bubbling mass cooking over a wood fire in a big black pot, reminiscent of Macbeth. Whatever it was smelled wonderful.

Muhith recommended the hard-boiled eggs and bananas, both of which were unopened.

We drove on. A flat tire stopped us. Bakta changed it—he declined our offer of assistance. We stood by the side of the road and chatted about the parasites that grew in the dirt and transmitted disease to a largely barefooted population.

The hill country around Gorkha must have been so named because the terrain is smooth, not jagged. The hills were certainly high enough and steep enough to qualify as mountains anywhere in the United States or Canada. Rocks speckled through the huge grassy mounds made green by the monsoon. We arrived late in the afternoon as the sun broke through the ever-present clouds just long enough for us to watch the green hills turn black.

At dinner, I thought about my hair dryer. How stupid I had been. Where on earth did I think I would plug it in? The homemade tapers that flickered and sputtered shed little light on the tables on the screened-in porch where we ate. They were the only source of light. We ate chicken and rice, I with beer, Muhith with Lemu. There were no other choices.

The innkeeper, carrying a candle in each hand, and Muhith preceded me through the inky blackness up the narrow stairs to my room. As the innkeeper stood aside, Muhith entered the room, raised his light above his head, and rotated in a full circle to look around.

"Please close the windows," he said to the innkeeper who responded by doing what he was asked. Muhith handed me his burning candle and an unlit spare. His parting words to me were, "You will be fine. I'll see you in the morning."

I put my bag on the bed, a ticking-covered mattress, no sheets. In the dim light I could barely see the door to the bathroom, but the stench was overwhelming. I closed the door.

I brushed my teeth without benefit of water and swallowed the toothpaste. I covered the mattress with towels from my bag, made myself as small as I could, and settled into the middle of the bed. Scared of the imaginary creatures that might come out of the dark to assault me, I read by the light of the taper until I fell into an exhausted sleep.

I woke early. Psychologically holding my nose, I managed to use the bathroom and wash my hair with water from the spigot that protruded from the gray, unpainted wall.

"Mr. Muhith, why did you ask the innkeeper to close the windows?" I asked when he joined me for a breakfast of hard-cooked eggs and boiling hot tea. His response indicated that he considered the screens to be inadequate protection from mosquitoes.

We finished eating as he explained that the village of Gorkha was the origin of some of the most fearless soldiers ever to serve in the armies of the British empire. Historically, the Gurkhas, as they were known, had given everyone who ever tried to invade Nepal a very bad time. During World War II, they served with distinction in the British army. Even today, they were prized as soldiers all over Asia.

Muhith and I were scheduled to interview development project managers in the Gorkha area that day. The first such manager was responsible for a series of projects related to the renovation and restoration of the Gorkha durbar. The durbar, a meeting place and the location of a temple where one of the ancestors of the current king was born, was located a couple of thousand meters almost straight up one of the "hills."

The project manager was in charge of a combination erosion control–trail improvement effort by means of which the gullies created partly by natural erosion and partly by foot traffic were paved with stones from the river bed in the valley below Gorkha. The resulting paved trail reduced the natural erosion and made it easier to get around on foot. Muhith mischievously pleaded ill health, leaving me to accompany the project manager on the hike to the top of the mountain and the temple.

The project manager had earned a master's degree at a university in Tennessee. Like many of his countrymen who were educated in the West, he returned to his country to try to help.

As we trudged up the stone staircase, he gave me a lecture, worthy of an entomologist, on the insects we encountered along the way. Only a few of them, I noted, were poisonous enough to require immediate hospitalization. Needless to say, I stayed in the middle of the trail and kept a sharp eye out for anything that appeared harmful.

By the time we got to the entrance to the durbar, an hour later, I was perspiring heavily even though it had been chilly, approaching cold, when we started. There was a sign on the entrance gate stating that Westerners were prohibited from entering the temple without the consent of His Majesty's government.

We passed through the gate into a courtyard that surrounded an ancient Nepalese temple. Pigeons all but covered the roof. A ring of pigeon guano several inches deep extended from the temple walls to the drip line of the eaves.

I should have been honored when the project manager told me that I could enter the temple. I was less than thrilled, however, at the prospect of removing my shoes and walking through the pigeon droppings to enter. To refuse to enter or to enter wearing shoes would have been an unforgivable breach of etiquette.

I removed my shoes, but not my socks, and stooped to enter the temple behind my Nepalese guide. It was cool, damp, dark, and reminded me of a stable with a very low ceiling and a dirt floor. It was the temple of a very down-to-earth God, not an exalted one distant from man. When we left the temple, I put my socks in the pockets of my lightweight, Eddie Bauer down vest, brushed off the soles of my feet, and put my shoes on.

Bakta drove us onward, into the Terai, after Muhith and I finished our other interviews in Gorkha. Our destination for the night was the guest house of one of the provincial leaders. The cinder block facility had electricity and odorless bathrooms. Chameleons clambered up the interior walls much like they did on the exterior walls at my parents' place in Florida.

A representative of our unseen host went to find a chicken for dinner. I showered, dried my hair, and joined Muhith for a cold beer in the lounge. He drank Lemu.

"The mosquito netting is very good. Be sure to use it," he said as we rehashed the day's events over drinks. I had been so preoccupied with taking a shower that I had failed to notice any mosquito netting.

"Mosquito netting is not exactly part of my culture, Mr. Muhith. Would you mind showing me what to do with it?" I asked. With that we walked down the hall to my room, where Muhith identified the protective screen rolled up and tied to the frame over my bed.

Following his instructions, I got onto the bed, untied the mosquito netting, and let it drop down like a tent around me. "Tuck it under the mattress when you get into bed," he said "it will also keep the snakes out." "Great!" I replied with a cheerful smile.

The chicken, which arrived live, was served with rice about an hour later. As a consequence of hiking around for most of the morning and feasting on another lunch of bananas, boiled eggs, and beer, I was starved. I slept better than I had the night before.

The next day we looked at a chicken farming project and a Brahma bull ranch. I walked the ditches, surveyed the control systems, and listened to lectures on how the pumps worked at several irrigation projects. As we traveled to each new project site, we moved north and west, eventually leaving the Terai and heading into the mountains that surrounded our destination for the day—Pokhara.

Although it is a small town, less than sixty thousand souls, Pokhara is the second-largest city in Nepal. It is spread out in a pocket surrounded by the Annapurna range of the Himalayas. Annapurna is a Hindi word meaning "provider of food to the world."

In the dry season you can see Mt. Annapurna, the jewel of the range, rising 26,500 feet to meet the sky. Annapurna is a mile higher than anything in North America and half a mile lower than Mt. Everest. I was hoping for a glimpse of any one of the Himalayas before I left Nepal. After almost two weeks in the country, I had only seen the bases of the mountains; the peaks were always covered by the clouds that dumped monsoonal rains much of the time.

Muhith and I stayed in a pleasant hotel just outside of town. Unlike the inn in Gorkha, it was recognizable as a hotel—it had conventional bathrooms, electricity, even air conditioning, and a restaurant. We stayed two nights.

By setting my alarm clock and getting up at 5:30 one morning, I managed to see Annapurna for about fifteen minutes before she disappeared back into her cloud cover. That was the only view I ever had of a Himalaya.

Muhith and I visited hydroelectric power project managers in and around town. We listened as design blueprints were explained to us. Project managers told us of the difficulty and expense associated with getting supplies and materials, especially cement, to the construction sites.

I learned about portable bridges that were trucked in, frequently from India, to span chasms in the roads created by walls of water that not infrequently descended down the gullies from the mountains. They told us of the problems they had getting labor and meeting payroll daily, in cash. I clambered over a couple of small dams and looked unknowingly at turbines.

On Friday, Bakta drove through pouring rain back toward Kathmandu. His limited choice of roads was governed more by the probability of washouts than by map. As Muhith and I walked in the rain behind the car, he traversed a couple of washouts with inches to spare between him and destiny. Larger vehicles had to turn around and go back until repairs were made. Still larger vehicles, unable to turn around, backed out or remained stuck.

We briefly drove the India Road, so named because it went into India, on our way to the last project, a cement factory in an industrial area outside of Kathmandu. Muhith provided a running monologue on the transportation infrastructure of the country.

The entire nation, a little larger than the state of North Carolina, had about fifteen thousand kilometers of roads, very few paved. During the rainy season, the roads between western and eastern Nepal regularly washed out, leaving opposite sides of the country accessible only by helicopter.

The China Road, which was originally built as the link between Nepal and Tibet, was missing three or four kilometers up north of Kathmandu. These vanished in a bad rain a couple of years back. Replacing them was a fantastically expensive, long-term proposition.

The sun broke through briefly as we arrived at the cement factory. It was a nearly new, modern facility that had been built as part of an overall development plan to help Nepal manufacture some of the materials it needed to build its own infrastructure. Manufacturing much-needed cement in the country created jobs and spared the government from the foreign exchange problems associated with importing it.

I was having trouble paying attention toward the end of the day. Although it had been an exhilarating trip, I looked forward to getting back to the hotel and finding out what Thomas Peter was doing.

"Mr. Muhith, what does one wear to dinner if one is being picked up by an elephant?" I asked over the phone.

On our return to Kathmandu, we were invited to dinner by Mr. Rimal, one of the people who worked for His Majesty's government. He instructed us to ask Bakta to drive us to the end of some road where we would be picked up and taken to the restaurant. Apparently the last leg of the journey was over a road accessible only by elephant.

Muhith informed me that jeans were quite appropriate under the circumstances. I was looking forward to dinner, if only for the ride. Unfortunately, even the elephant was rained out so we had to settle for dinner in town. I have never ridden an elephant.

We ate in a very nice restaurant where we ran into a World Bank employee, an Ethiopian, who was in the country on a different mission. After dinner Mr. Rimal, the Ethiopian, Muhith, and I were drinking coffee and considering leaving when we were boisterously greeted by the husband of the woman who owned and ran the restaurant.

Apparently he and Mr. Rimal were acquaintances. He had been to a reception at the Korean embassy and, judging by the way he swayed back and forth as he towered over the end of our table, he was more than a little tipsy.

He ordered a complimentary round of drinks for the four of us. In a polite interchange, he introduced himself and discovered that the Ethiopian and I were based in Washington. He seemed uninterested in Muhith's origin.

With no conversational transition, I suddenly found myself the focus of a heated monologue on the war in Viet Nam. Politics was never one of my prominent interests. I could go for months without discussing politics. I did not subscribe to a newspaper and rarely had time to read one. Needless to say I was startled at being accused of being a monger of the war in Viet Nam.

A waiter arrived with four shot glasses and a white plastic bottle about the size and shape of a container of transmission fluid. In spite of the dignified protestations of Muhith and the Ethiopian, who was a teetotaler, the waiter filled four shot glasses and placed them appropriately on the table. The clear liquid was tasty—strong, but quite tasty. I drank mine and switched glasses with the embarrassed Ethiopian. He smiled gratefully.

As I mentally tried to work my way out of the political box into which I had been cast by our Nepali host, he turned to the Ethiopian to vent his spleen—this time on race relations. The mild-mannered, soft-spoken, gentle Ethiopian was speechless in the face of a verbal assault that lambasted him for being a timid black token in a racist society.

As Mr. Rimal stammered in embarrassment, I rose aggressively to our defense and told the Nepali that not all Americans thought or acted alike, let alone thought or acted according to his peculiar views. Furthermore, the Ethiopian was not an American and had no responsibility or part in race relations in the States.

The Nepali settled down as he sat down at the head of the table. He ordered another round of transmission fluid. This time he was persuaded by Muhith's simple statement that alcohol was not his culture. He waved off the waiter who had reached Muhith's elbow. The Ethiopian sat silently, and Mr. Rimal and I continued drinking from the three never-empty shot glasses that remained on the table.

Years later, my children took me to see *Raiders of the Lost Ark* at least half a dozen times. Each time I watched Karen Allen in the bar scene, I was happily reminded of the remarkable evening I spent in the restaurant with the Nepali, the Ethiopian, Mr. Rimal, and Muhith.

Somehow, Thomas Peter managed to get through to me two days before I was to leave to return to the States. Whatever else he had to say was subconsciously set aside by the news that Sandy Kinsey was in the hospital in Paris.

He had few facts. All he knew was what Karen Nold had reported when she called. The baby shower that she and Judy Reach and I were planning for early November was off. There had been some problem that resulted in the baby being born unexpectedly, and very early.

The baby was also in the hospital—prognosis unknown. I told him I would try to get to Paris and suggested that, if appropriate, he might join me there since he had not been able to make it to Nepal.

Muhith and I met with Grant Slade to review the work of the last three weeks. Grant noted that Muhith and I had done all of the fieldwork in eastern Nepal, largely because washouts had prevented us from going into the western part. The dry season was approaching, however, and it seemed likely that we could get in and out of western Nepal uneventfully.

He asked if we wanted to do more fieldwork out west. "I'll make arrangements for a helicopter to get you out, if you get stuck," he offered. Although the prospect of a helicopter ride in the Himalayas was somewhat appealing, I was relieved when further discussion revealed no reason for additional fieldwork.

I asked Grant if he would send a cable, which he did: Madame Mornand. I am at your mercy. I will arrive Paris from Nepal day after tomorrow. I hope you can accommodate me. Ann Hopkins.

Muhith and I were going home. Late in the afternoon, he accompanied me to the airline office where I changed my tickets. That night we had a pleasant dinner together at the hotel. I ordered without need of his counsel.

I bought a Coke and what was advertised as an apple to stave off hunger during the long layover in Delhi. I peeled the apple with my pocket knife. As I crunched on what tasted remarkably like a pear, I struck up a conversation with some Peace Corps kids seated nearby. They were returning to the United States after a two-year tour in Nepal, where they had worked on small farm projects cultivating fruit trees. We swapped stories.

I was amused at their description of how they had remained relatively healthy. Initially, they had asked that their water be boiled and filtered. When their Nepalese hosts asked why, the volunteers explained that it was for health reasons, reasons that the hosts were unable to understand. They were, after all, healthy and they drank their water unboiled.

When the volunteers learned to answer "why" questions with "because it is my culture," debate stopped. Cultural differences are accepted and respected when reason fails, something that I had learned subconsciously but that only crystallized when the kids stated it so clearly.

Brigette and Jean Charles Mornand were expecting me. She greeted me with wild enthusiasm, and he came briefly out of the office to smile affectionately when I dragged into the lobby of the Gavarni after the twenty-hour trip from Delhi. I must have looked like a bag lady, with Thomas Peter's bag, a colorful Nepalese cloth bag containing the carefully wrapped masks, and two Nepalese rugs rolled into big tubes and tied with jute trailing behind me.

"But of course," I could stay at the hotel, Brigette said. I had the impression that she had lost someone else's reservation to make room for me.

She explained that everything was okay. Sandy and her mother, who had arrived shortly after the baby was born, were at the hospital visiting the baby. Brigette was thrilled that she was godmother to Sandy's son and that the boy was named after her own son, Christopher. In spite of her inclination to chat, she had my bags taken to the room and shooed me off for a welcome shower and an even more welcome nap.

I called home to be greeted with the happy news that Thomas Peter was coming to Paris. I tried talking to each of the children with the usual result. The conversation with Tela, who was eight, always began, "When are you coming home?" and ended with "I love you." In between there was silence unless I asked a question, in which case I got a yes or no response. The boys, at six and five, were even less communicative. The telephone is a dreadful means of communicating with children— they have to be touched and felt and looked at to make meaningful contact.

When I awoke, got my act together, and wandered down to the lobby, Brigette informed me that Sandy was back at the hospital visiting Christopher. I instantly recognized Betty Sprague, Sandy's mother, when she walked into the lobby from the street. She had a Florida tan.

I liked her a lot. She was an attractive, lively, white-haired lady with a broad mind and a naive sense of humor. She smiled easily and had a cheerful disposition.

Over a beer in one of the neighborhood brasseries, Betty told me the story of what had happened. Sandy, who was seven months pregnant, had been staying at the Gavarni while she managed the installation of REMS at the embassy. Somehow, she caught listeriosis, a very dangerous bacterial infection usually contracted from improperly treated dairy products.

The disease was passed on to the baby in utero. Sandy went into labor. The doctors at the American Hospital made every effort to hold back the birth until the baby's listeriosis could be brought under control with antibiotics administered to Sandy.

Christopher was born by Caesarean and had taken up residence in an incubator in the intensive care unit. He was still there, and it looked like he would be there for quite a while longer.

Betty and I wandered around Passy for a while before returning to the hotel. On our return Sandy and I greeted each other like the long-separated friends that we were. Brigette and Jean Charles had gone home for the day. The three of us went to dinner.

We talked a great deal about having babies and about doctors, hospitals, and medical insurance. Sandy's medical insurance was useless in France, but PW had made arrangements for Sandy to get the money required to pay the huge medical bills through the office in Paris.

Over coffee, Betty asked me, "When were your boys circumcised?" I was less than certain. I explained that it seemed to me that one of the few points at which an obstetrician came into contact with a baby was for the circumcision shortly after birth.

"I wonder if Christopher has been circumcised?" she pondered aloud. I told her that I doubted it. When she asked why, I responded, "It is not the French culture." When Sandy later investigated, more out of curiosity than anything else, she found that Christopher was uncircumcised and likely to remain so. Circumcision was not the culture.

Thomas Peter arrived with an injured ankle. He had fallen while jogging. Brigette was amused at the naive enthusiasm with which he attacked Paris—she referred to him as my fourth child. We took bus tours, which I hated and would never have taken with anyone other than Thomas Peter. We visited the designer clothiers. He looked wonderful in the new suits he bought. I worried about the money.

I had one more stop to make before returning to Washington. Long ago I had committed to visit Mom and Gil on my way home from Nepal. They had just bought a new summer place in Vermont near my sister's place.

Thomas Peter and I flew out of Paris on the same day with different destinations, I to Boston and on to Burlington, Vermont, he to Washington. He kindly relieved me of the burden of schlepping the rugs by taking them with him.

I intentionally went to Vermont alone. I had to make peace with Mom. She had been very upset when I was held; what hurt me hurt her equally. She was horrified when I sued. Since the day I told her about the lawsuit, she had never once brought up the subject, and she stopped the conversation or left the room whenever anyone else did.

I believe she thought I was pursuing a Joan of Arc–like course of action to the same inevitable end. Her attitude left me with an uneasy feeling. I would have preferred that she support my position, but she was entitled to her different and strongly held view.

I did not know what to expect when I gave Mom the pashmina shawl.

Buying a present for her was always a problem. She had elegant taste and already owned everything she wanted. I had bought the pashmina shawl because it felt good, it was handmade in Nepal, and because it was not dyed; it was a lovely gray color that would look good on Mom.

When she wore it over her bedjacket that evening as we sat around the roaring fire, I realized it was a better gift than I had planned. In addition to its other appealing characteristics, it was warm. We had a pleasant visit and established an uneasy peace over the lawsuit.

Trial 1

GETTING READY

"We got Judge Gesell," Doug said over the phone. He seemed to think that was good. By Doug's description the man was brilliant and thoughtful, loved the law, and managed his calendar.

I assumed that all judges were brilliant, thoughtful, and loved the law, so I asked what managing the calendar meant. In response to my question I was told that Judge Gesell brooked no nonsense from attorneys.

Evasiveness or delaying tactics would not be tolerated. After considering the wishes of the attorneys, the judge would set a schedule agreeable to all, and then everyone would stick to it. There would be no delays in his court. That sounded good to me.

On the day before Halloween 1984, Judge Gesell scheduled the trial for the week beginning March 25, 1985. He specified that discovery had to be finished in late February and that paperwork to support the trial had to be submitted at a pretrial conference the first week in March. When Doug called to keep me posted, I noted the dates on my calendar and went on about my business.

In November, I had the impression that Doug and the Gibson, Dunn, and Crutcher lawyers (known as GD) who represented PW were doing a legal dance. In the interrogatory and document production phases of discovery, Doug had asked for a lot of normally private or confidential data. His requests included compensation data for certain partners, data that might be needed to determine lost compensation or other damages. The GD lawyers were reluctant to turn over any personnel information that might be publicly exposed and were more than reluctant to provide any compensation data at all.

Doug had never taken on a national law firm of the prominence and size of GD. He certainly had no desire to irritate them—only the Lord knew what legal horrors they might unleash on him and me if we provoked them. So Doug and the GD lawyers made a deal to the effect that partner compensation data would only be provided if PW were found guilty of discrimination.

The GD lawyers had to live with whatever problem public exposure represented, however. Judge Gesell made it clear that any notion that proceedings in his court would be anything other than matters of public record was intolerable to him.

I usually dealt with Doug by phone—he kept me posted and I called every now and then on the off chance that something exciting might have happened. Very little of what took place required or profited from my involvement. Most of it was just "the lawyers lawyering" as Thomas Peter put it.

Legal documents that Doug wanted me to review, he sent to me by messenger. I usually read them without comment except to identify an occasional typo, which I noted over the phone. Legalese was Greek to me.

This time, however, Doug wanted me to come to the office. He had received some of the documents that we had asked PW to produce. He wanted me to go over them. Then he wanted to discuss what we were going to do next.

The downtown location of Kator, Scott, and Heller was much more convenient to me than had been that of Stein and Huron. I found the office just above Farragut Square with no difficulty. Funny little place, I noted as I proceeded through the small, unsecured hall that served as a lobby.

I took the closet-size elevator to the seventh floor. The elevator door opened into a cozy, cluttered area that served as a waiting room. It was partially occupied by people typing and others standing around in shirt sleeves talking to each other.

Doug greeted me and took me to see his new office. It was small, barely large enough for a couple of uncomfortable looking, overstuffed chairs and a drafting table. Seeing the drafting table with neat stacks of papers around the periphery on three sides made me realize that I had never seen Doug's office at Stein and Huron. Based on the height of the table, it looked like Doug worked standing up.

We wandered down the hall to meet my newly acquired second attorney, Jim Heller. When I entered the room he stood, walked around his desk, and shook hands firmly. He wore a white shirt with a slightly curling collar. The fact that it was unbuttoned at the neck was obscured by a nondescript tie.

Although he clearly came to work in a conservative business suit, his coat was nowhere to be seen. His grizzled bush of dark brown, gray-speckled hair seemed to fall naturally in an appealing state of disarray. He seemed very serious.

He fit perfectly into his cluttered surroundings. Boxes and piles of legal stuff covered most flat surfaces and a lot of the floor of his office. Only the center of his desk was relatively clear. It contained a yellow pad and a few loose yellow sheets covered with what can only be described as undecipherable black scribbling.

Jim asked questions from no apparent agenda. Many of them I had previously answered for Doug. When he seemed to have finished, I asked him what he thought of our chances. He explained that, as near as he could tell, there was no "smoking gun," no piece or pattern of evidence that screamed blatant discrimination.

He was reluctant to answer me until he had pored over the pile of materials that PW sent over in response to our request that they produce documents. He also said that the legal outcome might depend on the defense that PW offered. "If they argue that they just didn't like you, and that's why they didn't make you a partner, they might win," he said. Not liking a candidate was probably an acceptable basis for rejection, as long as it was used indiscriminately.

"This is more subtle," Doug said of the pattern of remarks in the long and short forms and other materials that PW had submitted. He had studied the PW paperwork for hours.

He did not use the word stereotyping at the time, but he toyed with the idea that perhaps no one person or situation had been decisive in my being rejected. Instead, he hypothesized, the entire selection process had permitted me to be evaluated in terms of how I compared to the conventional image of a woman, rather than how I met the requirements of a manager.

He thought the process permitted, even fostered, a biased evaluation of women. He wondered if there had been any research done related to discriminatory effects of derogatory characterizations based on race. If such research existed, he thought it might be applicable or extendable to women.

He told me that he had called Donna Lanhoff, an attorney at the Women's Legal Defense Fund, to discuss his theory and ask for suggestions. Over the years, she and Doug had worked together on legal matters in which they shared a common interest. She referred him to Sally Burns who then worked at the Georgetown Sex Discrimination Clinic, but shortly thereafter joined the NOW Legal Defense Fund.

It was Sally who suggested that Doug solicit the testimony of an expert on stereotyping. She recommended Susan Fiske, a Harvard Ph.D. who was an associate professor of psychology at Carnegie Mellon Institute. Sally had been impressed with her work and had planned to use her in a case involving the GAO. Dr. Fiske had never testified, however, because the GAO matter was settled before trial.

Doug planned to contact her, but he was unsure of the admissibility of the testimony of that kind of expert. With Dr. Fiske he was specifically concerned that she had never been qualified as an expert witness by a district court. He would have to give it more thought.

We discussed the need for expert witnesses, what they might cost, and how I would pay for them. Each expert, Doug explained, would probably cost a few thousand dollars in travel or other out-of-pocket costs and professional fees. He would try to minimize the travel costs by selecting local experts.

According to Doug, I definitely needed an expert statistician to determine and testify about the distribution of women on the staff and in the partnership. He had one in mind, a statistician he had used before.

We talked about depositions. Taking them could get expensive. I would have to pay the costs of transcription for any deposition that Doug or Jim took. Furthermore, there would be travel costs involved if they decided to take depositions of people who were outside the Washington area.

They wanted to keep the number of depositions to a minimum. My reaction to all matters related to experts or depositions was for Doug and Jim to do what they thought was appropriate and send me a bill.

In January, when PW's interrogatories and document production requests came in, Doug asked me to come to the office again. I had to respond personally to the demands. He wanted to go over everything with me and be sure we both understood what I had to do and by when. Furthermore, he wanted to make sure that I responded in a legally appropriate way—accurately, but in a manner that was as favorable to me as possible.

He and I reviewed the interrogatories that I was required to answer. There was nothing problematical: fewer than twenty questions, most of which asked for details to support statements made in the complaint I had filed to start the lawsuit. Most could be answered based on files in the possession of and maintained by PW.

The list of documents I was required to produce was minimal. Doug told me to answer the questions as specifically and narrowly as possible and produce whatever documents I had.

By then, Doug had spoken with Dr. Fiske over the phone. She agreed to review the material that had been available to the Admissions Committee. In late January and early February they had a few phone conversations to discuss the data and her evolving conclusions.

When Doug and I talked, he summarized and explained to me whatever she had said. I found it close to impossible, however, to understand an attorney's summary and explanation of the conclusions of a research psychologist related to a point of law. After each conversation with Doug, I called my brother, who earned a master's degree in psychology, for a lay interpretation of the psychological terms and theories that were being thrown around.

Depositions started in mid-February. Doug and the GD lawyers agreed to take all the depositions for Washington people at the GD offices. It made little difference to me.

When I went to the first deposition, it was clear that GD spent more money on its offices than did Kator, Scott, and Heller. GD was located in one of the best office buildings in downtown. I had been in the tall, new pink stone building with the multistoried atrium over the entrance many times.

I regularly met Bini Herrmann there when we had lunch together. Bini had worked for *Time* magazine since we graduated from college. *Time* had offices on a couple of the upper floors.

Doug and I presented ourselves to the receptionist who was more or less hidden on two sides behind a marble and mahogany structure. "We're here to meet Mr. Tallent for a deposition," Doug said.

She told us we could have a seat and she would call him. We stood beside the elegant, unsittable looking chairs. They reminded me of my grandmother's living room.

"The walk, talk, dress femininely stuff didn't hurt," Doug said as the revolving door whooshed behind us. The grin stayed on his face for most of the time it took us to walk the four or five blocks from the GD offices back to Kator, Scott, and Heller.

We had spent the entire day closeted in a windowless conference room while Doug took Tom Beyer's deposition. The remarks to which Doug referred were still fresh in his mind. They had been made at close to five o'clock just before we quit for the day.

It was a nice ending to an otherwise tedious proceeding, most of which consisted of Tom's description of everything I ever worked on. He gave credit where credit was due, but he also made every effort to shift the emphasis from me to the firm and the teams I worked with. He was carefully prepared.

The deposition was scheduled to continue early the next morning. As we waited to get started, I wondered what Kathy Ireland thought about Tom's advice that I wear fewer "power blues," as tailored, navy blue suits are called. She had been wearing such a suit and a white shirt that tied at the neck when he made his remarks the day before.

Kathy was one of four attorneys who represented PW. Ric Sullivan, PW's in-house assistant general counsel was the first. The other three were Kathy, Steve Tallent, and Wayne Schrader, all GD attorneys. She seemed to be the youngest and the most junior of the GD crew.

Tom must have been angry. The continuation of his deposition was held up more than half an hour as we all waited for Steve Tallent to show up. Tom was compulsive about being on time. In all the years I worked with him, he had the best track record for on-time performance of any partner I ever met, in spite of the fact that he was probably the busiest. Being held up by one of his own attorneys must have irritated him.

Steve, the senior partner on the case, left me with the impression of humility. He was in his forties. His warm eyes and scruffy gray-blond hair and goatee reminded me of one of Julia Randall's terriers.

When he occasionally took his coat off, I noticed that he was a little pudgy. He usually had attached to his belt a brown leather pipe holder that resembled a sheath for a small knife. He spoke softly in a low voice.

Unlike Steve, everything about Wayne irritated me. He was slender, of medium height, and had wispy, thin blond hair. His small, closely set, beady eyes and sharp nose reminded me of an aggressive bird. The naturally high pitch of his voice combined with hostile body language and an arrogant manner to make him offensive, even when he appeared to be attempting politeness.

From what Judy Reach and Sandy Kinsey said about him it sounded like he irritated more than just me. Somehow, in the process of trying to interview Sandy, he threatened her by saying that she had to cooperate or risk losing her job. She was so angered that she went straight to Tom Beyer and told him that she thought it was inappropriate for one of PW's attorneys to threaten its *female* employees.

She refused to talk to any attorney until she hired one to represent her. Sandy talked to no one in the absence of her own attorney. It cost her fifteen hundred dollars to meet with the various lawyers.

After Steve got there, Tom Beyer's deposition continued. It was hard for me to avoid squirming. Doug had asked PW to produce any contemporaneous notes that had been taken related to me or my candidacies.

One of the items that washed in was a set of Tom's handwritten notes taken at the final partners' meeting in which it was decided not to propose me in the second round. I made every effort to keep a poker face and sit still as Doug went through each item in the notes and asked Tom to explain.

I felt as if my personality were being dissected like a diseased frog in the biology lab. A meeting that had started off with the score twelve for, two opposed, Tom abstaining, ended with a unanimous decision not to propose me because the two opposing partners, Ben Warder and Don Epelbaum, were adamant in their positions.

An hour or so of personality dissection was followed by another equally lengthy period of discussion of all my technical and client problems. I had lived through the review process and knew the technical problems were bunk, but I did not enjoy hearing them resurrected.

Doug presented Tom with letters and memoranda prepared by or for State, all of which expressed satisfaction, in the good to laudatory range, with the technical work of my team. I was surprised when Tom dismissed them on the basis that either the client did not know what it was doing or PW's standards were higher than those of the client. I was more surprised to hear about the problems that I supposedly had with Roger Feldman, Austin McHale, and Fred Cook, my client on REMS.

I was relieved when the deposition ended at midday. Overall it had gone as I expected. Tom represented himself and the firm well.

The next week the attorneys and I reconvened in the same dimly lit conference room so that Doug could take Ben Warder's deposition. When Doug asked me what he could expect, I told him that Warder would waffle and he did. He sat quietly, responded carefully, and spoke in his characteristic monotone.

He disagreed with Tom about who had prepared the first draft of my partnership proposal. According to Ben he never had a role in the drafting. He also disagreed on the subject of profanity. While Tom acknowledged that there were some partners who swore a lot, as Ben saw it PW partners swore only occasionally for emphasis, but not as a general rule.

It was clear from everything that Ben said that he believed he was removed from the original State Department work because of my efforts, not his actions. It was equally clear he had never been a supporter of mine.

He was nonconfrontational and, therefore, perfectly comfortable saying nothing in public and recording negative views in private. The deposition was over in time for a late lunch. Doug told me we would probably never see Ben again—he would make a terrible witness.

I had to go in to the Kator, Scott, and Heller offices over the weekend after Ben's deposition. Jim and Doug wanted to make sure I was properly prepared for my own. The next week I would sit in the hot seat. It was the GD lawyers' turn to ask questions.

Jim gave me a typed sheet of standard instructions for people about to undergo depositions. He apologized for the impersonal nature of the sheet and explained that having the instructions typed out minimized his risk of forgetting to tell me something.

"Answer the questions specifically but don't volunteer anything," he said. Then we spent a few hours discussing the questions he believed I should expect.

We tried to practice: he would ask a question and I would answer. The practice session was a disaster. I had great difficulty taking the questions coming from Jim seriously. He seemed like such a warm and wonderful person.

He got a little fed up a couple of times when I laughed in response. His frustrated reaction cut short my nervous humor and made me focus. Everything about his manner said this was a serious situation.

When the deposition started late in the morning I was tireder than usual for a Friday. Someone was using a jackhammer on one of the floors above the GD offices. The noise conducted through the concrete superstructure of the building reverberated through the normally quiet conference room with nerve-racking irregularity.

Doug accompanied Jim who represented me in the deposition. His first legal action on my behalf was to comment, on the record, that if the noise got too bad we would have to move or stop and reschedule. He continued by objecting to the fact that Ric Sullivan, Tom Beyer, and Lew Krulwich attended the deposition.

Apparently Jim believed that GD or PW was in violation of some legal rule that restricted the number of participants from the opposing sides to one each. Jim must have been right because only one representative of PW attended subsequent depositions.

Steve Tallent began the inquisition on a low note, my claim of retaliation over being booted out of the Railroad Retirement Board. After half an hour of questions on that, he questioned his way through my early days at PW, from my arrival as a policy anomaly through Project Integrity and the original proposal to the State Department.

He seemed to be trying to get me to admit that I had no reason to expect to be a partner. He also made every effort to get me to state that my business success was, in reality, attributable to Tom or Ben or some other partner of the firm. I held the line—I was responsible for the successful efforts of a team.

Steve questioned his way through my recollections of the partnership evaluation process as it applied to me and on to my discussions with the partners after I was held. We broke for a late lunch as he was beginning to question me on my meeting with Joe Connor in New York.

Doug and Jim and I reviewed the events of the morning at lunch. Jim chastised me for saying, "Mr. Krulwich contributes to any activity he participates in," in response to Steve's question, "Did Mr. Krulwich do any work . . . or was he just a figurehead?"

I had permitted Steve's derogatory characterization of Lew to bait me into ignoring Jim's counsel. I had volunteered what I thought about Lew instead of simply answering the question with "He worked." Jim handled it kindly, but his reminder was stern enough to make me think twice about volunteering again.

Steve knocked off questions about my meetings with Joe, Pete

McVeagh, Ben, Tim Coffey, and Don Epelbaum by four o'clock. Then he abruptly changed subjects. He focused on the long- and short-form comments.

He jumped around from comment to comment asking that I identify comments I considered to be sexist or inaccurate. Occasionally he would ask if I agreed with some partner's characterization of me or if I could identify what of my own behavior might have caused a partner to characterize me negatively.

Three partners into that line of questioning, I concluded that the whole approach was an attempt to trap me. I believe Steve was hoping I would answer the questions on a partner-by-partner basis in such a manner that he could find an overall pattern that could be used against me.

He was probably hoping to be able to make a statement like, "She herself agreed with 60 percent of the criticisms," or "She herself stated that sex was not a factor in almost all of the short-form comments." About five, we quit for the day even though there were more questions to be asked—my deposition was to be continued.

The following Friday, Jim and Doug, without me, went to Philadelphia to take the deposition of Don Ziegler. The objective of taking Don's deposition was to understand the partner candidate evaluation process generally and specifically as it related to me.

I had no recollection of ever having met Don. I confused his name with that of Ron Ziegler who had been responsible for public relations at the State Department.

Don was, however, a very important partner. He was one of eighteen elected members of the firm's Policy Board. He was also the chairman of the eight-man Admissions Committee, a committee of the board.

Under his leadership, the Admissions Committee evaluated the information about the eighty-eight partner candidates in my year and recommended, to the board, whom to reject, hold, or admit. The Policy Board made a few changes to the recommendations.

On a three-quarters vote of the board, successful candidates were placed on the ballot for a formal vote of the partnership. Appearing on the ballot was the equivalent to being admitted—the vote of the partnership as a whole was essentially a rubber stamp process.

Doug, Jim, and I spent little time reviewing what happened at the Ziegler deposition. We had to prepare for depositions of Don Epelbaum and Lew Krulwich and what we hoped would be the end of mine, all of which were scheduled for the same day. What little we did discuss, surprised me.

The vote on me had never even been close. I started out as a hold on the verge of a reject. In the final analysis, I was a unanimous hold. Surprise at my own disposition was compounded by the fact that another OGS candidate proposed that year began as a hold but was admitted.

On the Friday after the Ziegler deposition, Don Epelbaum's began first thing in the morning. The man had a way with words. He had voted for my admission—sort of. On the long form that he wrote in September supporting me, he remarked, "At time[s], however, she can be abrasive, unduly harsh, difficult to work with and, as a result, causes significant turmoil." Jim characterized it as "damning with faint praise."

Only a month or two later, in November, Roger Marcellin, a member of the Admissions Committee, went to OGS to interview the partners about their candidates. According to the notes that Marcellin took that time, Don said, "I don't enjoy working with her. I avoid her socially." Yet in his deposition, Don commented that he "generally" avoided social contact with managers.

Jim and I both wondered why he had singled me out for comment on the long form. Although Don acknowledged that he had written most of the words in the OGS proposal that I become a partner, he was no fan of mine.

Furthermore, he had never been one. Nothing he said in his deposition was sexist. Everything he said seemed to be smoothly malevolent.

By the time the deposition ended, I was too nervous to eat lunch. Jim, Doug, and I discussed what to expect from Lew. "Dear, sweet Lew," I thought. "He will be honest, thoughtful, and carefully considerate," I said. I had no doubt that he would refute John Fridley's view of my integrity.

The deposition seemed to be excruciatingly painful for Lew. The fact that I was responsible for his being involved embarrassed me.

He seemed torn between the poles represented by the two sets of attorneys. He paused interminably after each question. Then he generally responded painfully and haltingly.

He was unable to recall specifics on a wide range of topics. It was clear, however, that he was a supporter and had always been a supporter. He had no reservations about my integrity.

At four that afternoon, after a brief but welcome break, my deposition reconvened. Kathy Ireland picked up where Steve had left off—on the long- and short-form comments.

She was more methodical than Steve had been. She proceeded in consecutive order. With the redundance of a broken record player she asked the same questions over and over.

Only the name of the partner changed. "Do you have any reason to believe that sex was a factor in recording these comments?" "Do you believe that his comments are inaccurate or unfair?"

In the case of Peter Hart, a tax partner, I answered, "Probably not," to the question Do you believe Peter Hart to be biased against females?

If ever there was anyone who had a wide-ranging tolerance for differences, it was Pete. In contrast to every other partner in OGS, Pete decorated his office with blond, modern contemporary furniture. It was a refreshing change from the heavy, dark, uncomfortable furniture everywhere else.

When Pete transferred from Washington to Philadelphia, I attended a riotous farewell party planned and organized by a woman who loved working for him. The centerpiece of the party was a writhing belly dancer. It was clear from his reaction that he was embarrassed, but he managed to enjoy the party without ever losing his dignity.

I responded similarly to questions about Norm Statland. In my view he was "not particularly" biased against females. He voted against almost everyone. To his credit, however, his protégée, Kay Lindstrom, was one of 7 females among 662 partners in mid-1984.

In other cases, I certainly thought there was reason to believe that gender might have been a factor. It seemed unlikely that Corky Hoffman would have suggested "a course at charm school" for a man. Pete McVeagh's backhanded compliment that I had "matured from a tough-talking somewhat masculine hard-nosed manager to an authoritative, formidable, but much more appealing lady partner candidate" must have been gender based, even though he voted for me.

In response to most of the questions, however, I waffled in a manner worthy of Ben Warder. The GD lawyers would have a hard time finding a self-incriminating pattern in my answers.

I was startled when Kathy switched, without transition, from long- and short-form comments to witnesses. I naively imagined litigation to be like business competition, a basic principal of which is never to reveal your tactical or strategic direction to the opponents unless required to do so. "Have you asked PW or State Department people if they would speak to your attorneys?" she asked.

"Am I supposed to answer these questions?" I asked myself as I shot a puzzled look to Jim. His lack of expression said Yes.

I answered the questions. I had spoken to Bob Lamb, Roger Feldman, Joe Linnemann, and Howard Renman at the State Department and Karen Nold, Sandy Kinsey, and Judy Reach at the firm.

Litigation differs from business competition. The judicial process seeks to make all the information, points of view, and arguments of each side available to both. To litigate is to debate in a public forum. There is, however, more at stake than a trophy.

At about seven in the evening, the deposition, a long week, and a long day ended.

Joe Connor, the chairman and senior partner of the U.S. firm of Price Waterhouse had a difficult travel itinerary. Business plans called for him to be out of the country during the week in which the trial was scheduled.

The GD lawyers wanted to move the trial date to April to accommodate Joe's plans. They raised the question in a hearing before Judge Gesell.

He managed his calendar. He was not available in early April. He suggested that Joe's deposition be recorded on video tape and that the tape substitute for Joe's testimony at trial. He extended the period for discovery by one week and slipped the date of the pretrial conference accordingly. The trial date remained fixed.

Doug and Jim reluctantly agreed to the video tape. They were unhappy with the agreement but more unhappy at the prospect of an appearance before Judge Gesell to argue with the GD lawyers about the presence of a witness who was probably less than critical to my case.

Jim went to the national office of Price Waterhouse in New York to take Joe's deposition. From what Jim reported on his return to Washington, Joe was good. He exuded confidence, prominence, and polish.

Apparently he had all of the media presence of a first-rate politician. He frequently answered a question that he preferred to answer instead of the question he was asked. He spoke of me and my problems sympathetically. Jim summed it up: "I understand how he became senior partner of the firm."

While Jim was preparing for and taking depositions in New York,

Doug concentrated on finishing our pretrial package, the name given to the pile of legal documents submitted before trial. It included a brief that outlined the legal arguments we planned to make in our case, a list of exhibits to identify documents we planned to submit as evidence, and a list of witnesses categorized as lay or expert witnesses. It was due to the judge and the GD lawyers two days after the Connor deposition and about ten days before trial.

"What's a rebuttal witness?" I asked when I read that one the of two experts would be called as a rebuttal witness. "The way the process works," Doug explained, "is we'll go first because we're the plaintiff. Our first round is called the 'case in chief.' When we finish making our case," he continued, "it will be PW's turn. When they finish, we'll have a final shot, called rebuttal, to rebut their arguments. A rebuttal witness is one called for purposes of rebuttal."

"Chill, Mom!" my children frequently say to me. I believe they are telling me to calm down—I have a less than laid-back temperament. Doug, on the other hand was so laid-back that it terrified me.

Although he had never met Susan Fiske, he planned to call her on rebuttal. Furthermore, he continued to express concern, but only mild concern, that Judge Gesell might not qualify her as an expert.

He also seemed only slightly troubled by the fact that stereotyping had never been used to support a claim of discrimination. Stereotyping was what he believed occurred and it was the basis of one of the arguments he planned to make.

The pretrial package of materials delivered for the March 14 conference before Judge Gesell identified Susan Fiske as a rebuttal witness. It stated that she would offer expert testimony to the effect that sex role stereotyping played a determinative role in the Admission Committee's decision.

Mike Kator was married in Georgia the weekend before the trial started. With one exception, all the attorneys at Kator, Scott, and Heller attended the wedding festivities for the senior partner's son.

The Friday before the trial, Doug met Susan Fiske for the first time. She came to Washington to prepare to testify.

He was in the office most of the weekend. He missed the wedding.

During the six-month period that preceded the trial, the positive and negative revelations and turns of events, inevitable in litigation, left me in an ever-changing state of wildly swinging moods. Two people, Toni Gibbons and Thomas Peter, were responsible for the preservation of my sanity during that period.

At our regular lunch meetings, Toni cheerfully dismissed as ridiculous PW's position. More importantly, she kept me so busy that I had little idle time to become morbidly preoccupied with the suit.

We finished the technical tasks related to the procurement, and State selected the contractor. There was a hiatus of a couple months while the contracting people plodded along, working out what seemed to be a never-ending series of contractual details. Just before the trial, however, the contract with the FNPay contractor was signed. Work on the new system could finally begin.

Thomas Peter was an unending source of moral support as I struggled through the derogatory diatribe that came with the document production process and the depositions. He was adorable at Thanksgiving when I was so busy with FNPay that I almost forgot our anniversary.

An impish grin was splashed across his face when we met for a drink at Tivoli's, a bar and restaurant near the State offices in Rosslyn. I could tell that something was up, but I never expected him to replace the beat-up Indian bands with a new set of wedding rings, a yellow gold circle of alternating diamonds and rubies guarded by two simple twisted rope bands. It was the first time he had ever given me a gift that fit so perfectly.

For my birthday several weeks later, he pulled another shocker—a surprise party that must have been hours in the planning. He invited people I had not seen in years, including Joey Biero, whom I had not seen since our wedding.

Christmas and New Year's were full of friends and relatives, fun and music. Thomas Peter had rented a piano while I was in Nepal. I basically disapproved of the acquisition until we all gathered around it and made music and merriment over the holidays. He was not a bad player considering the fact that the piano was his fifth instrument, after the banjo, the guitar, the flute, and the French horn.

Just before the trial Thomas Peter suggested that the children visit their grandparents during the proceedings. It was a brilliant idea.

Although subconsciously I knew that Tela, Gilbert, and Peter would all be out of school for spring recess, I had neglected to consider what we would do with them while we were in court. My mother agreed to have

Tela and Gilbert visit. She was, however, reluctant to handle all three, largely because of the swimming pool in her back yard. Mom had visions of herself in the middle with Gilbert and Peter on opposite ends of the pool attempting to drown.

Thomas Peter enlisted the help of his mother and sister Rose. Peter could go to Philadelphia to stay with them. They would be happy to help out and even happier to have Peter around.

The trial was one of very few occasions on which I ever permitted the children to be split up. I believe it is important for siblings to stick together. It was clear, however, that there was no reasonable alternative.

Thomas Peter made all the travel arrangements. Then, to provide moral support, he rallied friends and arranged, well ahead of time, for them to attend the trial on a staggered schedule. Mary Curzan, Ruth Hopper, and Vera Schneider were all scheduled to show up and sit through whatever they had time or interest to sit through. He did all that he could in anticipation of a difficult period.

Trial 1

MONDAY

Judge Gerhard A. Gesell must have been close to seventy-five the first time I stood to watch him stride with stately posture into his courtroom. His full head of perfectly groomed, snow-white hair was in stark contrast with his black ankle-length robe.

Alert, curious eyes sparkled out of his red face over an enchanting, genuinely warm smile. In a low, well-modulated voice he greeted the attorneys cheerfully, but formally, as he sat down.

I had watched the interaction between him and his marshal and court reporter at a couple of the conferences that took place before the trial. The steady-eyed, unfailing attention that they paid him gave me the impression that they worshiped the man.

My own impressions of Judge Gesell were supplemented by the admiring and respectful impressions provided by Jim and Doug. His parents founded the Gesell Human Development Institute. He graduated from Andover, where my nephew went to school, and Yale. He had been a partner at Covington and Burling, a prominent Washington law firm, on Pearl Harbor day (December 7) in 1967 when President Johnson appointed him to the federal bench. He could be impatient, especially with the irrelevant, and acerbic when irritated.

The morning of the trial, but before the formal proceedings began, Doug and Jim agreed to withdraw my retaliation claim. The lawyers from Gibson, Dunn, and Crutcher stipulated that I was technically competent. At the time, I was unaware of these actions.

Thomas Peter was the entire audience when I took the stand as the first witness of the trial. Tom Beyer, Ric Sullivan, and the three GD lawyers sat before the bar on the PW side of the courtroom.

Doug sat at the table on my side of the bench. Jim stood before me and the judge to ask questions that he and I had reviewed in preparation for the testimony. Under his direct examination, I gave my vital statistics, described my family and education, worked my way through aerospace, and into the Big Eight and Price Waterhouse.

Jim had told me to expect questions from Judge Gesell and warned against using technical terms or buzz words. I always prided myself on speaking English without relying on such jargon.

It never occurred to me, however, that "consulting staff" was not a well-defined term. It was a little unnerving and more than a little amusing when the judge asked for clarification. "Now, what kinds of staff are we talking about? Were they computer wizards or secretaries or what were they?

"I don't understand what a consultant is," he continued. "You see, anybody who really has any skill in Washington is a consultant. I want to know what were these people, what kind of people were they? How old were they? What did they do? What did they profess to be able to do?

"I'm not being critical, but you've got to get me in the atmosphere of this. I don't understand what a staff is unless somebody tells me."

Jim questioned me through the work with the Bureau of Indian Affairs, the requirements for the State Department, the award of the big FMS contract, the proposal in St. Louis, and the real estate management system. Except for an occasional interruption from the judge asking a clarifying question, my explanation was a regurgitation of what I had explained in my deposition.

When Jim asked about the meeting with Joe Connor, the judge expressed interest in what happened after the meeting. "Was Connor's plan implemented?"

"That was a new wrinkle," I thought. I had never viewed Joe's remarks as much of a plan and, as such, had never thought about implementation.

Shortly after lunch we picked up with Tom Beyer's memorable advice that I "Walk more . . ." and look like Sandy Kinsey. Jim questioned me out of Price Waterhouse, into my own business, and into my job at the World Bank.

When I described what I was doing at the bank, Judge Gesell asked in an incredulous tone that startled me, "And you want to leave that job and go back and join this crowd? That's what you're asking me to do, right?"

Jim finished his direct examination. Steve Tallent started cross-examination.

Steve focused on every comment ever made about my apparent failure to get along with people. The judge was curious, occasionally skeptical. "I don't understand where they had a chance to know that you were unpleasant except on the basis of something that somebody told them."

Steve turned to a discussion of profanity. I am absolutely certain that Lew Krulwich could not have imagined the Pandora's box he opened when he said, "Just because it's a lady using foul language," probably in response to a question about whether or not he found me to be profane.

Over years of litigation, my use of the English language was described in various legal documents and in the newspapers as if it were worthy of a drunken sailor who had smashed his finger with a hammer. I never understood what seemed to be a preoccupation with profanity and the extent to which I used it.

In my deposition, I had stated my general view on the subject in response to a question from Steve Tallent. I was talking about bad work products, not people:

> If the end product is sufficiently lacking in quality, that one or more people might have to stay up all night to get it fixed so that it can be delivered, then that product might be described as either a "screw-up" or being "screwed up."
>
> If the quality of the end product is such that the delivery date might be in jeopardy, then the product might be described as "fucked up" or a "fuck-up." None of this language, by the way, is startling in the consulting profession.

Steve next asked if I had been requested to resign. He probably wanted me to say that I quit. I told him I had been pressured, not specifically asked to leave.

I was startled again by how much Judge Gesell understood. He restated my options. "They said you could stay and not be a partner. You could stay and hope the lightning would strike and you would work for MacVeagh, or you could quit."

Steve made subtle attempts to discredit me, nothing flagrant. At one point he asked, "It's true, isn't it, that in—as you came up to the proposal stage in FMS-1 that Mr. Beyer told you that the State Department had asked that you not be proposed as the project manager on FMS-2?"

Steve's statement was true. His implication, that I was removed for failure to perform, was false.

Steve asked about the series of reviews by Ben Warder after I was held. The judge interrupted, "Well, now, is the issue in the case—I'm asking the plaintiff—of retaliation or is it not?"

I failed to understand the question. I knew I was the plaintiff, but I had never understood the retaliation issue to which he referred, nor did I know that it had been eliminated as an issue. I had no idea how to answer the question.

Fortunately, Jim recognized that the question was addressed to him or Doug, rather than to me. Jim answered, "She is not talking about retaliation."

Judge Gesell confirmed, "I understood that it had been withdrawn."

The judge had apparently expected Jim to object to the line of questioning as irrelevant. Jim explained, "I want to be precise about that though. Mr. Tallent is in an area where we do believe that there was a kind of confirming set of actions about not having reproposed her, that we think there was an attempt to justify that by a lot of late down reviews."

The judge, however, needed little explanation, "I understand that. You say they were making a record after the event."

About three o'clock in the afternoon Steve finished his cross-examination. The judge called a ten-minute break.

I was relieved to get off the witness stand, partly to escape the psychological heat. The cross-examination had taken longer than Doug or Jim planned.

Roger Feldman and Bob Lamb, who were scheduled to testify next, were cooling their heels in the witness room. I immediately went to find them. I wondered how long they had been kept waiting.

When I found them, however, they seemed to be enjoying a quiet conversation about old times. I apologized for keeping them at the courthouse. It did not seem to bother them. I was cheered by their patience and good humor.

Roger testified before Bob. The purpose of his testimony was to set aside any doubts raised about my role in PW's success at the State Department.

In response to Doug's direct examination, Roger confirmed my role on the original proposal for the financial management system, "The committee and team that determined the selection was very favorably impressed with her performance during the orals and also was very favorably disposed to the written proposals that came from Price Waterhouse."

He made clear that I had nothing to do with Ben Warder's removal from the project, "I believe that Mr. Gulli, who at that time was director of financial systems and principally in charge of the conduct of the project, asked Price Waterhouse to remove Mr. Warder from the project."

He explained State's reasons for requesting the removal, "It had to do with his performance, attitude, his presentation, and the lack of constructive contribution on his part to the efforts to that point."

He stated why the department wanted a partner, not a senior manager, as the project manager on the final project for State, "A partner would lend greater prestige to the conduct of the project. . . . There would be a need to require top-flight talent to be brought forth from throughout the firm. . . . A partner would be presumably well positioned to be able to tap on the different resources of the firm."

Roger gave his impression of me, "I would describe Ann as extremely competent, intelligent, a very capable person. Strong and forthright, very productive, energetic, and creative."

When Doug asked, "Do you know people who are partners at Price Waterhouse who have worked on FMS?" Steve objected. Roger, who was prepared to compare me to every partner he ever met, was prevented from answering the question by the objection from Steve.

Roger sat patiently on the witness stand as the attorneys and the judge discussed it.

Unbeknownst to either Roger or me, Price Waterhouse had stipulated to my technical competence. That stipulation rendered irrelevant any testimony about my competence or my competence compared to other partners at PW.

Steve did not cross-examine the comptroller of PW's $30-million FMS client. A baffled Roger Feldman was excused from the witness stand.

When Roger and I later discussed his testimony, I explained why it had been cut short. He described the awesome judge as "Moses towering over me." In my mental concept of Moses, he had a beard and carried the law on tablets of stone. If I ignored the beard, I could understand Roger's view.

Jim examined Bob Lamb. When the witness was called to the stand by name, Judge Gesell quipped, "Lamb. Not to the slaughter, I presume."

"That's up to your Honor," Jim replied.

Bob reinforced Roger's positive impression of me: "I thought she was a very good project manager. In fact, I've subsequently tried to hire Ann for the State Department because I thought she was so good. I thought she provided a good sense of direction, a good sense of leadership for the team."

He commented on his observations of my dealings with my teams on FMS and REMS. "Well, I never saw her cut anyone off, to use your phrase. I thought she was a broad-minded person.

"I think Ann—I liked Ann very much and I saw a great deal of her both socially as well as professionally because of the intensity and nature of the relationship that we had and I enjoyed that association because I liked her intellectual clarity. I liked her—she was a stimulating conversationalist."

Steve objected, saying that there was no question of my acceptance by the client at State.

Judge Gesell overruled his objection:

> Well, there wasn't until you raised the suggestion earlier today that she was taken off the work at the request of the State Department, implying that there was some lack of confidence in her work, which the prior witness explained.
>
> I do think, as I've said from the beginning, what these witnesses say about what they observed as to her relationships to the staff of Price Waterhouse, whatever it is, is the most important issue, and I think you've covered that.

Steve did not cross-examine the assistant secretary for administration of PW's $6-million REMS client.

Tom Beyer was called as a witness on my behalf. Under Doug's direct examination, Tom introduced himself and described my career at PW. I was impressed when Tom testified that under his leadership, OGS had grown an order of magnitude, to 350 people.

Tom must have been as startled as I when Judge Gesell interrupted the examination. "You spotted a star, right? Now then, what happened? What happened?"

Doug questioned Tom about my performance appraisals. Shortly after a discussion of a counseling session related to softening my image, Judge Gesell interrupted again, "Did you ever have a woman project manager work with you before on a major matter?"

Although he was unable to remember any by name, Tom, who I am certain cared only about results, and never about gender, responded, "I don't remember the sex of the—gender of the individuals. It was not particularly relevant to me."

Judge Gesell, chided him a little, "Well, that's not a very big thing, to tell the difference between a man and a woman, you know."

Doug asked the next question. The judge seemed to be stuck on the women project managers.

He interrupted, "The reason I asked, there was testimony before me that you suggested she change her mode of dress, her lipstick, her hairdo, and I thought perhaps that showed some consciousness of femininity."

Tom said that he "was trying to search for a way in which Ann could present a very positive, confident, and successful image to Mr. Connor." The judge initially misinterpreted what Tom said. Referring to Joe Connor, Judge Gesell asked, "*He* criticized her dress, as you understood it?"

That was not what Tom meant. Connor never criticized me at all. The judge confirmed his understanding of Tom's explanation, "You just thought it would make a better impression."

As Doug continued asking questions, Tom talked about St. Louis, REMS, winning St. Louis. The end of the day approached and Judge Gesell politely asked when Doug planned to finish. Doug said he expected to examine Tom for "in the neighborhood of twenty minutes."

Judge Gesell had other matters scheduled so he decided to reconvene in the morning. He ended the examination with a cheerful, "I think then we'd better pull the shades down for the day now."

Trial 1

TUESDAY

The next morning Doug continued his direct examination of Tom. The topic was notes taken at the meetings in which the partners of OGS decided not to propose me in the summer of 1983.

When Doug tried unsuccessfully to read Tom's handwriting, the judge tried to help Doug by saying, "Well, what does it say. Let's ask the witness to read his writing and see what it says. What do you understand it says?"

Tom's wonderful sense of humor emerged, "I may have as much trouble as you, sir." Judge Gesell returned an equally good-humored, "Well, you're the expert on your own handwriting."

As Doug and Tom slugged their way through the bad copy of Tom's ancient, hastily scribbled notes, the judge interrupted, "Now, a lot of your partners have talked about it and they've heard gossip, it reads to me as though someone at least had heard gossip in their offices."

"I don't know whether they've talked to people or not. . . . Did you ever have anybody come to you directly from the staff and say I can't get along with this woman or I want to be taken off the work or she's just kicking us around and I can't do anything about it?"

Tom gave an example, "One time was in 1980, the exit interview with Mr. Kaplan, Robert Kaplan, a young consultant who had worked with Ann Hopkins in Albuquerque. . . . He alleged that she screamed obscenities to him, four-letter words, continuous stream of them for up to forty-five minutes."

I cringed. I was angry at Bob when I talked to him. I have no doubt that I swore, but screaming obscenities was drama, not reality. I am unable to scream anything for forty-five minutes.

When Jim, Doug, and I later discussed the drama, they told me it was testimony not worth refuting.

Tom provided an example from FMS, "Karen Nold was one of the senior managers on that job and Karen said—was quite depressed about things and I tried to cheer her up and said, you know what is your problem? What's going on? And she expressed the sentiment that she just felt that Ann's overbearing style was smothering her attempts to be—to bring forth her ideas, her conclusions, her recommendations, and suggestions."

I cringed again, especially since Tom had told Karen to be more assertive. Tom continued

> Pat Bowman was attempting to bring forth some ideas in her area. Ann struck out at her. Inasmuch as to smother her commentary and say we don't need that now. Something to that effect.
>
> Pat, who is a very independent person in her own right and not about to be transgressed by anyone, struck right back and said something to the effect you can't treat me that way. Don't you dare treat me that way. We were all a little startled by it and the incident passed. Ann accepted it and it went on.

It was hard to maintain a poker face and avoid squirming. Pat Bowman and I disagreed all the time, but I still give her job references and we talk on the phone.

Doug expressed legal irritation at the fact that Bob Kaplan's exit interview was not part of the record and that the incident had not been mentioned in Tom's deposition. Tom said that he only recently remembered it.

The judge seemed to want to move the case along. He reminded Doug of his earlier estimate of the time required to complete the examination, "You said yesterday that you had twenty minutes—we've now been an hour."

Tom explained that Don Epelbaum had called him in the summer of 1983 to say that he would not support me as a partner candidate. Apparently Marge Gellar, Tom Colberg, Larry McClure, Steve Higgins all opposed me even though they had not worked for me since mid-1982.

As Doug led Tom through his notes, the judge asked about the partners in the meeting, "How did it break down sex-wise? How many were men, how many were women?"

When Tom answered that there were no women partners in OGS, Judge Gesell seemed a little surprised. "You had no women partners in your organization?"

Tom's testimony ended the first part of my case, in legal terms my case in chief. Steve entered a routine motion to dismiss the case. Judge Gesell took that under advisement. He would rule on the motion after both sides had finished.

Joseph E. Connor, the senior partner of the Price Waterhouse U.S. firm, testified on tape. The movie was interrupted, about two-thirds of the way to the end, by lunch. After lunch Wayne wanted to present Don Ziegler's testimony so he could go back to Philadelphia.

Judge Gesell's sense of humor showed again as he said, "All right, then we'll wheel the unlive witness away for the time being."

As the equipment required for the Connor movie was being moved around, Judge Gesell asked, in obvious admiration, "How old is this man? Does anybody know?"

Tom knew. "Fifty-three," he responded instantly.

Jim had predicted that Judge Gesell would be impressed by Joe. It seemed that Jim was right.

Donald R. Ziegler was called to the stand. Don described how the partners were canvased. A package containing the proposals for the candidates was distributed to each of the partners, usually in September. The partners who had comments submitted them on long or short forms. The length of the form was an indicator of how well the commenting partner knew the candidate.

Each form included a list of attributes for evaluation. There were far more attributes on the long form than on the short. Each commenting partner ranked a candidate on each attribute in a quartile, first being high, fourth being low.

The rank was supposed to reflect the commenting partner's comparison of the candidate with other candidates, successful or unsuccessful, in recent years, including the current year. "With no definition of what that is, whether it's three years or ten years or five years," asked Judge Gesell referring to the comparison period.

The partner comments were mailed to the Admissions Committee late in September. The Admissions Committee had an organizational meeting in September or October. At that meeting, Don Ziegler assigned individual partners to visit the offices with candidates. The purpose of the office visits was to review the candidates' personnel files and talk to the partners about the candidates.

While Don described the process, Judge Gesell studied the long form. "Well, now, I don't see on this form any place where you ask about the relations of the candidate to the staff on the entire form, isn't that right?"

Don first wanted to make sure that the judge was looking at the right form. The judge said, "Well, I have the long form. That's the most important because the other people, they don't know anything about her anyhow."

Don explained where the judge could find what he needed by identifying the section entitled "Profession Related" attributes. "Well, it's all lumped together," said Judge Gesell. "Suppose I was confronted with a candidate who had done an excellent job dealing with clients and had trouble with the staff. How would I know how to rank one, two, three, or four?" the judge continued.

Don identified separate attributes for acceptance by associates, partners, staff, and clients. Judge Gesell continued to question, "Well, that's under the heading 'Profession Related.' What is a profession-related acceptance by the staff? What is that?"

Judge Gesell reviewed the subheadings on other related parts of the form. "And how the candidate relates to civic activities and how the candidate relates to professional organizations?" he asked.

He seemed unimpressed with the form, "That doesn't have anything to do with 'Profession Related.'"

Wayne questioned Don back on track. In October the executive secretary of the firm prepares an extract of the comments from the long and short forms. The Admissions Committee member who visits a candidate's office takes the extract with him. The offices are usually visited in November or early December.

Wayne introduced, as evidence, the paperwork related to me. It included the extract, office visit notes, and the numerical tally of quartile rankings by attributes. Judge Gesell studied the paperwork.

He observed, "Well, on this document by far the bulk of the partners who apparently filled out this 'Profession' response indicated that she was better than most in her relations with staff and with clients and with partners. Right?

"She was always in the first two quarters rather than the last two quarters," Judge Gesell observed. He continued, "Compared to all the other candidates that have come along in recent years."

That, however, was not good, as Don tried to explain: "Yes, sir, but again, you know, when you compare this to where the other candidates fell you have to put that into perspective with respect to all the other candidates."

The judge saw an inconsistency, "You don't ask them to rate them against the other candidates of that year."

Don explained, "She ranked very low in relation to the other candidates."

Judge Gesell asked for specifics. "In her personal attributes over all. Congeniality, among others," Don replied.

When the judge commented that the other areas seemed "fairly strong," Don summed it up. "The strong candidates fall within the first or second quartile insofar as personal attributes are concerned and with the predominance being in the first quartile."

Don continued to explain the process. The Admissions Committee member who makes the office visits collects and summarizes what he finds in the office. That information is provided only to the committee.

Judge Gesell expressed surprise that the Admissions Committee kept what it found confidential. "Confidential from the other partners who are making the vote, right? Is that what you're telling me? That you don't tell your partners what the other partners think of people?"

Don explained:

> When we recommend that a candidate be held for further consideration or when we recommend that a partner-candidate not be submitted or not be considered further for the possibility for admission we do share with the Policy Board itself our reasons and the reasons why we reached that decision. We also prepare a memorandum which sets forth the most substantive reasons why we reached that decision.
>
> We provide those memoranda to the area practice partners who are asked to contact the partners in charge of the offices of the unsuccessful candidates so that the partners in charge of the offices understand why the Admissions Committee reached the decision it did reach and they are asked to explain to the candidates themselves essentially why the Admissions Committee reached the decision that it did, so we do share the information with them.

"After the decision," Judge Gesell confirmed.

Don stated that he visited the St. Louis office and that Roger Marcellin visited OGS. He explained the Admissions Committee process by which they met and discussed all the paperwork—how they weighed the extracts, the office visit notes, the statistics, and came to a conclusion.

Wayne asked, "Have those characteristics and comments about those characteristics been considered or weighted in the same manner and fashion for male and female candidates?"

Naturally Don replied, "Yes, there's no difference given to male or female candidates."

Judge Gesell wanted to understand. "How do you know that? How do you know that? How many women candidates have you ever considered in the course of the time you've been in this job?"

Don replied based on the current year, "Well, just this year alone, four."

Judge Gesell, however, wanted the answer for the period prior to the current year. "But how many before that?" he asked.

The numbers for that timeframe were no different. "Probably over, say, four years, fifteen," Don said.

Judge Gesell then asked, "Aren't there some partners that would prefer to go a little easier on what women they take in because there are not many women and some of them seem to say in here that this one would make a good lady partner or woman partner?

"Isn't it a factor that you consider in terms of your business? Do you need women partners? Do you have women clients? Don't you think of those things?"

Don responded, "I think we're very objective and successful at looking at the candidate and not necessarily whether he is of a specific religion, race, creed, or whatever the case might be."

Judge Gesell asked about the office visits. "When you make these field trips don't you find you run into people with prejudices and attitudes among your partners?"

"There are a few. . . . There are some partners who comment on a candidate because, let's say it might be a woman or they might not like their ethnic background, but on the whole I think that the partners comment more on the candidates' professional qualifications," Don said.

The judge asked a different question. "You don't have a very good percentage of women, do you?"

Don explained that the number of women in the pipeline to the partnership was small but growing. That accounted for the small number of partners who were women.

Wayne tried to get Don's direct examination back on track. Don explained that the Admissions Committee meets in December, in January, and again in February. In the February meeting, the committee recommends candidates to be put on the ballot.

In my case it was always a question of holding or rejecting, Don explained. Wayne plodded on.

He asked Don, "Do you recall any instances where a candidate who received large credit for the success of OGS on the FMS project and who had received high praise for work on the St. Louis FMHA project was recommended for a hold."

"One was Ann Hopkins and another was Nick Homer," Don said. I thought he was stretching the comparison a bit, but there was never any doubt in my mind that Nick should have been the partner he became in 1985.

Doug asked the questions on cross-examination. He planned to ask about certain remarks made in the paperwork PW had provided in response to my document production requests. He began his questioning with St. Louis.

When Don did the office visit in St. Louis, Tom Blythe was positive and Tim Coffey changed his recommendation from hold to admit. Doug asked, "So the only negative recommendation or conversation you had about Ann Hopkins out of these three was Mr. Fridley, is that correct?"

Don confirmed, "Fridley continued to think that she should not be admitted to the firm."

There was a memorandum in evidence that recorded the fact that Lew Krulwich was responsible for the time-recording or billing deficiencies that Fridley had attributed to me. Doug asked Don about the memorandum.

Speaking of the Admissions Committee, Don said, "We accepted Lew Krulwich's comments with respect to the matter." When Doug asked Don to confirm that Fridley's remarks were discounted by the committee, Don was tentative, "I don't know that his comments were discounted. . . . I think, at least in my mind, there still was an underlying feeling perhaps that since he was the partner responsible for the work that he was assuming the responsibility for that particular matter."

Doug prepared to ask Don questions about comments made about some of the men who became partners. The forms and paperwork that recorded the comments were all coded. The names had been marked out with a black Magic Marker.

A code in the margin identified the individual whose name could be found only on a single master list. The master list cross-referenced codes to names of people.

Doug had trouble when he originally tried to analyze the information. He expected that it would be hard to avoid confusion during the cross-examination.

He explained the cross-referencing scheme to Judge Gesell, "Your Honor, for the record, this, as a lot of documents in this case, was coded. The codes identifying who the candidates are are set forth in plaintiff's Exhibit 27."

Doug asked Don about Code 39 [Ernest Pushaver] who became a partner even though he suffered from "lack of maturity, wise guy attitude, headstrong, abrasive, cocky."

Judge Gesell interrupted with, "What number is Hopkins?" Don answered, "MO-12." The judge's humor surfaced again, "It all sounds like CIA agents, MO-12."

Without benefit of a question, Don commented, "which is the last of the MCS candidates on the page. . . . With respect to the MCS candidates Ann Hopkins . . . was the lowest-ranked candidate of all the MCS candidates that year."

Doug instructed Don to find a quote [Jerbasi on Diana Wilson], "Moving into the materials themselves I'd like you to flip through to the short-form comments on Miss Wilson to the sixth page of the short-form comments.

"The comment by Mr. Gervasi which begins, 'I have a difficult time believing these women are partner candidates. I have never met a woman at PW who was capable of functioning on a middle manager level' and so forth."

Judge Gesell interrupted, "What do you draw out of that?" Before Don could say anything, Doug stated, "I wanted to ask a couple of questions, your Honor."

Doug asked matter-of-factly, "Do you know how many partners in Price Waterhouse have attitudes similar to Mr. Gervasi?"

"I haven't the foggiest idea. I will say this, that the Admissions Committee paid absolutely no attention to Gervasi's comments," Don said.

Doug continued, "Did anybody talk to him about it?"

Don dismissed the remark, "I don't even think we considered it worthy of discussing with him. Just simply from the point of view that we didn't think a comment like that was germane to the consideration of any candidate, and we totally discounted it and ignored it.

"He made the same comment with respect to a number of women, all the lady candidates in that year, as I recall, if I'm not mistaken, and we paid no attention to it."

Don acknowledged that PW had no "stated policy prohibiting discrimination on the basis of sex in the admissions process."

With the end of Don Ziegler's testimony came the end of the second day of the trial.

Trial 1

WEDNESDAY

Joe Connor starred in the remainder of the Price Waterhouse movie for the first hour of Wednesday morning. It was so boring I was unable to sit through it.

There is very little in the way of a script for the movie. Steve Tallent summed up the condition of the transcript, "Your Honor, I think the record should be clear . . . if we ever want a transcript for any purpose we'll have to make another. It is totally unacceptable."

Jim, therefore, asked to read a few salient remarks into the record, "Your Honor, . . . the notes that were referred to for some period of time during that deposition I showed [to] Mr. Connor, and he looked at pages 5133 and 5134 of plaintiff's Exhibit 20, which are those notes by Miss Mertson, and since it's only three lines I wonder if your Honor would let me read the entry on Ann Hopkins into the record because it's at the bottom of the page and it may not be clear."

He continued by reading the summary comments of the policy board, "'A. B. Hopkins was discussed by DRZ,' and I believe that's Donald R. Ziegler, 'JRJ,' and that's Mr. Jordan, and I don't know his first name, 'observed that she had done a good job on a proposal. However, even with a lot of talent she needs social grace. PBG,' who is Paul B. Goodstat, 'stated that he would counsel her and he intends to get her involved in a number of projects. JEC,' who is Mr. Connor, 'said he would speak to her as well as PBG. Board concluded to hold.'"

Wayne Schrader asked that Roger Marcellin, the Policy Board member who did the office visit in OGS be called as a witness. Roger explained the procedures for office visits and for his discussions with the partners in the Washington area.

Judge Gesell asked, "Did you talk to any staff?" When Roger responded negatively, the judge followed with another question, "Well, I'd like to know why not. It's all secondhand. It's all secondhand. You're not talking to any of the people involved. You're talking to people who heard gossip from somebody else, aren't you?"

Roger explained that was not normal procedure. Judge Gesell confirmed, "So you had no direct contact with the people she was supposed to have difficulty with."

Wayne asked Roger about the memorandum that he wrote to the Policy Board. It recommended that I be held at least a year. Judge Gesell read the memorandum as the questioning continued.

He looked up as he said, "Well, this memorandum doesn't say what interpersonal relations you're talking about. If I were to pick that up and look at it I wouldn't know whether you're talking about clients or you're talking about staff."

As Roger started to say something, Judge Gesell interrupted, "Now, as I gather in this case—at least from what I've heard, other partners, other of your partners, and from the clients themselves there was no such problem with the clients."

Roger said that the comments were about interrelations with staff and partners. "You're not interested in how someone gets along with clients?" the judge asked.

Roger commented, "There were strong representations made that she got along well with clients. I personally found it hard to believe that someone who had this many problems with partners and staff would not eventually have the same problems with clients."

The judge posed an alternative assumption, "Wouldn't it have been just as easy to believe that since she got along well with demanding clients that the staff was responsible for the difficulty and not the lady?"

I had worked for only two clients, but I had worked with far more partners and staff was Roger's response. Judge Gesell pursued it farther, "She went all over the world talking to clients and she's all over the world talking to your people, though they're in some other kind of a corporation. You didn't even find out what they thought of her when she went to Timbuctu, or wherever it was?"

The judge returned his thoughts to the memorandum, "But reading this memo you wouldn't know where her problems were, would you?"

"I would have no doubt that Tom Beyer would be the one that would have to talk with her. He knew exactly what her problems were," Roger answered.

Jim did the cross-examination. He asked Roger to interpret the comments he had written about the office visit.

Referring to one of the partners [Haller] in OGS, Jim asked, "Was the thing you remembered most about your interview with him that he said that she brought her kids into the office?" It was one of three things that Roger remembered.

Jim asked Roger to explain his abbreviated comment attributed to Lew Krulwich. The comment read "Many male partners are worse than Ann, (Language and tough personality)."

Roger explained why he had raised the question of profanity: "Several other partners that I spoke with had brought up the use of profanity so that was one of the negatives that I was putting in front of the partners when I brought it up to Krulwich. That was intended on his part to explain away the profanity issue—and saying, I think, people are just focusing on that because it's a lady using foul language. She's no worse than any of the male partners."

Although he was unable to remember the conversation with Lew, Roger conjectured, "I probably said something like how bad a problem is it? Is she a dirty mouth? And he said, no, I don't think so. She doesn't use any worse language than any of the men do.

"Oh, yes," Roger said when Jim asked him if any male dirty mouths ever became partners.

Roger confirmed that Tim Coffey had changed his recommendation from hold to admit. He could not recall if Epelbaum changed his original recommendation from admit to hold.

Roger, however, was responsible for the report to the Policy Board, and that report recorded three admits and two holds. Because we knew that Tom, Tim, and Lew recommended admit, Doug, Jim and I concluded that Epelbaum must have changed his mind.

A break followed Roger Marcellin's testimony. I ran into Tim Coffey in the hall outside Judge Gesell's courtroom. He had changed little in the two or three years since I last saw him. I was glad to see him.

We shook hands. He drawled a greeting in his dramatic southern accent. "Sorry to see you under these circumstances," I said.

Under Wayne's direct examination Tim told the St. Louis story, pretty much the way I would have told it. He discounted the difficulty of the job, but then he was away for most of the effort.

I had no reason to cringe at anything Tim said. Not until almost the end of cross-examination when Doug asked, "Obviously I am pleased that you came down on the right side, but I am trying to see whether anything other than that certainty that she was very good at getting government business had been resolved in your mind to the point where you could say it's not any longer a hold, in my judgment it's a yes.

"Where had you had any change in your feelings about her as a person, as a person who could work with and supervise people?"

I had never seen Tim angry and I would prefer never to see him angry again. The question infuriated him. He reacted, out of control, "Well, when you said 'right side' I stopped listening to you. . . . It's hard for me to react to whatever you said beyond that. . . . It can be read back to me."

Doug asked another question. Tim calmed down and talked positively about how he changed his recommendation from hold to admit after the orals. I was embarrassed that we had so annoyed him.

The morning ended with Tim's testimony. After lunch, when the trial resumed, St. Louis was still the topic of testimony.

Kathy Ireland conducted the direct examination of Barrett Boehm. Barry as he was known, had worked on the proposal in St. Louis. He testified that the people in St. Louis had not liked working for me.

As the last question of her direct examination, Kathy asked Barry if he would want to work with me again. "Socially Ann and I are very good friends and we left the project very amicably. I think I would prefer not to. . . ."

As the first question in the cross-examination, Doug asked "Mr. Boehm, you did get to become good friends with Ann Hopkins, didn't you?" Barry replied, "Well, I wouldn't call it good friends."

He stuck with the party line, but he also acknowledged that I helped him out. When Doug asked him about it he said, "My father-in-law's ladder plant had been flooded several years ago and he was in an area that didn't qualify for federal government flood insurance and all of his inventory was damaged. . . . She gave me some very good information."

Price Waterhouse asked that Don Epelbaum be called to the stand. Under Steve Tallent's direct examination, Dandy Don did a marvelous job for Price Waterhouse. He was careful, articulate, well prepared, and awful.

Don advised me to "put a little sugar on your tongue" prior to my going to St. Louis. He testified that I failed to take his advice. "I think in November . . . she came back and told me that my advice was stupid. She had gotten better advice from somebody else and my advice was stupid."

Many people who originally worked for me transferred to Don when he became the partner on the State Department FMS job. Don testified about their reaction to me:

> These individuals indicated that in one case Ann had written on a flow chart "this individual is an FU," in the upper-right corner of the document. Do I need to describe what that means? Another individual had problems with, again, the nature in which she was treated by Ann.

> I had people from St. Louis after the FMHA job began over to my house and they talked about the turmoil that existed during the proposal process and in St. Louis and how they never wanted to work again with Ann. When Roger Marcellin came in November to interview me I made it clear to him that my strength of conviction for Ann had wavered and that in my opinion I was a hold.

Don testified about how I described my meeting with Joe Connor to him:

> She went on to tell me that Joe went through all of the partners who voted against her and editorialized the comments like Norm Statland, Norm Statland votes against everybody. John Fridley. Who is John Fridley? I don't even know who he is. Those are the kinds of comments that she made.

> Joe Connor used his chits up to admit Schick, Fred Schick and Henry Lum the last year and next year he's going to use his chit to get me admitted. Well, I had met Joe Connor. I had met with him on a number of occasions and I had listened to him talk about the bond between partners and the special relationship that partners have and I just could not believe that Joe Connor would speak that way about his partners to a senior manager and I could think of no other reason, and her tone also added to that, no other reason that she was going to tell me this story other than to try and intimidate me and I reacted very negatively to that.

Every meeting I ever had with Don was characterized negatively. It was brilliantly done—and devastating. Fortunately it ended, and with the end of Don's testimony PW rested its case.

Karen Nold was the first witness called on rebuttal. She had guts. The pressure on her must have been intense over the last four or five months while she was considered for the partnership. She became a partner the month after the trial. The decision was probably made by the time she testified, but it was not announced until April.

Karen testified that we were friends, that I cared about people who worked for me, that she learned from me, that she would work for me if I were a partner. She testified that I treated her like a human being.

In every brief PW ever wrote, she was always quoted, with negative connotation, for her answer, "Yes, I think she has a controversial style." She gave that answer in response to a question that Steve Tallent raised on cross-examination. He asked, "Would it be fair to say that, to your knowledge, as a senior manager that Miss Hopkins had a controversial style, management style."

On rebuttal, Sandy Kinsey made comments similar to those Karen had made. She responded differently to the style question. Sandy said, "I don't believe that it was controversial in the context of our engagement."

In every brief PW ever wrote, she was always quoted, with negative connotation, for her statement under cross-examination, "it requires a lot of diplomacy, patience and guts" to work with me. Sandy never considered the statement to be a derogatory remark.

When Judge Gesell asked, "What's your feeling about this outfit? Does a woman get a fair shake?" Sandy responded, "I think I have, your Honor."

Testimony for the day ended with Harry Barschdorf. Every statement Harry made about me was positive. He was not cross-examined. Harry is never quoted.

Judge Gesell asked Doug to explain the program for the next day. Doug said he planned to call two experts who would testify on rebuttal. The first, he said was a psychologist. The judge understood the second, "The other is just a statistical expert." He asked Doug to explain the planned testimony of the psychologist.

For a man who six months ago probably could not have defined the term stereotyping, I thought he responded beautifully:

> Dr. Fiske would testify, first of all, that there is the general phenomenon known in her field, social psychology, of stereotyping, that there's been a lot of research on it for the last fifty or sixty years, that there's a consensus in the profession about it. That there are certain antecedent conditions which generally give rise to situations in which stereotyping might occur. And that there's been a fair amount of research as to what those conditions are. That

it's also possible to observe certain indicators to see whether or not it is occurring, so she would give that background first, documented in the literature.

Second, she has been supplied with a lot of materials in this case, long- and short-form comments, that type of thing. Deposition extracts. And I believe that she will testify that based on her opinion both the antecedent conditions are satisfied for stereotyping on the basis of sex and that based on her analysis and her review of the materials she believes that this type of sex stereotyping was occurring, did occur at the time Ann Hopkins was being evaluated for partnership.

It would seem to us that if she's right about that, that if indeed there were a number of men who were reacting negatively to Ann Hopkins for the reasons she suggested, that they didn't really want to deal with an aggressive, domineering woman, that if that indeed is true that it's clear in the context of the Price Waterhouse partnership decision that just a few individuals who are strongly opposed can effectively block a partnership, partnership candidacy. And we think that's what happened here and we think it's based on those reasons.

Doug's grammar may have been less than perfect, but I thought he gave a remarkably clear summary in response to a random question at the end of a long day.

The judge warned Doug and Jim that they had some legal work to do. First, he said, "You've got to identify who you say are the discriminating officials. You haven't done it. . . . If you're laying the finger on Mr. Epelbaum, I suppose you are, and who else, I don't know that. . . . If you feel Mr. Connor is a sexual stereotyper you've got to tell me so. . . ."

Then he asked both sets of attorneys to help him interpret *Hishon v. King and Spalding:* "I'm trying to find out what the Supreme Court is talking about and I want to convey to you in a sense of wanting to assist you, not in a sense of wanting to create obstacles in your way, and I need the help from the other side as well."

The judge considered *Hopkins v. Price Waterhouse* to be a possible precedent for future cases. "I can't look at this case as just a case. I've got to think of whatever standard or whatever rule or whatever result I get. It has to have—I have to think of how it is going to affect comparable situations, how is it going to be consistent or inconsistent with the law, perhaps with the Constitution, which encourages freedom of association.

"I have to think about a lot of things and that's what I need. A lot of help." Each request for "help" meant that Doug would more than likely have to write a brief on the issue.

Judge Gesell seemed to have regard for the attorneys. He appreciated the way they had handled matters so far. "I think you tried the case that way . . . as, for lack of a better word, a nonsmearing effort, and I think the defendant has handled the case the same way."

He was professionally pleased to have what he perceived as a tidy legal issue:

> It presents a unique case, hopefully to develop some standards and of course you have your client's interest in mind, but I need, in addition, as much help as I can get and the more I get into the case the more I feel the need for help and I hope I'm conveying a message to you . . . and . . . also to able counsel on the other side because this looks like it may be the first case that comes along in this area after the Supreme Court that isn't so tainted with obvious excrescences that shouldn't be tolerated by a civilized person anyhow, any way. But I want to try at least to make the Court of Appeals understand what the problem is.

Doug told the judge that the attorneys had agreed to write briefs on the issues after the trial, "You had suggested yesterday afternoon that this would be a good case for post-trial briefing. . . . We talked afterwards and agreed with that whole-heartedly for the reason you expressed because it will provide us an opportunity to bring that up."

I was in a foul frame of mind when I got home at the end of the day. Carol Supplee, the downhill neighbor, was washing her car when I pulled into the driveway. I brushed off her greeting with a preemptory reply as I headed straight for the front gate and the door beyond it. Thomas Peter was right behind me. He could handle it.

On the few occasions that Carol and I had talked, she seemed like an okay person. Her husband prevented us from becoming better acquainted. He was an arrogant, condescending, uptight pill. It was no loss, I had thought, when he walked out on her several months ago.

"How are things with Ann? She seems upset," Carol asked.

"As well as they could be when you have to sit through a trial while everyone says what a toad you are," Thomas Peter responded.

Doug had decided to call the statistician to testify even though the statistics were legally useless. The expert had analyzed at least ten years of data in great volumes, only to discover that any conclusion he tried to draw was not statistically significant.

The number of women at the partner level, even the number of partner candidates, was proportionately tiny compared to the number of men. The data, however, were statistically inconclusive.

Trial 1

THURSDAY

First thing on Thursday morning, my expert statistician was called to the stand. He testified for an hour or two. Stacks of paper were introduced into evidence.

My impression of the testimony was the same as Judge Gesell's when he said, "Well its unintelligible to me. If you want me to consider it, I have to know what it is. It doesn't make any sense at all. It looks like gibberish.

"I am sure it is important in terms of analyzing something, but what is its evidentiary value is what I am getting at?"

Susan Fiske, she gave as her name. She earned her undergraduate degree from Harvard just before I joined Touche. She earned her Ph.D. there in 1978, about the time I joined Price Waterhouse. One of Doug's first questions was to ask her to explain her expertise in the field of stereotypes.

"What did you call the field so I understand it?" the judge asked.

Steve Tallent objected, "Your Honor, I have grave doubts as to whether this is proper rebuttal."

Judge Gesell failed to share Steve's doubts. The judge explained, "I know you have made that position clear before. It seemed to me that if one assumes, as I do at this stage, that a prima facie case was shown, . . . and that what has happened is that you have come forward with an explanation and that the question now before me is the burden of the plaintiff to show that your explanation is pretextual, it would seem to me entirely appropriate at this stage to examine your defense in light of the expert testimony of this witness."

Steve caved in. "I have no objection to the expertise of the witness," he said.

Doug had predicted he would have a tough time with his direct examination of Susan Fiske. Her area of expertise encompassed its own vocabulary. He would have to handle the examination in some way that would ensure that Judge Gesell understood her.

Even if the judge understood what Susan said, he might not accept her conclusion. And if he accepted her conclusion, he might not accept Doug's theory of the case—that if stereotyping is the basis for an employment decision, the decision is a violation of Title VII. But it was essential, in any case, that the judge first understand Susan's testimony.

If the judge asked me to define "consultant," I wondered how he would react to Susan Fiske's jargon. Not far into Doug's direct examination, we all found out.

Judge Gesell frowned as he said, "You are not telling me anything. You have got to talk to a layman, ma'am. You have got to talk to a layman. You are not talking to one of your colleagues and so I have got to understand what you are saying, you understand."

Susan responded with a pleasantly feisty, "Can I try again on that one?"

Judge Gesell tried a top-down approach. He turned to Doug and asked, "Why doesn't she give me her opinion? And then tell me what she bases it on," he suggested. He was trying hard when he continued, "If we did that then I think I would have a better understanding of where you are getting."

Susan stated her professional opinion: "I am confident that stereotyping played a role in the decision about Ann Hopkins," she stated.

That was not specific enough for the judge. He asked, "Well, now, what kind of a role and how confident? Are you able to say that you are confident within a reasonable degree of certainty in your discipline?"

In addition, he wanted to know, "What part? I don't know how you would express it in your discipline percentage-wise or how you would express it, but minor, major, middle?"

Susan was more specific when she said, "Well, in lay language I would say it played a major determining role."

Judge Gesell pushed for absolute specificity. He extended her opinion into a question, "A major determining role, with reasonable certainty?" That was her opinion she said.

Susan commented on antecedent conditions, conditions that foster sex role stereotyping. She defined the first condition, rarity. "If a person is a part of an unusual category they are more likely to be perceived in terms of that category."

She explained the context in which I was part of an unusual category. "Ann Hopkins was one of eighty-eight people being proposed for partner at that time. She was the only woman, which makes it extremely likely that she would be perceived in terms of her gender. . . . The very . . . small number of female partners at Price Waterhouse . . . would tend to make being female extremely salient in that setting."

Susan described stereotypes:

> The overall stereotype for feminine behavior is to be socially concerned and understanding, soft and tender, and the overall stereotype for a man, all other things being equal, is that they will be competitive, ambitious, aggressive, independent, and active.
>
> So if a woman behaves in a way that is, in quotes, masculine, if she behaves in a competitive, ambitious, aggressive, independent and active way, . . . she is often likely to be perceived as being unfeminine on the social dimension.

She described ambiguity as a second antecedent condition. "The more ambiguous the criteria and the more ambiguous the information the more room there is for selective perception and I am an expert in selective perception."

Susan commented on the nature of the partner candidate evaluation criteria:

> Some of the task-related criteria are not ambiguous, they talk about the amount of money one brings to the organization for example. That is [a] very objective criterion.
>
> If you talk on the other hand about people's personality traits or "having an excellent reputation" or "outstanding attributes" or comparing individuals, I would submit that those are rather vague criteria.

Susan refined her definition. "Categorical thinking, which leads to stereotyping, is trying to maximize the differences between two groups of people, say, males and females, and minimizing the difference within a particular group. So in other words, advising a woman to behave more like a woman and less like a man is a way for people to reinforce their categories."

Susan discussed male-female-neutral stereotypic dimensions:

There is a social dimension that has typically [been] deemed to be the province of women and a task dimension that typically seems to be the province of men.

Given that the majority of the comments regarding Miss Hopkins were related to her social skills or perceived lack of social skills but they were not related to irrelevant dimensions like stereotypically neutral dimensions like honesty and integrity. Honesty and integrity are not part of either the male or female sexual stereotype so the focus of the comments were on the kinds of personal traits that are related to sex role stereotyping.

She discussed selective perception and its impact on me:

There seems to me to be a very interesting case of selective perception going on here. When I looked at the ways the two different groups of people described the very same behavior, it was striking to me that her supporters described her behavior as, on the long and short forms, outspoken, sells her own ability, independent, courage [of] her convictions, stamina. All attributes you would think of as positive.

Her detractors or the people who voted hold or insufficient or no on her described that very same behavior as overbearing and arrogant and abrasive and running over people, so to me that is a warning that there is selective perception going on. . . . The very same behavior—behavior is ambiguous enough that it can be perceived in more than one way. . . . And given that her nonsupporters were perceiving this sex role incongruent behavior in negative ways, behavior that in a man would be—typically might be considered to be more adaptive because it is congruent with being a manager to be ambitious and aggressive and so on.

She concluded with, "It fits extremely well with the literature that I know [that] says there is a penalty for behaving in sex role incongruent ways and people who do that are disliked."

Susan said that intensity of negative remarks is an indicator of stereotyping:

There are some other indicators, . . . the intensity of the negative reaction. The literature on stereotyping of people who are rare in organizations indicates that the negativity of the response becomes disproportionately negative.

That somebody who is being seen in terms of a stereotype will be seen in intensely negative ways and it seemed to me that some of the comments by the nonsupporters were rather remarkably negative. Disliked by virtually everybody she knows. But that clearly wasn't true, because there were other staff people who were saying positive things. She is very tough-minded and no nonsense and I can get along with her.

In summary she stated, "the nonsupporters were seeing her in a real black-and-white kind of light and that is a consistent indicator of stereotyping, especially in these rarity type of cases."

Just before lunch Judge Gesell asked, "So this was all decided ahead of time and they just went [on] to confirm it is what you think happened?"

Susan deserved better than a lunch in the courthouse cafeteria. That, however, was all that time permitted.

After lunch, Doug's direct examination of Susan ended on the subject of how hierarchy and stereotypes are related. "Some of the oldest research in stereotyping indicates that people who are very concerned with hierarchy, who are either concerned that other people—especially concerned that other people be deferential to them are also extremely deferential to people above them in the hierarchy, are especially likely to be stereotypers, to be people who engage in stereotyping."

Steve Tallent cross-examined Susan. In response to his questions, Susan said she spent about twenty hours preparing for testimony. She told him that she reviewed all the paperwork on me and spent two or three hours looking through the paperwork on male candidates. She stated that she and I first met that day.

In her testimony Susan discussed what she referred to as a double bind—a conflict between the assertiveness and aggressiveness required to get the job done and the image required to fit the female stereotype. She said that the effect of this double bind might be reduced in an organization that included a lot of women. As part of that discussion, she said, "What I would tell her is to work in a department that has a substantial number of women in it."

I am sure that Doug wished she had made her point differently. The statement later became a humorous opportunity for interchange between the judge and Steve, with Susan in the middle.

First, Judge Gesell commented, "You understand that if this organization that we have in front of me now said, well, there [are] some stereotypes around here so all the women will have to work together, I would have more lawsuits."

Susan tried to make her original point a little differently, "If you have a critical mass of women in a particular department and the research literature indicates above 15 or 20 percent at a particular level then these [stereotypical] effects are really undercut quite a lot."

Before she finished her thought, Steve chimed in with, "You don't have many lawyers researching this area do you?" Under the circumstances, it was a very funny exchange.

Steve asked on what Susan based her opinion. "I believe that it is based on the same evidence that the Admissions Committee used."

He started on a different tack when he asked in a mildly sarcastic tone, "Are there abrasive women? Are there mean women? Are there arrogant women? Women who are just plain rude?

"Now, if I run across one of these women and I comment that she is just plain rude, what must I do to ensure that my own reactions are not springing from some deep-seated stereotype that I am carrying around in my bosom?"

With no hesitation, Susan answered right back, "Well, if you say she is the rudest person you ever met you should pay attention to what she said because she is unlikely the rudest person you ever met. When people say extreme statements like that, they should be re-examining the basis for those statements."

Steve asked about Susan's review of the forms for some of the men: "Did you sample that in any scientific way that I can take an empirical number to see if you had a scientific basis for that?"

No and she didn't count them either, she said. She used no empirical data base and no statistics. She observed, however, "I am an expert in observing behavior and at drawing conclusions from written documents."

Furthermore, she stated, "You don't need to have a sample in this particular case because I have the entire population of comments that were made about her."

Steve seemed mildly sarcastic again when he asked, "Some of these folks describe Miss Hopkins as . . . overbearing, arrogant, self-centered, abrasive, thinks she knows more than anyone in the universe, and potentially dangerous. Would you think it would be somehow a stereotypical decision to exclude such a person from the partnership, if that was in fact true?"

She certainly scored a point with me when she answered, "I am not qualified to say whether or not it is true."

Judge Gesell actually asked far more difficult questions than did Steve. At one point he asked about the situation Tom Beyer had described in earlier testimony. "He had a group of managers in the company talking about how the job was going, women, new managers, including this plaintiff. He was asking for suggestions on how they ought to proceed. And another woman spoke up and she was told by Miss Hopkins to keep still. It wasn't relevant. So he said, look, we are all trying to work on this. You shouldn't be so assertive. A stereotype?" he asked.

"I would suggest that the same behavior coming from a man would be less likely to be focused on as much of a problem," she responded.

The judge seemed angry when he said, "Well, he probably would have fired a man. I agree with that. If a man had done it, he probably would fire him but other than that I don't understand what you are talking about." Susan must have been relieved when we took a break shortly after that one.

Doug had a few questions on redirect examination. He asked what an organization could do to reduce the likelihood of stereotyping. She explained. "It is clear that the organizational environment can discourage people from stereotyping by creating an incentive situation not to do that."

Having and enforcing a policy helps she said.

> To me the fact that there was no policy with regard to sex suggests that the organization was not making an effort to undercut sexual stereotyping. That Mr. Gervasi, who made the rather extreme comment about the women who were coming up, apparently people ignored him, but the fact that he was able to make that almost verbatim same comment two years running and nobody said to him, look that is really not an appropriate thing to say in this context, suggest[s] to me that the organization is not discouraging people from stereotyping.

Under recross-examination, Steve asked what sounded to me like a snide question, "The plaintiff suggested to you that this might be an occasion where your expertise might be used to find some stereotyping, is that correct?"

Susan answered directly and succinctly, "Yes, that has been suggested to me before too and I have declined to participate." Susan only testifies out of conviction. By profession, she is an academician.

The day ended on a dull note: PW's opposing expert statistician. Jim and Doug had told me on a number of occasions that Judge Gesell "glazes over" when confronted with statisticians, especially those that testify about statistically insignificant numbers.

The judge was unimpressed by my statistician and he was unimpressed by PW's statistician. I found it hard to blame him.

Trial 1

Jim and Doug believed that Judge Gesell had been impressed with Don Epelbaum and his testimony. They decided to put me on the stand as a rebuttal witness in hopes of leaving the judge with a more positive impression.

Don had done a spectacular job. I had no notes from any of the meetings. I certainly never remembered calling him or his advice stupid. "Stupid" and "chits" are words I never use. Furthermore, although my presence to some people may be intimidating, I never made a conscious effort to intimidate anyone.

When Steve Tallent and Judge Gesell pinned me down on the "stupid" remark and asked me how I knew I did not make it, I remembered the time frame that Don had tagged to the remark. I testified that I was out of town around that time frame.

Initially, I could not understand why Judge Gesell was so angry at the end of the trial. What I failed to realize was that in trying to offset the negative impression that Don left, I effectively called him a liar. Apparently most Title VII cases involve opposing sides calling each other liars.

Judge Gesell was really angry. What began as an interesting legal problem involving stereotyping became in the final minutes a garden-variety Title VII case.

He explained his annoyance.

240

Somewhat to my regret the whole thrust of this case changed today from what I understood it to be and I have therefore no suggestion to make to you as to how we ought to go. I had obviously naively assumed for the first time I had a case where the parties weren't calling each other liars. Now I've got that and so I'm back in the old familiar discrimination case which has nothing to do with most of the issues we've litigated.

. . . We're now calling people liars. We've got questions of credibility. We have a case that is in many ways a garden-variety case. I was disappointed, but that's plaintiff's choice.

I think it's quite changed. You've got your discriminatory official now and you've called him a liar. That's what we are and I didn't think that's what we were—I didn't think that was what we were trying and I had hoped for once I wouldn't have to have to deal with it, but we have it now and I'm going to have to deal with it.

I was very impressed with the fact that there was none of that on the defendant's side. There was an obvious clear desire on the part of the defendant to have the merits of their system and their approach to those things looked at in terms of running this partnership and in terms of meeting their responsibilities.

Now it's all gone. And I don't have to reach all these cosmic problems if I accept [your witness's] testimony, so we have quite a different case.

"I made a mistake," I thought. I got one year confused with another. "What do we do about errors?" I asked Jim, as I walked out of Judge Gesell's courtroom through the door that Jim politely held open for me.

"If it's material, we'll have to amend the record," he said absently. We were both dejected as we walked across the hall toward the door that led to the escalator. The wrath of Gesell I experienced that afternoon had to be worse than the wrath of God to which I had never, to my knowledge, been subjected. I should have asked what it meant to be "legally" material.

Jim preceded me on the escalator going down. Facing me, with his back to the bottom, he said, "You've seen our last bill. We'll never send you another one." He turned, stepped off the escalator and ambled slowly toward the main entrance to the courthouse as I trailed along behind, speechless.

At that time, the price of the litigation was $57,686.83. Out doors at last, the brisk March air sent an anxious chill down my spine. I forgot about mistakes and legal materiality. It was over. The outlook was less than promising, but the trial was over.

I knew there would be no results before fall. Based on what Jim and Doug told me, the legal paper process would take most of the summer. The typed transcript of the trial was scheduled for delivery in April. In May my proposed "Findings of Fact"—the facts as seen from my legal point of view—would be submitted. Shortly thereafter my legal arguments in the form of a post-trial brief were due.

PW would counter my proposed facts with theirs and respond to my brief with a brief in reply. The judge would ask both sides to identify any proposed "facts" that they had in common. Each step in the sequential process would take a couple of weeks.

It was the end of May before the judge had all the paper required to make a decision. If stacked, it would have been a pile four or five feet high. We guessed that the ruling would be out in July or September. Nothing happens in August. Our best guess was September. We waited.

Dyslexia

When I got back to work after the trial, all Toni knew was what Roger had told her about his testimony and what she read in the *Washington Post* on March 29. To fill in the details, I joined her for a lunch meeting that she had already scheduled with Gilda Feldman. Toni and Gilda, who had more than a passing interest in the litigation, had been friends for years. Gilda was Roger's wife and an attorney who worked in consular affairs at State. Over time, the three of us became a regular trio at lunch.

The FNPay contractor, for which Toni was responsible, got off to a slow start. Several months were required to get a full complement of appropriate people assigned to the project. Once assigned, the people had to learn all about the international payroll operations of State. The FNPay team used the original FMS contract as a model for plans to visit a large number of posts overseas.

I objected. Although I had been to twenty or thirty posts, I believed the incremental benefit of fieldwork decreased dramatically after visits to the first few posts. For whatever reasons, I was overruled. Toni's delegate and the team began developing a plan that included extensive fieldwork. As they formulated travel plans, I developed specifications for the work products to be produced in the field.

Spring turned into early summer as the FNPay people made ready to leave the country. My work slacked off a little, just in time for the first of the activities that mark the beginning of summer—the Girl Scout camping trip.

I admired the Girl Scout troop leader, Merrily Hardisty. Although she had never been a Girl Scout or a camping enthusiast, she founded the scouting program at the school that Tela, Gilbert, and Peter attended. She spent hundreds of hours going through Girl Scout training programs, including those required for certifications of competence in first aid and troop camping, certifications required before a troop could use Girl Scout facilities. Throughout elementary school, Tela benefited from the time that Merrily committed. Tela loved the Girl Scout program, especially camping.

I was unwilling to devote regularly scheduled or evening hours to scouting, but I had considerable camping experience and liked camping, so I volunteered to serve as Merrily's assistant on outdoor trips. To everyone's benefit, Thomas Peter, Gilbert, and Peter usually came along, the boys as ex officio scouts and Thomas Peter in the role of singing minstrel.

Merrily planned the events in excruciating detail, scheduled the sites, bought the food and supplies, rented the equipment from the Girl Scouts, and delivered everything to the camping area. She had everyone's task assignments, sometimes in fifteen-minute intervals, neatly printed by hand on index cards. She was then prepared to set up camp, build the fires, cook the meals, clean up, and ensure that twenty scouts had a wonderful time. I was afraid that Merrily would drop from exhaustion before the camping started.

My nature prevented me from managing the camping activities the way Merrily seemed inclined to manage them. My first official act as chairman in charge of the great outdoors was to enlist the management talents of the mothers of my daughter's two best friends. The first of these was Vera Schneider, a middle manager at IBM. The second was Susan Riley, a housing lobbyist. We became a management committee. We established a few objectives: bring everyone back alive and without major injury; teach the scouts the value of independence and teamwork; build self-confidence.

"Let the girls handle it," we told Merrily when she tried to do some chore. We had delegated responsibility for almost everything to the scouts. We taught them how to do what was necessary, but we did nothing for them. They quickly learned the relationship between building fires and eating dinner. They developed great enthusiasm for cleaning up when we told them that they could sing around the campfire or go to sleep only after the grounds passed inspection.

The first day was rough. Scouts ate food that ranged from raw to burned. Only the adults sang around the campfire. We had to do three inspections before everything passed. It was after midnight when everyone finally went to bed. Thereafter, the scouts, including Gilbert and Peter, handled the camping activities much more efficiently. In the process they developed a sense of confidence, competence, and independence.

With the chores out of the way, the children could enjoy themselves in the outdoors. Peter discovered a luna moth in transition from chrysalis to adult. For four hours, he lay close to motionless on the ground with his chin tucked in his hands, propped on his elbows, eyes fixed on the struggling insect. At intermittent intervals, the other scouts quietly joined him to check on progress, but none of them had his patience with or interest in the entire process. As the audience changed around him, he gave a continuous, soft-spoken lecture on entomology.

Merrily took groups out to make plaster casts of animal tracks, abundant in one of the marshy areas on the grounds. We other adults spent much of the time sitting around the fire circle. Thomas Peter played the guitar and orchestrated songfests. Susan applied Band-Aids and other first aid. Vera and I named the plants and insects that individual scouts dragged in for identification: poison ivy, Queen Anne's lace, toads and frogs in a range of sizes.

At one point I carefully described, to a rapt audience, all of the unique characteristics of a particular variety of tick I had found. "Do ticks fly?" asked Vera skeptically as the insect flew off the palm of my hand. "No," I said. Everyone had a good laugh at my expense. Susan, who grew up in Chicago, spent ten years in a convent, and could barely differentiate a tick from a tiger, still enjoys reminding me of that confrontation with my own error. The "flying tick" experience taught me to confirm all identifications by asking Peter or using a bug book before issuing a definitive pronouncement.

Hollins' graduation, and with it my twentieth reunion, followed shortly after camping. I never missed a reunion. Thomas Peter and the children always attended. They enjoyed being out in the country. The children, from an early age, had the run of the campus. I never had any concern for their well-being. They enjoyed the freedom and had, over the years, made friends with the children of some of my classmates.

A little before the reunion, the boys wandered into the kitchen looking for me. Gilbert had a mischievous expression on his face. "May I have a snake for my birthday?" Peter asked as Gilbert stood silently by, watching for my reaction. I assumed they had visited the snake house at the National Zoo, one of their more popular haunts around the neighborhood.

"I had better answer that question carefully," I said to myself. I remembered an occasion on which Peter and I were driving out Connecticut Avenue running errands one Saturday. He was eighteen months old when he asked, "Mom, do dinosaurs eat babies?" Thinking fast, I responded, "No, babies make too much noise when they holler." For about two blocks, he sat silently and contemplated the seat belt that held him in place. Then he chirped in with, "What about sleeping babies?"

I wanted to address the snake question properly so that I could close the issue without raising more, and more difficult, questions. "You may have a snake only when you can demonstrate to me that you know enough to be a responsible pet owner." Then I explained that he had to know all about snakes: how to house them, what they ate, where to get the food, and how to feed them. He also had to have a budget for their care and feeding and a plan to earn the money required by the budget. There were no more questions.

After the reunion, we traded the mountains of Virginia for the mountains of Vermont. Thomas Peter and I took the children to survey the fifty or sixty acres of woodland that Mom and Gil had bought. Gilbert and Peter happily traipsed around behind Gil as he showed them the sugar maple trees and the places where the porcupines hid.

He arranged for the children to have a private tour of the adjoining dairy farm. The cows' plopping splattered manure all over the curious children as they peered through the guard rails to watch the milking. On the way back to the house from the farm, the children wrote their names on a huge, half-moon-shaped fungus that had fallen off one of the dead trees. When they stomped up the back stairs to shed their stinky clothes on the porch, someone proudly presented me with the fungus, which I ignored until they gleefully pattered off to play in the bathtubs.

"You better do something about this," Gil said to me pointing to something on the surface of the fungus. Peter's name was spelled with only one "e" and most of the letters were reversed. In that single instant I understood why Peter showed little interest in looking at the pages of the books that Thomas Peter and I read to him and why he spent an extra year in the four-year-old's nursery class at school. It was not because he was uninterested in reading or, as the school had said, because he had small motor development problems that made it difficult for him to "color within the lines." It was because Peter was dyslexic—unlike Tela and Gilbert who had learned to read long before they reached Peter's age, Peter was unable to read. Furthermore, he was unlikely to learn to read without serious intervention in his learning process.

On our return to Washington, I was astounded to discover how much Peter knew about snakes. He named half a dozen varieties that were commonly kept as household pets, from pythons and boa constrictors on one end of the size spectrum to garter snakes on the other. The bigger snakes would eat live mice, which, so he told me, were conveniently available from the local pet store. Smaller snakes ate similarly available goldfish. I mentally flushed the price he quoted for the mice—there would be no mouse-eating serpents in my house. Goldfish, he said, cost about seven cents each. A garter snake could be expected to consume an average of two or maybe three fish per week. He could pay for everything with his allowance.

He presented me with lists of information, which he could recite but not read. "Now may I have a snake for my birthday?" he asked. He would prefer a boa constrictor.

I had been taken. The two boys must have conspired against me. Upon further questioning, I determined that Peter had endeared himself to the herpetologist at the zoo, from whom he obtained the printed lists. Gilbert read the material to Peter who memorized it as fast as he heard it.

Peter got a garter snake for his birthday. We named him Oscar. Oscar was housed in the kitchen in a terrarium with a removable screen lid. His food supply circled in the water-filled, ceramic dog food bowl in the center of the terrarium.

During the work weeks between trips I reviewed the material coming in from the FNPay team, which was with the delegate somewhere overseas. The products consistently failed to meet the specifications that I had prepared and that Toni had approved. I told Toni there was trouble brewing—I had no confidence that appropriate work was being done. From meeting to meeting, she conveyed growing irritation with her delegate who was supposed to be managing the contractor. The delegate failed to report in. Toni became concerned that she was losing control of the contract.

"We're going to Paris next week," Toni said. Something was very wrong—Toni rarely traveled anywhere. It was a little before eight in the morning when I walked into her office, unopened coffee container in one hand, briefcase in the other. She was almost finished with her tea. Her empty in-basket and the altitude of the neat stack in her out-basket told me that she had been at work for quite a while. Her tone of voice when she verbally pounced on me told me she was very angry.

"What on earth is wrong?" I asked as I tossed my briefcase on a chair, seated myself on her sofa, and opened my coffee. Toni explained that the delegate was somewhere in Africa and planning to go to Paris. Word had drifted back that the delegate wanted to consider using the foreign national payroll system installed in Paris as the basis for the worldwide FNPay. That approach had been considered and rejected months ago. It should have been a dead issue. Furthermore, even with the entire diplomatic telecommunication system at her disposal, Toni had been unable to make contact with the delegate, to whom she had not spoken in weeks.

I listened as she expressed her concerns that the project was out of control and headed in the wrong technical direction. Her major fear, however, was that the FNPay team would return without having collected appropriate information and would then have to go back overseas. The reason she was going to Paris was to make sure that the team had what it needed before it returned to the States.

Expounding on the basis for her anger and frustration seemed to have a calming effect. Her normally unflappable, cheerful disposition returned. "Can you go to Paris?" she asked tentatively. When I explained that my passport had expired she chided me with, "We issue them across the river at Main State."

Toni had a cable sent to Paris. It read simply, "Please arrange accommodations for Mrs. Gibbons," and specified the dates late in July. It offered no reason for her arrival. I called Brigette to ask if I could stay at the Gavarni. She responded as if the hotel were empty even though it was the height of the season.

John Gibbons delivered Toni and me to Dulles. On the long drive out, we talked about the post-trial brief that Doug and Jim had recently delivered to Judge Gesell. John was an attorney who practiced employment law. In fact, he and Jim had worked for the same law firm years ago. He always spoke of Jim with obvious respect and he seemed to know more about Jim than I did. I never knew, for example, that Jim had gone to Harvard until John told me.

John was a quiet man who spoke slowly and softly. He was pensive—always thought before he began to speak. He had a charming but subtle sense of humor. He was a master of the one-liner delivered with a poker face. I valued John's ability to interpret, articulate, and offer opinions about the outcome of my attorneys' legal efforts. I had asked John to read their latest legal product and explain it to me some day—in English. When he returned home from the airport, he carried with him a copy of the post-trial briefs, mine and PW's.

Tela was nine that summer when she asked to have her ears pierced. At some time between birth and adulthood, I came to believe, probably under the influence of my mother, that piercing one's ears was only a short step away from prostitution. Many of my friends, including my sister, had pierced ears. I never held it against them; pierced ears were just not for me. A consequence of my belief, and the fact that clip-on and screw-on earrings hurt my earlobes, was that I never wore earrings. I explained my position on the subject to Tela without responding to her request. She suggested that I come out of the Stone Age and think the matter through.

"Tela wants to have her ears pierced," I said to Toni, whom I had never seen wearing earrings. "What do you think?" The plane had just lifted off from Dulles and we had seven hours to consider the issue before we landed in Paris. Having one's ears pierced was considered to be "below the salt," according to Toni's upbringing, born in Iowa, devout Catholic, educated at a women's college.

She retrieved a small bottle of Rose's lime juice from her Wang bag in anticipation of mixing up a gimlet when the opportunity presented itself. "What does below the salt mean?" I asked. She laughed at herself as she defined the origin of the expression. In medieval times, social status was apparently measured at the dinner table by proximity to the salt. People seated between the head of the table and the salt were socially more prominent than those below the salt.

Two hours, two gimlets, and a lot of personal history later we reached the same conclusion that Tela had: we were anachronistic in our views. To correct our historical biases, Toni and I decided that we would join Tela and the three of us would go together to have our ears pierced. The remainder of the flight was spent planning the schedule for the week ahead of us.

We landed in Paris early Sunday morning. Although we were tired after the all-night trip, Toni called an early afternoon meeting with the FNPay team. The purpose of the meeting was to lay out the plans for the week. The delegate could not be reached by phone and was unavailable for the meeting, sick in bed with the measles or chicken pox or something.

On Monday morning, Toni was told that the delegate had returned to the United States. She was in a state of disbelief when she explained the situation to me. In spite of her almost daily efforts, over a period of more than a month, to make verbal contact, she had failed to do so. I was speechless. I wondered what the delegate was thinking while being pursued half way around the world by the boss, a member of the Senior Executive Service with the rank of deputy assistant secretary.

By the time we returned to Washington, Toni was less uneasy about the project. The review in Paris sent the FNPay team scurrying after missing information, all of which was available at the Paris RAMC. She was secure in the knowledge that the team had information adequate to ensure that additional fieldwork would be unnecessary. The delegate disappeared from the project and eventually from State.

July ended. There was no word from Judge Gesell.

When the work-related dust settled, Toni called her doctor and I called mine, only to discover that ear piercing was not a medical procedure. To perform the task we had to find a jewelry store. That done, the three of us met at what by all appearances was a sleazy little shop at a suburban mall in Virginia.

"Who's first," said the woman with the oversize staple gun in her hand. I gently nudged Tela toward her. "She is," I said to the woman, "and," I anxiously warned Tela, "if you so much as wince, I'll turn around and run straight out of here." Although neither Tela nor Toni winced, I cringed visibly. We three left with ugly surgical steel pegs through our earlobes, some bottles of stuff, and instructions on how to use the contents of the bottles to prevent infection of our wounds.

Toni must have followed the instructions. Although I had to help her get earrings in every now and then, especially when we bought new ones at the little jeweler around the corner from our office building, she never developed an infection. Tela, however, developed infected earring holes, singly or in pairs, one after the other, for the remainder of the summer. Each infection represented a problem unsolvable by me for two reasons. First, my bad eyesight made it hard to see the solution. Second, I was afraid I might hurt my daughter, a fear compounded by her loud protestations as I approached her with alcohol in one hand and earring in the other.

Sandy Kinsey, who had dropped by the house for a visit, came to the rescue with the first infection. She had pierced ears for years and therefore understood the problem. Her eyesight was good enough and she was undaunted by Tela's hysterically expressed anxieties. "Stand still!" she said as she gently but tenaciously grasped Tela's ear and swiftly inserted the sterile earring, with unerring accuracy. We went back to our conversation around my kitchen table. Tela went about her business, none the worse for wear.

On the Friday after the onset of the next infection I was having one of those regularly scheduled lunches with Toni and Gilda. I recounted the story of Sandy's solving the problem the first time and expressed my frustration over the fact that Sandy was out of town, hence unable to repeat the process. Toni laughed merrily and indicated that Tela's anxiety was enough to prevent her from volunteering to help. Gilda, in mock disgust at my temerity, told me to bring Tela by her house the next morning and she would take care of it—and she did.

Discrimination

I was exhausted and relieved when school started. Judge Gesell signed a memorandum recording his "Findings of Fact" and "Conclusions of Law" ten days later, on September 20, 1985. I was euphoric. Judge Gesell found that Price Waterhouse had discriminated when it decided not to make me a partner early in 1983.

> Whenever a promotion system relies on highly subjective evaluations of candidates by individuals or panels dominated by members of a different sex, there is ground for concern that such "high level subjectivity subjects the ultimate promotion decision to the intolerable occurrence of conscious or unconscious prejudice. . . ." Such procedures "must be closely scrutinized because of their capacity for masking unlawful bias. . . ." This scrutiny comprehends examination of evaluation procedures that permit or give effect to sexual stereotyping. Differential treatment on account of sex, even if it is not obviously based on a characteristic of sex, violates Title VII. . . . An employer who treats a woman with an assertive personality in a different manner than if she had been a man is guilty of sex discrimination. . . . A female cannot be excluded from a partnership dominated by males if a sexual bias plays a part in the decision and the employer is aware that such bias played a part in the exclusion decision.
>
> This is not a case where "standards were shaped only by neutral professional and technical considerations and not by any stereotypical notions of female roles and images. . . ." Discriminatory stereotyping of females was permitted to play a part. Comments influenced by sex stereotypes were made by partners; the firm's evaluation process gave substantial weight to these

comments; and the partnership failed to address the conspicuous problem of stereotyping in partnership evaluations. While these three factors may have been innocent alone, they combined to produce discrimination in the case of this plaintiff. The Court finds that the Policy Board's decision not to admit the plaintiff to partnership was tainted by discriminatory evaluations that were the direct result of its failure to address the evident problem of sexual stereotyping in partners' evaluations.

"I guess you won, but I'm not happy with the opinion on 'constructive discharge,'" Jim said. Because of that loss I was not entitled to reinstatement as a partner. "Will I get my attorney's fees back?" I asked. When Jim answered affirmatively, as I expected, I responded, "What more could I ask? I could have lost."

John Gibbons and I finally got together to discuss his interpretation of the pile of legal documents that I had left with him en route to Paris in July. We met at Germaine's because it was within easy walking distance of his house in Glover Park. We each ordered a beer. I gave him the judge's memorandum before he had a chance to order lunch. I fidgeted quietly while he scanned it.

"I do not understand 'constructive discharge.' What is it?" I asked as he flipped the final page and looked up. I referred to the judge's ruling.

> . . . She has the burden of proving that she was constructively discharged. If the plaintiff resigned voluntarily, and not because Price Waterhouse made working conditions intolerable and drove her to quit, she is not entitled to an order that she be made a partner. . . . Being denied partnership was undoubtedly a professional disappointment and it may have been professionally advantageous for plaintiff to leave the firm when it was unlikely she would not [sic] obtain her ultimate goal. Disappointments do not constitute a constructive discharge, however. . . . Plaintiff's failure to show a constructive discharge requires the Court to deny plaintiffs [sic] request for an order directing Price Waterhouse to make her a partner.

We ordered lunch. Based on John's lay explanation of the law, I formulated my view of the issue: "Did she jump, or was she pushed?" Did I walk out or was I pushed out the door? If I jumped, I was entitled to no remedy. If pushed, I was entitled to be invited back into the fold. To this day, Jim Heller cringes every time I use that trite question to state the issue.

Over coffee I told John that I was puzzled by another part of the judge's memorandum. It dealt with an issue referred to as "back pay." Judge Gesell decided that I was entitled to be paid the difference between what I made as a senior manager ($70,000 per year) and what I would have made as a partner (roughly $100,000 per year) for the period between July 1, 1983, when I failed to become a partner, and January 1984, when I left the firm. By my calculation, the "back pay" to which I was thus entitled amounted to about $15,000—peanuts. He further decided, however, that no evidence was submitted at trial to enable him to compute the entitlement amount. Therefore, he awarded nothing and wrote:

> The parties have represented that, without the knowledge or consent of the Court, they agreed to defer resolving the amount of backpay until the issue of liability was resolved. But the parties do not have the authority to structure a trial for their own convenience. Issues can only be separated for a separate trial by order of the Court. . . .
>
> No such order was ever requested or granted in this case. A party who makes an "unauthorized determination not to go forward on issues that were properly in the case does so at his own peril."

I asked John to explain. He was unable to do so. He conjectured, however, that both sets of attorneys had agreed to bifurcate the trial, that is split it into two parts, one dealing with liability and another dealing with remedy. Then, he hypothesized, someone failed to get the judge to order the bifurcation. John told me to ask Doug or Jim.

While we waited for the check, John walked me through the near-term steps for an appeal from a decision of a district court. Both sides had a month during which they could appeal. If no one appealed, it would be over.

Desertion

Toni and I left for Paris again two weeks after Judge Gesell published his memorandum. We were excited. Except for occasions when she had to play hostess at dinners organized to maintain the morale of the FNPay team, she and I spent most evenings enjoying our good spirits. We usually ate together.

I always asked Brigette to make dinner reservations, a task she enjoyed because it gave her a chance to show off her beloved Paris. Unlike tourists, Toni and I sought quiet restaurants frequented only by Parisians and we ate late.

At the end of the work week, the senior French national at the embassy invited Toni and me to his home for dinner. We were honored but dismayed. "What do you take a French man and his wife when you are invited for dinner?" I asked Brigette. "A California wine," she replied. Brigette found and wrapped a couple of tasteful bottles.

Dinner was an elegant six-course event impeccably prepared by the lady of the house. It began at eight with hors d'oeuvres and kir, ended at midnight with espresso and cognac, and included a different wine with each intervening course. We staggered back to our hotels, exhausted.

Two days after my return to the States, Jim and Doug appealed Judge Gesell's order. A week after that, PW appealed. At the time, I believed the appeals were filed in the opposite order. I never had any intention of appealing the judge's ruling on constructive discharge unless PW appealed the ruling on liability.

Doug later explained to me that as the end date for filing an appeal approached, he and Jim acted on the assumption that PW would appeal. Had the lawyers from Gibson, Dunn, and Crutcher called to say stop the litigation, it would have been over.

By Halloween the record of the case was sent to the U.S. Court of Appeals for the District of Columbia circuit. By Christmas Judge Gesell had put the case into legal limbo to await action by the circuit court.

After the holidays, Doug and Jim geared up the brief-writing process. They had to argue the two issues, constructive discharge and liability, separately. Thus, they had to write twice as many briefs for the circuit court as they did after the trial. They had plenty of time. The arguments were scheduled for October 23, 1986, a week before Halloween.

About the time the brief writing started, Thomas Peter began to assess the learning disability testing centers in the Washington area. He hoped to identify one that could help with Peter's reading problem. He looked at every available option and selected what he considered to be the best.

Peter had a Wechsler, a Kaufman, a Beery, a Bender, a Jordan, a Wepman, a Slingerland, and a few others. The tests took the better part of a day. The resulting report contained almost as many words as one of Doug's shorter briefs. It was opaque. Reading law books was surely easier.

After scrutinizing a thousand long words, all I could conclude was that Peter was unable to read. "Hell, I already knew that," I thought. The report recommended that he go from kindergarten to first grade, where he would need lots of help from a specially trained teacher. Furthermore, he should be tested again in a year. "This is crap!" I said to Thomas Peter.

We met with the diagnostician. She was as unenlightening in person as she had been in her report. Thomas Peter handled most of our end of the conversation. I was too angry to engage the woman. She offered nothing new and nothing useful by way of counsel.

I pressed her a little—for a diagnosis, a prognosis, a plan—anything. "We'll wait until he's eleven to see if he has a problem," she responded. "Maybe you'll wait," I thought. "Me, I'm going to assume there's a problem and do something," I said to myself. Unfortunately, I had no inventory of good ideas about what to do.

Thomas Peter and I walked down the stairs and out the front door. If I was angry on arrival, I was enraged beyond control on exit. For lack of a better option, we enrolled Peter in the summer reading program at the center.

"Nothing French," I said to the man from Ridgewell's. Toni and I decided it would be gauche to take the French nationals out to dinner after being so graciously entertained at home while we were in Paris. Neither of us wanted to cook. We agreed to split the cost and hire a caterer. We would have the party at my house, only because it was bigger than Toni and John's. I told Ridgewell's we wanted something typically American, right down to the wines.

Monday afternoon Ridgewell's showed up with linen, flatware, dishes, food, liquor, staff—everything you ever imagined necessary for a wedding reception, let alone a seated dinner for eight. Under the careful scrutiny of the amused staff, the children hung around the kitchen.

They tasted the food as it was unpacked. With the exception of the crab claws, boiled shrimp, and chocolate-covered strawberries, they declared it all to be unpalatable. Until the arrival of the guests, most of their time was spent lying on the floor crunching strawberries as they watched carbon dioxide curl over the edge of a Paul Revere bowl containing water and dry ice.

It was a science experiment, they told me when I asked what was going on. The children and the people from Ridgewell's were a mutual entertainment society.

At dinner Toni and I sat at opposite ends of the table, each with the other's spouse seated at left. The French nationals were seated in protocol-dictated positions between us. We had a lovely dinner, perfectly cooked and elegantly served. A different California wine complemented each course.

The conversation was light and humorous. Thomas Peter was at his entertaining best. I had fun. The French nationals had fun. Toni and John enjoyed themselves. The children gave the evening rave reviews.

Thomas Peter left me on Wednesday, two days later. I was absolutely blindsided. Karen Nold had canceled dinner plans that morning. Thomas Peter suggested that he join me instead. We met in Rosslyn at Windows, a tasteful restaurant with an expansive view of Washington and its monuments. What I expected to be a dreamy evening with my husband of more than ten years became a nightmare of soap opera proportions.

I was destroyed. Blinding tears ran down my face and covered my glasses with salty translucence. I raced from Windows onto the street into the traffic where I hailed the first available cab. Panic gripped my diaphragm, making breathing difficult and uneven. My stomach was heaving from nervous nausea when I arrived home.

Thank God the children were asleep. Against all hopes, I thought that perhaps the situation would change by morning so I could avoid dealing with them. By then, however, the situation had deteriorated. Thomas Peter had spent the night on the sofa and delivered the bad news to the sleepy children when they staggered down for breakfast.

He then moved out. Behind he left a black cloud of depression and a hurricane of emotional turmoil over and around the family.

The hysteria of the children forced me to exercise control over my own emotions. Fortunately all the things we had to do diverted my conscious attention from marital problems. In less than a week I had to take charge of the Girl Scout camping trip. After that I had just enough time to unpack the camping gear and pack business suits before leaving for Paris. When I finished a week's business, Tela was supposed to join me for ten days of mother and daughter goofing off.

Although Thomas Peter joined us, the children and I spent the camping trip cowed and cringing under the influence of his departure from the house. He stayed at home when I left for Europe. Toni and I flew to Paris in relative silence. There was no fun in the design review.

Tela and I spent a miserable week in the Gavarni. We were each preoccupied. I made hopeless plans to fix the unfixable. She worried nervously about the future. Brigette's effusive enthusiasm, normally charming, grated. Each day I counted the hours until I could get home and begin working on the problem of saving my marriage.

The first day of Peter's summer reading program was the Monday after Tela and I returned from Paris. Peter said he was sick. He wanted to see the doctor. The child looked fine to me. Upon examination, I mentally diagnosed a case of acute hypochondria, a disease that often afflicts children confronted with an undesirable task. The symptoms can be simple—an intermittent limp that moves from side to side is an example.

These, however, were complex: stomachache, headache, and foot pain. I offered Peter my medical opinion. "In my experience, this disease doesn't call for a doctor until your left big toe starts to hurt. Let's see how you feel in the morning."

When Thomas Peter vacated the house, I was left without a car. Being carless posed no immediate problem. I hated cars. Parking was a pain. I often found myself several feet from the curb. Drivers got wet in the rain. The cab I usually took to work dropped me at the door. Cars were expensive. The round-trip cab fare down town was cheaper than the parking lot fee. There was no such thing as a "quick" errand by car. Half the time was spent parking and walking between the car and the errand.

On the other hand I liked motorcycles, except when it rained. I never rode in the rain. I had been riding since 1969. My first bike was a Suzuki 70cc. It was followed by the Yamaha 175cc that I had when Thomas Peter and I were married. Bikes were cheap. When it was new, I only paid fifteen hundred dollars for my red 1981 Honda 400. Gilbert had picked the color. A bike could be parked anywhere. It was the perfect vehicle for running errands. Bikes were interesting. I could always count on one of the children wanting to go along on the bike. Each of them learned to ride at age two.

With Thomas Peter gone, my only means of personal transportation was the motorcycle. Peter showed no signs of illness when he donned his helmet. He seemed fine as we rode the short distance to the school. In no apparent pain, he hopped off the bike. "Mom, we have a problem," he said as he stood in the street on the threshold of his summer learning experience. I could barely see his eyes under the sun visor.

"What is it, Peter?" I asked. He removed the headgear. "It happened," he said pointing to his right foot. "My big toe hurts." I dismounted the bike and gave him a big hug. "You've got the wrong foot, Peter. Don't worry. You'll have fun at camp." With his helmet under my arm and his left hand in my right, I walked him to the door.

I spent the summer learning to live with the likelihood of being a single parent. I found it impossible to do all the things that had formerly been done by the two of us. In an attempt to preserve the children's activities, I eliminated all but essential, generally work-related activities from my own agenda.

I slept less. I developed a tolerance for mess around the house. Laundry was done less frequently than it had been. The children and I ate out more. The phone list was extended to include the local Chinese and Italian carry-outs. I bought a freezer to reduce the number of trips to the store.

Doing anything as a family of four is impossible on a motorcycle. I told Thomas Peter I needed a car, wanted a Toyota van, and expected him to provide one. He did.

As much as Peter enjoyed anything that summer, he enjoyed reading camp. He was, however, no better able to read at the end of the summer than he had been at its beginning.

The new school year started hopefully. Thomas Peter suggested marriage counseling. My mood swung to the high end of elation. Maybe things would work out.

Appeal 1

The U.S. Court of Appeals for the District of Columbia Circuit consists of about twelve judges if there are no vacancies. Appeals from decisions of a district court are usually handled by a panel of three of the twelve. If the circuit court is very busy, a district judge may sit on a panel with two circuit judges.

John Gibbons met the children and me in the lobby outside the courtroom. Toni had too much work to do to join us. Jim and Doug were waiting on familiar turf. We were across and down the hall from Judge Gesell.

The circuit courtroom was narrower than the district courtroom. No jury boxes usurped space along the walls. An elevated platform with three high-backed, leather-looking chairs enclosed behind a waistwall dominated the far end of the room. Dark, austere portraits of dignified, black-suited men hung on both side walls. Engraved plaques identified former judges of the circuit.

After one look at the courtroom, the children decided they would prefer to kill an hour in the cafeteria or explore the halls of justice rather than enter. The court had scheduled an hour for the arguments. According to Doug, that was a little unusual. Half an hour was customary. I gave the children Coke money and told them to behave. They scurried off.

John and I entered the court. We sat on one of the blond wooden benches in the middle of a middle row. He and I were alone on my side of the aisle. The lawyers sat or stood around opposing tables before the bar that separated the audience from the participants. Doug and Jim spoke inaudibly.

On the other side, Steve Tallent quietly watched as Wayne Schrader supervised several fresh-faced, junior professionals. The youngsters carried boxes and briefcases around and positioned them in rows according to some plan evident only to them. It looked like an awful lot of files to support a presentation of only an hour's length. Jim and Doug, by comparison, had one case each.

I clutched John's arm as we stood when my three judges, Edwards, Williams, and Green, entered the court. Judge Edwards was a stately man. Standing on a platform several feet above the courtroom floor, he seemed very tall. Had we been on equal footing he still would have been tall. He was black.

Doug and Jim had called him Harry Edwards when they explained that he was one of the smartest and most respected judges on the circuit. Judge Edwards was the chief judge—he sat in the middle chair.

Circuit Judge Williams sat to his right. Neither Jim nor Doug knew much about him. He had only recently been appointed to the bench by the Republican president. He was an academician: he had taught, rather than practiced law. A head of curly hair topped an open, nice-looking face. To me he seemed intense, very serious.

Joyce Hens Green, a district court judge, took the remaining seat. Jim and Doug always referred to her by her full name. I assumed they did it to avoid confusion with another Judge Green. They respectfully described her as articulate, experienced, knowledgeable, hardworking, and tough-minded.

Judge Edwards smiled. In a lilting voice, he welcomed everyone to the proceedings. The attorneys introduced themselves.

A light atop Jim's podium turned green. He seemed completely at ease as he opened the folder containing his black scribbles. "Two minutes into my prepared statement, I'll be interrupted with questions. The trick then is to answer the questions and still make my points before I run out of time," Jim had said.

He was wrong. The questions, mainly from Judge Williams, started forty-five seconds after the light turned green. They were related almost entirely to liability. Jim, however, wanted to argue about constructive discharge.

According to his legal theory, resignation by an employee confronted with a career-ending situation was constructive discharge. Jim believed that Judge Gesell made a mistake when he concluded that I left voluntarily and was, therefore, not subjected to constructive discharge. Measured by the number of questions on the subject, none of the judges seemed interested as Jim expressed this point.

By the time the yellow two-minute warning flashed, Jim had finished what he had to say. He asked if there were questions. There were few. He reiterated the points he thought were critical. A red light ended his argument. Jim returned to his place at the table with Doug.

The light turned green on Steve Tallent. Shortly after he finished his first sentence, Judge Edwards politely interrupted to explain the role of the court of appeals. That court is prohibited by the Supreme Court from resifting the facts found by the district court. It is further prohibited from coming to new conclusions based on a different interpretation of the facts. Unless Judge Gesell missed something major or concluded something absurd, his findings and conclusions on liability would stand.

Steve knew that. He persisted, however, in rearguing liability anyway. First he argued that some of the stereotypical remarks were really gender-neutral. Charm, as an example, is equally prized in men and women. Even if some remarks were sexist, he continued, they really had nothing to do with the decision. After all, the remarks were made, with few exceptions, by my supporters. Opponents made no sexist comments.

Judge Edwards observed that Susan Fiske had reached a different conclusion. In her expert opinion, stereotypical views were a determining factor in the partnership decision. Was Steve now challenging the expert witness who had been unchallenged at trial? Steve vehemently asserted that he was not.

He was having a rough time. I was anything but sympathetic.

Judge Edwards asked about Tom Beyer's memorable advice that I walk and talk and dress differently. Steve argued that Joe Connor, not Tom, told me, in gender-neutral terms, what I had to do to take corrective action. According to Steve, Tom was speaking as a friend. His views did not represent those of the partnership.

Judge Green had been relatively silent to that point. She had disappeared deep into her chair. She held her left hand in front of her face, index finger across upper lip, thumb lightly touching her cheek, other fingers hiding her mouth. The body language said contemplation, skepticism or disbelief.

Clasping both hands, she leaned forward. "Tell me, Mr. Tallent, in a partnership which partners do not speak for the firm?" she asked, mildly incredulous. She seemed unable to buy the Beyer-was-speaking-only-for-himself argument.

The lights seemed to flash through the remainder of Steve's argument and through the rebuttals. Suddenly it was over. I was more disappointed than relieved. It was like the end of an exciting movie. I had enjoyed every minute of it.

John commented on the apparent futility of rearguing liability as we left the courtroom in search of the children. "By the time Judge Edwards finished with him, the only argument Steve had left was that Tom Beyer never said anything at all," John mused through a broad grin.

I polled the attorneys. John, Doug, and Jim were each of the opinion that the vote would be two to one in my favor on liability. Everyone was perplexed by the apparent lack of interest in constructive discharge. They declined to offer opinions on the outcome.

Coping

The cab waited in front of the house. "Oscar must have escaped again," I thought. The screen cover on the terrarium was ajar, the snake nowhere in sight. There was no time to look for him. I grabbed my briefcase from its normal resting place on the floor under his vacant home and went to work.

As a familiar cab driver prattled about the state of the economy and the weather, I did a mental search for Oscar. Where could the damn snake have gone? The children would be upset. They were always upset when Oscar got lost.

I once retrieved him dangling over the gutter outside my bedroom window. I suspected that Peter routinely removed Oscar from the terrarium and played with him while watching television in my bed-room. There was simply no other explanation for the snake "escaping" on the second floor and being found on the fourth.

It was hard to believe that Tela or Gilbert would even consider taking Oscar from his glass cage. If asked, Tela was willing to hold the snake while the terrarium was cleaned. She was, however, unlikely to handle the animal for any other reason. Gilbert preferred to leave Oscar alone.

"Ask the children to find the snake" hit my mental notepad about the same time that I stepped into the elevator en route to my office on the sixth floor. I had to prepare for a meeting at ten. I was running late.

Dawn Parrish was as compulsive about being on time as I was. She had been a client since the spring. We had a meeting on the tenth floor to go over one of the several technical specifications for procurements that I was tasked to write.

Dawn worked for Howard Renman. She was a good client and a very decent human being. Everything I did for her she reviewed carefully. That was especially important during the months just after Thomas Peter left. I had trouble focusing. She caught some real bloopers, which she pointed out matter-of-factly. I was a wreck and she knew it.

We frequently had lunch together, sometimes several times a week. She and her roommate invited me to the house for dinner. Her roommate was a special education teacher and took an active interest in Peter's learning problems. She made suggestions and clipped articles on dyslexia for me.

I had spent Labor Day weekend with them in West Virginia. The children were with Thomas Peter. Dawn knew I would have stayed home and been miserably lonely had she not invited me. I was lonely anyway, but I appreciated her thoughtfulness and kindness.

At three minutes before ten, exactly on schedule, Dawn walked into the office to pick me up to attend the meeting. Simultaneously I found Oscar. He was in my briefcase. I had blindly felt around the bottom of the leather bag looking for a pen and encountered the snake instead.

We found a clean brown paper bag, no small task in an office building. I put the misplaced reptile in his temporary home and stapled it closed. We were fifteen minutes late to our meeting. The excuse Dawn offered for our tardiness was worth the wait.

As the end of the school day approached, I called the house every ten minutes until the children got home. I was afraid they would be unnecessarily upset if they arrived to find Oscar gone. They had been emotionally jerked around by Thomas Peter's absence and continued to be jerked around by the marriage counseling process.

My sister-in-law first made me aware of just how intensely it affected them. On one of her visits, she had gone to the zoo with the boys. In the monkey house they watched the black-and-white Capuchins. Sheila called them Dominican monkeys because their coloring reminded her of the habit worn by the order.

A pair of parent monkeys watched as three little monkeys ran around, squawked, and pestered each other. The father got fed up, turned and walked away. Gilbert characterized the interactions of the monkeys as those of a dysfunctional family. I was astounded at his correct use of a term that I had to ask Sheila to define.

When it started, I knew marriage counseling would be a trial. I despise inward-focussed, backward-looking, subjective analytical processes. I am loath to deal with middlemen. I much prefer to deal directly with problems and people.

I always slept badly the night before a counseling session. My mind cycled through endless agendas and plans for the next day. Exhaustion helped me overcome depression and get to sleep the night after a session. I never had control over the agenda. None of my plans worked. Although I usually entered sessions hopefully, my hopes were inevitably dashed.

One day each week, for an hour, I sat with Thomas Peter and a humorless, dispassionate marriage counselor. I listened to his tearful descriptions of his childhood and problems with his "family of origin," a term that differentiated the children and me from him and his mother and sisters.

In one of the sessions, I hysterically asked what family of origin discussions had to do with the problem at hand. Men marry people similar to their mothers, women their fathers, so I was told. The purpose of the discussions was somehow to interpret our marriage in light of our families of origin to some end that was never clear to me. All I wanted was for the talk to end and Thomas Peter to come home. Unlike Thomas Peter and the marriage counselor, I never viewed the counseling process as an opportunity to learn something about myself.

I lived from session to session on the faint hope of a positive sign. When Thomas Peter or the counsellor rescheduled, I went into a temporary funk. Between sessions I threw myself into my work and the children. I cooked breakfast every morning and was home for dinner every night.

I gave only a rare passing thought to the court of appeals. The likelihood of a ruling before mid-January was nil.

When I agreed that the children could spend Thanksgiving with Thomas Peter, Sheila asked me to come to Arkansas to spend it with her. My family had also invited me. I was torn between the awful prospect of being alone on my favorite holiday and the equally awful prospect of traveling during the worst travel period of the year. I was also anxious at the thought of imposing my gloomy self on my family.

Self-preservation dominated. There are occasions when friends are more helpful than family. Sheila and I had struggled through ten years to friendship. I spent the holiday taking naps and reading murder mysteries at her house. I had no responsibilities, no tasks or chores. We usually ate at restaurants.

Sheila was no cook. She had a culinary repertoire of about two dishes, which she prepared infrequently. We had a peaceful Thanksgiving dinner hosted by two of her friends. Somehow, being at the table of strangers directed my mind away from my problems.

The marriage counselor was astounded. Shortly after Thanksgiving, Thomas Peter decided to return on a trial basis. I was euphoric until he said he would keep his apartment and he would not come home before Christmas. The children and I would have to spend the holidays without him. The normally joyful holiday chores of Christmas shopping, tree trimming, baking fruitcakes, opening presents under the tree, cooking turkey and stuffing looked like a mundane task list of immense proportions.

My sister's invitation was barely uttered when I accepted it. Tela, Gilbert, Peter, and I flew to Vermont. I rented a car to drive from Burlington, the nearest airport, to Susan's place outside Middlebury. The children slept through most of the trip. That was fortuitous.

I got lost leaving Burlington and again in Middlebury. Susan's address was Bristol Notch Road, Top of the Notch. On a dry day in summer at high noon, my driving was barely up to the standards required to maneuver the dirt road that wound its way up the mountain to her place. I was over my head at midnight in the first major snowstorm of the winter.

I misjudged several hills and had to back carefully downhill to start over. "Aren't we going the wrong direction, Mom?" Gilbert asked sleepily when he waked during one of the backing stages. He sat up, paid attention, and guided me through the final mile. We arrived after midnight to spend a white Christmas with Susan and her family. I love my sister.

Thomas Peter returned, only to leave forever six weeks later on President's Day weekend. We had spent that weekend with the children, skiing in Bayse, Virginia, just south of Toni and John Gibbons's retirement home near Front Royal and a long way north on the route to Hollins College.

David Hopper must have thought I was crazy. The children thought I was sick. At two in the morning I had delivered a letter written over a large volume of Canadian Club to Thomas Peter's apartment. It was snowing lightly. On my return the van almost made it up the driveway before it sideslipped into a perfect position to block all access to the cul-de-sac. I went to bed. David had to deal with it in the morning.

A couple of days later, Thomas Peter and I walked along the bike path in Rock Creek Park where he discussed the difficult decision he had to make. Someone, either I or his junior partner, with whom he was having an affair, would be horribly hurt by his decision. I lost.

I did learn one thing in marriage counseling: the definition of a passive-aggressive personality—one who passively expresses covert aggression. For what it was worth, it explained a lot.

In the early summer my business at the State Department started to collapse. I estimated that by the end of the year I would encounter a six-month business void while I competed for new work. Going six months with no income while paying the expenses of running my office in Rosslyn was untenable.

It seemed certain that Thomas Peter was never coming back. Although he contributed mightily to the financial support of the children, I would soon be without health insurance, and shortly thereafter without an income. It was time to recognize the reality of single parenthood and get a more conventional job.

My morale was about as low as I thought it could be when Betsy Hishon called. She and I had touched base irregularly since my first call to congratulate her on her May 1984 Supreme Court victory. I had called to tell her when Judge Gesell issued his favorable opinion and again to share the excitement after the arguments before the court of appeals. Betsy's upbeat demeanor and southern accent always cheered me, but this time her voice on the phone was particularly welcome.

She called to tell me that she'd been asked to speak as part of a panel of women involved in prominent legal issues. She wanted to know if I might join her on the panel. I told her I would welcome the diversion from my gloomy professional situation. That settled, we talked about job searches while in litigation. From what she said, my prospects were not good.

Within a month, I received a call from an organization associated with the Carter Library of Emory University. I was invited to a symposium to be held in Atlanta. The subject was women and the Constitution. If I accepted, I would be part of a panel that included Betsy and Sara Weddington, the attorney who, at the age of twenty-eight, argued *Roe v. Wade* before the Supreme Court.

I jumped at a chance to get away from Washington. It would be fun to meet Betsy and Sara Weddington. The symposium also offered a chance to see Justice O'Connor, who was scheduled to be one of the main speakers. Furthermore, if Sully could get to Atlanta, I could take Tela and the two of them could have a reunion.

What fun I thought. When Sully agreed to take the five-hour bus ride from her home in Hinesville to Atlanta, I told Tela about the trip. She was ecstatic.

Schedule conflicts prevented Tela and me from hearing Justice O'Connor. We did, however, have dinner with President Carter and Rosa Parks. It was hardly intimate. As I recall there were about three hundred people at dinner.

President Carter and Mrs. Parks sat at the head table. Tela decided she wanted to shake hands with the former president. She walked the twenty yards across the hotel dining room to discuss the matter with a security officer at one end of the table. President Carter and Tela spoke, shook hands, and he kissed her on the forehead.

Tela was less interested in discussions of women or the Constitution than she was in the glass elevator that ascended twenty-plus stories through the atrium. Until Sully arrived, Tela spent most of her time in the elevator. Afterward, the two of them disappeared to renew old acquaintances. They spent most of the symposium weekend goofing off.

In mid-June, shortly after Tela and I returned from Atlanta, the entire family descended on Mom and Gil in Vermont to celebrate Gil's eightieth birthday. I puttered around, painting, plastering, and making small repairs. The children split their time between Mom's place down in the valley and Susan's up on the notch.

The woodpile at Mom's was overrun with garter snakes. Peter caught and carried them around in twos and threes. Initially Gilbert watched suspiciously, but after a while he learned to like them. Mom had to ban snakes from the house.

I worried that there was a larger variety of snakes on the notch. Visions of the boys' capturing copperheads came to mind. "Oh Mom, what do you think I am, stupid?" was Peter's response to my expressed concern. There followed a lecture on the anatomical differences between poisonous and nonpoisonous snakes.

The pond on the notch was the real problem. All the children knew how to swim, but the pond was a lot bigger than the pool in Florida. Using inner tubes and other flotation devices, the boys routinely managed to get stranded in the center of the forty-by-seventy-five-foot pond. Once again, I practiced lifesaving.

Brother, Susan, and I talked about the lawsuit. They wondered what was taking so long. I relayed Jim's usual answer to my questions on the subject: the circuit judges had heavy caseloads and a great deal of other work to do. I hoped for the opinion soon. If July passed without its being published, it would be September. Nothing, of course, ever happens in August.

The World Bank, as the International Bank for Reconstruction and Development is more commonly known, reorganized in the summer of 1987. To reduce the number of people employed by the bank, it offered incentives, in the form of generous retirement packages to certain employees.

I found out about the reorganization on a sunny, breezy Saturday. It was cool for late June. David and Ruth were drinking iced tea on the terrace behind their house. A brick wall retained my garden at chest height above theirs. Dry rot and a storm had knocked down the fence that once separated us. Ruth and I decided we liked the atmosphere better without the fence. We had talked about putting up a captain's ladder to make it easier to go back and forth between the two gardens, but we never got around to it.

On David's invitation, I hopped down to join them. He had decided to retire. Some of his colleagues had already thrown a retirement party for him when they were together at a meeting in Paris earlier in the summer. He and Ruth planned to sail their boat from Annapolis, where it was moored, through the intercoastal waterway to the Caribbean and back. They would return in September in time for Ruth to start law school at Georgetown University.

It was a short retirement. The next week David agreed to become a senior vice president. One of the organizations under his management was responsible for planning and budgeting. After the new organization settled down, I was retained to do a few consulting projects in budgeting.

Constructive
Discharge

When July ended, I mentally prepared myself to wait until September for the opinion of the court of appeals. It had been more than nine months since the arguments. The children left to spend August with Thomas Peter.

"We won! Affirmed, reversed, and remanded," Jim said. His ebullient tone of voice told me more than the legal terms did. On August 4, 1987, the court of appeals affirmed Judge Gesell's position on liability, reversed his position on constructive discharge, and remanded the whole mess back to him to deal with the issue of remedy.

As the attorneys had predicted, the decision on liability was split two to one. Judge Williams dissented. The decision on constructive discharge, however, was unanimous.

Unlike many of the briefs and other legal documents, the majority and dissenting opinions were readable. In fact, much of what was written was humorous. The majority opinion was written by Judge Joyce Hens Green.

Early in the opinion she reiterated, in writing, what Judge Edwards had stated so clearly at the oral arguments. The court of appeals does not retry district court cases. "In order to overturn a determination of liability, we must conclude that it is 'based on an utterly implausible account of the evidence.'"

She then proceeded to knock off PW's arguments one by one. I found laughable the firm's first argument, that Judge Gesell made an error when he interpreted certain comments, including "charm school" as a sexist characterization.

In college days, my hackles always rose when Hollins College was referred to as a "girls' school" or a "finishing school" or a "charm school." The institution was, and for that matter still is, a liberal arts women's college. The other terms are at best inaccurate. I find them derogatory and offensive. Judge Green might have agreed with me.

> Price Waterhouse . . . suggests that one partner's comment that Hopkins needed to take a "course at charm school" is not sex-indicative, because charm is a quality admired both in men and women. This argument borders on the facetious. . . . The sexist import of the comment is patently clear, particularly as charm schools are inextricably linked, both historically and philosophically, with the antiquated notion that women should devote their energies to social and cultural affairs rather than business or professional endeavors.

The firm's second argument was that Tom Beyer's comments about walking, talking, and dressing femininely were personal remarks made by an individual and a friend. PW argued that Judge Gesell made an error because Joe Connor, not Tom, was the firm's spokesman and Joe advised me in gender-neutral terms. The majority disagreed.

> The firm argues that the District Court erred in stating that Beyer was "responsible for telling her what problems the Policy Board had identified with her candidacy. . . ." Price Waterhouse claims that this task officially fell to the firm's Senior Partner, Joseph Connor, who made no reference to Hopkins' femininity in his meeting with her. . . . This contention not only rests on the artificial assumption that Beyer, the chief partner in Price Waterhouse's Washington office and Hopkins' leading supporter, would be kept completely in the dark as to the Policy Board's views on her candidacy, but is directly contradicted by the testimony of Roger Marcellin, a member of both the Policy Board and the Admissions Committee at the time of Hopkins' nomination, who stated that he had "no doubt that Tom Beyer would be the one that would have to talk to her [Hopkins]. He knew exactly what her problems were. . . ." Beyer's advice, of course, speaks for itself.

The lawyers from Gibson, Dunn, and Crutcher had created their own trap on the third argument, that Dr. Fiske's testimony was without evidentiary value. At trial they accepted her as an expert in her field. They presented no opposing expert to refute her testimony. They made no attempt to disqualify her on appeal—a course of action likely to fail. There was no way out.

> Disclaiming any intention of denigrating Dr. Fiske's field of expertise, Price Waterhouse attempts to dismiss this evidence as "sheer speculation" of "no evidentiary value. . . ." This is so, the firm contends, because Dr. Fiske failed to compare the stereotypical comments made about Hopkins with similar comments made about male candidates; she lacked information concerning the authors of these comments; and she had never met Hopkins. . . . Dr. Fiske testified that she was an expert at evaluating written comments, that reliance on such written documents was a standard practice in her field, and that she did not need to observe Hopkins or meet her critics because she had the entire universe of reactions to Hopkins before her. . . . This information, along with other "convergent indicators" of stereotyping— such as the extremely small number of female partners in the firm; the absence of any other female candidates among the eighty-eight nominated along with Hopkins; the exaggerated and extremely intense negative reactions of Hopkins' critics to behavior supporters perceived as positive; the ambiguous criteria the firm used to evaluate a candidate's personal qualities; the absence of complaints from Hopkins' clients; and the positive assessments of Hopkins in areas where performance could be measured objectively . . . provided Dr. Fiske a sufficient basis from which to draw her conclusions that Hopkins was the victim of stereotyping.

Finally, the firm tried in vain to argue that Judge Gesell made an error by accepting, as evidence, sexist statements that were irrelevant. The firm maintained that comments made in prior years or about other female candidates were irrelevant because they had no effect on the decision to hold me. The argument failed.

> The firm challenges the District Court's reliance on comments partners made about other female candidates, contending that the trial judge intentionally misconstrued these statements in order to find in them evidence of stereotypical thinking. One partner stated that he could never vote for a female partner. One successful candidate was criticized for being a "women's libber," and two other unsuccessful women were characterized as . . . "Ma Barker"; and "one of the boys. . . ." It is impossible to misconstrue the

sentiment behind a categorical opposition to all female partnership candidates. Despite the fact that the firm took no steps to admonish this partner for his statement, which he made just one year before Hopkins came up for consideration, Price Waterhouse suggests the comment is essentially irrelevant because it was obviously ignored by the Policy Board and was "of no further concern . . . by the time that plaintiff was proposed." The firm also argues that the comment about one candidate being a "women's libber" cannot be viewed as evidence of discrimination because the woman in question became a partner. . . . These arguments miss the mark. The District Court did not purport to find that any of these comments determined the fate of the women in question, reflected the views of the Policy Board itself, or had a direct impact on plaintiff's candidacy. Rather, the court relied on them as evidence that partners at Price Waterhouse often evaluated female candidates in terms of their sex. We find nothing erroneous in such reliance; on the contrary, we believe it is eminently correct.

On these same remarks, in his dissenting opinion, Judge Williams disagreed with the majority. He did it with humor.

> These included one [remark] plainly beyond the pale—a remark by a partner that he "could not consider any woman seriously as a partnership candidate and believed that women were not even capable of functioning as senior managers. . . ." So we know that, at least at some time in the past, there was one male chauvinist pig rampant among the Price Waterhouse partners. But there is no evidence that this troglodyte ever influenced a single other partner.

Doug's brief and Jim's oral argument on the issue of constructive discharge must have been persuasive. The issue received as little attention in the majority opinion as it had at oral arguments. Judge Williams agreed with the majority in a dismissive footnote to his dissent. In summary, the court decided in my favor. "Price Waterhouse's decision to deny Hopkins partnership status . . . coupled with the OGS's failure to renominate her, would have been viewed by any reasonable senior manager in her position as a career-ending action. Accordingly, it amounted to a constructive discharge."

I finally understood why Jim became mildly irritated every time I phrased the constructive discharge issue as "Did she jump, or was she pushed?" It was not necessary that I be pushed. The fact that I found myself in a career-ending dilemma after the discriminatory decision amounted to constructive discharge, even if I left voluntarily. The constructive discharge ruling in *Hopkins v. Price Waterhouse* established a legal precedent in the District of Columbia Circuit.

John Gibbons and I met, once again, for lunch at Germaine's. This time we met to discuss what I could expect next. I had few questions about the opinion of the court of appeals. I understood it better than I had initially understood Judge Gesell's memorandum.

According to John, the firm was likely to request a rehearing by the court of appeals en banc, that is, all twenty-four judges meeting as a group. Several weeks or months could pass before the court processed the request. He believed the request would be declined.

The firm could also request a writ of certiorari from the Supreme Court. Processing that could take six to nine months. "I don't think they'll get one," John said "but they can spend a long time trying."

If the Supreme Court granted certiorari, the case would not be heard this session. The current calendar was full.

At best, I could hope the case would be heard at the start of the new session in the fall of 1988. Even in that situation, the Supreme Court might not rule until the end of June of 1989.

A trip to the Supreme Court could take two years. If I won, I would be in the same legal position I was in now—facing a trial on remedy in Judge Gesell's court.

Based on what John said, Doug was about to become a very busy beaver. During the entire course of the litigation, Doug wrote all the major legal documents written on my behalf. Shortly he would be required to write briefs or other material related to a litigation on three legal fronts: the district court, the circuit court, and the Supreme Court.

Until some legal order stopped the process, Doug would proceed with the first phases of a trial on remedy with Judge Gesell. At the same time he would fight requests for a rehearing by the court of appeals en banc. Later he would file whatever legal documents were required to oppose the inevitable request for a hearing by the Supreme Court.

For the first time since I had met the two men, I recognized a separation of duties that had escaped me because Jim and Doug functioned seamlessly like the team they were. Simply stated, Doug wrote the words that defined the legal positions that Jim argued orally.

The children, who had no trouble differentiating between the men, occasionally confused what the men did. To make it easy for them to remember I described Doug and Jim as a "song and dance" team. Doug wrote the lyrics and Jim danced for the judges of the various courts.

For Tela and Gilbert, the analogy was effective. Peter was usually confused. "Does he sing or dance?" Peter frequently asked about one or the other with equal likelihood.

Like any oversimplification, the musical reference was inaccurate. Every brief Doug wrote was better for Jim's contribution, review, and revisions. Every argument Jim made improved as the result of Doug's critique.

Custody

Toni and John were considering getting a dog, she told me over lunch. They thought it might be good company and fun to have around their country home in Front Royal.

The children had asked for a dog every Christmas for the last several years. I had maintained that no child under the age of seven could responsibly handle one. Caring for escaping snakes was easy. Until Peter reached the age of seven, I told the children, I refused to consider a dog. When Toni raised the dog question, however, Peter was seven.

The idea of having a dog suddenly appealed to me. Since the age of two, Gilbert had been terrified of dogs. A friendly pooch had jumped on him. The dog tried to lick his face as he lay strapped in a stroller. It was a small dog, but to Gilbert, trapped on his back, it was gargantuan. He screamed. I assumed that incident was the reason that Gilbert sat on the piano or sought some other high place whenever there was a visiting dog in the house. Gilbert would get over his fear if he watched a bumbling furball grow to be a big dog.

Toni and I decided it would be fun to take the families and go dog hunting together. I told the children to study dogs and let me know what they recommended. The house was instantly full of dog books, collected largely by Tela.

Even as my business at State wound down, Toni and I continued to get together weekly. Dogs and dog magazines became a popular topic of conversation. Although the children did a great deal of dog research, we relied on that done by John. All things considered, he recommended a standard poodle.

The children and I got a black, eight-week-old standard poodle puppy from a breeder. We named him Fidelity-Amandine Lucile Aurore Dudevant of Cathedral Avenue, Fidelity-George for short. We call him George. In six months, the dog outweighed Gilbert. Gilbert is no longer afraid of dogs.

Toni and John never got a dog. She was diagnosed with breast cancer at Thanksgiving and had a mastectomy after Christmas. I was terrified when Tela and I went to visit her in the hospital. When she was released, a dark cloud, in the form of a small bright spot on an MRI, left everyone nervous and uneasy.

Peter got good grades at school. In some classes, his grades were better than those of his siblings. His test scores were at the national average in some areas, considerably higher in others. He scored in the fifty-eighth percentile on reading comprehension in spite of the fact that he could read only five words.

Homeroom was one of the few classes that he attended with his second-grade classmates. At least two periods several days each week were spent in the resource room, the private school equivalent of special education. I paid for outside tutors who worked with him daily, at the expense of his lunch hour and physical education class.

All three children knew Peter was dyslexic. We had discussed it. As we sat around the kitchen table, I had asked Tela to write her name using her right hand while holding her left behind her back. Tela is left-handed. She had written her name badly and with difficulty. I had made a similar request of Gilbert with similar results.

"Dyslexia, like handedness, is a condition, not a disease," I told them. "The condition never goes away. It's the reason Peter reads badly and it makes learning to read hard for him." Peter knew he had to work harder than most children.

I was as concerned over the potential impact of dyslexia on Peter's self-image as I was over its impact on his reading. I knew there was a risk that he might conclude he was stupid if he were unable to keep up with his class.

Spelling seemed to be the area of greatest risk. Peter hated spelling. Every week he had a spelling test that he was almost guaranteed to fail.

I mentally projected the devastating impact that twenty or thirty consecutive failures might have on his confidence. As a preventive measure, the children and I started a program to ensure that Peter passed his spelling tests.

On Monday, with Peter standing by, Tela neatly printed the spelling words, one by one on separate index cards. On Tuesday, Gilbert went over the words with Peter, card by card, until he had most of them memorized. On Wednesday, Peter and I went through the cards.

Thursday was spelling test day. As I drove the children to McDonald's on the way to school, someone called out the words for Peter to spell. When he spelled a word correctly, he was handed the corresponding card which he gleefully tore up and threw over his shoulder. By the time we got to school, he could spell the words.

Shredded index cards accumulated on the floor of the van. Peter passed his spelling tests, frequently with perfect scores. Twenty-four hours after any test, he was unable to spell a single word. Against bad odds, his self-esteem and confidence held their own.

Mine, on the other hand, were severely tested. After working with the State Department for seven years, I understood the organization, knew hundreds of people and a great deal about departmental operations. Budgeting was one of a broad range of subjects about which I was only generally informed.

At the World Bank I knew nothing and no one. I was supposed to be or become expert on the single subject of budgeting. I was surrounded by talented professionals who were better informed than I and, in many cases, probably smarter.

I was not sure that anything I had ever learned applied at the bank. It is a unique organization and, as such, inclined to do even the most mundane administrative functions differently from any organization with which I ever worked. Words that defined what I thought were conventional business terms had different meanings.

I felt lost. It was months before I began to feel comfortable working with the bank.

To say that I was financially insecure is to make an understatement of immense proportions. I had two years to run on the lease of my office in Rosslyn. Although the office was useless because I worked downtown, it cost me a thousand dollars a month, which I could ill afford. Short of declaring bankruptcy, I was unable to get out of the lease.

And I was alone.

I always needed a good friend, a stiff drink, or both to keep me company when I read the legal paperwork that PW's lawyers produced. The description of my interpersonal skill problems in the petition for certiorari was as vituperative as any I had ever read. I have seen child abusers more kindly described.

Lunch at Germaine's was more solemn than usual. Toni was doing remarkably well, John told me. She decided to undergo reconstructive surgery.

I had a lot of questions for John. Aside from being offensive, the petition left me wondering what the case was about. It was by far the most legalistic document I had ever read. Furthermore, it was written by a different set of attorneys and the Gibson, Dunn, and Crutcher lawyer on the front page of the brief was no one I had ever seen. I wondered why PW had changed its legal representatives.

John explained that the new law firm, Mayer Brown, was a very high-powered Chicago firm with an office in Washington. It specialized in appeals to the Supreme Court. PW had probably retained them because of that specialization. That was consistent with what Jim had told me. Price Waterhouse was bringing in the big guns. The new kid on the GD lawyers' block was Theodore R. Olson, President Reagan's personal attorney.

"What a shame," I thought. I had secretly hoped that Gibson, Dunn, and Crutcher had been fired.

There are some pretty specific conditions that must be met before the Supreme Court will accept a case. John referred to the acceptance as "granting cert," short for granting a writ of certiorari. He discussed the general conditions. I knew the Court interpreted the Constitution. I also knew it resolved issues where the constitutionally granted rights of one party conflicted with those of another. But I never thought of the Supreme Court as the overseer of the lower courts. It is.

The Supreme Court settles matters of law when the courts of appeal in the circuits across the country interpret federal law inconsistently. John qualified his remarks by saying that it had to be an important law and the inconsistency had to make a big difference. After all, from thousands of requests the Court only accepts one or two hundred cases each year.

PW's constitutional rights had not been violated. The issue between the firm and myself was hardly a constitutional conflict. However, Title VII of the Civil Rights Act of 1964 was an important law. I only hoped that my case would be viewed as insignificant, indifferent, and unimportant. I had never been in the Supreme Court building and I had no interest in a personal guided tour.

After the refresher course in high school civics, John explained Mayer Brown's case and the legalese they used to describe it. They argued the evidence. To be discriminatory, there must be an intent to discriminate. The court of appeals goofed by upholding Judge Gesell when he found discrimination based on unconscious stereotyping. If, however, the law prohibits employment decisions based on stereotypical evaluations, they argued that PW was still innocent. Under this legal scenario, the circuit court goofed by upholding Judge Gesell when he failed to recognize that I was too disagreeable to be a partner.

They argued the burden of proof—who had to prove what. Judge Gesell found that once I presented enough evidence to show that discrimination played some role in the partnership decision, the burden of proof shifted. PW then had to prove that absent all discrimination, the firm would never have made me a partner anyway. The circuit court agreed. Mayer Brown argued that, on burden shifting, the lower courts goofed again. The burden of proof should have been on me to prove that, absent discrimination, I would have been made a partner. Price Waterhouse should never have been required to do anything except demonstrate that it had a legitimate reason for its decision.

They argued the evidentiary standard. Even if the burden properly shifted to the firm, the judge erred by making it too hard for the firm to prove its point. I only had to present preponderant evidence to prove my point. When the burden shifted to Price Waterhouse, however, the judge found that it had to prove its point with clear and convincing evidence. In this case, the circuit court and Judge Gesell goofed by not applying the same standard to each of us.

John's opinion was unchanged. He, Jim, and Doug were still in accord: it was unlikely that the Supreme Court would grant cert. The legal issues were technicalities, unlikely to be important enough to warrant review by the highest court in the land.

My ability to understand and retain information outside the realm of my experience is limited. Hearing the facts described in different words or interpreted by different people helps me learn. Doug and Jim had explained the law. John had also explained it, differently, and from a different point of view.

"Why don't you call Greg?" asked Ruth. I had dropped the Supreme Court papers through her mail slot earlier in the week. We were ensconced in her living room sipping tea. Although she was only halfway through her first year in law school, she was as good a legal tea-leaf reader as anyone I knew. On the petition for cert, however, she offered no opinion.

"He's an attorney. See what he thinks," she continued. I had met Ruth's oldest son, Greg Zagorin, when he and I were both invited for dinner or holiday functions. We were about the same age.

He and I spent a few hours together when a combination of carpenter ants and a summer storm sheared a forty-foot locust tree from its base and left it leaning precariously against the back of Ruth and David's house. It was Fourth of July weekend. At the time, the Hoppers were in Italy on business. The distraught housekeeper had relied on Greg and me to do something. Based on his handling of the tree crisis, he seemed like a calm, considerate man.

Greg and I had dinner at one of the neighborhood restaurants. He carefully qualified his opinions by stating that he practiced contract law for the Department of Defense. He and I discussed, in substance, the same issues that John had patiently explained to me.

Greg, however, reached a different conclusion. He believed that the Court would find either burden shifting or evidentiary standards important enough to take the case, but that the real interest of the Court was the stereotyping issue.

"Shit!" echoed over the secretarial bays in front of Bob Picciotto's office. I looked around nervously to see how many people might have heard me. The only person in sight was Bob's secretary who had called me from a meeting for an urgent phone call from Doug. The last time I was similarly summoned, I was told that the court of appeals had declined PW's request for a rehearing en banc.

"The Supreme Court took the case," I said in an attempt to excuse my bad language. Fortunately Bob was away and out of earshot. Not that Bob would have been offended—startled probably more than offended.

Bob Picciotto was the director of planning and budgeting. His name could strike fear or rage into the hearts of most managers at the bank. He had influence, if not control, over how much money they could spend.

Furthermore, he exercised it, not always in accord with the desires of the managers.

He was my client. In spite of his somewhat fearsome reputation, he was a personal pussycat, a lovable human being. When the children ran around the office, he always spoke to them cheerfully and expressed a genuine interest in what they said. He dealt kindly with me as I struggled to learn the bank. With patience he poked holes in my analyses and identified errors, but he did it so that I never felt personally assaulted.

Bob was unassuming and unpretentious. Wispy, graying hair seemed to be patted in place. When it fell to his forehead he unconsciously pushed it aside. Although he dressed as one would expect a banker to dress, he never quite fit properly into his clothes. A collar curled up or a shoelace dangled. Something was always ever so slightly misplaced. It contributed to his humanness.

At the same time that Bob initiated the personnel paperwork to convert me from a consultant to an employee of the bank, Jim and Doug started writing briefs for the Supreme Court. It seemed likely that I would be employed by the time the Court heard arguments in the fall of 1988. If not, there was a distinct possibility that financial pressure would force me to move from the District where I could put the children in public schools.

The children's school went only through sixth grade. Tela was in her last year. In the spring of 1988 she applied to other schools, one of which, the Maret School was two blocks from home. The location made Maret my first choice. It would simplify my life greatly to have a school within walking distance.

Tela decided to go to Maret. I encouraged Gilbert to apply even though he was only in fourth grade and could have stayed where he was for two more years. I considered moving Peter, but decided against it because of the lack of special programs.

Gilbert was enthusiastic about Maret. When he was accepted, I unilaterally decided that he would change schools. I had no attachment to the current school. Among other things, I was always irritated when the headmaster insisted on calling me Mrs. Gallagher. The misnomer is understandable and completely acceptable from my children's buddies. From the headmaster, it was unforgivable and intolerable. I did not like the man.

Thomas Peter was less than thrilled with the old school. He characterized the institution simply: "Purveyors of education to the rich and famous." He was, however, an active participant not only in the school program but also in activities of the related church. He resented my decision to move Gilbert. Gilbert decided he hated the new school as soon as he realized that Thomas Peter opposed the transfer.

One Saturday morning when the children were with Thomas Peter, I was served with legal documents notifying me that he intended to sue me for custody of the children. I went ballistic.

As long as Thomas Peter and I were married, I harbored some hope for reconciliation. For that reason I never planned to divorce him. In fact, I had no plans to divorce him when I discussed the custody matter with Jim Heller. It would indeed be peculiar, Jim told me, to litigate custody without divorce, and Thomas Peter had sued only for custody. Jim helped me realize that I had to face facts. As long as I had to litigate, I should oppose the custody suit and countersue for divorce.

Gilbert became disruptive at school. Peter started a fire in the institutional laundry room. The school demanded family therapy as a condition of Peter's reenrollment in the fall. We spent six weeks in family therapy. I hated it, but Peter was reenrolled.

According to Jim I was never in any real jeopardy of losing custody of the children. The threat I imagined, however, was worse than the one that was real. Thomas Peter eventually withdrew his custody suit.

Tela's best friend was thinking about going to sleep-away summer camp. Tela wanted to go. I worried over the decision. I had to send Peter to reading camp. Gilbert and Tela were scheduled to attend the summer program at school. The idea of Peter in one camp, Gilbert in another, and Tela in still another, this one on the eastern shore of Maryland, troubled me. Tela had never been away from home. She was only twelve. I rationalized; then I let her go to camp.

My house is conveniently located along the most direct route between Jim's home and office. In May and June, as I grappled with the problems of getting the children from school into their summer programs, Supreme Court briefs drifted in, usually delivered by Jim in his beloved, beat-up yellow Volkswagen Rabbit. I dumped them in heaps, sometimes in the kitchen, usually on my desk. In mid-July, when I finally had all of them in final form, I culled the drafts and sat down to review the material, some of which I had never read.

"Blue v. Pink," I mused when I stacked up the ten briefs submitted to

the Supreme Court. The five-by-eight-inch, individually bound pam-
phlets were color coded. As petitioner, Price Waterhouse's brief was
required to be blue. As respondent, mine had to be red, close enough to
pink to evoke the color comparison. Red suits my coloring better—I look
washed out in most shades of pink.

The pile included a dirty brown brief filed by the Department of
Justice. My government was not on my side. A yellow brief recorded my
counterarguments to the blue brief. All the rest were green.

The green booklets were colloquially referred to as amicus briefs,
from the Latin amicus curiae. The term describes an uninvolved party
who offers advice to the court. Betsy Hishon told me she had twenty. In
Price Waterhouse v. Hopkins there were five.

Although amicus briefs sometimes raise relevant legal points unnoticed by the parties involved in a litigation, their general purpose is to
represent the interests of a constituency. The briefs tend to be aligned
with one side or the other. In PW's case, the amicus score was four to one
in my favor.

The score is no predictor of legal outcome, but it made the children
feel better. Children will keep score on anything. The introduction to
the AFL/CIO amicus brief describes the "125,000 working men and
women" represented by the union. At Peter's request I read the opening
paragraph while the children and I waited for the pizza we had ordered
in a local restaurant. Peter rapidly lost interest, but not the number.
"Does that mean you have a hundred and twenty-five thousand votes,
Mom? How many do we need to win?" he asked. "No, Peter; and we
need votes from five Justices of the Supreme Court to win," I replied.

Doug's colleague Donna Lanhoff who had helped with the search for
Susan Fiske, coordinated an amicus brief prepared by the Women's
Legal Defense Fund. It represented the interests of forty women's
groups.

The American Psychological Association submitted an amicus brief.
As a tactical matter, that was important to me. In PW's brief, Mayer
Brown had consistently enclosed stereotyping in quotes, as part of an
obvious attempt to put clinical psychology in the same legal credibility
class with voodoo and witchcraft.

When they were asked, both Doug and Susan helped the APA
attorneys by reviewing or exchanging drafts. Susan's presence in town
gave the three of us a chance to get together over lunch. I was surprised

when she told me that although she had been asked, she had never given testimony on another matter. Flattered, I asked why she testified for me. "I had never seen anything so egregious," was her simple reply.

As an attorney, Doug was pleased that the New York Bar Association filed a green booklet on my behalf. Women are horribly underrepresented in the partner ranks of the legal profession. It was sobering for me to realize how much effort was expended on my behalf by people whom I never knew.

Once again, John and I ate lunch at Germaine's. Greg Zagorin and I had dinner at a neighborhood restaurant. Betsy Hishon and I got together for drinks and a chat at the Sheraton downtown where her husband, a tax attorney, was attending a business meeting. We glibly referred to each other as "Landmark One" and "Landmark Two." We shared hopes that the outcome in *Price Waterhouse v. Hopkins* would be favorable to me.

After many reviews of the colorful piles of Supreme Court briefs, there was consensus on one item. Everyone, including Doug and Jim, believed that my weakest legal position was related to the evidentiary standard issue.

William Glaberson from the *New York Times Magazine* introduced himself over the phone. He called me at home. Like most private citizens, my phone number is listed in the local directory. He had an idea for an article that he had mentally and very tentatively entitled "Profiles in Tenacity" along the lines of a book written by John F. Kennedy. I laughed as I said, "If you're writing about tenacity, you should be talking to someone at Price Waterhouse. The Supreme Court case is theirs, not mine."

I explained that *Price Waterhouse v. Hopkins* was a case that PW brought before the Supreme Court. My case was *Hopkins v. Price Waterhouse.* I had been on a winning streak in the lower courts. The last thing I wanted was a Supreme Court case.

The press called infrequently during the three or four years that Jim and Doug and I slugged it out in the lower courts. Granting media requests for interviews only became an issue when I was dragged before the Supreme Court. Jim told me I could do what I wished, but he advised against my talking to the media until the arguments were over.

I had retained Doug and Jim to represent me. They were professionals. I believed that my interests were ill served if I tried to second-guess them or if I ignored their counsel. On those rare occasions when we disagreed, they did it my way. This, however, was not the time to ignore their advice.

I told Bill that, on advice of counsel, I avoided discussions of the litigation. I declined the interview. In several phone conversations over the next few weeks he convinced Doug and me that his interest was more in the people involved in issues before the Court than it was in the legal questions. He had enough tenacity to persuade me to talk to him, but only with one of my attorneys present.

It was August, hot and humid. There was something wrong with the air conditioning in the house. Doug and I nearly boiled during the interview. The children wandered in and out at will to ask a question or to listen. Between interruptions, I discussed personal matters. What Bill wrote about the litigation he learned from the public record.

His article, *Determined to be Heard,* appeared in the *New York Times Magazine* on October 2, 1988, the day before the Supreme Court term started. After that, Jim and Doug eased off a little from their position that I avoid the media.

Al Kamen, a *Washington Post* reporter persuaded Jim with the simple argument, "It is, after all, the local paper." They consented to my talking to the *Washington Post,* but advised that I keep the tone of things straight-laced and serious.

After the interview, a *Post* photographer came by the house to take a picture of me and the three children. As I tried to keep a straight face while encouraging the children to smile, we struggled with George, who bounced on and off our laps. When our picture was snapped, the expression on my face was grim. After seeing it on the Saturday before his argument before the Supreme Court, Jim commented, "In the future, smile." The photograph went into the *Post* files.

Price Waterhouse
v. Hopkins

Halloween was a Monday in 1988. It had also been a Monday in 1983 when Betsy Hishon went before me. Five years to the day separated our hikes up the thirty-six steps to the Doric-pillared portico that dwarfs the main entrance to the Supreme Court building. Most of my family made the trip to Washington and walked up the steps with me.

Over the years, my sister and brother and I have spent only a little time together. The memory of that time is treasured.

Susan and her husband both work, as do Brother and his wife. We all practice our professions seriously and with commitment. The demands of work and family have consumed most of our time and energy. However, when one of the three of us needs the others, as I needed them then, we set aside other priorities and band together against all obstacles.

Barely six weeks into the school year, it was grossly inconvenient for Susan to take time away from her teaching. Dressed as a witch, complete with stage makeup and spray-painted hair, she presided over her classes the Friday before Halloween. The frantic trip to the Boston train station left her covered with a gooey mess of makeup mixed with perspiration. The toilet facilities on the train to New York were inadequate for the task of cleaning up.

"You look like a witch, Aunt Susan," said Brother's oldest child when Susan finally arrived late Friday to spend the night with Brother and his family. The next day when she and Brother strolled up the driveway to the house on Cathedral, she was her usual attractive self: clean blond hair, unnoticeable makeup, deftly applied.

Saturday night the children went to bed earlier than the adults did. Due more to boredom than exhaustion, Tela, Gilbert, and Peter retired when the topic of conversation turned to legal issues after a chaotic and very late dinner.

Susan, Brother, and I sat up for a long time talking about the history of the case. I eventually succumbed to exhaustion, leaving them with a multicolored pile of briefs to review. They sat reading in my living room until just before dawn.

Sunday evening was consumed by planning. My neighbor Carol joined us for dinner. Vera Schneider wanted to be there, but she had to go to Annapolis on business for a couple of days. That made Carol the only in-town resident with a car.

I decided to stay outside the logistical loop. Carol had to coordinate the efforts required to make sure that George, Tela, Gilbert, Peter, Sheila, Susan, Brother, and Vera's two girls wound up in the right places at the right times on Supreme Court Day. When I went to bed, the planning process had advanced only to the point where everyone agreed that George would stay at Carol's house.

The family was noisily wandering to and from showers upstairs as Carol arrived early on Supreme Court Day morning. It was cold. I was making huge volumes of coffee.

Sheila drifted into the kitchen. I poured coffee for Carol and then for Sheila. The three of us sat talking about how cold it was until Tela arrived, hair still wet from the shower. "We're going down to hold a place in line. I didn't come all the way from Arkansas to miss the show," Sheila said as she, Carol, and Tela left to catch a cab downtown.

I heard Brother thump down the stairs to the first floor to wake the boys who had fallen asleep with the television running in the recreation room. He thumped by once again in the process of getting the boys into the shower.

"Don't worry about it, Sis. I've got everything under control," Brother said. By all appearances, his statement was false. Barefooted, with his shirt unbuttoned, and a tie draped over his shoulders, he poured himself a cup of coffee. Apparently the boys could only find one tie and were unable to find any socks at all.

"Get out of here. We'll handle it," said Susan as she coaxed me to leave the house. When the door closed behind me, Brother, still barefooted, was making plans to borrow a tie from David Hopper.

A cab dropped me at Kator, Scott, and Heller. Jim looked wonderful. He lowered his chin in shy reaction when I commented to that effect. His wife must have helped him buy that shirt I thought. Over the years, Jim's wife, Bobbie Heller, and I had gently, but persistently teased him about his boring shirts. He always responded with indifference—shirts were irrelevant to him.

Susan, Sheila, and Carol were relieved when I caught up with them shortly before noon at the front of the line that stretched for hundreds of feet at the base of the steps. They had arrived at ten o'clock for the midafternoon argument. Vera's girls, who had arrived even earlier, were with Tela taking their turn picking up hot chocolate to stave off the cold. "Where's John?" they asked in unison.

No one had seen Brother since he took the boys and left the house on a mission to buy socks en route to the Court. Fortunately, he and the completely dressed boys arrived as the line was released to proceed up the stairs and into the Court.

In pairs, Sheila and Carol followed by Susan and Brother preceded the boys and me on the quiet walk up the stairs. Vera's girls and Tela were somewhere in front, nowhere in sight.

The line going through the security checkpoint just inside the door backed up, forming a crowd on the portico. Although the boys were pooped from playing with relatives all weekend, they stood patiently beside me between two of the twenty-foot-high pillars.

Family and friends disappeared through the door and into the building. Susan and Brother had reserved seats in Justice Brennan's box. She got them through the efforts of a colleague whose family had for generations been friends of the Brennan family. I was impressed with her cleverness and her good fortune.

I was also a little envious. Jim had obtained passes from the Court that guaranteed seats for Ruth, me, and the children somewhere in general seating. Ruth, who spent the morning in law school, met the children and me in the office of the chief marshal. From there we were escorted into the courtroom to the middle of fifteen or twenty rows of highbacked benches by a young, very serious, female marshal.

Ruth sat to my left, Gilbert and Peter to my right and along the aisle.

Bobbie Heller was later seated in a chair at the edge of the bench across the aisle. Friends, supporters, and the rest of the family were sprinkled around the back of the full house.

It was evident from the outset that Gilbert, Peter, and I would be unable to see the argument before the Court. The seating was designed to observe the justices, not the attorneys.

To the horror of the stern marshal who seated us, the boys, unable to see past the bench in front of them, decided to chat with each other. On her quiet command, I moved Peter so that my body separated the two bored boys.

The ceiling in the courtroom was easily eighteen feet high. Draperies, dark purple, shaded toward burgundy, hung from the ceiling behind the justices' seats and along the sides of the general seating area. I wondered what the acoustics would be like as I stood and coaxed the boys to stand.

The justices of the Supreme Court entered through slits in the drapery. Chief Justice Rehnquist sat at center. The other justices sat in seniority order, Justice Marshall to the chief justice's far right, Justice Scalia to his far left.

Somewhere near the center, Justice O'Connor's eyes stared through deep gray rings on a ghostly white, stoically expressionless face. In spite of a mastectomy ten days earlier, she was on the bench. The press had speculated that she might be absent.

I expected the arguments to be lively and interesting, similar to those before the court of appeals. Jim was ready. During the previous week, he and Doug had brought in several respected attorneys to play devil's advocate at a mock court session. They criticized his prepared argument and his delivery. They tried to ask the most difficult questions they could imagine from the point of view of each of the justices.

The boys' falling asleep met with another stern command from the marshal. Sleeping in the Supreme Court is prohibited. "She must be childless," I thought as I reluctantly shook the boys into consciousness.

The arguments were a disappointment. The justices listened as Kathryn A. Oberly presented her argument for Price Waterhouse. She finished, right on time. Jim presented his argument. He finished, very early. There were no questions. He sat down.

Between the dreadful acoustics and the badgering marshal, I barely heard the arguments. There were few questions, none of them entertaining, to interrupt the proceedings. Susan and John later told me that from their vantage point they could hear and see everything.

According to those who could see him, Jim was calm, poised, eloquent, and articulate. Had he been taller they might have described him as elegant. Since he and I were close to the same height, most characterized him as urbane.

It was clear where my friends' loyalties lay. By comparison to Jim, they characterized Kathryn Oberly as dowdy. Her pale complexion might have benefited from makeup. She wore an awful black suit and no jewelry. She stooped or slouched. According to them, her arguments were unpersuasive. Some wondered if having a female argue before the Supreme Court was a tactical ploy. In the spirit of the season, she should have had a witch's mole on her nose.

In point of fact, an attorney, regardless of sex, must wear black to argue before the Supreme Court. Proceedings before that Court are very formal. I am told that when the attorney general appears, he wears a morning coat. Kathryn Oberly had no choice. Black does not suit her coloring and no amount of makeup or jewelry would have compensated for that.

In the years since Supreme Court Day, I have had the pleasure of meeting Kay Oberly, as she refers to herself, on several occasions. "Nothing personal. Litigation polarizes," she said when we were first introduced. The warmth of her smile and the sincerity that radiated from troubled eyes banished any recollection I may have had of her posture or what she wore.

I gave her a ride to the airport once. I was driving to work and noticed her unsuccessfully trying to hail a cab. We chatted about being single parents and the trauma of divorce proceedings, matters that we had in common. I like Kay.

I never believed that her arguing *Price Waterhouse v. Hopkins* was a ploy. A different attorney, Paul Bator, was originally slated to argue the case. She was on brief.

The argument was initially scheduled for the first week in October. Paul Bator had another argument before the Supreme Court that same week. For that reason, PW's case was rescheduled to Halloween. I believe that he was terminally ill when the case was argued. He died around Halloween.

The sleepy boys were relieved that the arguments were over. Tela joined us as we worked our way through the crowd back toward the portico where I had agreed to meet Brother and Susan.

Instead of Brother, I found Sheila; standing with her were two white-haired ladies, one of them, Louie Spencer, was an ancient friend of my mother. Mom and Louie had been close friends since they lived in Galveston when Louie's son and I were born, only weeks apart. The last time Mom and Gil were in Washington, three generations of Louie's family enjoyed burned barbecue on the deck at my house.

Louie had taken the train down from Princeton specifically to attend the arguments. I invited Louie and her friend, Rachel, back to the house and asked Sheila to make sure they got there.

A light breeze alerted me to the fact that we were outside on a sparkling bright cool autumn day. Tela, Peter, Gilbert, and I joined hands. I inhaled deeply before speaking.

"Okay children. See that crowd at the bottom of the stairs?" I asked. They acknowledged the existence of the three or four completely equipped and set-up television crews who seemed to be waiting behind an invisible barrier that prevented them from coming up the thirty-six steps.

"We are going to walk all the way down, right through the middle of the crowd, over to the corner, and hail a cab. Stand up straight," I said. We took the first step in unison.

Running into Louie had so startled me that I forgot about Brother who hastily caught up with us on the second step. I was afraid to look down through my bifocals for fear of falling. To my relief, Brother stepped out a little ahead of us. Sheila, Carol, and the rest of the group were right behind the children and me.

"At least if I trip down the steps of the Supreme Court on national television, Brother can catch me," I said to myself. With Brother one step ahead, his attention split between the children and me uphill and the media downhill, the children and I walked with even, uninter-rupted stride to the bottom.

I recognized Rita Braver in the crowd. She was wearing an ear-to-ear grin. "Easy, Brother," I cautioned as I nudged the children to move in front of me into single-file formation. The path through the crowd was not wide enough for us to pass four-abreast. Something about the rigid cut of his jaw gave me the impression that he was prepared to engage anyone who got too close.

Brother fell into line behind me as we wormed our way through the press corps. In descending order by height, the children walked directly to the curb. Each raised a hand to hail a cab. Brother opened the rear cab door for us.

"Think like a school bus," I said to the startled cab driver as he eyed the three or four cameramen who appeared in his rearview mirror. "We're going to Georgetown Day School, followed by St. Patrick's, followed by the Maret School," I continued as he pulled away from the curb. He kept an eye on the mirror that tracked the progress of the cameramen running after him down the middle of the street.

The children and I hugged each other excitedly. After we picked up their friends, we were going to a party.

Divorce

Peter had been digging for worms in the garden. Ruth and I had been tending azaleas and talking back and forth over the wall when the idea struck. Fighting off PW's attorneys had been quite a strain on Doug and Jim, and whereas they worked hard to keep my spirits up, I wondered what kept them from the doldrums.

"I'm thinking about having a Supreme Court party to cheer Jim and Doug on," I muttered in the general direction of Ruth. At the time I was considering cold cuts and other deli delights from the local grocery store.

"That's a great idea, Mom. Why don't you call Ridgewell's?" chirped Peter. Ruth agreed.

"The menu must include crab claws, jumbo shrimp, chocolate-covered strawberries, and dry ice," I told the woman from Ridgewell's. "Beyond that, you're on your own," I said with a laugh.

I explained to Ridgewell's representative that the children and I had decided on a three-purpose party. Tela and Peter would celebrate Halloween. For Gilbert, who would be eleven at the end of the week, it would be a birthday party. My purpose was to pay homage to Doug and Jim. I elaborated only to the extent necessary to respond to her curious questions. Even for Ridgewell's, the party seemed a little unusual.

Tela, Gilbert, and Peter were each allowed to invite ten friends, so she could expect twenty or thirty children, ages nine to thirteen. Although it was a wild guess, I estimated forty to sixty adults. She was laughing when we hung up.

"No pumpkin muffins, no multigrain buns, no pasta salad, no fall vegetables," I said as she read the proposed menu a little later that day. "But you've eliminated all the starches. It won't be a balanced meal," she responded in horror.

I stopped any thought of a debate with "they can eat a balanced meal some other time." She informed me that she would have to check with her supervisor. I had the impression that she was concerned that Ridgewell's image might be tarnished by a menu that paid inadequate attention to the various food groups.

The supervisor must have agreed with me. After one more phone call the menu was set. There were no more nutritional discussions.

The taxi-cum-school bus was loaded well beyond the legal limits when it delivered us to the party almost an hour after we left the Supreme Court. Eight children and I piled from the car and onto the driveway. Fortunately I added a generous tip to the thirty-dollar fare because the excited children left all their book bags and jackets in the trunk of the cab. Hours later, the driver returned to deliver the forgotten belongings.

The setting in the house was worthy of Ridgewell's. In the recreation room, carbon dioxide oozed eerily through the appropriately scary eye, nose, and mouth openings of a four-foot plastic pumpkin that looked real enough to use for pie.

On the second floor, spotless white linen, impeccably pinned to fall in scallops, covered every major flat surface, including the badly stained porch table on the deck. Tasteful arrangements of fall flowers, the same kinds that the bridesmaids had carried at my wedding, offset the whiteness of the linen on the bar and porch table.

I realized how hungry I was when I inspected the sterling flatware carefully arranged in symmetric patterns around the precut turkey and ham on the serving table. There was an empty tray for the filet— Ridgewell's thought that should be served hot. Flowers, fruit, and cheeses added color.

My children were on a first-name basis with half the staff I encountered in the kitchen. By the time I arrived to survey the scene, the youngsters were eating chocolate-covered strawberries and petits fours, a new addition to the menu. I sampled the crab claws and shrimp that were being elegantly laid out on trays with cocktail sauce.

The voice I had heard only over the phone introduced herself and informed me that she would personally supervise the party. She asked me to make a few last-minute decisions before the adult guests arrived. By then five or ten more children were underfoot.

"By profession, I am a management consultant, not a caterer. Please exercise your best professional judgement," I requested. I nearly tripped over a couple of nine-year-olds on their way up the stairs as I started down to answer the doorbell. "By the way, please assign your staff so the younger children don't run around upstairs," I commented.

People filled the living and dining rooms. They overflowed through the doors opened wide onto the back deck. Some even escaped the crowd upstairs by retiring to the recreation room. It had been abandoned by the children, most of whom were playing ball in the driveway under the careful supervision of a liveried waiter serving crab claws, Cokes, and petits fours.

Jim and Doug, each surrounded by ever-changing groups of four or five, told and retold the legal story, to the Danzigers and the Gibbons, and the Renmans. Roger Feldman entertained with descriptions of the trial on liability and his recollections of Judge Gesell as Moses. He also talked a lot about loons—Roger was a loon fan.

Bini Herrmann and Sally Keene Craig renewed acquaintances with Brother and Susan, whom they had not seen since my wedding. Thanks to their late-night reading, my brother and sister were able to answer the dozens of questions that my college classmates and Louie Spencer and Rachel raised.

As she inevitably does, Mary Curzan brought flowers. She came without Mike. He was out of town on some project for Arnold and Porter. I thought fondly of Mike and the fact that he brought Doug to the party, so to speak, when he recommended him to me more than five years ago.

Mary and Sheila talked about growing up Catholic with Susan Riley and other friends from Girl Scout days. I remembered when I met Mary at my wedding in 1974. She and I had become friends over the years since.

About the time she left, sometime after midnight, the formal party ended, almost unnoticed. One minute there were a dozen of so friends and family members sitting around, the next minute I heard a polite question, "Do you need anything else, Miss Hopkins?" The kitchen was spotless as were the deck and the dining and recreation rooms.

Brother took the Schneider girls and Louie and Rachel home. Ridgewell's vanished, leaving the family sitting in the living room talking quietly over coffee and cognac. I went to bed.

When he called in mid-November, Jim commented once again about how lovely the party had been. I knew it was his attempt at subtlety. He wanted to talk about a distasteful matter, the divorce. I tried to avoid the issue in hopes that it would go away.

Divorces do not vanish. They are scheduled. Mine was due to be heard in the D.C. Superior Court in late winter or early spring. Jim had sent papers over for me to review. I filed them with barely a glance. Other than to note that Thomas Peter's lawyer had misspelled Thomas Peter's last name, I had no comments.

"We have seven children—her four, my two, and you," David said when he extended the invitation for Thanksgiving with the family. Ruth must have known how hard it would be for me to be alone. David delivered the line but it must have been Ruth's idea to invite me.

I cooked escalloped potatoes and a pair of pies for the dinner. It kept me busy and focused my mind on something other than the absence of my family. I enjoyed dinner. Greg and I chatted about legal matters. I went home early.

Sheila came for Christmas. For some reason that to this day I am unable to understand Thomas Peter was very angry. Sheila is a pragmatist. Her brother's wrath would not separate her from his children. She loves Thomas Peter, the children, and me. Disputes between Thomas Peter and me never changed that.

Price Waterhouse's Supreme Court case was the topic of only a three-minute conversation. There was no hope for an opinion before April. I expected it late in June.

We actually had a pretty good time at Christmas. Maybe I was becoming accustomed, to the extent possible, to being alone. The children dressed George in their Christmas clothes. The day Sheila returned to Arkansas, she undecorated the tree and put away the boxes of trimmings while I was at work. That was the best present of all.

"I won't specify an amount and I don't care what the law allows," I commented angrily to Jim when he raised the issue of child support. Jim was only trying to protect the future interests of the children. It was inappropriate for me to vent my frustration on Jim.

I forced myself to calm down. "Let Thomas Peter name the numbers. His Catholic guilt will drive him to a higher number than I would ever pick," I said. Jim consented sadly.

The divorce proceedings took place on St. Patrick's Day. Maybe the Irish celebrated. I did not.

Jim was shocked when I became hysterical in the hall of the D.C. Superior Court building. He had seen me shed a few tears, go into temporary states of depression, and drop a number of well-placed expletives during the various interactions with Price Waterhouse. Never had he seen sadness, depression, and rage converge as they did that day. I came within a hair of leaving him standing before the judge without a client.

The unsettled calm that Jim had talked me into lasted only until I left the room at the end of the hearing. Thomas Peter's lawyer had used salary information obtained from the accountants who worked for his company and my company and who had for years prepared our joint tax returns.

The legal point was immaterial. I was, however, outraged at the use of what I considered to be confidential information, especially since my income was overstated by 50 percent. Although I had filed a joint return with Thomas Peter the year before, I decided that I would never use the accountants again. Furthermore, whether or not it was to my financial advantage, I would file my own tax returns.

That was easier said than done. I have no recollection of ever filing tax returns. I always had them prepared and filed for me. Shortly before taxes were due, I was in deep *kim chi.*

I called Jim. I had forgotten that his wife was a tax accountant until he told me that she might be able to help, even on short notice at the busiest time of the year. In spite of the fact that I had hired Jim, not Bobbie, she pitched in and helped out. Somehow they got me through.

Jim does not practice family law. Mine may have been the only divorce he ever handled. I was a dreadful client.

What's New, Charlie Brown? was selected to be the Maret School spring musical. It had a core cast of four, two girls, a boy, and a dog. I expected Tela to audition. She auditioned, usually successfully, for all the plays.

She had played the title role in *Annie* the year before at St. Patrick's Episcopal Day School. The matter of orphans aside, she was type cast:

a caring child who could never pass a homeless person on the street, a child whom others naturally followed, a mischievous child with a wry sense of humor.

A two- or three-octave voice range and stunning red hair also helped. Unfortunately, Tela's hair, although naturally wavy, does not kink. The school wanted her to wear a wig. Tela resisted. My hairdresser of many years came to the rescue. He set her hair in ringlets for the dress rehearsal and each of the performances.

To my surprise Gilbert also auditioned for *Charlie Brown*. Both children were successful. Gilbert played Linus to Tela's Lucy. They were both typecast. The script of the play could have been written in my kitchen.

During the late winter and through the spring, chaos reigned at the house. Homework, spelling drills, and meals had to be scheduled around play rehearsals that ran several hours, several days each week. Peter frequently attended rehearsals and coached Gilbert on his lines. By the time Gilbert and Tela had their lines memorized, Peter knew all the lines of all the characters.

"Watch me. You and Gilbert are half the cast. I'm sure I can get tickets," I said when Tela told me that *Charlie Brown* was sold out. The ticket application form must have come home in some book bag. With the swirl of other activities around me, I either missed it or failed to process it. Tela was very upset at the prospect of my missing a show.

Tickets were readily available and relatively plentiful. Peter went to the dress rehearsal. Carol Supplee and I attended all four performances. Susan Riley and Vera Schneider attended one each. *Charlie Brown* was the most entertaining event of 1989.

Evidentiary Standards

My only acquaintance with evidentiary standards was gained from reading murder mysteries and watching Perry Mason on TV with my grandmother when I was a kid. As I recall it, the prosecutor always had to prove beyond a reasonable doubt that the defendant did it.

As an evidentiary standard, I understood what "beyond a reasonable doubt" meant. Clear and convincing was harder for me to understand. Preponderance was a word I had to look up in a dictionary. The difference between clear and convincing evidence and a preponderance of the evidence escaped me completely.

I had asked Doug and Jim and each of the other attorneys I knew to explain the difference. The question reduced what I generally considered to be intelligent, articulate practitioners of the legal profession to babblers. To this day I do not know the difference between the two evidentiary standards.

I had a headache on May Day 1989 when the Supreme Court announced its judgment in *Price Waterhouse v. Hopkins*. The day before, a couple of friends and I had gathered around eleven in the morning at the Old Angler's Inn for brunch to celebrate Carol Supplee's birthday. The waiter, who was unaccustomed to people ordering beer at brunch, told us that the beer was warm. Undaunted, we asked him to bring out the wine coolers to chill the Becks.

When we put the party together we had specified brunch, not a specific time, so by the time all the people who were coming got there and ate, it was four in the afternoon. The celebration continued at a leisurely pace with marguerites and a Mexican dinner at L'Auriol Plaza in Adams Morgan and ended at my house with coffee and cognac at two the next morning.

At 9:00 A.M., I was tired when I got to my office. By the time I returned from my first scheduled meeting of the day, I had missed the first pot of coffee, which was usually made at 8:30 or so by the division chief's secretary, Gopol.

When I returned from dumping the old coffee grinds, washing the pot, getting fresh water, and waiting for the new coffee to brew, I found among the messages on my desk one that told me Jim Heller had called. I had a knee-jerk reaction to telephone messages from either of my attorneys: drop everything and return the call.

The clerk of the Supreme Court had called, Jim said. The opinion had come down. Someone from Kator, Scott, and Heller, was en route to the Supreme Court to pick up a copy. He had no clue what the opinion said.

My next call was to Ruth Hopper. I told her what little I knew and asked if I could come by for a cup of tea when I had the opinion in hand. I wanted to escape the press corps until I could calm down, and I would appreciate her reading the opinion and telling me what it meant.

My stomach was flipping. "Who needs this?" I said to myself. I left the coffee on the desk, walked from my office, and waited while Evalyn, who had not been with me long enough to know what was going on, finished taking a message for one of the other people she worked for. I told her that I had to go see my attorneys about unspecified legal matters. If she got any phone calls from people outside the bank, I asked her to tell them that I was out and she did not know how to reach me. If bank staff called, she was to take a message and I would call back.

It was raining. I never carried an umbrella or a raincoat. I took a seemingly endless cab ride ten blocks across town where I jumped from the cab and raced into Jim's building. Walking through the dry lobby gave me a chance to shake off the wetness and regain some composure.

I felt like I had most of my act together when I walked into the Kator, Scott, and Heller offices. Jim, I was told, was in the Xerox room. Sure enough, when I walked into the Xerox room, there he was, reading disjointed bits and snatches of the Supreme Court opinion as the copies trickled from what had to be one of the slower copying machines I had ever seen.

I tried to help Jim with the Xeroxing and only succeeded in interfering with whatever organizational concept he had in mind. He told me he had been too busy copying the opinion to read it. Furthermore, it was going to take some time to figure out what the Supreme Court had said.

What I thought was "the" opinion was actually four opinions. The judgment of the Court was written by Justice Brennan. Justices Marshall, Blackmun, and Stevens joined in that opinion. A second opinion was written by Justice White who concurred with the judgment of the Court. A third opinion was written by Justice O'Connor who also concurred with the judgment of the Court. A fourth opinion, dissenting with the judgment of the Court, was written by Justice Kennedy and joined by Chief Justice Rehnquist and Justice Scalia.

All I knew was that the vote was six to three. When Jim finished making copies, I took one and left him to pore over the sixty or seventy pages of opinions. There were clearly three justices who were of the opinion that PW had not discriminated. The problem was that I did not know what the various opinions of the other six were or, more importantly, what the opinions meant to me.

I took a cab back to the bank parking lot to pick up my car. With a rather crumby copy of the opinions of the Supreme Court on the car seat next to me I headed for the house.

Halfway home on the Rock Creek Parkway, the local all-news radio station announced that Ann B. Hopkins had won a major victory over Price Waterhouse. On one hand I felt better. On the other, I was skeptical and wondered how the local news station had figured out the answer before my attorneys had. The local news station must have had better Xeroxing facilities.

When I got back to the house I found Sonia puttering around the kitchen. I asked her to tell anyone she did not know that I was out, indefinitely. She should take messages. I was going next door for a calming cup of tea before the impending press storm. If Jim or Doug called, she should give them the neighbor's number. A smiling Sonia continued wiping the kitchen counter.

"Mrs. Hopper is in the bedroom," the housekeeper told me when she let me in the front door. I hiked the stairs to the third floor where I found Ruth sitting on the sofa, reading. She greeted me warmly and then more or less ignored me as she focused her attention on the rain-bespeckled Xerox of the opinions.

As I waited for her to wade through the legalese, I fidgeted or stared vacantly out the window at the Washington zoo grounds across the street. She read with concentration interrupted only occasionally by a raised eyebrow, a snicker, or a grin. When she finished, she explained that overall I was fine. I had won on one legal issue and lost on another.

On the personally critical issue of burden shifting, I won. PW maintained that the courts should not have shifted the burden to them to prove that interpersonal skills problems, all by themselves, were the basis for the denial of partnership. They maintained that it should have been my burden to prove that discrimination, not interpersonal skills was the real reason for the denial.

In short, the burden of proof should have never shifted from me to them to prove anything. It was essential that I win this point; had I lost, the litigation would most likely have been over and I would have lost the case, not just the legal point.

On the issue of evidentiary standard, I lost. PW had maintained that even if the burden to prove something did shift to them, they had been held to a standard of proof that was too tough. Judge Gesell had required that the firm prove its case by clear and convincing evidence. The appellate court had agreed with Judge Gesell.

The Supreme Court disagreed with both lower courts: the firm should have been required to prove its point with only a preponderance of the evidence. Of all the possible legal errors that PW suggested to the Supreme Court, the evidentiary standard error was the one that my attorneys had told me to expect and also the one that was least likely to affect me adversely.

Ruth told me what I needed to know in summary without going into an analysis of the broader legal implications of the decision. Many months later Jim explained some of the fine points.

One point was related to the circumstances under which an employer was liable for attorneys' fees or damages in a discrimination case. The Court held that if an employer carried its burden of proof by the appropriate evidentiary standard, then the employer could not be held liable for either attorneys' fees or damages.

That meant, as an extreme example, that if a person sued a company for discrimination in hiring because several managers of the company repeatedly said "We don't hire . . . " (fill in the blank with any protected group), then the company would not have to pay the person's attorneys' fees if the company proved that another legitimate reason (the person could not read) would have prevented the person from being hired.

In the final analysis, I was not affected by that aspect of the Supreme Court's decision. The Congress, however, was sufficiently concerned that it overturned the decision in the Civil Rights Act of 1992.

It was almost a year before I learned that, technically, PW won the Supreme Court case. Because of the evidentiary standard error, the Court reversed the judgment made by the court of appeals against PW and sent the case back to the appellate court to get the error fixed. That error cost me $3,946.61, which I had to pay for costs incurred by PW to print materials submitted to the Supreme Court.

It could have been worse. The D.C. Superior Court ordered my divorce on May 10, 1989. That cost almost $7,000.

Healing

"Hi, Mom" echoed down the stairs as I hurried back into the house. The children, who had spent the weekend with Thomas Peter, had come home after school. The boys were in the kitchen with Sonia.

"Hi, guys. The Supreme Court opinion is out," I responded. "Great! What happened?" they said, peering down at me over the stair rail on the second floor. "I'm not sure, but the radio says I won." I reviewed the garbled phone messages.

I immediately returned Evalyn's call. She was accumulating a stack of inquiries. They had to be from the media, I explained, because neither of us recognized any of the names. I asked her to tell people that I was out, indefinitely, but that I would get back to them. From what little I could tell, all of the messages that Sonia had attempted to record were also from the media.

I returned Nina Totenberg's call. She was with National Public Radio, which had been my client in my last days at Touche. On Doug's advice, I had declined her request for an interview before the Court ruled. At that time he and Jim had both advised against my dealing with the media. I told her that I would consent to an interview when the ruling was published, largely because Doug seemed to respect her.

Most of the national press corps was packed like sardines into small quarters downtown at the federal courthouse waiting for developments in the Oliver North trial, Nina explained. Apparently the press corps had irritated Judge Gesell. It had been banished to some cramped space and been told to stay there.

After expressing a genuine desire not to inconvenience me, she asked if I would be willing to meet her at the courthouse. There we could find a quiet place to talk. I agreed—my only alternative was to fidget around the house until Jim and Doug could fill in the picture that Ruth had sketched.

As the cab driver slugged his way through the late afternoon traffic compounded by the drizzling rain, I tried to focus on reading the opinion. It was hopeless. I returned the legal papers to my briefcase and stared mindlessly out the window.

When I found the room that Nina had identified, I understood what she meant about the cramped quarters. I had to step over and around people sitting on the floor, leaning against walls, and bumping into each other as they tried to move around.

By the time I found Nina I realized that I had dived into the national press pool. After several years of avoiding the media, I met most of its representatives all in one afternoon.

Several reporters followed us down the hall until I explained that my interview with Nina was related to matters personal, not legal. I told them I was unprepared to discuss the as-yet-unread opinion.

In deference to the Supreme Court of the United States, which had spent six calendar months preparing the opinion, I would not discuss it until I had read it. They pleasantly and politely returned their attention to Oliver North. I am unable to recall what Nina and I discussed that dreary afternoon in the badly lit vending machine room somewhere in the bowels of the courthouse.

Tela had joined the boys in the kitchen by the time I returned home. They were all eating cereal at the kitchen table. More messages had stacked up.

Tela had a neatly prepared list. She also conveyed verbally her opinion about what I should do with each person whose name she recognized. I returned all the calls and scheduled interviews.

"Tonight's television crews will be here in less than an hour," I remarked. Three excited children planned the logistics for the evening. They set up staging areas in the living room on the second floor and in my office on the fourth floor.

Tela greeted people at the front door. Gilbert ran the elevator to carry equipment from the front hall to and from the staging areas. Peter directed the television crews and me to the proper locations. George followed around everywhere knocking over photographic equipment.

My headache was back. I glanced in the bathroom mirror as I took two aspirin. I looked better than I thought I would after running around in the rain most of the afternoon. It was a credit to my hairdresser.

Only one more television interview stood between me and falling into bed. This one would be different though. I knew Bob Strickland, the CBS reporter who covered the local news for Channel 9. We were hardly intimate acquaintances, but I had met him at a Christmas party at Carol's house. We had chatted as people do at those kinds of events. He had been calm, soft-spoken, and thoughtful—an easy conversationalist.

Unlike all the other interviewers, who came with a producer who told everyone what to do and seemed to be in a hurry, Bob was alone with his cameraman and behaved as if he had all the time in the world. It was less than forty-five minutes to air-time.

We sat on the sofa in the living room. I must have looked tired because Bob asked, "How're you doing?" before the interview began. I briefly described Carol's birthday party and its relation to my current state of exhaustion. I told him that the Supreme Court opinion was still unread, so I would prefer to refrain from discussing it. He unrolled a wire service report on the case and handed it to me to read while he and the cameraman discussed the placement of lights.

The interview was brief. Toward the end Bob asked if I could lose the case when it was reconsidered by Judge Gesell. "I could lose," I said.

I turned on the TV before I crawled into bed in hopes of seeing myself on the news. I missed it. Jim Heller saw some of it, though. The next day he chastised me a little for commenting that I could lose.

That same day my stepfather offered his condolences on having lost after seeing one of the national news programs that had so stated. He was relieved when I told him I had not seen the program to which he was referring but I was delighted with the outcome.

Although I generally avoided the media, I agreed to talk to *Time* magazine, only because Bini Herrmann worked there. The children liked the article because they liked the picture.

Vera Schneider read the article over a calm, quiet, pleasant dinner in one of the neighborhood restaurants. The children were with their fathers. She and I had walked home at a leisurely pace and settled down with cognac and coffee, when the phone rang.

I listened carefully as Thomas Peter explained that he and Tela were at Fairfax Hospital where Peter had been delivered by ambulance. He had been admitted with a compound fracture of his left arm. Gilbert was at some event up at the school. "I'll pick Gilbert up and be right there," I said.

A brief conversation between Vera and myself revealed that neither of us knew how to get to Fairfax Hospital. "Why the hell would anyone take a nine-year-old to Fairfax Hospital instead of Children's?" I asked rhetorically as I picked up the phone.

I called next door and reached Ruth. About fifteen seconds into a set of detailed instructions on how to get to the hospital twenty miles away, she changed subjects. "Meet us out front. David and I will take you." Less than ten minutes later we had Gilbert in the car and were on our way to Fairfax Hospital.

"Will Peter need blood?" Gilbert asked anxiously. "I don't know, Gilbert. But if he does, all of us can donate it," I said, responding to both his stated question and his unstated fear of AIDS. He breathed an audible sigh of relief. A conversation about types of blood and who had which type followed.

Peter was in the orthopaedic ward of the hospital crumpled up in the vertex created by the flat bottom and elevated top of the hospital bed. A pile of bloody clothes cluttered up the floor in one corner of the room on his side of the curtain that separated him from his roommate. A loose piece of blood-splotched linen was strewn across the foot of the bed.

Stuck into his right hand and taped down was a needle connected to a clear plastic tube through which he was being intravenously fed and medicated with fluids that dripped from plastic bags hanging from a rack at the head of his bed. The purpose of the medication was to stave off infection that might have crept into the three-inch gash created when the broken humerus penetrated the biceps. Tela and Thomas Peter, both clearly upset, were standing between Peter's bed and the window.

"Hi, Mom. Hi, Gilbert." he said quietly and without whining. I attempted to introduce a cheerful tone into my voice as I asked, "How are you, Pete?" "I hurt," he said, and he started to cry.

Gilbert was terrified. I spent just enough time with Peter to stop the crying. Then I walked from the room looking for someone who knew what was going on.

"Please get all the bloodstained materials out of there and flatten the bed," I asked of the first hospital employee I met. At the nurses' station, all I could find out was that surgery was required and they were waiting to hear from the surgeon.

David, Ruth, and Vera were lined up along the wall in the hall when I returned to the room. "Someone had better take charge," Ruth said quietly but forcefully—the implication was obvious.

I told Thomas Peter that Tela and Gilbert had to leave the hospital. He decided to take them to his house. It was pushing eleven o'clock. A check back at the nurses' station indicated that the orthopaedic surgeon was still nowhere to be found.

I thanked the Hoppers, told them I would be okay, and asked Vera if she would be willing to come pick me up in the morning. Everyone left.

The orthopaedic surgeon was located at just about the time I was considering becoming extremely hostile. When Peter went into surgery to have the bone set and pinned, I called my sister.

My nephew, Bo, was scheduled to come for a visit. He was a senior at Andover and my legal predicament was the topic of his history paper. In addition to preparing a list of questions that he wanted to ask me, he had made arrangements to talk to Doug and Jim on Monday. I told Susan that we had to cancel Bo's trip.

While Peter was in the recovery room, I talked to the surgeon. Peter was going to be in the hospital for a week, plus or minus. He would need at least two more operations.

In a day or two, when all danger of infection had passed, the surgeon would close the wound. Sometime thereafter he would operate to remove the two crisscross pins that currently held the bone together. If the bone failed to heal properly more surgery might be required in six months or a year.

I called Susan back and asked her to send Bo anyway. I was going to need all the help I could get to keep Peter company in the hospital.

That weekend Vera sent balloons to the hospital to cheer Peter up. Bo sat with him for hours on end while I got some sleep. The surgery to close the wound took place at two in the morning on Sunday or Monday night. By the next weekend Peter was home. I was relieved of the burden of making the forty-mile round-trip to the hospital once or twice each day.

Unfortunately, the orthopaedic surgeon had offices five or ten miles southeast of the hospital. The round-trip for weekly checkups was fifty or sixty miles through some of the worst traffic in the Washington area.

More unfortunately, the surgeon, who seemed to be quite a good surgeon, knew nothing about children other than their bone structure.

He advised against Peter's going to King's Dominion for his birthday, a trip that had been planned for weeks. He advised against Peter's going to Camp Echo Hill with Tela and Gilbert. "Holy cow," I thought. "The arm may heal, but the kid will die."

"Peter is dyslexic," I said to the surgeon. "This was supposed to be the first summer in four years that the kid would escape 'Johnny Can't Read' camps and do something normal with his brother and sister." I asked him to reconsider his advice in light of the whole child.

He consented to permit Peter to go to camp if Peter would sit quietly and stay away from other people—interaction with others might lead to a raucous fray and further injury to the arm. I wondered what a pediatric orthopaedic surgeon at Children's Hospital would have said.

I followed my nose and ignored the surgeon's advice. About a month later, on his birthday, Peter threw away his fourth cast when it got wet on one of the water rides at King's Dominion. All the children went to camp. Peter was waterskiing in mid-July. Bo earned an A on his history paper.

"Why is it taking so long?" I asked Jim, who asked himself the same question. When the Supreme Court reversed the judgment of the court of appeals on liability, it remanded the case back to that court for further proceedings. By July the Supreme Court's order should have wended its way back to the court of appeals where a routine paperwork process should have passed the matter back to Judge Gesell.

"I don't know. I only guarantee one thing. This time next year we won't be arguing before the World Court," Jim retorted, trying to introduce a little humor.

One evening late in July, the phone rang. "Lisa works with children like Peter. She knows a school that seems to get remarkable results with children who can't learn to read. Why don't you give her a call and discuss it," Ruth said. Lisa Gentry, Ruth's best friend's daughter, lived in Madison County.

I knew where Madison County was only because I wrecked a car there my freshman year in college. The ambulance took the injured to the University of Virginia Medical Center in Charlottesville. I called Lisa first thing the next morning.

After a little telephone tag and some searching around, Lisa came up with the name and number of the school. I dialed the number of Oakland School.

The phone rang three times before I found myself talking to Mrs. Dondero, the head of the school. I told her all about Peter's school history and summarized what I remembered from all the testing results and reports. It sounded to her as if Peter and Oakland were a perfect fit. "Why don't you bring him and his academic reports and test scores down so we can talk?"

After five years of patiently tracking down leads in the heretofore fruitless search for anything that could help Peter learn to read, I had a time crisis of considerable magnitude. It was Monday, August 1, 1989. Peter was at his father's house with Tela and Gilbert. On Wednesday they were all scheduled to fly to California where they planned to vacation for three or four weeks. I told Mrs. Dondero that Peter and I would be there in the morning.

The drive to Boyd's Tavern, fifteen miles east of Charlottesville gave me a couple of hours to prepare Peter for the possibility of going to boarding school, a prospect that I found heart-wrenching and tear-jerking. Although he was enrolled in and expected to go back to the school he had attended since he was four, he could probably handle changing schools.

He and I had visited or discussed every special school in the Washington area. He knew that if I found one acceptable, he would leave his current school. Boarding school, however, that was a different matter. Peter was skeptical.

I turned off the pavement onto the gravel road that split the grounds, leaving large open meadows on both sides. Whatever I had expected Oakland School to be, it was not.

Working horses grazed on the top of the back hills of what must have once been a farm. Widely spaced buildings ranged from two to two hundred years in age. We pulled the car onto the grass at the edge of the gravel circle in front of the Manor House, an elegant colonial, prominently located atop a hill overlooking the meadows.

Joanne Dondero met us at the front door between the pillars on the veranda. She escorted us to an upstairs bedroom that served as a lobby and meeting room for visitors. Peter and I chatted with her for a few minutes. Then I gave her the manila folder labeled "Schools" that I had hastily pulled from my filing cabinet at home. We left her to review the contents while Peter and I inspected the facilities.

We walked through the Manor House and the surrounding outbuildings of various sizes. Each contained tiny classrooms and an occasional office. We ambled up the hill to the cinder block dormitories that were barely noticeable beyond the meadows, at the edge of the woods. We marveled at the huge modern gymnasium completely hidden in the trees.

On our way back to the Manor House we toured the almost brand-new dining hall. I was reminded of Hollins College, only on a much smaller scale. Oakland had fewer than one hundred boarding students.

"I note that you made good grades in college," Mrs. Dondero said to me as Peter and I trudged up the stairs heading back to the lobby-bedroom. She stood at the top grinning down on us. The "Schools" file contained everything that might reasonably be classified under that heading, without regard to family member. She had read the academic records and test scores for every member of the family, as well as school-related correspondence and probably the elementary school play programs—the file contained a lot of extraneous matter.

"I think we can help Peter," she said. I was sold then and there. No one had said that in the five years that I had been seeking help. I did, however, ask what the curriculum would be. "*His* curriculum," she said, making it very clear that each of the students had a unique curriculum, "will consist of ten forty-five-minute classes each day: reading, reading, reading, reading, reading, and reading—because he can't—math and math—because he's good at it—and PE and PE because every kid needs it."

Peter perked up, "You mean I don't have to take spelling?" There followed a lively dialogue, the gist of which was that it was rather difficult to teach spelling and a lot of other subjects to a child who was unable to read. Peter would take reading—period.

"What do I do next?" I asked. Based on my experience with the half a dozen or more schools I had dealt with in the past, I expected to be presented with reams of forms, a description of the admissions process and schedule, and an "I'll get back to you" message. Instead, she said, "You can give me a deposit of four hundred dollars and bring Peter back to start school in September or you can think about it and give me a call." I wrote the check.

Peter sat silently for a while on the drive back to Washington. As the miles tripped by he gradually spoke more and with growing enthusiasm about taking horseback riding, going fishing, and not having tutors and not having to struggle with homework, in general, and spelling, in particular.

Although he was leery of being away from home, he knew he had to learn to read. With mixed emotions, he accepted the fact that he was going to boarding school when he got back from California.

There are few children under the age of nine at Oakland. Younger children are usually unable to overcome homesickness. No child can focus on academic matters when in the throes of an attack of loneliness and longing for home.

I lined up the family to combat what I was sure would be a lonely time for Peter. By the time school started, Mom, Gil, Susan, Bo, Ami, John, Cathy, and Sheila were prepared to maintain a steady stream of cards and letters into southwestern Virginia. Peter had to know he was part of a family that supported him in his quest to learn to read. Everyone had the address and instructions to print short words and short messages.

"Peter will adjust faster than you will," was Mrs. Dondero's parting remark in mid-September when Tela, Gilbert, and I left Peter and his trunk in her care. She discouraged phone calls and visits during the first four weeks. Peter would need that time to get school focused. He would be unlikely to spend the week thinking about the next call or visit home if he knew for certain that there would be none.

We missed Peter terribly. During the first week of boarding school, Gilbert had trouble sleeping without his constant companion. I called Mrs. Dondero for daily progress reports, which I conveyed to Tela and Gilbert at dinner.

The first week in October Judge Gesell held a scheduling conference. By all appearances he was angry. He expressed himself accordingly.

He was extremely displeased with the legal mess that the court of appeals and the Supreme Court had dumped on him. With the exception of a bankruptcy case or two, *Hopkins v. Price Waterhouse* was the oldest case on his docket.

He wanted to be rid of the matter. He set dates for briefs and oral arguments for him to reconsider liability by the new evidentiary standard. Simultaneously he scheduled the legal steps preliminary to a trial on remedy.

Judge Gesell said he intended to conduct the trial on remedy without first announcing his judgment on liability because he was certain that anything he did would again be appealed. I had the impression that he planned to tie the remainder of the case neatly with a legal ribbon and then let the court of appeals deal with it. He never wanted to see *Hopkins v. Price Waterhouse* again.

Unfortunately, he indicated, his schedule was clogged up with criminal cases until February, five years less a month after the original trial. He set February 26, 1990, as the date for the next trial.

Doug, Jim, and I left the conference half relieved, half worried. We had long been concerned that PW might ask for a new trial on liability or attempt to force the remedy trial to wait until the liability issue was reconsidered and resolved. Judge Gesell managed to eliminate those concerns. We were relieved that the trial process finally had a fixed end date.

We were, however, more worried than ever at Judge Gesell's apparent anger. Even after five years it was undiminished. We took no consolation in the fact that the anger was impartially directed at both sides.

Peter came home for a visit the first weekend in October. His initial homesickness had diminished rapidly and then vanished. He was a cheerful, happy child who liked school, especially horseback riding and fishing.

Just before Thanksgiving, Jim reargued liability for the fourth time. Kay Oberly who had replaced Steve Tallent as Jim's debating partner was, in turn, replaced by Theodore R. Olson.

Ted Olson, as he introduced himself, had never been to charm school. When I first met him I was seated on one of the benches in the back of Judge Gesell's courtroom waiting for Jim and Doug after a conference. Ted walked up, extended his hand to shake mine, and introduced himself. I gave a passing thought to letting him stand there with his arm extended. Instead, I shook his hand. Had he gone to charm school he would have known that handshaking protocol required that he wait for me, as a woman, to offer my hand.

Ted was likable, though, in as much as any attorney can be likable. He was tall, trim, blond—reminded me of a skier—and had a never-ending grin that looked just sincere enough to avoid being classified as a "cocktail party smile." There was something boyish about the way he held his chin down and peered upward with his eyes.

Ted was no match for Jim in the oral arguments. In fairness to the new man from Gibson, Dunn, and Crutcher, there were few novel ways to present the same old evidence.

Almost five years ago, Judge Gesell had not been clearly and convincingly persuaded that PW would have rejected me had discrimination been eliminated as a factor. Common legal sense said he would not be preponderantly convinced either. However, he seemed so irritated that no one would hazard a guess about the outcome.

I was cautiously optimistic as Thanksgiving arrived. Sandy Kinsey and Christopher were in town for a visit. They came for the day. She and I stuffed and cooked a turkey in spite of the fact that Tela and Peter wanted honey-baked ham and roast beef, respectively. Fortunately Peter was home for three evenings over Thanksgiving. I managed to satisfy the culinary requirements of each child over the long holiday weekend.

Jim and Doug were madly collecting data at the time. PW had to provide whatever they needed to estimate the extent to which I had been financially "damaged" by the discriminatory decision. Judge Gesell had scheduled the discovery process to end on December 15.

It was a tough job for them, in part because PW was inclined to provide as little as was legally possible. What made it more difficult, however, was figuring out what to ask for. Jim had to learn enough to understand PW's very unusual partner compensation and retirement programs.

Partners are not salaried. Instead, each partner is entitled to a portion of the profits of the firm based on the number of shares that are assigned to him. Unlike securities, the shares are not assets and may not be bought or sold.

A share value is computed at the end of a fiscal year based on the profits made in that year. Each partner is paid an amount equal to the share value multiplied by the number of shares he holds.

I helped them understand and interpret the annual compensation system. I was, however, useless on the retirement program. I knew nothing about it. Furthermore, I wanted to be reinstated, not paid some current value for a future benefit.

"If you insist on reinstatement, it will make the case harder to win," Jim had said on more than one occasion. "So be it," I always replied.

While Jim swapped correspondence and telephone calls with the GD lawyers, Doug searched for an economist to interpret the data, make estimates, and offer expert testimony about financial damages. Bob Picciotto, my boss at the bank, helped in the search for an expert.

When the period for discovery ended, Doug and Jim had the data they needed. They also had an expert economist from Georgetown who could interpret the data and estimate damages.

About that time, I drove to Oakland to pick up Peter for the Christmas holiday. We bought the family tree on the way home. I planned to have a crowd for Christmas dinner.

Just before Christmas, Kayong called, as she was prone to do several times each year. Sully had returned to Washington, this time to stay. Kayong's children were scheduled to be home for the holidays. She wanted to bring her children and their boy- and girlfriends to visit.

"Bring the whole family for Christmas dinner," was my response. The number of people at dinner tripled. I bought a bigger turkey. We put all the leaves in the dining table, which we joined to the kitchen table to form a T.

We covered the T with white linen cloths set with the good china and silver. Sheila, Carol, the children, and I had a very merry, oriental Christmas.

Because I accepted Mrs. Dondero's forcefully stated visiting guidelines as rules, I only brought Peter home every third weekend. I drove to Oakland to pick him up after classes on Friday and took him back late Sunday. As the trial date approached, I decided to make an exception.

"Would Peter's intellectual ability be permanently impaired if I brought him home on an odd weekend and let him play hooky for the trial," I asked in mock seriousness. "I doubt it," was her reply.

Tela and Gilbert were as excited about playing hooky from school as they were about Peter's coming home. I predicted that schoolwork was going to take another nosedive.

In spite of my best supervisory efforts, Gilbert's homework and sleep schedule suffered whenever Peter was home. I frequently caught the boys late at night enjoying thrillers, usually by Stephen King. They propped themselves up with pillows in one bed or the other and snuggled together as Gilbert read and Peter listened.

The morning of the trial the two boys were asleep in a pile in Peter's bed. An open copy of *It* lay on the floor.

Trial 2

WEDNESDAY

Vera, Carol, and I went shopping the weekend before the trial. They served as stylistic advisers in my quest to buy two new suits, one for each day of the proceedings.

I bought a conservative, light-brown, plaid Freedberg suit and a two-piece linen dress with a red jacket and navy skirt. Tela still refers to the Freedberg as "boring brown."

The day before the trial, after I picked Peter up at Oakland, I dropped by the Hoppers' to ask Ruth's opinion on the suits. Tela and Carol had voted for the red jacket on the first day. Vera leaned toward brown.

Ruth's advice was in line with my intuition—I should wear the brown suit on the first day. I gave her a hug. She wished me luck. She and David were leaving the country the next day.

The legal proceeding to arraign Marion Barry, then mayor of the District of Columbia, began at the same time and on the same day as the trial on remedy. The army of police and media people and the drastically increased security for the mayor's arraignment slowed efforts to get to Judge Gesell's courtroom.

Doug, Jim, and I arrived later than we planned. Carol, Vera, and the five children were all sitting on the front row. "The boys were going to be a handful," I thought.

We put our briefcases on our table. I left Jim and Doug to organize and stack their exhibits, files, and scribblings and went to address the children.

Vera's girls and Tela knew to take matters seriously. The boys, however, were more enamored of playing hooky and enjoying each other's company than they were of the proceedings at hand.

"Listen up, kids," I said quietly from across the waistwall that separated us. "The rules here are not as tough as the Supreme Court, but you have to follow them." I looked straight at my two mischievously smiling sons. "You do what Carol says. She knows the rules."

I was relieved when the children responded to the marshal's "All rise." After that, when I took my seat at the table with Jim and Doug, I was no longer able to see them without turning. They were on their own. I had to focus on the bench.

"Glad you were all able to get in. I put a lot of police out there to protect you," Judge Gesell started on a cheery note.

Jim introduced himself, for the record only. Everyone before the bar was well acquainted one with another. He explained that he and Doug would present my case with three witnesses, me, my former husband, and my economist.

I would testify that I wanted to be reinstated, as a partner. I would describe the efforts I had made to get work to earn an income. Thomas Peter would corroborate what I said about certain of my job searches.

My economist, Joe Tryon, would testify to his estimates of back pay amounts to which I claimed to be entitled. Joe would also testify about estimated "front pay," a financial substitute for the partnership for which I sued. Front pay estimates would only be needed if the judge decided not to order that I be made a partner.

Although Doug had made it very clear in his briefs that I was suing for reinstatement, not front pay, Jim wanted to be sure the judge focused on that fact during the trial.

Jim stated my position. "You will hear more from Mr. Tryon by a great deal than it takes Miss Hopkins to say she would still like to be a partner in Price Waterhouse. The volume of testimony about front pay should not deceive your Honor. That is not our primary goal in this case."

On behalf of Price Waterhouse, Wayne Schrader introduced himself. He raised an administrative matter. Before the trial began, Doug and Wayne had stipulated to noncontroversial documents and exhibits. Doug refused to stipulate, however, to certain lists of former PW managers who had made partner at others of the Big Eight, which by then had shrunk to the Big Six.

Earlier in the week, when I asked for an explanation of the refusal, he had explained his reluctance. He was concerned that the lists might be used for some unexplained purpose. He wanted to know how each list was prepared and what might have been excluded. He wanted to preserve the option of asking questions about individuals on the lists.

Failure to reach a stipulation would require that PW call, as witnesses, someone from each of the Big Six to introduce the lists as evidence. Wayne thought that Doug's position was unreasonable. Doug told him to take the issue to the judge.

Wayne did so. "We have identified a number of individuals who left Price Waterhouse as managers or senior managers who went on to become partners in other of the what I'll call the Big Eight; . . . if we can't reach a stipulation on that I'm going to have to bring in witnesses from those various firms to testify to the uncontrovertible fact that certain people identified are partners in their firm."

Judge Gesell acknowledged Wayne's complaint. The trial began.

According to plan, Jim called me to testify. He and I had been over and over the questions he planned to ask and the responses I intended to give. "Why do you want to return to Price Waterhouse?" he asked.

"Management consulting is my profession and Price Waterhouse is preeminent in my practice area." I had made that statement many times.

Guided by Jim's orderly, calm, patient questioning, I talked about how I approached the job market when I knew I would not be a partner in 1983. I described informal exploratory meetings with the Owner, Jeff Baldwin, and other partners I knew at Touche Ross.

At the time of those meetings, years ago, I had concluded that I was a pariah in the Big Eight. I never moved past the exploratory stages with Touche, and I never pursued any of the others.

At trial, however, I understated my conclusion, by saying that I was not left with an optimistic feeling after my meetings with Touche people. Judge Gesell seemed mildly irritated when he implicitly asked me to be more direct.

First he asked, "Well, did you apply for a job at any of the Big Eight? I mean did you go and say I want to work for you?" Then he followed up with, "What do you mean you weren't left with an optimistic feeling? Did they tell you there wasn't a job?"

I could be no more specific. No one ever told me, "You can't sue one member of the brotherhood and go to work for another." Still, I had that clear impression. Thomas Peter and I had spent hours talking about the glum prospects at Touche and others in the Big Eight.

I explained to the judge that I never explicitly asked for a position because Thomas Peter and I had concluded it would be pointless. I became irritated when Judge Gesell gave me the impression that Thomas Peter could or should have influenced the process.

Referring to Thomas Peter and Touche, the judge commented, "So I imagine he put in a good word for you." He continued, "They had talked to him. They had trusted him, right?"

Over the years I was married, I was annoyed every time my career became snarled with that of my husband's. Having been deserted, sued for custody, and forced into an unwanted divorce, I struggled to be civil as I answered the question. "Sure, but people do not normally check with my husband on me. They could check with me."

When Jim got back on his planned track, I described my early job searches and my reasons for forming my own consulting firm. I answered all the questions Jim wanted to ask in less than an hour.

Theodore Olson introduced himself for the record. I should have been flattered at being cross-examined by President Reagan's personal attorney. Instead, I wondered what it cost the firm on a per question basis. It had to be expensive.

Unlike Jim's line of questioning, the purpose of which I understood, I had no clue where Ted was going and he had no obligation to tell me. Furthermore, his objective was to persuade the judge that I had not tried very hard to be comparably employed after I left Price Waterhouse. If he could prove that I was a dilettante, PW might escape liability for back pay.

He began with Pete McVeagh and the three options that Tom Beyer proposed and I rejected when I decided instead to sue the firm. I thought we had covered that years ago at the original trial.

So did Jim. He protested calmly, but it was a noticeable protest. "Your Honor, let me note for the record we're well beyond the scope of direct and I do believe we're retrying the case we tried back in 1984."

Ted countered Jim's comment. "I understand, your Honor, but we're talking about the remedial phase of this case. That includes the alternatives."

The judge agreed with Jim. "Well, you'll have to get the remedy from new facts, not from trying to retry old facts."

When Ted tried to argue—"I'm not attempting to retry old facts, your Honor"—I began to enjoy Judge Gesell again. He ended the argument with, "Well, I'm telling you you are because all those facts you're asking about are settled in the record today."

Ted began to ask questions that I expected. He asked about my profession and my qualifications. Naturally I described myself as a consultant.

I was amused by the way the judge asked me to be more specific about the kind of work I wanted to do when I left PW. "Well, now, Miss Hopkins," he said, "living in Washington as you and I do we know there are all kinds of people going around with the name consultant. The question that you were asked was what is it that you individually were looking for? The word consultant covers, you know, everything from ex-congressmen to—"

Ted confronted me with a statement that purported to describe the work I wanted to do. Apparently, it appeared in the pretrial brief that Doug had written in January, about a month ago.

Ted asked me if I had made the statement. I knew I had not because it referred to money, a subject on which I had for years carefully avoided comment.

I had no idea where he was going with the line of questioning. I was, however, suspicious. He was trying to trap me in something, but I was unable to figure out what.

He asked me to confirm the words that appeared in Doug's brief. "My question is did you reasonably believe in 1984 that the only place that you would be able to obtain opportunity comparable to that available at Price Waterhouse in terms of future earnings and work in your field was with another Big Eight firm?"

I thought I had more or less answered that question in my testimony. I would have answered unequivocally "yes" but for the term "future earnings."

When I hedged a little, Jim came to my rescue. "I think she's answered that."

Ted disagreed with Jim. "I don't think she's answered it, your Honor. I would like to have her answer it."

I was confused. I lost track of the question I was supposed to answer. I racked my mind trying to figure out what Ted wanted. "Are you trying to make some subtle point, Mr. Olson? Because I don't understand it."

I believe Judge Gesell was trying to help me when he asked: "You don't remember what you said before, is that right? Is that what you're saying, or do you remember what you said before? If you remember what you said before would you tell counsel what you meant to say or convey?"

Although I probably read the pretrial brief, I was unable to recall a single thing it said. The question that Ted asked seemed unrelated to my ability to recall the specifics of the brief. I was baffled when I asked: "It's about memory?"

Ted must have been frustrated at my reluctance to confirm a statement printed in my own brief. He appealed to the judge. "Your Honor, this is an argument made in her brief filed on Miss Hopkins' behalf."

Judge Gesell seemed to recognize my dilemma. I failed to recognize the statement in question. "I know. That's the trouble with lawyers. They make arguments. She didn't make the argument."

Ted believed, rightly so I learned years later, that I was responsible for every statement in the brief. "It was made in this court on her behalf. If it's not her position then—"

The judge, however, was more pragmatic. He could differentiate between me and the attorneys. "Did you tell the lawyers what to put in the brief, or did they put it in?"

The question was almost rhetorical. I responded with amusement. "The attorneys wrote the briefs."

By then the judge appeared to be as confused as I was. "Apparently they're talking about something your lawyer said. Did you tell him what to put in the brief about what you thought were your best opportunities or was that his judgment about what he understood you to mean to him?"

I continued to be amused. "It's most likely to be my attorney's judgment and my attorney's words and what my attorneys put in the briefs."

As I sat in the witness box in a state of amused confusion, Jim rose. He addressed the bench. "I think I'm the guilty author of that statement, your Honor, and I don't think it is a fair translation of what she went through and perhaps I hadn't interviewed her sufficiently before that. I apologize."

When Ted continued to press for an answer, Judge Gesell offered his explanation of what he thought I had said. "Well, I think she's answered that. She's answered that the big bucks [were] in the Big Eight and the kind of thing she wanted to work on were things backed by big accounting firms because they could do the accounting aspect of the development of the information that would be useful for her when diagnosing major problems needing computer system analysis. That's what she's been saying, as I understand it. Is that generally what you've been saying?"

"Yes, sir." I was relieved to agree with him.

I read no legal significance into the judge's comment to Ted. Judge Gesell continued, "So now, that hasn't anything to do with whether or not there may have been other opportunities that partially or completely could have mitigated her distress, but she was looking for the big companies with the big bucks, she says."

I agreed with Ted when he responded to Judge Gesell. "Well, I think that the point is established that what she was interested in was the Big Eight accounting firms and that by profession, by discipline, by education, and by opportunities—"

I mentally disagreed with the judge when he attempted to extend what Ted had said. "Well, also they had the organization I understand it from the witness, the accounting organization to provide the material that was necessary if you were diagnosing a complex situation. So that you could know what it was the computer had to do or could do."

I had never worked with the audit people. Consequently I had no reason to consider an accounting organization to be useful in the consulting business.

I felt like a bystander a tennis match. Then Ted turned to me to ask if I agreed with the judge. "That is your position, Miss Hopkins, that—"

At the same time, the judge interrupted him. "That's what I understood she said."

The question that Ted finally asked me was different from what I had previously heard. "Those are the only organizations that would provide you with the kind of back-up for the kind of work you wanted to do?"

It was too restrictive. "Only is a very narrowly restrictive word. The statement that I made is that—"

I must have blown it because Judge Gesell seemed irritated again. "Maybe," I thought, "he was just frustrated at coming to an understanding, only to have it vanish." He turned to Ted. "Then I don't understand it. I'm in your position now. I don't understand it. If that isn't what she was saying, then I don't understand what she was saying either. So you may pursue it."

Whatever trap Ted had set, he seemed satisfied that I had fallen into it. He turned to the judge. "Thank you, your Honor."

Ted asked me to identify all the people I contacted in my job search early in 1984. He asked how many newspaper advertisements I had pursued. He wanted the names of recruiters or placement organizations I had contacted or used. I plodded through. There were no obvious traps.

He questioned his way into 1987 when I started consulting with the World Bank. When Ted asked why I closed up my own practice to join the bank, I told him. "Because my family situation was such that I had difficulty dealing with the varying workload, the bad cash flow, and I decided to go to work for the World Bank."

He, however, seemed interested in something else. That same year I turned down an offer to start a consulting practice for a small local accounting firm.

Ted tried to put words in my mouth. "It's also for maybe those same reasons you just identified you didn't want to be in the position of having to develop a practice."

Jim rose to my defense. "Your Honor, that's not what her prior testimony was. This is 1987 and she's testified very clearly about a change in family situation and a problem that she was encountering in her own consultancy and the reasons for going to work for the World Bank. I think Mr. Olson is trying to twist this."

Ted took the offensive. "Let's see if I'm trying to twist that. Do you recall having your deposition taken on November 22, 1989?"

He wanted me to read from my deposition. When the litigation began, I wore bifocals. By 1990 I needed reading glasses. They were in my briefcase on the table where Jim and Doug were seated.

"I'm sorry, if I'm going to have to read something I'm going to have to get another pair of glasses," I explained to Ted and the judge. I wondered if I needed permission to leave the witness stand or if I should ask Jim or Doug to hand me my glasses.

Judge Gesell was almost chivalrous in his handling of the situation. "Well, you can get down and get your glasses. There's no rule against getting your glasses."

Jim rose and responded in kind, "Thank you, your Honor."

I prepared myself for another trap. It had been three months since my deposition. Ted handed me a copy as Jim retrieved his from his orderly pile on the table. "First of all, Miss Hopkins, back on page 21 so that you have the context of this, it refers—the segment of this conversation begins with the reference on that page to Arenson, Fetridge, Weigle, and Stern."

I found my place and acknowledged that I understood. Ted continued. "And then on Page 23—"

Once again, I acknowledged that I had followed along in the text. "I would like you to read to yourself the portion beginning at line three and ending at line eight."

Unaccustomed as I am to reading depositions, I got lost. "I'm sorry, you would like me to read what?"

He repeated his instruction. "The portion beginning at line three and ending at line eight"

"Okay," I acknowledged. "I read it."

Nothing seemed controversial about what I read. I was waiting for the bear trap to close. Ted asked me to confirm my testimony. "Is that your testimony?"

It was. Furthermore, it was exactly what I remembered. I was nervous. "Where was he going?" I asked myself.

Ted read the text into the record of the trial. "Let me read it into the record. 'Question: Did you ever reach the point of discussing what the compensation arrangement might be if these discussions had come to fruition?' 'Answer: No, because as I recall it they wanted me to develop a practice and that was not something that I wanted to do.' Was that your testimony?"

It seemed to be a date trap. Ted attempted to point out an inconsistency between the deposition and something I had said earlier. "... She had indicated one year during her deposition and now some other date."

Judge Gesell figured out what Ted was trying to do long before I did. "I just want to know as of what time did she make that statement? Because that depends—on that depends whether or not it is inconsistent with anything she said before."

He and Ted asked each other for the year that I decided I did not want to start a consulting practice with the small accounting firm. Each acknowledged his ignorance to the other.

Once again, Jim came to my rescue. He had been reading the cited pages in my deposition as Ted grilled me. "Your Honor, if Mr. Olson had asked her to read the next four lines which I will do on redirect I think the times—"

Judge Gesell dispensed with the legal formalities. "Well, you can read it now. We don't have a jury here. I'm trying to get at the truth. I'm not trying to get people trapped."

Jim stumbled for an instant. "I'm sorry, I lost the line count."

The judge had, however, already figured it out. "Well, you're supposed to pick up at line nine."

Jim read from the deposition according to Judge Gesell's instructions. "I wanted to—I was considering other options at the time and I had better options. What were those options? Being an employee of the World Bank."

The judge figured out the year in which I stated that I did not want to start a practice. "Yes, so it's in '87."

Jim seemed pleased that he had kept me out of trouble. He agreed with Judge Gesell. I was glad to see Ted get caught out of context—he could have read the next four lines himself. "Yes, that's right, your Honor."

Ted tried to recover by generalizing my attitude in 1987 back three years in time to 1984. "Well, your Honor, I submit it has to do with this witness—the plaintiff's efforts to get alternative employment not just in 1984 but we're talking about a period of time—"

Judge Gesell was not persuaded. "You're confronting her with whether or not she had taken opportunities and suggesting that she should have because she wasn't interested in practice and she has been saying she was interested in practice and that her interests changed for reasons she's explained, so the date is crucial. Thank you." Ted dropped that issue.

My tax returns were next. I was certainly glad I had never prepared my own tax returns. Any slip of the pencil would probably have been portrayed as bank robbery or fraud.

I believe that Ted was trying to make me look disreputable. He raised the subject of the computer that Thomas Peter bought for me just before I left Price Waterhouse. It was recorded as an asset of my company on my early tax returns. "I believe your tax returns or material associated with your tax returns indicated that you bought a computer in October of 1983, a business-type computer that cost something in the neighborhood of $5,000. Does that ring a bell at all?"

Once again, I wondered what Ted was trying to prove. According to my tax preparer, the cost of the computer was properly recorded and depreciated. Maybe he thought I was buying assets to hide my true income.

Whatever Ted's point was, it fell way short of the mark. Judge Gesell had little interest in my computer. "Well, I don't know any significance about having a computer. Most everybody has one strapped on their back or in their briefcase or something all the time. If you don't have one of those you're not clued in. You're never going to find out what's going on in the world. And it's a very small computer. It's $5,000. If she spent $250,000 and had it taking over the whole attic I would be interested, but really everybody has computers. I even am thinking of getting one and I don't even know how to type. That's a minor matter."

Ted tried feebly and unsuccessfully to indicate that a five-thousand-dollar computer may have been a bigger deal in 1983 than it was in 1990. The judge continued to express disinterest. "I would suppose she couldn't do her work at Price Waterhouse without having a computer at home to bang things out and then take those 'sloppy discs' and bring it into Price Waterhouse. I just want you to know you haven't made a big impression on that."

"I gather," Ted responded with a bashful grin. "At least the man can laugh at himself," I thought.

Ted changed subjects. "Do you feel today, I believe that it's implicit in what you said before, that you feel today that you are qualified to be a partner at Price Waterhouse?"

"What a stupid question," I thought. Was I dealing with another trap? If I answered Yes, he might ask me to explain how or why I was qualified. Other than drinks, dinner, or holiday visits with Karen Nold, Judy Reach, Sandy Kinsey, and occasionally other people at PW, I had had no contact with the firm for years.

I told Ted that I was qualified in 1983 and that unless there had been some dramatic changes in the nature of the practice, I should be qualified in 1990. Ted pressed the question. He wanted to know if I believed that I was qualified in 1990.

Judge Gesell at least understood my reluctance to answer. "Well, it turns out if they're no longer in the management consulting business, Mr. Olson, if they're now running a bunch of racehorses I think you ought to tell her because she might not want to go there."

The judge was clearly troubled at the prospect of my returning to the firm. He interrupted my testimony to ask a question. He referred to Joe Connor and the lawyers at PW's table.

> I'm just talking to you as a person and trying to understand. Not trying to say they're right at all, but they're all sitting here to keep you out of the partnership and you're an intelligent woman, you've got a lot of experience and you've got—you've shown you [can] make a living on your own. You've probably shown they were wrong, so what is the point of wanting to put yourself into a position of future friction?
>
> That's what I find so difficult to deal with because my responsibility here is an equitable responsibility. It's a matter of trying to understand and be fair and you—it just seems to me that I've got two people that have got their minds made up. They're going to butt heads together and I have to say to you that if you go back to the partnership, and you may as a result of these proceedings, I'm not saying one way or the other about that, but we'll be back in here again and again on problems relating to your relationship with these people that don't want you. Now that's my trouble and I can't get an answer.

All I could say was "I may be deluded, but I feel that there are people there who would be happy to practice with me and there certainly are lots of them there that I'd be happy to practice with."

I left the witness stand and returned to my table with Jim and Doug. Jim passed me a scribble that said I had done fine.

Just before lunch, Jim called Thomas Peter as a witness to corroborate my testimony that I had worked hard to find a comparable job after I resigned.

Thomas Peter managed to testify to his name, age, address, and other facts. For most of his time on the stand, however, Judge Gesell addressed the attorneys on a range of legal issues. Thomas Peter sat looking dumbfounded as the legal jargon rattled around him.

The judge seemed to be concerned about when it became my responsibility to mitigate damages after I left PW.

> It appears to me from what happened this morning that it is the position of the defendant that the obligation to mitigate commenced in 1984. That's certainly the impression I got from all the questioning. I don't see that there's any obligation to mitigate in 1984.
>
> There wasn't any obligation to mitigate until somebody said she had some rights, and I didn't give her any rights. The Court of Appeals finally decided that she had some rights . . . and the date of that opinion was almost at the time this man no longer was very closely involved with your client. . . .

I don't believe there was ever a real question about when my duty to mitigate began. It began in 1983 or 1984. I also believe that the judge was less concerned about mitigation than he was about being reversed by the court of appeals.

He used mitigation as the issue to express his frustration with the circuit court's decision:

> I found after the trial that she was not forced out of the case. Therefore, she had no longer any rights and I said that since neither side had presented any evidence of damage she wasn't entitled to any damage, and then when you got upstairs a new notion of law developed of which I was not apprised, which was that the failure of lawyers to present proof was not an excuse for finding there wasn't any proof and therefore the matter was reopened and we began to have another trial. . . .
>
> She lost the case. All she had gotten was a declaratory judgment that there had been sex discrimination. That's all she had.

Then he chastised both sets of attorneys.

> Both sides walked out of this courtroom with a private agreement that they hadn't told me anything about and so while she had established a principle of law and had a declaratory judgment that stereotyping was a violation of Title VII, that's all she had. She had no rights. . . .
>
> It was only when the Court of Appeals determined that she had been constructively discharged did she get any rights because under Title VII law unless she was constructively discharged she wouldn't have had any right to back pay. And so lo and behold the most decisive thing that was decided by the Court of Appeals adversely to the defendant was something that the defendant did not choose to appeal.

He complained about the Supreme Court.

> We tried a case, I'll go back over what I told you again, we tried a case on the question of whether or not there was stereotyping in connection with the decision affecting her not getting a partnership. I made it perfectly clear in my opinion and everything else that the partnership process was a continuing one. . . .
>
> You went up to the Supreme Court or somebody went up there with the idea of upsetting the whole apple cart by turning the whole thing down to the initial decision, which is most unrealistic in terms of the way Price Waterhouse operates as a partnership and it had no relation to what I had decided in my case and so eventually a new case was constructed by able counsel on both

sides, not the case that was tried down here, and it came back down with a remand from them to do something that was not in focus in my court and never was in focus in my court.

He complained about PW's failure to appeal constructive discharge to the Supreme Court.

> You could have appealed the constructive discharge. She had no right, absolutely no right to any back pay ever, if she was not constructively discharged. I held in your favor and said she wasn't. The Court of Appeals' decision said I was wrong. The plaintiff won the Court of Appeals' decision and you never appealed it to the Supreme Court.
>
> I even had—you weren't here, Mr. Olson, it isn't anything personal, but I even tried to persuade . . . counsel for Price Waterhouse not to go to the Supreme Court in the middle of the stream. I said they were going to muck up the case if they did. They ought to go on through and get a damage decision and then take the whole thing up and I was told I didn't understand the process. I obviously didn't because you got cert. I didn't think you were going to get cert. And then you made your own notion of what the issues were in the case and took it to the Supreme Court and you changed all the rules. Now, that's what happened.

But Judge Gesell accepted the circuit court's ruling on constructive discharge.

> . . . You never appealed it and you never even gave them a chance to say, and the law of constructive discharge is all over the lot. . . . Now we're talking about going back up to the Court of Appeals that believes there was a constructive discharge. . . .
>
> If that issue is open, we're not litigating it. I decided it on the facts I had. They told me I was wrong. What do you expect the trial judge to do? To say, well, I'm going to say it just the way I did before and then they have a second chance of chewing the cherry? That would be a ridiculous way to run a lawsuit. . . .

In spite of Judge Gesell's obvious belief that the court of appeals' ruling on constructive discharge was the law governing this case, Ted Olson politely disagreed. The judge declared his intention to go to lunch.

I left Jim and Doug to confer about the legal issues that so aggravated the judge. I joined family and friends who ate in small groups all over the courthouse cafeteria. We sat in groups of three or four because the place was so crowded.

Mary Curzan and I had a salad together. I was so distracted that I had not seen her enter the courtroom. After consuming the tasteless salad, I hopped from table to table to check on the children.

The boys thought everything was boring. The girls thought everything except the judge was boring. The adults were fascinated, especially by Judge Gesell.

He must have had a very light lunch I thought. When the court reconvened, Judge Gesell skipped his normal greeting. Instead he reaffirmed his belief that the court of appeals' ruling on constructive discharge was the law of the case. "It's just as clear as day," he said. He must have spent most of the lunch period reading legal material.

For all practical purposes, Thomas Peter never testified at all. The judge thought he had a vested interest. Anything Thomas Peter could say about me, I had already said. Ted objected to almost everything else as hearsay. He and the bored boys left very soon after lunch.

Jim called my economist. Joseph L. Tryon was a Georgetown University professor. He held advanced degrees, including a Ph.D. from Harvard. By comparison to the dozens, maybe hundreds, of economists I met at the World Bank, Joe was the most unassuming.

Although Doug always referred to him deferentially as Professor Tryon, Joe referred to himself simply as "a teacher." He never qualified the term, not college teacher or economics teacher; he was a teacher. He never referred to himself as Dr. Tryon or Professor Tryon, or even Mr. Tryon; he was instead Joe, nothing more.

Doug's wife, Amy Wind, one of the attorneys at Kator, Scott, and Heller, had worked with him on a different case. With enthusiasm and without reservation, she had referred Joe to Doug. I was personally impressed when we met to discuss the possibility of his testifying. I had the impression that he interviewed me to determine if I was acceptable as a client.

Joe reminded me of Mister Rogers, although he was probably a little shorter and bigger boned. In age he could have been a young grandfather. He spoke softly. Complicated principles of economics were explained in simple terms, but he was never condescending.

As Jim predicted, Joe's testimony took more time than did mine. From just after lunch until very close to the end of the day he testified. The bottom line according to Joe amounted to a little more than $.5 million in back pay and about $2.5 million in front pay.

Under Doug's careful examination, Joe did a first-rate job. He had mastered the complexities of the compensation and retirement systems of both the World Bank and Price Waterhouse. He seemed to respond beautifully to the steady stream of questions from Judge Gesell.

He was helped by his own reasoned, reasonable estimates. Joe never cluttered up the testimony with specious, impressive sounding numbers or fake precision. Every interest rate, discount rate, cost of living or other factor that he used was taken from an unassailable source.

Although Joe managed to keep Judge Gesell's attention, he lost that of the girls. When Jim rested my case at the end of Joe's testimony, they were gone.

Doug never did agree to the stipulation on the Big Six lists. Wayne had to call representatives of each of the firms to introduce the evidence he wanted in the record.

I guess he wanted to show Judge Gesell that I could or should have tried to become a partner at one of the other big accounting firms. Part of the evidence to support that hypothesis was a litany of former PW staff who became partners elsewhere.

Bill Beach was the first of the representatives of the brotherhood. He presented the list on behalf of Deloitte and Touche, the firm that resulted from the merger of Deloitte, Haskins, and Sells with Touche Ross.

I knew Bill, liked him. He was the partner to whom I submitted my resignation when I left Touche Ross. Although I never worked for him, we had had a few beers together on a few occasions.

Ted had an opportunity to use Bill to throw a dart at me. I have no memory of ever insulting Bill and I doubt that he does. I did, however, walk out of a bar, probably close to hysterics after he and I had a conversation about my not being able to go back to Touche as a partner.

By the time Ted finished with the examination, I was characterized more as rude than as distraught. It was a small point. "Litigation polarizes," as Kay Oberly said.

Ted gave the judge a copy of the list of half a dozen or so Deloitte and Touche partners who had been managers at Price Waterhouse. It was marked "Confidential."

Judge Gesell frowned as if he were growing angry. "Why is this marked confidential? What possible confidentiality—" He was interrupted by Ted's saying, "I think it was not meant in the governmental sense. I suppose in the process of putting it together—"

The judge would have nothing off-the-record in his court. "It's not confidential as of this moment, all right?" he declared. Ted made no argument.

Jim cross-examined Bill, largely about compensation. I was surprised at how little Bill knew. He could only guess at what managers and partners made, but it sounded like at least 25 or 30 percent less than comparable PW people.

Bill's testimony put a slightly sour twist on the end of what was otherwise a great day in court. Carol, Tela, and I ate Mexican food at a restaurant downstairs from Germaine's. The boys wanted to stay home. They tried hard to talk me into letting them play hooky without making an appearance in court the next day. I refused.

Trial 2

THURSDAY

I could not justify the children's playing hooky from school unless they at least showed up at the courthouse. On the other hand, the testimony promised to be pretty boring. I let the boys leave immediately. Tela wanted to remain a while.

I was relieved of all legal responsibility on the second day of the trial. In my red jacket, I sat with controlled posture at the table with Doug and Jim. Most of the remainder of the brotherhood testified in the morning.

Representatives of Coopers and Lybrand, Ernst and Young, and Arthur Andersen paraded to the witness stand to present their lists and answer Jim's questions about compensation. Coopers and Lybrand had nine partners who came from PW. A new partner earned around $100,000 to $120,000 per year, about what a new partner at PW made.

The man from Ernst and Young identified the ten people on his list. He had been with Arthur Young before the merger with Ernst and Whinney. As a senior manager, he had no knowledge of partner compensation. Furthermore, he was reluctant to state his own. With a little help from Judge Gesell he said that as a senior manager he made in the range of eighty to ninety thousand dollars per year.

Tela must have gotten bored and left by the time Wayne prepared to call the partner from Arthur Andersen. The judge seemed to be approaching boredom. He said, "Are we going to have another one of these?"

Wayne responded affirmatively and hinted that a stipulation was in order. Judge Gesell tossed a small dart at Doug and Jim. "Oh, you can't get a stipulation. You'd better put the witness on. They won't agree to anything."

The man from Andersen identified the two partners on his list. He also stated that he made $160,000 his first year as a partner, up from $100,000 the previous year.

The person from Peat Marwick had a schedule conflict. He never made an appearance.

A man representing the human resources function at Price Waterhouse testified next. There was nothing cohesive about his testimony. He presented a few interesting facts. There were nineteen senior managers who earned more than $150,000 per year. Ten of the forty-seven men in my class who became partners had withdrawn, including three of the consulting partners. I had trouble imagining what the testimony accomplished.

Ted Olson called Joe Connor to the stand. He seemed to have aged prematurely and he looked tired. As he walked to the stand, I realized he was shorter than I. I had always known that but it was not so obvious when he testified on television at the first trial.

Joe introduced himself as a representative of Price Waterhouse world firm. I wondered why no partner from the Price Waterhouse U.S. firm would testify. That was the firm I sued. The PW world firm had nothing to do with the management of the U.S. firm. Continuity, I assumed, must be the reason.

Joe's testimony was smooth, dignified, and polished. Some of what he said was either funny or unnerving.

He bleakly commented on the uncertainty of the accounting business. "So the economic attractiveness of the profession is quite different today than it was even as recently as ten years." I suppressed a laugh as I thought, "I wonder if the partners know they're going broke?"

He commented on the law. ". . . We would observe whatever the Court directs us to do and I think we would try to do that with—in the best spirit possible. It is in my personal opinion doubtful that there would be acceptance of Miss Hopkins as a partner."

In spite of the fact that he was probably unable to differentiate between a computer and a condominium, he commented on my technical skills. "I now have some question as to her ability to perform as a partner. . . . Ann had good technical skills six years ago, if I have the right number of years. But the practice in OGS has now become so technically cutting edge, the size of the systems that we're doing, the methodology the firm now uses, all [of] which has been developed in the last six years[,] has moved so rapidly. . . . I think she probably is rusty now in the system area."

When Jim rose slowly to his feet, I barely noticed it. At some point he was seated beside me, then he was standing before the judge speaking calmly. "Your Honor, what I heard Mr. Connor saying, and I think I'm entitled to explain it since we have been criticized [for] the way the case comes to you, some case was going to come to some judge this way, what I heard Mr. Connor saying is we don't accept the fact that we may have mistakenly or discriminatorily evaluated Miss Hopkins, for we don't think she's entitled to be a partner and we'll resent it if you order it. I heard that. I heard that quite clearly, if not in those words."

Judge Gesell disagreed.

> I understood him to say something [different]. I understood him to say that although he was personally more favorable to your client's admission, that he felt that the judgment made by the partners that she had interpersonal relationships that were disadvantageous to the firm would not disappear if I ordered that she be made a partner.
>
> . . . And they will not disappear because they were matters that they had reached a conclusion on and whether or not that conclusion in part in accordance with my findings which I gather are now accepted contain some people who are influenced by sexual stereotyping does not mean that your client was devoid of interpersonal difficulties, and you know from the record that's clear.

Jim refused to be diverted from his point.

> There isn't a Title VII defendant in the world that doesn't think that they made a good judgment. There are a few caught in an act and feeling guilty about it. Not very many of them don't believe that they honestly made that firing or promotion decision which some court has now told them was not valid and was illegal. If every court sits and listens and they say we just can't accept that we did that wrong and therefore there's going to be difficulty accepting your Honor's decree undoing that wrong, then I think Title VII is nullified by personal attitudes which just simply are unreconstructed as a result of the case, and I can't believe that that is where the law is and I didn't mean to suggest anything more, your Honor.
>
> I don't think anybody is quite responsible for the posture of this case.

Certainly I am not saying that the two lawyers together bear all of the responsibility for it. Somebody was going to get the first partnership case. This is the biggest partnership anybody could have imagined to have that case happen to. *Hishon v. King and Spalding* could have had it happen to it. It was a firm of about a hundred people with a former Attorney General who I'm sure didn't believe that they violated the law. That woman decided not to press that issue, but somebody was going to do it because it's an important part of Title VII.

Now I really do think, your Honor, that if you hear testimony and take it to heart, and again I shouldn't cut off a judge in a bench trial, but I do want to note for the record, if you take to heart Mr. Connor's, meritorious partner that he is, projection of how the Policy Board which he no longer serves on will deal with a decision which might come down in Miss Hopkins' favor saying not only was there enough discrimination to warrant relief but I ordered the relief, because that is what the law calls for, and if that's where your Honor comes down and it the Policy Board of Price Waterhouse says we can't accept that, we're sure we were right before, then I don't know where we're ever going with these cases but it's going to be true in every other Title VII case, corporate versus partnership level at this size level doesn't make any difference.

When Jim returned to his seat, his eyes were focused on the bench, his back toward me. I whispered my approval of his remarks in the general direction of his right ear.

Joe rambled pleasantly onward, guided by Ted's continued questioning. He spoke with evident concern about the fluctuations in share values over the last several years. We broke for lunch when Ted Olson finished soliciting Joe's gloomy view of the business world.

"You were terrific," I said to Jim when we broke for lunch. He was rattled, visibly shaken. I failed to understand.

"That speech either lost the case or made you a partner," he said. "Now if you'll excuse me, I have to go make peace with my partner." Jim went to find Doug in the cafeteria.

I was astonished. Jim had lost his temper. That was what precipitated "the speech." I had known the man for years and never noticed that he lost his temper. He seemed to have been completely under control.

Carol and I dubbed it the "Martin Luther King speech." We may not have done justice to Dr. King. Jim was not that good, but those of us who listened to his speech were impressed.

By the time he started to cross-examine Joe Connor after lunch, Jim had loosened up considerably. He asked three questions to solicit answers from Joe that made clear the fact that Joe had no management role in the Price Waterhouse U.S. firm, and that he had had no such role at any time since mid-1988.

Jim's fourth question was, "Tell me, is the firm really going down the tubes?" Thereafter Jim asked short questions and Joe gave long-winded responses for another fifteen or twenty minutes. I paid little attention to the remainder of Joe's testimony.

Joe was followed by a pair of expert witnesses, one representing an executive search firm and another an outplacement counseling firm. The executive searcher testified that I should easily have been able to find a position at eighty thousand to two hundred thousand per year when I left PW in early 1984. Furthermore, my annual income in 1990 should have been at least two hundred thousand.

The outplacement counselor offered his expert opinion that I should have sent out at least fifty to sixty résumés as part of my Washington-based job search. In addition, I should have contacted two hundred search firms nationwide.

If Judge Gesell believed the two experts, then I clearly failed to mitigate damages at all. By that logic, I should be entitled to no back pay, zero. On one hand, I should have been able to earn a lot more money than I did. On the other hand, I had failed to look hard.

"Where were you two experts when I needed you?" I thought. I believed them not at all.

Jim asked the outplacement counselor how he would advise a person to handle a litigation situation such as mine. His response was, "Oh, I would never advocate that anybody offer that as a piece of information in seeking a job."

Jim pushed the point a little by asking what advice he would give to the litigant who had to participate in depositions, trials, or other legal proceedings. He responded, "I would probably ask them to stretch their imaginations and say that they had some sort of legal business to take care of. I would not suggest to them to say that I am suing a company that I was employed by."

The final expert and final witness for the day and the trial was "the figure man" as Judge Gesell referred to him. Ted Boutrous stated it more arrogantly, "He'll be testifying on economic statistics."

By contrast to Joe Tryon who was an "economist," Dr. Paul J. Andrisani was a "labor market economics and statistics and human resource management" specialist.

Ted Boutrous and Dr. Andrisani irritated Judge Gesell about five minutes into the direct examination. Dr. Andrisani was testifying to what he believed I should have earned had I stayed at PW and been nominated for the partnership the year after I was held.

The judge protested.

> I don't understand this whole scenario. It doesn't bear any relation to this case. We're talking about somebody else's case. We're not talking about this case.
>
> This woman couldn't have stayed at Price Waterhouse. She was forced out. She was constructively discharged. So all of that supposition is [purely] hypothetical. In addition, if you carry it on as he apparently is about to do, he's carrying it out in a period when I've been hearing testimony all day that they don't want her anyhow.
>
> So you're talking about something that has no relation to the case and I'm willing to have you make it as an offer of proof and I'm not critical of the witness because he's doing what he was asked to do, I'm not going to pay any attention to it. It hasn't anything to do with this case. It's just off the mark.

Ted Boutrous tried to recover. "If I can just briefly explain the underlying rationale. One, as I understood it, you didn't want to get back into whether or not the constructive discharge issue was alive or dead. So I'm—"

Then Judge Gesell realized that the constructive discharge issue remained unresolved. "You're assuming that—the assumption is that she wasn't constructively discharged?"

He reiterated his previous position on the issue. "I thought she was. Then I was wrong. I thought she could have stayed. I thought she could do just what this man was talking about. But I was told I was wrong. And that's our system.

"I was told by the Court of Appeals that I was wrong. And that's an accepted fact in the case and I don't see why we can go ahead—"

Ted Boutrous explained that Dr. Andrisani's testimony also supported an alternate theory of the case, under which the judge might order my return to the firm as an eligible partner candidate, instead of a partner.

Apparently Judge Gesell was not so inclined at the time. He gave his views on the alternate theory. "Well, you see, you've asked—you've proposed to me that I declare that she's eligible—to be considered eligible for partnership and then Mr. Connor got on the stand and indicated that they'd obey an order to make her a partner but otherwise he made it clear she would never be a partner, so making her eligible to be a partner would be utterly nonsensical. . . . That's the only way she's going to be made a partner, by order."

Ted Boutrous dropped that line of questions and moved to the next scenario. A few minutes later, the topic of examination was front pay. A key element of front pay is an estimate of future earnings. The calculation involves factors similar to those used to predict the growth of the economy of the United States.

As any newspaper will tell you, these futuristic estimates are wildly unreliable. Ted suggested a structured settlement or a structured award as a means of getting around the estimating vagaries.

The idea failed to appeal to Judge Gesell. "Well, you could, I suppose, fashion a front pay approach that would wait until the year's gone by and then each year come into court and we'd have another lawsuit and talk about it and fix the figures for that year in relation to the taxes and the interest rate and then we wait for another year and another judge would do it. Maybe some of my law clerks would have children and maybe they'd become judges and they'd be doing it. . . . That would be called a structured settlement"

At the beginning of the trial, Jim and Doug had considered calling an additional expert witness to rebut the testimony of the executive searcher and the outplacement counselor. When they finished cross-examining Dr. Andrisani, they decided against the rebuttal witness. Their decision was based only partly on lack of perceived need.

For either party to introduce any more witnesses would require that the trial continue into the next day. Jim and Doug were reluctant to prolong a proceeding that Judge Gesell clearly wanted to end.

The attorneys for both sides declared their cases closed. They stood before the judge and agreed on the post-trial procedures and schedules. As part of the discussion of post-trial procedures, Judge Gesell predicted the outcome. "I am of the view that since the case is obviously going to be appealed again on and on to the Supreme Court and back again, maybe that getting into the question of attorney's fees at this stage is probably not a wise thing to do."

Judge Gesell retired to his chambers. Friends and family went home for a respite before the celebration. Doug and Jim stood at my table talking to the GD lawyers, trying to agree on schedules for the next round of paperwork.

I sat, waiting for Jim and Doug, on one of the benches on my side and near the aisle. Although I was elated that the trial was over and relieved that it seemed to have gone well, I could hardly wait to get out of the courthouse.

The legal conference seemed to be breaking up. I stood up in anticipation of leaving with Jim and Doug. Ted Olson ambled toward me.

"If I lose this case, I'm going to call you and insist that you put me in touch with your employment experts to help me find one of those many high-paying jobs," I said with a grin.

He returned my comment with a good-natured chuckle. "That's fair," he said. "We should have to put up or shut up." He continued down the aisle and through the courtroom door into the hall.

Jim, Doug, and I left the court in splendid humor. We returned to the Kator, Scott, and Heller offices. Doug and Jim went their separate ways to clean up other legal matters. I was after all, not their only client. We agreed to meet later at the party.

As I was leaving, I ran into Joe Scott, one of the other partners. He told me how well the case seemed to be going. I asked him why the GD lawyers persistently asserted that Gesell could revert to his original opinion that I was not constructively discharged—especially in light of the judge's explicit statements to the contrary.

The GD lawyers, I assumed, were not stupid. I asked Joe if they knew something that we had missed. He said that we had missed nothing on that issue. The GD lawyers were arguing a technical point. It related to the wording in the order that went from the court of appeals to Judge Gesell after the Supreme Court ruled. They wanted to interpret the wording to mean that everything Judge Gesell had done had been vacated, leaving him free to do what he wished.

Joe said categorically that the argument was futile. It would not prevail. I would be all right. Constructive discharge, at least, was in the bag and unlikely to leap from it.

In no particular hurry, I went back to the bank to check for messages before going to the party. It was late in the day.

The half of the people in my division who came in very early in the morning were gone. Only the late half were still at their desks. The relative quiet was restful.

A review of the pile of pink message slips on my desk revealed nothing of an emergency nature. I returned a few calls, then I walked the two blocks to Harvey's, the Restaurant of Presidents.

Peter picked Harvey's for the party. It was his favorite restaurant downtown. The child had expensive taste. I occasionally ate lunch at Harvey's with Sandy Kinsey, but I avoided eating there regularly because the food prices were on the high side.

Judy Reach and I regularly met for drinks at Harvey's. Sometimes Karen Nold or others from PW joined us. It was across the street from the PW offices. The place was tasteful—a little on the dark side, but quiet. Furthermore, it was the cheapest bar in the area.

I would have preferred to have people come to the house, but Wayne Schrader's schedule had nixed that. He was involved in another trial that overran its schedule. The GD lawyers had asked the judge to slip the original trial date.

I was irritated when Jim told me about the request. "If those bastards can drag me through years of litigation, they oughta be able to show up in court on the scheduled date. Let him move the other case," was my reaction. Jim more or less ignored me on that point. He did not resist the change.

The trial only slipped a few days. Until the week it happened, however, there was a level of uncertainty about the date that prevented me from calling a caterer or inviting a lot of people. I decided to invite a few friends who had flexible schedules to join Doug, Jim, and me for dinner at a restaurant.

Gilbert liked fish, so Peter's choice of restaurants met with his approval. Tela would have preferred Mexican food, but she went along with the boys.

The children, who came with Carol, met me at Harvey's as I was confirming that there would be twenty to twenty-five people for dinner. The maitre d' explained that he would put us in a separate room where the group could expand or contract, if necessary.

Tela, Gilbert, and Peter took on the job of making sure that everyone had a good time. They sat at a separate round table with Vera's girls.

The purpose of having all the children at one table was not to segregate them from the adults. It was to give them the freedom to move around and talk to the adults, some of whom would be pinned against the wall by a long L-shaped configuration of abutting tables. The children knew that once I sat against the wall in the middle of the longer leg of the L, I would be trapped for the evening.

Jim and Bobbie arrived first. He sat next to me. Bobbie wisely sat on the outside of the table. Toni and John Gibbons sat to my left, John next to me.

Doug and his wife, Amy Wind, sat along the other L of tables. Doug and Jim were always wonderful about splitting up at the parties. It gave twice as many people a chance to ask questions about what had happened.

I discovered early in the litigation that I was incapable of giving a decent explanation of the latest legal event to more than the first two or three people who asked for one. The fourth person was likely to get a tired answer.

My friends, who stuck with me and provided the moral support that enabled me to endure, deserved better than a tired answer. In addition to paying homage to Doug and Jim, the parties served the purpose of giving my friends a chance to get the answers they deserved in the detail they wanted.

Joe Tryon and his wife came. On first impression, an impression that lasted, she struck me as a charming woman. They both told me how flattered they were to be invited. I was far more flattered that they came. Mary Curzan sat and chatted with them.

Mike Curzan was in town for a change. He sat opposite his referral. All evening Mike examined and cross-examined Doug on the legal issues of the case. Frankly, I think they had fun as "just lawyers, lawyering."

Most of the children ordered lobster and ordered early. Cokes flowed in abundance. When they finished eating, they flitted around making sure that everyone had everything that was wanted. They must have given the waiters cause for concern over there jobs.

The children became bored of the event long before the adults did. They decided to go home. Because they did not want to bother me, they asked Carol to give them the cab fare to get home. Carol walked them outside and to the curb. They hailed a cab, which she prepaid. We all tucked each other into bed when I got home an hour later.

Reading

Peter's vacations only occasionally fell at the same time as those of the Maret School. As a result, there were periods, sometimes as long as a week, when Peter was on holiday from school and everyone else was in school. To minimize the diversion from schoolwork, I tried to encourage Peter to play with me instead of Gilbert or Tela in the afternoons and evenings.

One diversionary tactic that I used often and with considerable success was to invite Peter to join me for a late lunch followed by a round of errands. Peter enjoys eating out, especially if he can eat dishes, such as Thai or Indian, that I seldom cook. If we met across the river in Rosslyn for lunch at 1:30 and if he then did a few chores at different subway stops along the line, he might be diverted until supper time.

Tela and Gilbert were in school for the entire week of Peter's spring break shortly after the trial. I enlisted Toni Gibbons and Pat Popovich as co-conspirators in the diversion of Peter.

Peter wanted a new pair of tennis shoes. I told him to use the subway system to find a store that sold what he wanted. Further, I asked him to determine the price of the shoes before he met Toni, Pat, and me at Tivoli's in Rosslyn for lunch. My plan was to give him the money after lunch and let him get the shoes and go from the shoe store home.

Toni and Pat drank wine to my beer. We discussed Peter's reading scores. He read at third-grade level. In six months at Oakland he had made more progress than he had in the preceding five years and three grades supported by resource rooms and tutors.

We were unworried when Peter arrived fifteen minutes late. He sat down at the table and ordered a Coke. "What would you like for lunch?" I asked as I handed him the menu.

Toni and Pat grilled him about the details of his subway ride. From what I could piece together, it seemed as if he had taken the right train going the wrong direction at his first transfer point. He was late because he had to change trains three times to work his way back to Rosslyn.

The three of us reacted with broad grins as he enthusiastically described all the places he had been. What should have been a straight shot through four stations on the blue line became, instead, three transfers and a dozen stations along the yellow, red, and blue lines.

"What's feh-nell?" he asked, referring to one of the specials on the menu. Mirth and amusement turned instantly to amazement. I was so startled, I forgot what fennel was. Toni recovered fast enough to explain that it was a spice that tasted vaguely like licorice.

"Skip that," said Peter. He ordered something else—but he read it from the menu, something he had never been able to do.

When the four of us split up after lunch, I walked into the Rosslyn subway station with Peter. We stood facing the station map. He read, sometimes with difficulty, the name of every station on the map.

"Now that you can read, Peter, you have to learn to rely on reading," I prodded, "otherwise you may spend a lot of time making unnecessary transfers." I asked him how he planned to get to the shoe store. He traced his route as he read the station names.

I returned downtown to my office at the bank. He went the opposite direction, to buy his tennis shoes. He got home in a lot less time than I had hoped. He and Gilbert played most of that afternoon.

Partnership

On Sunday, May 13, 1990, I made the familiar trip to Oakland to bring Peter home for a five-week break before the summer session. The next day, Judge Gesell published his "Findings of Fact" and "Conclusions of Law on Remand."

Doug called me at the office to tell me that he and Jim were headed to the federal courthouse to pick it up. He glibly noted that he had asked the clerk of the court if she would give him a clue as to what the judge had found. She had declined, he said.

I called Ruth and asked her to stand by. As soon as I had a copy of the memorandum, I wanted to come by the house for tea.

The two attorneys, Jim driving, roared from the parking lot in Jim's trusty Volkswagen Rabbit. They raced down Pennsylvania Avenue.

While Jim sat, double-parked in front of the courthouse, Doug fumbled his way through security. He skipped the steps up the escalator to the second floor where the clerk was located.

He screeched to a halt outside the door to the office of the clerk of the court. Calmly, trying to give the impression of composure, he entered the office and picked up the memorandum.

At a pace approaching an undignified run, he retraced his route back to Jim in the car, madly flipping pages as he went. There was no answer on the last page, where he usually found it. "Damn," he thought; there was no answer on the first several pages either.

Doug finally found the answer in the middle of the thirty-three-page document. Like Gilbert reading to Peter, Doug read to Jim as they drove back to the office.

"Well, it looks like you're gonna be a partner," Jim said when he called. "Holy shit! I'll be right there," I said.

I immediately called Ruth. All she could manage in response to the news was "I don't believe it." Her tone of voice made it clear that what she failed to believe was that the end of the litigation was in sight rather than the outcome.

Ruth called David. David called me. He sounded at least as happy as I felt when his call caught me on my way out the door en route to Kator, Scott, and Heller.

Pandemonium reigned from the minute I walked into the office until I left carrying several copies of Judge Gesell's latest ruling. I started hugging and kissing people just the other side of the main entrance door.

What looked like every member of the firm was standing in the halls wearing irrepressible grins. A wedding reception would have been glum by comparison.

I gleefully bear-hugged the women who had so carefully and professionally typed and proofed and copied the piles of paperwork over the years. As I hugged Doug I pounded him on the back so hard that I almost knocked him over. I was close to joyful tears by the time I got to Jim.

Later, in the quiet and calm of Ruth's living room, she and I read Judge Gesell's memorandum. He stated the liability issue that he resolved.

> It is established at this stage that Price Waterhouse intentionally maintained a partnership evaluation system that permitted negative, sexually-stereotyped comments to influence partnership selection. . . . Against this background, the Court must evaluate the March 1983 hold decision to determine whether Price Waterhouse has shown by a *preponderance* of the evidence that it would still have placed Ms. Hopkins' candidacy on hold even in the absence of sexually biased evaluations.

He also provided a legal definition of the evidentiary standard: "Preponderance of the evidence 'means such evidence as, when weighed against that opposed to it, has the more convincing force' that something is more likely so than not so."

Until I read further, I was almost convinced that to be preponderant a body of evidence had to be "more believable" than whatever it was being compared to or weighed against.

"The clear and convincing standard is much more demanding; it requires 'a degree of persuasion higher than "mere preponderance of the evidence," but still somewhat less than "clear, unequivocal and convincing" or "beyond a reasonable doubt."'"

My hopeless confusion returned.

"Perhaps," I thought, "the definitions were perfectly clearly expressed in legal terminology." To my mathematical mind, however, the definitions were all circular. Each was defined in terms of the other.

As if to chastise PW's lawyers, he described what they might have done to counter Susan Fiske's testimony or to separate sexist from nonsexist evaluations. According to his thinking, PW could have called an opposing expert or paraded a stream of witnesses to testify to the accuracy of the negative comments.

> Price Waterhouse could have presented testimony from an expert . . . , thus providing some basis for this Court to make appropriate findings. . . . While it was apparent at the time the case was originally tried that sexist remarks were involved in the process, Price Waterhouse had made no effort to suggest guidelines for identifying sexual stereotyping.
>
> Just as the Admissions Committee failed to investigate whether any of the negative partner comments on Ms. Hopkins were based on sex stereotyping, . . . Price Waterhouse has failed to separate out those comments tainted by sexism from those free of sexism. . . . Nor have those partners making negative comments been presented for appraisal of motives underlying their comments.

Ruth and I set aside our copies for a moment to rehash the pretrial conference. I suppose that the GD lawyers could have made an effort to reopen the evidentiary record of the original trial. Maybe they could have asked the judge to permit them to bring in an expert or a host of new witnesses.

At the conference, however, he certainly provided little encouragement along those lines. Ruth and I both had the clear impression that any proposal to retry the case or reopen the record would have been met with extreme hostility, if not a buzz-saw from the bench.

The judge dismissed PW's argument that comments made by women about me must be free of gender bias. PW had succeeded in convincing Judge Gesell that at least Sandy Kinsey, Karen Nold, and Pat Bowman thought ill of my interpersonal skills.

He failed, however, to accept their views as necessarily unbiased: "As Price Waterhouse notes, the record revealed that a number of female staff members complained about Ms. Hopkins' interpersonal skills. But Price Waterhouse does not address the issue of whether the perceptions of these women reflected male-dominated standards governing how women were supposed to behave."

Ultimately, the evidentiary standard made no difference. Price Waterhouse was unable to unscramble the omelet, as Doug so nicely put it. The sexist and the unbiased were inseparable. Judge Gesell was unconvinced by PW's arguments. "Ms. Hopkins must be deemed to have failed to receive partnership at the time she was held over because of sex discrimination, in violation of Title VII."

Having dispensed with liability, the judge turned to what I thought was PW's legally laughable proposition that Judge Gesell could now overturn the court of appeals' unanimous ruling on constructive discharge. PW never appealed to the Supreme Court on that issue.

In his memorandum, the judge carefully cited six cases in the District of Columbia Circuit where my case was the legal basis for the definition of constructive discharge. Then he diplomatically stated why any notion of his reconsidering the issue was preposterous.

> . . . the Court of Appeals' decision in *Hopkins* has been repeatedly cited in this Circuit, in every case on the precise issue—constructive discharge—that Price Waterhouse now wants to avoid. . . . It would be difficult to argue that they are no longer good authority on the constructive discharge issue because a wholly distinct aspect of an opinion they cite was reversed by the Supreme Court. The Court also notes that the Court of Appeals declined to rehear *Hopkins* en banc, . . .
>
> Price Waterhouse did not appeal this holding to the Supreme Court. . . . This Court is bound by it.

If asked, I am certain the Jim Heller would specify the changed law related to constructive discharge as the greatest accomplishment of *Hopkins v. Price Waterhouse*. The circuit court ruling on an obscure term that followed the argument that only John Gibbons and I watched was dwarfed by the attention paid to PW's Supreme Court case.

That ruling, however, is the reason that Judge Gesell even considered ordering the partnership. He was probably reluctant to do so—he believed I quit. The circuit court, however, had ruled differently.

"Thus Ms. Hopkins, having now the benefit of her constructive discharge, may claim back pay, both before and after her resignation from Price Waterhouse, . . . and she may press her claim to be made a partner by court-ordered injunction. . . .

Judge Gesell was torn between two forcefully stated, opposing positions on the partnership. He was reluctant to order it: "She insists this has always been her goal, but Price Waterhouse has equally insisted it does not want her as a partner."

In spite of PW's arguments to the contrary, he had the authority to order Price Waterhouse to correct its illegal decision and make me a partner. He exercised his discretion to use that authority and stated his intention to so order.

> . . . the Court's authority to do so is clear. *Hishon v. King & Spalding* . . . firmly established that partnership admission decisions are subject to the reach of Title VII.
>
> The Court will order that Ms. Hopkins be made a partner of Price Waterhouse effective July 1, 1990. Upon admission, Price Waterhouse must grant Ms. Hopkins sufficient partnership shares so that she will receive . . . the average compensation given management consulting partners admitted on July 1, 1983.

"I'm sure glad Betsy Hishon started in 1978," I thought silently.

Ruth and I put papers aside again to discuss the concept of a legal obligation to mitigate damages. Title VII requires that an employee who sues an employer make every effort to offset damage that might result while the suit is resolved.

The legal consequence of failure to mitigate is to lose entitlement to financial damages. As an example, suppose that I had taken up building birdhouses, while I awaited settlement of my dispute with PW. That would most likely have been considered a failure to mitigate damages.

Frankly, I first became aware of my obligation at the second trial. I was far more motivated by concerns over financing my children's school and paying the mortgage than any legal obligation I acquired when I sued. Judge Gesell, however, was persuaded by PW's evidence that I was less than perfectly diligent in meeting my obligation to mitigate: "Price Waterhouse has presented significant evidence challenging Ms. Hopkins' claim that during this long, uncertain period she took reasonable steps to mitigate her loss of partnership."

The differences between Epelbaum and me over the "chit calling" conversation came back to haunt me once again.

"Ms. Hopkins misstated the substance of a meeting . . . between herself and Joseph E. Connor. . . . Ms. Hopkins misleadingly implied that Mr. Connor had disparaged certain partners who opposed her candidacy and that he had warned of adverse consequences his partners might experience for opposing her the next year. Mr. Epelbaum felt immediately that Ms. Hopkins had misrepresented Mr. Connor's position. . . . "

This time, however, what was legally material became numerically material. Judge Gesell decided that misrepresenting the meeting with Joe to Epelbaum was a failure to mitigate damages. Accordingly, he decided ". . . she must be deemed to have forfeited any back pay claim for the fiscal year 1983-1984."

The judge was also persuaded by PW's expert testimony that I could have earned more money had I pursued the market more diligently. He set one hundred thousand dollars per year as the annual salary that I could or should have earned: ". . . her back pay award for each fiscal year shall be determined by subtracting from the average Price Waterhouse partnership salary for her class as stipulated, $100,000 or her actual earnings, whichever is greater."

In numerical terms that statement translated into lost wages amounting to $244,000. He effectively valued the failure to mitigate at $234,000. For the record, he included average partner compensation and my earnings for PW's fiscal years 1984 through 1989.

Fiscal Year	Average Partner	Net Earnings	Cost of Loss	Award	Failure to Mitigate
1984	107,157	80,015	27,142	0	27,142
1985	111,000	56,112	54,888	11,000	43,888
1986	124,240	54,299	69,941	24,240	45,701
1987	159,265	68,842	90,423	59,265	31,158
1988	176,420	46,524	129,896	76,420	53,476
1989	172,957	67,106	105,851	72,957	32,894
Total	851,039	372,898	478,141	243,882	234,259

Whatever the amount of lost wages, it was subject to interest, to be computed based on the year in which the individual annual amounts were "lost." Judge Gesell stated that he would rely on Professor Tryon to compute the current value of historically lost wages according to the assumptions that he testified to at trial. He would order the back pay after Professor Tryon computed it.

"No final order can be issued at this juncture, because the Court lacks adequate data to compute the substantially reduced back pay to be awarded. . . ."

"A status conference is set for May 25, 1990, at 2:00 P.M. in Courtroom No. 6, at which time the Court will approve a final order. . . ."

When Ruth and I finished our tea and reading, it was time for the children to be home from school. I hopped over the retaining wall and went through the back door into the kitchen, where I dropped the memorandum on the counter.

Gilbert, accompanied by Peter who had spent the afternoon at Maret waiting for his brother, bounded up the stairs and into the kitchen in search of food. I told them the latest legal news and referred them to the ruling.

"Does this say that Price Waterhouse owes us all that money?" Gilbert asked. "The amount hasn't been determined yet," I remarked, "But don't hold your breath waiting for the check."

Although I was relieved by Judge Gesell's opinion, I knew that there would be another appeal. Still, things were fine—I could have lost.

Order

"That's a terrible picture," Gilbert said. He referred my picture on the front page of the *Washington Post*. "May I have the sports page?" he asked rhetorically.

He flipped the grim persona, taken from the *Post* photo files, over on the kitchen table as he searched for the baseball scores. "What would you like for breakfast?" I asked. He had pancakes.

On every street corner downtown I stared from newspaper vending machines as Washington went to work. I spent the day on the phone fielding calls from family, friends, and the media.

One of the few things that I accomplished that day was to organize the party. It had to be scheduled for the next week because of the schedule conflicts that inevitably come with the end of the school year and the beginning of the summer vacation season. I called Ridgewell's.

Someone from a morning show called me at home that evening. She wanted me to appear on television the next day, in New York. I told her it was impossible for me to get to New York. Furthermore, I had to take the children to school.

She suggested doing the show remote from Washington and volunteered to send a car and make sure the children were delivered to school. Tela, Gilbert, and Peter thought that was a great idea.

The family was picked up and delivered to various television stations several times before the week was out. Tela was thrilled at the opportunity to talk for fifteen or twenty minutes with Mitch Snyder, the now tragically dead homeless advocate whom we met in one of the waiting rooms.

On one occasion, when a producer asked me to step down the hall for makeup, a startled Tela asked, "You're not going to do that are you, Mom?" She seemed even more startled at my reply: "Tela Margaret, that woman is in charge and I'm going to do what she says."

After one interview I asked the children what they thought. Peter's response was, "Don't laugh anymore, Mom. When you laugh, your eyes disappear."

In the time between Judge Gesell's opinion and the party, I accomplished very little, if any, work. The phone rang continuously. Anyone could dial the main number at the World Bank and get through to me.

Her experience with the Supreme Court left Evalyn proficient at separating the American press from my colleagues, family, and friends. She had quickly figured out the priorities: children interrupted anyone, bank people interrupted anyone other than another bank person, everyone else left messages.

Prior to the opinion, I had never received an international call as an employee of the bank. When Judge Gesell ordered the partnership, the international press seemed to take an interest in the case. I began to receive several international calls a day, usually from the London press.

Evalyn was reluctant to ask what might be a bank person calling from overseas to call back. The first two or three members of the London press were quite surprised when they were instantly connected with me. Evalyn soon realized that none of the overseas calls were business-related. They too entered the message pile.

Evenings at home, the children answered all calls. They failed to record messages from anyone they considered to be undesirable, frequently without asking my views.

When I got to the office the next morning, I usually returned calls based on the messages I could interpret. Those were mostly recorded by Tela. Peter used no vowels and Gilbert had unreadable handwriting. It was actually easier for me to figure out Peter's vowelless notes than Gilbert's Sanskrit.

Although Jim and Doug were no longer opposed to media contacts, they preferred that I not be quoted by journalists in the United States. There were, after all, more legal proceedings ahead, at least the court of appeals, and possibly another trip to the Supreme Court.

The American press never pestered me and usually reported most of the facts correctly. Occasionally I was the wrong age and sometimes the legal analysis was a little shaky, but people were interesting and always considerate and polite. No statement I ever made off-the-record ever appeared in the media.

In dealing with the American press, however, I infrequently spoke on the record. For the record, I was usually just "delighted" with the most recent outcome.

I became sensitive when I read some of the nastier pieces of PW's briefs in the newspapers, but all that material was part of the public record. I also became sensitive when I was characterized inappropriately.

I do not own, let alone carry, a handbag. I did once, but when I was at Touche commuting to Chicago, I stopped carrying handbags and umbrellas. Originally I carried a portable typewriter, a handbag, a briefcase, a suitcase, and sometimes a trial case for working papers or a coat for the cold.

Something was always getting lost, usually an umbrella or a handbag. More than ten years ago I transferred the contents of my last handbag to my briefcase. The last umbrella I lost was the last one I ever owned. Advances in technology permit me to carry a seven-pound computer in lieu of the old portable typewriter and the trial case.

Jim and Doug were puzzled when I complained about my briefcase being characterized as a "beat-up brown" briefcase in some newspaper article. That same article characterized me a little unpleasantly too. Overall, however, my attorney-friends believed that the press generally characterized me positively. They had trouble understanding my concern over a briefcase.

Toni Gibbons and I had bought it at a shop near her club in Georgetown after lunch there. I paid no attention to the shop. I selected one we both liked. I carried it for years before I realized it was an "in" thing. The man who wrote the article should have been able to differentiate between a brown Coach bag and a "beat-up brown" briefcase.

I was more comfortable and less inhibited with British and Japanese journalists and with women journalists. One such person, a British woman whom I had met a year or two ago at a block party for the neighborhood children, called to ask for an interview.

Because of her publication deadline and my schedule we agreed to meet at the house early the next morning just after I got the children out the door and on their way to school. She asked if she could dress casually. I told her that would certainly not bother me as long as she promised not to characterize my attire unfavorably. We laughed.

The interview was a day or two before the party so my normally untidy house was spotless. She arrived on a bicycle, wearing cycling shorts, tennis shoes, a T-shirt, and a helmet. She apologized for the appearance of her hair when she removed her headgear. She looked a little funny, but she knew what a Coach bag was and characterized my house as tidy.

The short notice for the party made it hard for Brother or his wife to get away from work. The end of the school year made it close to impossible for Susan to leave. I told them that there would probably be another party. I was less in need of their support than I had been on Supreme Court Day.

I invited a number of people whom I had gotten to know at the bank to join the festivities. As a result, the group at the second party in honor of Jim and Doug would be larger.

The night before, Carol and I sat planning logistics for the day of the party. She observed that there was too much furniture in the living room to accommodate the group.

When she suggested that we enlist the help of the Ridgewell's staff and volunteered to take care of it, I leapt at the opportunity. Carol managed Ridgewell's. Ridgewell's handled the party. When they left, the sofas and coffee table were in their original positions. The kitchen was as bare as a bowling alley.

The day after, Peter wandered around the kitchen sampling the party leftovers. Tela and Gilbert were at school, probably flunking their exams. Carol and I sat wearily in the kitchen drinking coffee.

I planned to drive 250 miles to Roanoke for my twenty-fifth college reunion as soon as Tela and Gilbert finished school for the day. What I really wanted to do, however, was sleep for a week.

"Fly," said Carol as she reached for the phone. Five minutes later, I was less tired and the family had airline reservations. Although I had no cash in the bank to pay for the tickets, I decided to worry about it later.

"Let's go down to the courthouse and watch the judge issue the order," I suggested to Carol. The flight left after four o'clock. Judge Gesell had scheduled a conference in the early afternoon. We barely had time to make it.

The proceedings were underway when Carol and I slipped quietly into the courtroom. Jim and Doug occupied their usual positions at the table on my side. Ted Olson, Wayne Schrader, and Ric Sullivan sat at the opposing table.

The question before the judge was attorney's fees. Doug and Wayne had agreed on Kator, Scott, and Heller's costs of $426,407.93.

There was no legal argument. The problem was one of simple arithmetic. Ted Olson presented the almost forgotten $3,946.61 cost of printing Supreme Court documents. Because I had lost, I had to pay.

Jim acknowledged that the roughly $426,000 amount should to be reduced by about $4,000. When he made the calculation to the penny, however, he got the wrong amount. With a twinkle in his eye and a broad grin, Judge Gesell said, "I don't seem to agree with your number, Mr. Heller."

Ted Olson suggested that the lawyers work out the details and get back to him at a later date. Judge Gesell would have none of it. He made perfectly clear the fact that he was going to sign the order that afternoon, even if he accomplished nothing else.

Wayne Schrader made another attempt at the calculation—still wrong. Ric Sullivan, Price Waterhouse's in-house counsel, who had never uttered a single word in all the years of litigation, finally computed the right number, $422,460.32.

"It always helps to have an accounting firm handle the numbers," Judge Gesell remarked. He was in a jovial mood.

The attorneys retired to Judge Gesell's chambers, where the order was printed and signed on the spot. Doug gave me a copy when we met in the hall afterward. He and Jim went back to work.

Poetry

Carol stood by while I called the house to make sure the children were packing for the trip. As we walked away from the pay phones, we ran into a woman who worked for Judge Gesell. She smiled warmly and said, "I hope you enjoy your new job, Miss Hopkins."

Carol drove me back to the house to pick up the children en route to the airport. I slipped the order, a single page, through Ruth Hopper's mail slot. "This litigation may yet end," I thought.

The reunion was fun—almost three-fourths of my class attended. The children's periodic playmates were there. It was hot, even at night. To escape the heat, the children played cards in the corridor of the dormitory where we stayed. No one slept much.

When we got home, I was weary, physically and emotionally bone tired. Ruth and David invited me to spend a week or two with them at their summer place in Canada.

I refused. Even the thought of driving six hundred miles alone was tiring. Flying to Ottawa and renting a car to get to their cottage would be too expensive.

Canada, however, seemed more appealing as the summer wore on. The heat and humidity increased daily. Work went into the summer doldrums. I took Tela and Gilbert to camp. With Peter still in school, I was alone, lonely, and a little bored.

One Friday I got home from work—late. I was in a bad mood. It was sticky after a summer thunderstorm. I put my key in the lock. The bundle of papers that was tucked under my arm escaped my control and landed on the water-saturated indoor-outdoor carpeting that covered the floor between the gate and the front door.

As I dropped my briefcase to the ground and unceremoniously bent over to pick up the soggy papers that enumerated the latest version of the budget of the World Bank, I found a wet, crumpled note. Soggy mess in hand, I entered the house, kicked off my wet heels, picked up the mail, and headed for the kitchen to scrounge around for something to eat.

A survey of the refrigerator yielded nothing interesting. I flipped on the TV and spread the soggy papers out to dry, readable side up, on the kitchen table and counters. The crumpled note caught my attention because the even pattern of the print was occasionally interrupted by undecipherable black scribblings, immediately recognizable as Jim's.

My mood changed from one of sullen glumness to mild amusement to outright mirth as I read.

> There once was a woman named Ann
> who was told to act less like a man
> told to be very sweet
> and to dress oh so neat
> and to walk with a shake of her can
>
> she said ***! enough is enough!
> by nature I am very tough
> so to law I will go
> expert counsel in tow
> and dispense with all of this fluff
>
> thus was the saga begun
> and for many long years it has run
> with papers in reams
> up to the Supremes
> and at each step of the way Ann has won
>
> and now the end is in sight
> yet still more briefs to write
> a partner in a flash—
> or rolling in cash
> with Price Waterhouse bowed to her might
>
> So to all who reach for things stellar,
> But are hampered by not being a feller
> There's hope in the end,
> If you choose not to bend,
> and instead, hire Kator, Scott & Heller

The note was signed, "This doggerel writ by a committee led by Joe Scott."

Over the course of the next week or so, I tried in vain to compose an appropriate response, an activity that left me so frustrated that I abandoned it. I tucked the doggerel into my briefcase.

I was on the verge of changing my mind about going to Canada when Ruth suggested that her grandson Karl and one of his friends from school ride up with me. That clinched it. I took the two boys and drove to Lac Gatineau in Quebec, about an hour from Ottawa.

It was close to impossible to worry about anything that far into the boondocks. David and I discussed the mathematical theory underlying the washboarding effect of cars on the roads.

He paddled Ruth and me around the lake in a canoe and talked about the history of each of the cottages along the shore. While I was there, one of them burned down in a tragically spectacular display of fireworks late one night.

Kuwait was invaded. We had a hard time following the story though. Just about the only radio station we could receive was the BBC in London. Even the BBC faded in and out.

Ruth and I talked about work and family as we puttered around the kitchen. We both enjoyed cooking. I got through several murder mysteries. She read the *Economist.*

When the time to leave came, I was emotionally much more settled than I had been when I arrived. I decided to break up the long trip by dropping in on people on my way home.

Susan's place in Vermont was only a few hours from Ottawa. I spent a weekend with her and the family. Then I worked my way three hours south to North Bennington to visit Julie Randall and her dogs.

It was hot at Julie's. In rare deference to my desire for air conditioning, Julie took me to one of the few restaurants in town. That was the only time in the history of our twenty-year relationship that I ever remember eating out when I was at Julie's. She always cooked.

The next morning as I was preparing to leave, I retrieved Joe Scott's well-traveled doggerel from my briefcase. I asked if she would help me respond.

"I don't do poetry on demand," Julie quipped. I explained that an instantaneous response was not required. I needed something by the first week in September when the argument before the court of appeals was scheduled.

She reconsidered the words on the well-worn page. "I hope they're better lawyers than they are poets," she said, "The meter's all wrong."

"What is 'Kator, Scott, and Heller'?" she continued without looking up. I told her it was a law firm named after Irv Kator, Joe Scott, and Jim Heller. She glanced at the calendar over her desk. "I ought to be able to come up with something," she said as she placed Joe's work on top of one of several tidy piles on her kitchen desk.

It was a long drive from Bennington to Yorktown Heights, New York, where Brother and Cathy and their family lived. I had never seen their house. They had lived there only a year or two.

Cathy was still at work when I arrived. She usually worked until around 8:00 at night. Brother got home shortly after 4:00, but he left for the office at 5:30 in the morning. His two little girls and I sat at the kitchen table while he fixed spaghetti for their supper. After Cathy got home, the children went to bed and we three adults ate.

The next morning Brother was gone by the time the family and I got up. On her way to work, Cathy led me to the thruway going south as she dropped the girls off, one at school and the other at her day care center.

The trip had been pleasant. The memories rolled over in my mind and kept me company as I headed south toward the children and home. My stays in Canada, Vermont, and New York were nothing exciting, just families being families.

I battled the traffic down the various toll roads to the eastern shore of Maryland to pick up the children at camp. Summer was over.

A week before the second argument before the court of appeals, I received a letter from Julie. I recognized it by the tiny impeccable handwriting on the envelope. She said:

Dear H. -

This is the best I can do, under pressure of 2 house-guests & 1 puppy. It is very hard to write occasional verse when the occasion is not your own, so you can chuck it. At least the meter is right.

Thanks for coming by—

XX. Haste

J.

Her limericks, typed not-so-neatly on her ancient portable Underwood typewriter, were enclosed. They read as follows:

Dear Kator and Heller and Scott
Will Shakespeare you surely are not
Though you try very hard
to out-numer the bard
You don't put old Hop on the spot.

Remember he frequently had
To disguise a young lady as lad,
When at last she came clean
(As she always had been)
The Hero was startled but glad.

Unlike P and Water who wanted
Their boys to be roarers undaunted
But their girls to be girls
Blessed with permanent curls
and with bangles and—bits to be flaunted.

You have helped to reveal the true whiz,
For as well as promoting the biz,
I've produced T. and G.
and the redheaded P.
Who belong to a hers, not a his.

Through briefs and replies and rebuttals,
S. Courts and appeals and tut-tuttles,
Remaining a friend
And staunch to the end,
We sing you our singular chorals.

And now let the curtain come down,
For we have defeated the Crown,
And the boards and the lights
Where I stood for my rights
May they presently vanish from town.

I conclude in the place I began:
I was never but never a man,
Dear Joe, Jim, and Doug,
Mike and Irv, here's a hug
and a kiss from yours faithfully Ann.

One of the men at the office typed Joe's doggerel, under the title "Brief," facing Julie's limericks under the title "Reply Brief," on a single page, suitable for framing. The weekend before the argument was scheduled, I delivered several copies to Toni's favorite art shop, located next door to Germaine's.

That same weekend, Carol Supplee, Vera Schneider, Susan Riley, and I got together for a party-planning session. The argument date had already changed once. The guests all knew that the date of the party might change at the last minute and were prepared.

I was, however, reluctant to call Ridgewell's without a specific date for the party. Brother's wife, Cathy, planned to come from New York, leaving Brother to man the home front this time. Sister Susan planned to fly from Boston. The planning group decided that if we split up the work, we could do without Ridgewell's. Carol volunteered and was elected project manager.

Appeal 2

When my case reached the court of appeals for the second time, a rough translation of its legal name was *Hopkins v. Price Waterhouse, (District Court for the District of Columbia 1985), affirmed in part and reversed in part, (Court of Appeals for the District of Columbia Circuit 1987), affirmed in part and reversed and remanded in part, Supreme Court (1989).* In the D.C. circuit it is more generally known by its shorter name, *Hopkins.*

Oral arguments were held during the first week of the new court session. The existence of August made it close to impossible for the arguments to be held any sooner. The court of appeals was only slightly less anxious than Judge Gesell to be rid of the case.

Ruth called the night before the argument. "Why don't you ride down with David and me in the morning," she said. She suggested that I let the family get from the house to the court on their own.

"That's a wonderful idea," I said. "I'll meet you in the driveway in the morning."

David drove Ruth and me downtown. Normally he would have driven the little car because it maneuvers easily in traffic. On September 7, 1990, he drove the Lincoln. He wanted a calm, quiet dignified atmosphere for the trip.

He dropped us at the door where we waited while he parked the car. The three of us entered the courtroom arm-in-arm, me in the middle.

The front row on my side of the aisle was largely occupied by a crowd of children, my three, Vera's two, and Susan's two. I saw Carol, Vera, Susan, and another friend sandwiched between laughing children waving at me. There was no block of three seats available on my side.

"Are there any partners on PW's side?" David asked. The only people I recognized at a glance were the in-house lawyers, Eldon Olson and Ric Sullivan. "None that I recognize," I replied. (At the time I was unaware of the fact that Eldon Olson was a partner.) "Well, there should be," he commented turning right into the middle of PW's side. As we sat down he smiled broadly and said, "And now there is at least one."

I glanced to my left where most of Kator, Scott, and Heller sat with friends and family. Bobbie Heller smiled a greeting. Mary Curzan did the same.

John Gibbons arrived just before the time scheduled for the arguments. Seeing him raised a tear as I remembered our first trip to the court of appeals when he and I sat together.

The three-judge panel entered the packed courtroom a few minutes late. This time it comprised three circuit judges.

Chief Judge Abner Mikva seated himself and greeted the attorneys in a friendly mellow voice. He leaned over the bench to introduce Judge Karen L. Henderson, the newest member of the court of appeals. It was her first day on the job. Judge Harry T. Edwards, who sat to Judge Mikva's right needed no introduction. He had been the chief judge at the last argument.

Ted Olson went first. Ann Hopkins had genuine and serious interpersonal skills problems. Her problems and the complaints about her were not a pretext for discrimination. They were real and serious and gender-neutral. These same problems had been grounds for holding or rejecting males. Some of the criticisms of Ann Hopkins did show some indication of sexual stereotyping, but it was unconscious.

Her serious problems and stereotypical biases both contributed to the decision to hold her over for consideration in the next year, a common practice. She was not rejected. She had a chance. Eighty-five percent of those held over became partners the next year. She, however, blew it.

Her own unreasonable conduct destroyed her chances for the partnership. She left. Although she had plenty of opportunities to work elsewhere, she ignored or rejected them.

I had heard it before. I had read it before. The same vitriolic diatribe was being presented to the court of appeals once again.

Ruth's hand in mine was cold. She has low blood pressure. David patted my right hand which still clutched his left arm. He smiled supportively. Ruth squeezed my hand.

Ted continued. Price Waterhouse may have committed an error in the evaluation process. It did not, however, commit an error in weighing the negative against the positive factors.

Gender-neutral issues were overpowering. Twenty of twenty-one comments were negative in some manner. When Price Waterhouse investigated, it found a pervasive theme: unacceptable interpersonal relationships. Three partners testified to that effect at trial.

Judge Edwards, who had sat back in his chair to this point, leaned forward on his elbows. He, too, had heard the story before.

He proceeded to have a very polite legal fit. "Mr. Olson, your argument would be more properly presented to the district court. Judge Gesell asked you to resubmit your evidence there. Now you raise factual arguments before the Court of Appeals." He restated the position of the court in 1987: "This Court of Appeals can't go through the entire record. What you are asking for is impermissible."

Ted argued not that Judge Gesell reached the wrong answer, rather that he never weighed the evidence. I wondered how Ted could make that argument with a straight face.

Judge Edwards contradicted Ted. He noted that the judge reviewed the trial transcript, considered briefs prepared by both sides, and listened to their arguments. At best, Judge Gesell considered the facts to be in equipoise. Price Waterhouse did not meet its burden by a preponderance of the evidence. The court of appeals cannot reassess the trial record.

Ted continued. Judge Gesell failed to evaluate gender-neutral comments. The judge stated that those comments were tainted.

Judge Mikva joined Judge Edwards and the two took turns reading quotes from Judge Gesell's opinion and that of the Supreme Court. The evidentiary record was in balance. The record was not discarded. It was in balance. Judge Gesell said so. Justice O'Connor said so.

The dialogue between Ted and Judges Edwards and Mikva had the characteristics of conversation between a native and a foreigner across an impenetrable linguistic barrier. The native speaks to the foreigner, who fails to understand the language. The native repeats his words, slowly and more distinctly, in hopes that better pronunciation will overcome the barrier. When that fails, the native speaks more loudly.

No matter how slowly, distinctly, or loudly the words are spoken, the words fail because the foreigner does not understand the language. In this case, it was as if Ted Olson spoke Chinese to a panel that spoke only English.

Ted tried again. Although some comments were affected by stereotyping, others were unaffected, he argued. Judge Gesell considered none of the comments. Ted summarized his argument with a metaphor, "It's like throwing out all the apples in a barrel because of a few bad ones."

"If you could hear yourself, you'd see that you're going in circles," commented Judge Edwards. He continued by explaining that Judge Gesell did not take the evidence off the scales. A district judge cannot refuse to consider evidence. "You did not show evidence that would have persuaded the Court in any event," he remarked.

Judge Mikva joined the fray. "You didn't submit any more evidence." With one arm over his head, he expanded on the apple barrel metaphor, "How hard is it to hold up an apple and say 'This is a good apple?'"

Ted commented that additional evidence was unneeded. There was adequate evidence in the record.

"You were told by several judges that no matter how good you thought your evidence was, it wasn't," Judge Edwards retorted. "The Supreme Court didn't disagree with Gesell, so you lose again."

Ted's light had turned yellow a couple of apples ago. He was running out of time when he got to his arguments on the nature of my legal injury and the related remedy.

He argued quickly about the lack of injury. Ann Hopkins was not rejected; consideration of her partnership was deferred. Her own actions, as opposed to an act of the partnership, resulted in her not being proposed the second time.

When Ted got to remedy, he referred the panel of judges to PW's brief, which he summarized in the few seconds remaining. Partnership as a remedy is not described in Title VII or its legislative history. Partnership is an inappropriate remedy where the plaintiff took herself out of the running. She unreasonably prevented herself from being a partner.

She also failed in her duty to mitigate, Ted argued. She refused to go on interviews. At most she is entitled to receive back pay for the one year that she was in suspension.

Jim rose and approached the podium to take his turn. He corrected or restated a few facts in response to remarks made by Ted Olson.

"The Supreme Court said that Price Waterhouse didn't explain how the evidence was preponderant," Jim said. It was PW's burden to show that it was preponderant.

"Price Waterhouse is autistic," Jim declared calmly. I was taken aback. Jim seldom uses obscurities. The word autistic is infrequently used and even more infrequently used correctly.

Jim, however, used the word to perfection. It means "a pervasive development disorder characterized by impaired communication, extreme self-absorption, and detachment from reality." I knew the meaning of the word only because Brother John worked with autistic children for years. I hoped the panel got the message, one way or the other.

According to Jim, Price Waterhouse ignored stereotyping. Judge Gesell recognized that some statements that seem to be gender-neutral may not be. He merely asked PW to identify or explain the nonstereotypical comments.

Judge Mikva frowned. He seemed concerned that perhaps PW had an impossible quest. Perhaps no evidence existed that could be used to separate the stereotypical from the other. "What kind of evidence could have qualified?" he asked.

"Relevant evidence might have included expert evidence saying 'we don't agree that there was stereotyping.' Lay witnesses could have been called," Jim answered.

Judge Mikva asked about the lay witnesses. "How would you expect someone to respond, after the fact, when asked to explain if the language was discriminatory?" seemed to be the question that bothered him.

"Subject the witnesses to cross-examination," Jim said. That, he conjectured, should give a judge enough information to reach a conclusion.

Jim cited some sample questions. "How long did you know Miss Hopkins? Did you ever tell a man to go to charm school?"

"Many who criticized Miss Hopkins knew her for only five minutes," he continued. "We'd ask: 'On what do you base your criticism?'"

Jim summed up his point. The job was legally possible. PW simply decided not to call opposing experts or the authors of the comments to testify.

Judge Edwards asked, "If we give her a partnership, can they remove her six months later?"

Jim explained what the judge must have known. Title VII regulates the conduct of the firm. It contains provisions governing retaliation and insincerity of promotion.

Judge Henderson was troubled by Epelbaum. "How can Epelbaum trust Hopkins as a partner, or be forced to, as an equitable form of relief?"

"He said he didn't trust her," Jim responded.

"And Judge Gesell said he was right," Judge Henderson continued.

"She stumbled on the extra lap, and she had to take the extra lap because she was a woman," Jim argued.

Judge Henderson persisted. "Shouldn't a partnership depend on trust?"

"That there was one nose out of joint should not affect the remedy," Jim responded. "Judge Gesell said that there wasn't such hostility that she shouldn't be made a partner. He gave short shrift to Epelbaum," Jim said as the light on the podium turned red.

My government sat on my side of the court of appeals in the person of an attorney from the EEOC. Ms. Starr was responsible for an amicus brief filed on my behalf by her agency. PW had unsuccessfully opposed the brief.

Before the arguments, the EEOC asked Jim and Doug to relinquish a little of the time allocated to them. The EEOC wanted to participate. Jim and Doug reluctantly refused to give up the time. They wanted to be sure that they had all the time available to counter whatever the GD lawyers came up with.

The Court decided to add time to the schedule to permit the EEOC to argue on my behalf. Ms. Starr stated the legal position of the EEOC: partnership can be ordered as a remedy under Title VII. Furthermore, monetary relief would be insufficient to deter future discrimination. The arguments were not novel. It was, however, nice to have at least some part of my government on my side.

On rebuttal Ted reiterated the heinous nature of my interpersonal skills by citing the page numbers for nondiscriminatory, gender-neutral comments. He characterized them as substantial evidence.

He said that witnesses at the original trial were asked if sex was a consideration in making the comments. Those witnesses denied it. Furthermore, male candidates were treated equally.

Judge Mikva pointed out that if ". . . you put someone on the stand and ask 'Are you a bigot?'" he would be surprised by any answer other than a denial. The judge told Ted that his argument was not shedding any light on the issue.

Ted continued to try. He explained that the witnesses were subjected to cross-examination.

Regarding opposing expert testimony, Ted seemed to believe it unnecessary to make PW's case more persuasive. He commented that the Supreme Court regarded such testimony as "icing on the cake" and that it would have been of dubious value.

Judge Edwards reiterated a point made by the Supreme Court. The Supreme Court endorsed the notion that people who stereotype often are unaware of or unconcerned about their actions.

Price Waterhouse made the right decision, Ted argued in return. If a person, who is not a partner is abusive, she should be given a second chance before a partnership.

"If someone said 'I hate blacks,' it might be clearer to you, but you seem to suggest that sexual stereotyping is different from race stereotyping. What PW did is like saying 'nigger,'" said Judge Edwards.

Ted continued to explain. There were legitimate problems and therefore reasons for the deferral. He was undaunted. He did, however, change the subject to remedy.

Ted's position was that partnership was an inappropriate remedy. Judge Gesell acknowledged that Price Waterhouse had some legitimate concerns. Congress never addressed the issue of partnerships when it passed Title VII. Congress, not the courts should decide if a partnership can be ordered under Title VII.

"You must be out of your mind!" I thought. After two trials, two appeals, and a trip to the Supreme Court, Ted Olson wanted an act of Congress.

"Suppose that an employer said, all employees who do 'such and such' are eligible for a $50,000 bonus and a person was denied it because she was a woman. Would that violate Title VII?" Judge Mikva asked Ted.

Ted acknowledged that it would.

"What in the statute prohibits the same remedy if partnership is substituted for $50,000?" he asked.

According to Ted, financial damages were appropriate. Partnership was inappropriate.

Judge Mikva changed the example, "What if it were a vice presidency of a company?"

Ted argued that an employee could be reinstated. A partner was not an employee. Therein, as Ted saw it, lay the difference.

Judge Edwards stated that, under Title VII, ordering a partnership was permissible. "You don't think that a court can order the remedy?" asked Mikva rhetorically. "Until a few years ago, we couldn't order universities to give tenure," he quipped.

The university situation is an employer-employee relationship, Ted explained. Price Waterhouse partners are not employees.

"So a court could order someone to be made president of General Motors but not a partner in an accounting firm?" Judge Mikva asked. He seemed skeptical to me.

"Not until Congress recognizes nonemployee relationships," replied Ted.

I exhaled as I stood when the judges left the courtroom. I exhaled as if I had held my breath through the entire proceeding. Then I nervously released Ruth and David and stood on my own.

Celebration

Later that morning, family and friends reassembled back at the house. Carol arrived with a long list of tasks and everything she believed we needed for the party. We expected the customary group of fifty or sixty people.

It was a spectacular, cool dry sunny day. Cathy scrubbed mildew off the deck furniture on the back porch. Vera and Susan Riley peeled and pared vegetables. Sister Susan and Carol steamed and deveined twenty or thirty pounds of shrimp. I washed and ironed linen tablecloths most of the afternoon. Anyone with spare time polished silver.

A light banter of sarcastic humor filled the air all day as we went about our chores. Cathy was branded "anal retentive" for the fastidiousness with which she applied the Ajax to the white wire chairs. After spending three hours on six chairs, she decided the windows between the house and the deck needed to be washed. She proceeded to do so.

Sister Susan and Carol engaged in mock argument over the best technique for deveining shrimp. Vera and Susan Riley complained bitterly about the menialness of their jobs. They wanted to hire the Girl Scouts to replace themselves.

At the end of the work day we cleaned out the accumulated garbage. We shed our scullery maid outfits, showered, and dressed. By the time the first guests arrived we looked like the ladies we all were. Based on what the house looked like and the elegant fare, meticulously displayed in the dining room, Carol was as good as Ridgewell's.

The family and friends must have cleaned up. I certainly have no recollection of being involved. The next morning, Sister Susan, Cathy, and I sat peacefully in the kitchen for a few minutes before they took the subway to the airport. We all returned to our respective homes to await the outcome.

As it usually does, September flew by. My energies were absorbed getting the children clothed and supplied for school. Gilbert was a seventh-grader. He seemed to have grown so fast that nothing from the previous year fit. He and Peter could no longer wear the same size.

Tela entered her freshman year of high school. Although some of her previous year's clothes fit, their style suddenly became obsolete. The only color any freshman female seemed to wear was black.

I drove Peter back to Charlottesville for his second year at Oakland School. He was enthusiastic. The apprehension of the previous year had vanished. He was excited at the prospect of taking a science course and reducing the number of reading courses to five.

Peter had no grade, the students at Oakland are ungraded. He could, however, read well enough to look up the movies, determine the address, and make a selection. The year before he would have dialed "411," asked for the numbers of a few local movie houses, and called the numbers in sequence until he found a movie he liked.

October was busy at the bank. We had to begin the first-quarter budget review. I had little time to worry about the opinion of the court of appeals.

Jim and Doug thought it extremely unlikely that the opinion would be published before Halloween. On the other end of the probability spectrum, they were reasonably certain it would be out by Christmas.

Christmas sounded good to me. After all, the previous opinion emerged from the judicial process about nine months after the arguments. Halloween passed uneventfully.

By November, I began to get anxious, but only on Mondays and Tuesdays. Most opinions are published on those days.

The children spent Thanksgiving with Thomas Peter. I was alone and nervous. To divert my attention, I baked forty pounds of fruitcake. I was certain that the opinion would be published the Monday or Tuesday following the holiday. Nothing happened.

Reaffirmation

On Tuesday, December 4, 1990, the court of appeals unanimously affirmed Judge Gesell's order on all issues. I could no longer lose. The liability issue had been to the Supreme Court. It was dead.

The opinion of the court of appeals was written by Judge Edwards. In the first sentence of the opinion, I immediately sensed a desire to be rid of the matter: "This case, before this court for the second time, arises from a decision by appellant Price Waterhouse to deny partnership to one of its employees, appellee Ann B. Hopkins. We are again asked to review a finding by the District Court that Price Waterhouse's denial of partnership to Ms. Hopkins violated Title VII of the Civil Rights Act of 1964, . . . and to assess its shaping of an appropriate remedy."

Unlike Judge Gesell's memorandum, it was not difficult to find what the court of appeals decided. Very early in the opinion, Judge Edwards wrote the overall ruling of the court on the issues of liability and remedy.

> On remand, the District Court first offered to permit Price Waterhouse to introduce new evidence concerning nondiscriminatory reasons justifying the denial of partnership to Ms. Hopkins; Price Waterhouse declined this offer, choosing instead to rely on the evidence already introduced at the first trial. The trial court then reviewed that evidence and found that Price Waterhouse failed to carry the burden placed on it by the Supreme Court. . . . Having found appellant liable under Title VII, the District Court

ordered Price Waterhouse to admit Ann Hopkins and to pay her $371,000 in back pay. On this appeal, Price Waterhouse challenges both the District Court's finding of liability and its remedial order that Ms. Hopkins be made a partner. We can find no merit in either of these challenges.

He then proceeded to move through Price Waterhouse's legal assertions and knock them off one by one. Liability he eliminated first.

Specifically, Price Waterhouse asserts that the trial court sidestepped its responsibility to reweigh the evidence by emphasizing Price Waterhouse's failure to produce *new* evidence suggesting that it was moved by legitimate, nondiscriminatory concerns in denying Ms. Hopkins partnership in March 1983. Second, it asserts that, even if the trial court did reweigh the evidence, it committed clear error in not being persuaded by Price Waterhouse's showing. We disagree on both counts.

For the second time, the court of appeals stated its position on constructive discharge. The position was unchanged: "We find no error in Judge Gesell's finding that Ms. Hopkins was constructively discharged when Price Waterhouse informed her that she would not be renominated for partnership."

I mentally thanked Betsy Hishon once again. Judge Edwards wrote that Judge Gesell, in fact, had the authority to order a partnership: "Price Waterhouse also asserts that the District Court had no authority to order admission to partnership to remedy a Title VII violation. . . . Given the Court's judgment in *Hishon,* and after a careful review of Title VII, its legislative history and the case law interpreting it, we find that the District Court clearly acted within the bounds of the remedial authority conferred by the statute."

The opinion rejected a long list of other arguments. The claim for protection of the constitutionally guaranteed freedom of association was rejected. An argument that common law principles were violated was dismissed. The court of appeals decided that Judge Gesell did not abuse his discretion by ordering a partnership, nor did the judge commit an error or abuse his discretion in determining back pay.

The final page of the twenty-nine page opinion summed it up nicely:

For all of the foregoing reasons, the judgment of the District Court is affirmed.

So Ordered.

It was all over but the shouting. I wanted to have another party. Sheila was conveniently coming for Christmas. The house painter was inconveniently arriving the day after Christmas, when the children were scheduled to go skiing with Thomas Peter.

To paint the entire interior, alkyd on the walls and high-gloss enamel on the woodwork, would take a week. Allowing for a little schedule slippage and an airing out period, the party could not be scheduled before the first week in January.

Briefcase

"Are you sure you want to have a party that soon?" asked Jim referring to what I planned to bill as "the Last Party." He was concerned that the appeal period might not have passed.

I was reminded of his earlier comment about the World Court when I asked what avenues of appeal were left. He saw none, but allowed that the matter could probably be dragged out for months by another, almost certainly hopeless, request for a second writ of certiorari.

There was no need for consultation with John at Germaine's. Ruth Hopper was relieved of the burden of interpreting the opinion. I would do without legal prognosticators or tea-leaf readers.

A joyful Christmas and a period of chaos preceded the Last Party. The children all wanted leather jackets for Christmas. That presented something of a problem for the boys. When Sheila and I searched, we found nothing they would like in any of the children's or boys' departments. We eventually bought the smallest women's petite we could find. Tela's jacket fit; the boys' jackets were a little long in the sleeves.

Sheila and I ate out every night between Christmas and New Year's. We slept with the windows open in spite of the winter chill. The cold was a better alternative than asphyxiation.

The schedule for the painting job slipped to the point where the painter finally cleared out the last of the drop clothes and paint buckets as the purple Ridgewell's truck pulled into the driveway to deliver the equipment the day before the Last Party. The painter had to return later to finish a couple of unnoticeable doors. Carol and Sheila spent the day cleaning up after the painters and reassembling the house.

A professional cleaning crew arrived at seven in the morning to fine-tune the cleaning job. The crew had to work around a couple of my neighbors who spent the afternoon of the Last Party constructing a floral arrangement that stood almost four feet high when finished. The cleaning crew left about an hour before the Ridgewell's staff arrived.

When the guests began to arrive, everything seemed calm, quiet, and dignified. George had been banished to the doggie hotel for the night. Sheila had spent the day at the hairdresser recovering from the dirty duties of the previous day. She looked like she stepped out of a magazine for elegant women. The Ridgewell's staff looked like permanent fixtures.

The Last Party was the first time that Jim and Doug were not surrounded with groups of people asking about the next legal strategy or counterstrategy. Instead, the topic of conversation was what would I do next.

I was going back. Although I heard from Jim that Price Waterhouse would consider settling for $1 million, I told him to wait until they agreed to $3 million and even at that price, I would never agree to nondisclosure or any term that resembled a gag order.

Marty Danziger cheerfully delighted in his erroneous projection ("You'll never win, kiddo") of the outcome. Mary Curzan explained that her daughter was studying the case in law school. Howard Renman and other people from the State Department told me that, on my behalf, they had cabled Bob Lamb, now the American ambassador to Nicosia. Roger Feldman was with us in spirit although he was physically in Florida.

Joey Biero relayed stories of my high school antics to Bini Herrmann and Sally Craig. Susan Riley and Vera Schneider stood by in amused horror as their children listened in disbelief to Joey.

A friend from the World Bank took Polaroid pictures of most of the guests. Based on the pictorial record, which shows me hugging and kissing Doug, Jim, David, and a number of other friends, I was too excited to engage in any serious conversation.

As the Last Party drew to a close, Jim asked for everyone's attention.

He fished a few pages of folded white notepaper from his jacket. Jim then gave the only inarticulate speech I ever heard him make, a speech that he read from the black scribblings on the papers. He presented me with a brand-new "beat-up brown briefcase" to carry back to Price Waterhouse.

Epilogue

It takes more than a court order to make a partner.

Under the best of circumstances, the transition from partner candidate to partner is rough. The candidate has a business base: clients to serve and teams of people to care for. Of necessity, the candidate knows who the partners are and is likely to have professional or personal relations with many. Sponsoring partners watch out for the candidates. The professional staff knows who the candidates are and treats them with regard.

The candidates are the top of the nonpartner professional staff.

On the first day of the firm's fiscal year, when the aspiring candidates become partners, the paradigm shifts. What was at the top of one heap goes to the bottom of another.

The new partner may be relocated to a new city. More than likely, the former candidate's clients continue to be served by the partners who previously served them. The project teams are cared for by replacement project managers. The new partner has to find new clients and compete with more senior partners for staff to serve those clients.

Paychecks are distributed and reported differently. New partners have trouble interpreting what they are paid. The complexity of the compensation system, especially as it relates to taxes, is legendary. The firm offers instruction to explain the intricacies of partner compensation.

All new partners are assumed to be average until they do something to differentiate themselves from others in their "class"—those who became partner in the same year. Selling work, serving clients, managing people are more important that ever and there is competition for the opportunity to sell, serve, and manage. New partners have to learn to create opportunity.

There is no training program on how to be a partner. There are no descriptions of duties or responsibilities. The firm has an oral tradition. The partner role is learned from knowing and watching the more tenured partners and other members of the class. There is no master information or communication system for the new partner to rely on. Information resides somewhere in the partner network. The key to success is knowing who has the information and how to communicate across the network. To become a partner requires help from other partners.

The circumstances under which I became a partner were less than ideal. When Jim Heller told me that the GD lawyers were prepared to negotiate my reentry into the firm, I suggested that the time for middle-men was at end. I asked Jim to rid me of the lawyers. His charge was to find a mutually agreeable partner with whom I could work out the reentry details.

Around new year, 1991, I met with Lew Krulwich in the café at the Bethesda Hyatt, an easy subway ride from home. Lew would be my mentor and help me with reentry. Over his coffee and tuna fish sand-wich and my beer and burger, we discussed options. Family consider-ations eliminated any thought of leaving Washington.

In the Washington area, the firm had two consulting practices: OGS and the private sector practice. I was reluctant to return to OGS because Lew and Tom Beyer, the partners I knew best, were no longer there. Lew was in charge of consulting in the New York area and Tom headed all consulting in the United States. Lew and I agreed that I would join the private sector consulting practice as soon as I could finish my work at the World Bank. There was no hurry.

On January 16, 1991, I met Jim in the lower lobby of the building where Gibson Dunn had offices. He had picked up checks to cover my back pay and the Kator Scott legal fees incurred over the years of litigation. He gave me a pink check for $389,207.15: $243,000 awarded by Judge Gesell plus accumulated interest of $145,000. We arranged a time the next day for him to return the $58,000 I had contributed to the legal fees, which in the final accounting came to around $500,000.

I proceeded to Hunan on K Street for Chinese food with John

Montefusca, who managed printing operations for the World Bank. After lunch, John and I strolled back to his office where he made several color copies of the check. One of the copies, suitably framed, hangs in my dining room.

A call from the World Bank Credit Union caught me when I got back to my office. They would charge my checking account $16.50 for insufficient funds and asked that I make a deposit. I tried one of the bank's ATM machines, but they only accept deposits up to $10,000. At the Credit Union office, the polite teller informed me that individual checks over $30,000 are subject to a confirmation delay. In the interim, I would get no more insufficient funds charges.

In good spirits, I called Jim to ask him to write two checks, each under $30,000 when he refunded the legal fees. I am unable to recall my income for 1991. Only my accountant knows. It got so complicated that I turned over all my records to her and asked her to figure it out. I do remember paying $170,000 in income taxes.

Shortly before I left the World Bank, my friends and colleagues held a going away party. The farewell speeches were interrupted by a phone call from Tela's school informing me that Tela would have to undergo counseling with a psychologist or psychiatrist as a condition for staying in school. Tela was a rebellious fifteen.

In February 1991, more than half way through the firm's fiscal year, I rejoined Price Waterhouse. My first day on the job I reported to the firm's training center in Tampa, Florida, where I was to spend a few days studying marketing and methodologies. I stayed with Sandy Kinsey, who administers the national training program and lives in Tampa.

The two dozen students included a few other partners. Three were memorable. The first of these was an audit partner, a few years older than I. On one of the training breaks, he introduced himself with a firm handshake and a warm smile. As we chatted he asked "What did you do while you were" — he stammered a little, awkwardly searching for words — "on sabbatical?" I laughed and answered his question. To this day, I refer to the seven years I spent in litigation as my "sabbatical" from the firm, even though I know I misuse the word.

The second was also an audit partner. In similar circumstances, he welcomed me to the firm and gave a running commentary on his reactions to what he had read about the case in the media over the years.

In a state of obvious amusement, he remarked "My favorite quote was your son's question 'How many times to we have to win this thing?'"

The third was a consulting partner. He neither shook my hand nor introduced himself.

Training ended. I said good-bye to Sandy and Christopher, and returned to the cold in Washington.

In April, I took the children to the Virgin Islands for a vacation. Tela chose the location. Shortly before we left, she had her head shaved, except for a tuft of hair just over her forehead.

I had a temporary office and a secretary whom I shared with another partner in the firm's Bethesda office. It was in the boondocks, a long way northwest of downtown Bethesda. Downtown Bethesda is an easy to get to, near-in suburb of Washington, conveniently accessible by public transportation. The Bethesda office was a forty-five to sixty minute commute from home. Three times the first week, I got lost en route to work.

It mattered little. When I got to the office, there was nothing to do. I had no clients, no project teams, no constituency. The phone rarely rang. There was little sign of life on the whole floor that surrounded me. The place was badly lit and most of the offices were vacant. What was once a fountain, stood dry and empty in one of the halls.

Aside from the secretary, the only other person in evidence was the partner next door. He was a very funny man with curly black hair streaked with gray. By firm standards, it was unconventionally long. When he was around, he was good company, but I seldom saw him because he traveled constantly.

There was no one to go to lunch with and going to lunch was a trip. The office was surrounded by other office buildings and acres of parking lots. There were no city streets to facilitate shops, restaurants, or other signs of urban life.

Fortunately my stay in Bethesda was short. Those of us in private sector consulting practice moved to an office in Falls Church, Virginia, very near the hospital where Peter's broken arm was repaired. The commute was better than it had been to Bethesda. My trip was against traffic on Interstate 66, so I could cover the twenty miles in half an hour or so.

Although everyone seemed to travel a lot, there were more people in Falls Church. The partners, my former Bethesda neighbor included, were all together on "partner row." I knew a few of them by name and a few more by face. The people were nice enough, but very busy. No one had the time or the charter to help me out. And I certainly needed help.

What should have been easy was hard. The firm's administrative systems were initially confused by my having two staff numbers, one assigned before the sabbatical, the other assigned afterward. Time sheets and expense reports were an enigmatic sea of unfamiliar codes. The firm's standard packages for electronic mail, word processing, spreadsheets and the like were all different from the ones I had used for years. The voicemail system was impenetrable to the children. (I got a cellular phone so they could reach me.) Getting to routine meetings in unfamiliar settings in downtown Washington, Columbia and Baltimore, Maryland, Philadelphia, and New York required more time for advanced planning than I wanted to spend.

Everything else was even harder. The World Bank hired us to do a small cost accounting project. Other than that, I had not accomplished much by the end of the fiscal year in the summer of 1991.

Toni Gibbons died of congestive heart failure. John was taking her home from one of her all too frequent hospital stays when she collapsed. I met some of her family at the airport when they came in from the Midwest for the funeral. The sad memorial service offered a brief opportunity to see John and my old State Department friends.

While the children were in camp, Carol Supplee, Sheila, and I went to Europe for a couple of weeks. We flew into the Cologne airport and took the bus and train into the city. Sheila, who had never been to Europe, was startled to discover the cathedral towering above as we walked the steps out of the train station. We saw the Rhine and its castles from the decks of a hydrofoil. A leisurely ride on the train took us to Paris for a stay with Brigette and Jean Charles at the Gavarni. We toured all the famous churches and several that are only well known to Parisians. Between churches we walked the Seine, stopping frequently in the brasseries for rest and refreshment.

I attended the new partners' meeting for the class of '92 on Long Island later in the summer. The registration forms offered sailing, golf, tennis, and lounging by the pool. When I submitted my forms, I recorded my choice, "none of the above." I was later advised to take deck shoes, sunglasses and a hat. My secretary told me that "none of the above" was not an option. She had changed the forms and picked sailing.

The crowd of new partners, all strangers to me and most of them ten years younger than I, made me a little uncomfortable. However, they turned out to be a cheery lot and their good humor was a calming influence when we sailed around Long Island Sound. I sat near a mast and clutched the steel cables to avoid falling, or worse still, losing the contents of my stomach.

Just after the start of the school year, came the annual partners' meetings, called sectionals because the meetings are held in sections at several resorts around the country. When the partnership was smaller the partners met as a single group. As the partnership grew, it became increasingly difficult to get everyone together at the same time, in the same place. The sectionals are held for three or four days, overlapping into a weekend, in two time slots usually a week apart. Individual partners choose a location and time slot to suit their schedules and resort preferences. Spouses are invited and there is a program to entertain the spouses when the partners are in business meetings.

Leaving the children created logistical problems, so I chose the sectional meeting in Washington. Tela, who did not want to stay with Thomas Peter, could spend nights at the hotel with me and maintain her routine during the day.

I was more comfortable at the Washington sectional meeting than I had been at the new partners' meeting. I knew a few people, including a couple of the women in the partnership, one of whom had served the State Department in the days before my sabbatical. The women and their husbands were interesting, entertaining people. I listened to their funny stories about what happened when the male spouses were assumed to be partners or the female partners were assumed to be spouses.

I too fell prey to the role confusion. Dinner one night was served on one of the charter tour boats that offer meals and entertainment as part of a cruise on the Potomac River. I joined a group of women smoking on the deck and discussing the spouses' tour of the Supreme Court scheduled for the next day. The group was excited at the prospect of meeting Justice O'Connor. I managed to keep a straight face when asked if I was going. "I've been," I replied.

The next month, Mom died from a blood clot that lodged in her lung after routine surgery for gall bladder removal. She was seventy. My family was unable to reach me because the phone was off the hook to avoid homework interruptions in the form of calls from the children's cohorts. In desperation, Brother John called the Hoppers. Everyone was asleep when David rang the doorbell and pounded on the front door to deliver the news.

I was devastated, incoherent, out of control. I made plans to cover the children and coordinated plane reservations for Susan, John, Cathy and me to leave Boston, New York, and Washington and converge on El Paso, Texas. From there we would drive the 150 miles to Silver City, New Mexico, where Mom died. She and Gil had moved to "Silver," as it was called, to be near friends, many of whom were army families that had retired around El Paso.

Gil asked that Susan, John, and I deal with Mom's personal effects according to her wishes. He also asked that we each spend some time talking about her at the memorial service. We were up most of the night preparing for the service. The day after, at 4:00 A.M. on a moonless black morning we left for El Paso to fly back east. The tribulations of Anita Hill played out on the radio of our rented car.

Before Mom died, I had been pretty lonely and miserable at work, but I had her to talk to. We talked about little things: how much water to use to cook a cup of rice, the humming bird count in Silver, custard recipes for chili rellenos, what to do about the latest pattern of rebellious behavior by one or more of the children, Peter's progress at Oakland, the children's theatrical performances. We talked a couple of times a week. I always knew what was going on with the whole family. Mom was at the center of the communication network. The center was gone.

At work I had a list of companies, a charter to go sell consulting services, little idea of how to do it, and less interest in cold calling. After being out of consulting for seven years, the market, the partners, the staff, the business were largely unfamiliar to me. I wondered if I could go back to work for the World Bank.

Gilbert, who was going on fifteen, became a rebel and a discipline problem at school. I was called to a meeting about one escapade or another at least once a month. I came to fear the phone.

In the gloom of late winter 1992, when spring was about to break, I talked to Lew. He and I had been in touch irregularly. I was reluctant to bother Lew—he was a very busy man with responsibility for a major consulting practice. I believed it to be my job to figure out how to be a partner. But something had to change. I was floundering around, using a lot of energy, with no result.

It took months to work my way into the office of Dom Tarantino, the partner who dealt with people issues in the partnership. Dom was part of the triumvirate that ran the firm. I attribute the time it took to hectic schedules rather than to any intent to delay.

When I met with Dom in his office in New York, he seemed direct and sincere. I told him that I felt like I was being managed as a liability and that I wanted to be an asset to the firm. With evident good nature, he commented that I did have a few partners "walking on eggshells for fear that someone might say 'Good day,' when it wasn't."

With a smile, I raised my right hand and gave Dom my word that I would never again engage in litigation with the firm. I had had it with litigation. I wanted to get on with the job.

I was up, way up, when I left Dom's office and headed back to Washington. I knew I was on my way back to OGS. It might take awhile, but it would happen.

The Maret School called and suggested that I not apply for Gilbert to be admitted to the freshman class at Maret. Gilbert had no academic problems but he was a pain in the administration. I told them if they wanted to boot him out, then they would have to do so. I planned to reapply on his behalf. A little later, I got a letter from the headmaster at Maret. In overwritten, contorted language, the letter said that the school would not hold Tela's admission hostage to Gilbert's. Tela could be a junior at Maret, but Maret was not in the cards for Gilbert. In September 1992 he started his freshman year at Gonzaga College High School. He was going to meet the Jesuit tradition.

In October Tela took the family van and disappeared one afternoon. After being up half the night with the D.C. police or on the phone with various of her friends, I concluded that she and her best friend had taken off for New York. She called the next day to say she was okay. The wayward twosome returned the day after. In my relief, anger seemed inappropriate. I congratulated her on successfully making a trip that I was not sure I could have made at her age.

At about the same time, I learned I was going back to OGS. It had taken awhile, but Lew, Dom, Tom Beyer, and probably a number of other people had arranged a transfer.

Although I had left the Price Waterhouse offices on K Street in downtown Washington nine years earlier, I felt like I was returning home when I showed up in November 1992. My transfer was effective in December. In the interim, I was officeless. It made no difference.

The travel time from home to the OGS offices downtown was twenty minutes at worst. People and piles of files and papers filled the over-crowded facility. Half the staff were women, a quarter were other protected groups. The partner in charge was black and the partner group reflected the diversity of the staff, although not in quite the same proportions.

The paging system routinely announced international calls or mes-sages for people, some of whose names I recognized from presabbatical days. Although I still lacked clients to serve and staff to serve them, I knew a few people and understood government operations. I was confident that I could still write competitive government proposals. Furthermore, I was convinced I would have a chance to do so.

OGS offered another advantage. From downtown I could respond instantly to the frequent calls from Gonzaga, where Gilbert was regu-larly in trouble. He was confined to detention hall after school or on Saturdays for the slightest infraction. JUG they called it—"Justice Under God."

Through the winter in early 1993, I had a steady diet of proposal writing with more than the average number of all-nighters. But I was working with teams of people who gained confidence in themselves and me with every effort—and we won, not always, but often enough, although usually after months or years. The federal procurement pro-cess is widely and publicly criticized for the time required to award a contract.

My first client did not result from the proposal process. It was given to me by a man who made partner the year before I did not. The client was an intelligence agency. I had to be investigated, polygraphed, and otherwise scrutinized to protect national security interests before I could really go to work. The clearance process took several months and the transition from him to me took a little longer, but I finally had a client.

In the spring, Peter had a role in the Oakland play, *Yo, Romeo!* an elementary school takeoff on the Shakespearean masterpiece. Tela played in *Little Shop of Horrors.* I was convinced that most children aged fifteen and up were horrors. Police in the driveway at midnight were routine, usually looking for someone's misplaced child or investi-gating an incident of teenage mischief.

Peter graduated from Oakland in the summer of 1993. A few days before graduation, a prospective client summoned us to a meeting to explain our proposal. The meeting was immovable. It was scheduled for 1:00 P.M., in the Washington area, the day Peter was to graduate at 4:00, in Charlottesville. Starting before dawn, Tela, Gilbert, and I drove the 110 miles to Charlottesville. I left the three children together. By cab and plane I returned to Washington where I attended most of the meeting and retraced my path back to Charlottesville in time to watch Peter graduate. It was late when we packed up four years of boarding school memories and possessions and brought Peter home.

About the time that Peter and Gilbert left for camp, the prospective client became my second client.

Tela was too old for camp. She and I had planned a trip to visit Gil in Silver City. We had our tickets and were prepared to leave when Gil decided to move to Cape Canaveral, Florida. He was eighty-six and frail. In Florida he would be near his children who could oversee his care. He had arranged the sale of the house, which, under the terms of Mom's will belonged to Susan, John, and me.

Tela and I flew to El Paso. Our mission was to tell Allied Van Lines what to move where and to drive Gil's car to his new home. We picked up the Lincoln at the airport where he left it on his way to the Cape. At Mom's house it took less than eight hours to close down a lifetime of memories. Late at night, Tela and I left Silver. I could not stay there with the ghosts. We spent the first night of our journey to Florida in Demming, a very small town about fifty miles southeast of Silver City.

The trip across country was unplanned. Each morning before departing, I called the office to ask the secretary to make reservations for a hotel in the target city for the day. In the afternoon, I phoned in to be told where we were staying that night. Cruise control managed the Lincoln's rapid progress along the same interstate highway that goes from El Paso to Jacksonville, Florida.

We deviated from that highway for a couple of nostalgic days in Galveston. I renewed some old acquaintances by phone. Others Tela and I met for drinks or dinner. She was amused by old friends telling tales of my antics as a teenager and into my twenties. When she wanted to escape the adults, Tela walked the beach or swam in the hotel pool.

After San Antonio, Galveston, and a long run from New Orleans, we stopped in Orlando to rest ourselves and rid the Lincoln of 2,400 miles of dirt and weather. In Cape Canaveral, we returned the car to a tired, jaundiced Gil. He explained that doctors had told him he most likely had pancreatic cancer. A tearful Tela told me she was sad: "You'll be an orphan, Mom."

We returned to Washington. Further testing indicated that Gil was cancer free.

Two clients kept me and the client service teams hopping through the fall of 1993 and into the spring and summer of 1994. We bounced between the OGS offices downtown and client sites in suburban Maryland and Virginia.

At client sites we collected data related to the problem we were tasked to solve: how much paper was in piles of what size and how long did it take the paper to get through some process. Most of our time was spent standing before groups of client employees listening to them describe the cumbersome processes by which they did their work. These we drew on flip charts, blackboards, paper-covered walls, or computer terminals depending on what was handy or what was most likely to be effective in the client setting. We helped reconcile the different perspectives brought by each person in the client group, until we had consensus on what the process under scrutiny looked like. Sore feet and the mental exhaustion that comes with resolving differences among people, some hostile, signaled the end of each week.

At the offices downtown, we analyzed the data and pulled together and cleaned up the evolving process pictures. These we summarized and packaged as presentations to client management.

When everyone agreed on what the process problem looked like, we rejoined the client employee groups to lead discussions about solutions. We carefully analyzed optional solutions and summarized, packaged, and presented results to management for disposition. Depending on what client management decided, we wrote plans to make needed changes and helped implement those changes.

When we did our job and if the client followed through, the client would have solved a problem. I would have a happy, but former, client. I worked on more proposals, waited, and hoped for positive results.

The firm's fiscal year roughly coincides with the school year. The former runs from July 1 through June 30, the latter, from Labor Day till Memorial Day. With two clients to serve and proposals to write, fiscal year 1994 was work. By contrast, the 1993-94 school year was a physical and emotional endurance run.

Peter started eighth grade at the Field School, a mainstream school. He could read, but the act of writing was a struggle and spelling was torture. Although he had never had a history class, he had to write history papers. His success as a tennis player and general interest in athletics offered a diversion from academic focus.

A severe case of acne plagued Tela's senior year and threatened her self-esteem and confidence. The normal anxiety around the college application process was compounded by conflicting views, mine and her's, over where to go to college. These escalated to conflicting views on almost everything else. A bright spot was the theater. Tela excelled in the choral group and played one of the three little maids in *The Mikado*.

Gilbert had his worst year ever. With scores in the high ninetieth percentile on every standardized test he ever took, he made mediocre grades. He consistently stayed out after curfew and ran with a crowd of kids, some of whom I found scary. Gilbert showed no interest in anything.

During the week, off-work hours were consumed by routine dinner preparation and homework supervision, and periodically by history and literature papers and science projects. Although the papers contributed to a few all-nighters, in retrospect, they were worth the effort. I hated the science projects. They hung around the kitchen or the garage for weeks and they always seemed to generate dirt and mess.

Weekends were anything but relaxing. I was either up half the night waiting for Tela or Gilbert to get home, or awakened from unintentional slumber by their tardy arrival.

Doing ten or fifteen loads of laundry every Saturday drove me into a rage, not because I mind washing clothes, rather in reaction to the stuff that I extracted from the children's pockets. I routinely dumped marijuana packets, full or empty into the toilet. Cleaning the children's rooms revealed a wide range of colorful marijuana paraphernalia or assorted beer or malt liquor bottles.

When confronted with the evidence, the children usually denied knowledge or ownership and tried to follow up with philosophical discussions of marijuana and morality. These only elevated the tension.

The highlight of the school year was the cast party planned to be held after the last performance of *The Mikado*. Tela drove the family van to rehearsal at school, which was a few blocks away and on my normal driving path for errands.

When I later drove past the school, I thought it strange that the van was nowhere in sight in spite of several empty parking places directly in front of the theater. (Teenagers, and Tela was no exception, generally park cars close to their final destination.) A quick tour of the neighborhood revealed the locked van parked on a side street. Its contents included a sealed gallon freezer bag of marijuana, several cases of Zima, and a keg of beer, no tap.

When I got the contraband back to the house, I disposed of the marijuana by the usual method. I waited till after dark to handle the liquor. I was reminded of Elliot Ness as I hammered a screw driver through the seal on the keg and drained the contents onto the driveway. Water from the garden hose washed away the smell.

Not all adults share my views about teenagers, marijuana, and alcohol. A couple of parents later commented critically that I put a damper on the cast party.

At summer's end, in response to a call from the camp director, I picked Peter up at camp. He was sent home after being caught with a joint.

Fall of 1994 marked the start of major change to the business environment in Price Waterhouse and in OGS. The firm would change its career model from a tenure-based one to one based on skills and abilities. The performance and compensation system for partners was under evaluation. A new senior partner would take the helm at the end of the fiscal year. Reorganizations and realignments were underway.

The partner-in-charge of OGS would assume new, national duties. Years of discussion about moving OGS out of downtown ended with a decision to move across the Potomac River to Arlington, Virginia.

To make matters more interesting, the numbers by which OGS performance was measured were lackluster, partly due to the fact that people were spending more time than planned on work other than client service. As a group, the OGS partners were concerned that lackluster performance might jeopardize compensation or diminish OGS's stature in the firm. Some of the group questioned our ability to get our partner candidates admitted. Partner pressure to improve performance and solve problems that adversely affected performance was intense.

Tela started her freshman year at the University of Vermont, a happy compromise on the choice of colleges. Although she was singularly uncommunicative, she valued her freedom from parental supervision and seemed to appreciate it. The developing music program at Gonzaga captured Gilbert's fancy and began to consume his time. He was elected head of the choral group and had a major role in the musical *Into the Woods.* Peter was adjusting to the Field School. He was into sports and the coaches demanded discipline and focus, athletic and academic. He infrequently started but he played on a number of varsity teams. The home pressure eased.

By Christmas 1994, I was running out of clients. Work for numbers one and two was finished or nearly so. I hoped the logjam on the proposal backlog would break—some of our proposals had been out-standing for a year and a half.

As was her custom, Sheila came a week before Christmas to help me arrange a happy holiday season for the children and to orchestrate all the routine household repairs that I saved for her visits. As soon as we got the tree down, the children left for a week of skiing with Thomas Peter and Sheila returned to Arkansas. I spent the remainder of the holidays in Florida with Gil. He seemed very tired. Between chats, he napped and I baked and froze pies to keep him in sweets until my next visit.

Winter ended with a flurry of proposals with remarkably short time lines. Two requests for proposals allowed only a couple of weeks to respond. We were awarded contracts within weeks of proposal submission and expected to start work within days of award. By Easter 1995 I had all the client work I could handle.

Gil died that spring. Susan, John, Cathy, and I stayed together for a long weekend in Florida where we attended the memorial services. Gil's sons decided to scatter his ashes at sea from the bow of a family boat. We motored, then sailed out of Port Canaveral to put Gil to rest in calm, murky blue-green waters in sight of his beachfront condominium. I was sick all the way back to shore.

The school year ended with promise. Gilbert was up with a high B average. He took two summer jobs, alternating between lifeguard and bicycle courier. Peter held his own academically and went to camp vowing to stay out of trouble. Tela had a lackluster freshman year, but seemed committed to improvement. She took a financially untenable job in Burlington so she could stay in Vermont and away from home.

At work I was busier than I had ever been in my career. I felt as though I were fighting a losing battle with exhaustion. The August heat and humidity actually brought relief—my workload eased as the government work force escaped Washington for vacation. The business pace slowed with the increased temperature and humidity, but not for long.

In September, we were awarded a contract on a proposal that one of my teams had written more than a year and a half earlier. A flurry of activity ensued, but partisan political squabbles that resulted in a government shutdown offered time to get organized as the 1995-96 school year began. The fact that the children seemed to be operating on an even keel helped. Peter, as a high school sophomore, made decent grades as he played varsity soccer that fall. At the same time, Gilbert came close to an A average while he played Nathan Detroit, a gambler, in *Guys and Dolls.* Tela earned a better than B average her first semester as a sophomore at the University of Vermont.

By Thanksgiving the dozens of people on the teams I worked with were prepared to deal with the onslaught of demand for service. Christmas came and went. For the first time ever, Sheila and I managed matters so that the family's shopping was finished before the crowds developed in the malls.

The 1996 new year brought two blizzards and a continuation of the political squabbles. Together these created more government shutdowns and a stream of continuing resolutions on the federal budget. Fortunately, these events effected my client agencies less than others. In the meanwhile, Tela, with the help of the internet, started to keep in touch. Peter played varsity basketball and Gilbert prepared for the male lead in *The Fantasticks.*

Today, work and family continue the battle for time and priority in my life. My clients got less attention when Tela came home for spring break as Gilbert went into the final rehearsals for what was a fantastic week of theatrical performances. Peter's papers on Frankenstein, Rousseau, the dissection of a squid, and Quasimodo, the Hunchback, preempted Gilbert's recitals as I fell behind on my internet messages to Tela. Client activities almost always win the conflict with Peter's tennis matches. But life works.

May 1996 marked seven years since the Supreme Court decided *Price Waterhouse v. Hopkins* and six years since Judge Gesell ordered that I be made a partner. More than five years have passed since I returned from sabbatical. These years made me a partner—and an orphan.

Washington, D.C.
May 1, 1996

Index

Adams, Jack, 67
Admissions Committee
  chairman Donald R. Ziegler, 200
  comments of Daniel Gervasi, 221
  comments of Lew Krulwich, 220
  confidentiality, 218
  decision memoranda, 218
  evidence reviewed by Susan Fiske, 237
  explanation of decisions, 218
  failure to investigate negative comments,
    351
  material on ABH, 195
  meeting schedule, 220
  member Roger Marcellin, 201, 274
  organizational meeting, 216
  process, 219
  schedule to mail partner comments, 216
  sex role stereotyping, 204
  visits to partner candidate offices, 217,
    218
Allen, Karen, 186
Alton, Leslie, 128, 135
amicus briefs, 287, 372
AMS (American Management Systems)
  defined, 57
Anderson, Lea, 91
Andrisani, Paul J., 341-43
Arthur Andersen (one of Big Eight), 26, 57,
  108, 124, 125, 337, 338
Arthur Young (one of Big Eight), 26, 337
Atkins, William A. (The Owner), 28, 32, 34,
  51, 166, 322
  on Burroughs, 37
  criteria for successful engagement, 34, 58

on errors, 35
interviewing ABH, 28
project partner, 28, 34
Touche partner-in-charge, Washington,
  D.C., 51

Bakta (driver), 177-80, 182, 184, 185
Baldwin, Jeff, 31, 51, 58, 61, 101, 322
Barry, Marion, 320
Barschdorf, Harry
  hired from AMS, 116, 127
  personal characteristics, 127
  and REMS, 127-29, 134, 135, 142, 150,
    151, 157, 159, 160
  resigns from Price Waterhouse, 162
  testimony at trial on liability, 228
Bator, Paul, 294
Beach, Bill, 335, 336
Beyer, Thomas O.
  ABH as admirer, 118
  ABH denied partnership, 137, 140
  ABH's assignment waiting for FMS, 78
  ABH's mentor, 125
  ABH's options after rejected partnership
    proposal, 323
  ABH's partnership proposal, 125, 126,
    150, 156, 157, 198
  ABH's project partner, 148
  ABH's success not attributable to, 199
  advice to be more assertive, 215
  advises ABH to act more feminine, 148,
    208, 213, 263, 274
  apparent fierceness, 77
  approach to growth, 77

attorney threats to female employees, 197
cancels partner breakfasts for FMS
    requirements, 105
counsel to ABH, 148
deposition, 196-98, 215
directness, 79
discuss meeting with Joseph Connor, 142
as firm spokesman, 274
fiscal year promotion celebration, 118
and FMS, 77, 86, 92, 114
Judge Gesell questions Susan Fiske about,
    238
John Gibbons on Judge Edwards's
    questions about, 264
Judge Green on argument that Beyer was
    speaking only for himself, 264
handwritten notes, 197, 214, 216
kept in dark by Policy Board, 274
Roger Marcellin testimony about, 225
OGS partners' votes on ABH, 197
presence at ABH's deposition, 199
Price Waterhouse partner-in-charge
    Federal Management Advisory
    Services, OGS, 77
Price Waterhouse partner-in-charge U.S.
    MCS, 384, 390
relationship with Roger Feldman, 85
removal of Ben Warder from FMS project,
    92
REMS proposal and project, 122, 123,
    143, 150, 157, 158, 161
resignation of ABH, 163
resignation of Harry Barschdorf, 162
on spouse policy, 105, 115
State Department request to replace ABH
    as project manager, 210
support for staff, 77, 79, 104
termination of Bob Lam, 143
testimony at trial, 208, 212, 213, 214, 215,
    216
transfer from Boston, 77
transfer Judy Reach, 78
vote on ABH, 141
"Yertle the Turtle," 118
Biero, Joey, 8, 49, 205, 381
Big Eight
    anachronistic policies, 61
    big bucks, 326
    brotherhood, 166
    client, 27
    computer systems, 25
    consulting, 61, 166
    definition, 25
    definition by name, 26
    engaged, retained by clients, 27
    partner focus, 79
    Price Waterhouse as one, 33
    Price Waterhouse spouse policy, 61

Price Waterhouse managers who made
    partner in, 321, 322
Touche Ross and Co., 25
vocabulary, 33
Big Eight and ABH
    ABH as pariah, 166, 322
    ABH as reject from, 174
    ABH's application to, 322
    ABH's entry into, 208
    ABH's ignorance of, 25
    ABH's interest in, 326
    ABH's interview with, 25
    ABH's opportunities in, 324
    glum prospects of ABH, 323
Big Six, 321, 322, 335
Blackmun, Harry A., 305
Blythe, Tom, 123, 124, 220
Boehm, Barrett, 226
Boutrous, Ted, 341-43
Bowman, Pat
    ABH's relationship with, 215, 351
    Bureau of Indian Affairs, 63, 64, 92
    firstborn child, 106
    and FMS, 86, 92, 96, 104
Braver, Rita, 295
Brennan, William J., 31, 292, 305
Brown v. Board of Education, xii
Burns, Sally, 194
Business Week, 17
Butcher, Alva, 16, 17
Butcher, Bruce, 17

Caplan, Bob, 67
Carter, President Jimmy, 270
Carter, Tom, 25, 28
Coffey, Tim, 220
    cross-examination by Doug Huron, 226
    direct examination by Wayne Schrader,
        225
    evaluation of ABH, 126
    and FmHA, 124, 127, 128
    meeting with ABH, 200
    partner in St. Louis, 123
    testimony, St. Louis, 225
    vote on ABH, 128, 141, 225
Colberg, Tom
    Bureau of Indian Affairs, 63, 64, 65
    and FMS, 108, 109, 112
    hired from Office of Management and
        Budget, 62
    opposition to ABH as partner, 215
    replacement for Pat Bowman, 106
Connor, Joseph E.
    ABH comments on, to Don Epelbaum,
        227, 354
    ABH image, 213
    ABH integrity, 141
    ABH's rejection, 137

on ABH's return as a partner, 331, 339, 340, 342
absence at trial on liability, 203
award ceremony for FMS, 117
comments to Policy Board, 223
deposition, 203, 204
discriminating official, 229
explains rejection, 137, 138, 140-42
as firm spokesman, 274
FmHA proposal in St. Louis, 141
gloomy business propects, 340
impression on Judge Gesell, 216
meeting with ABH, 142, 199, 227, 263, 274, 354
plan for ABH, 150, 208
quality control review results, 157
resignation of ABH, 163
selects Don Epelbaum for FMS, 114
testimony on trial on remedy, 338, 340, 341
videotape testimony, 203, 216, 223
world firm, 338, 341
Cook, Fred, 129, 130, 133, 197
Coopers and Lybrand (one of Big Eight), 26, 337
court of appeals
affirms on all issues, 377
affirms on liability, 273
affirms partnership order, 378
arguments on appeal from district court, 261, 363, 367
and en banc, 277, 284
reverses on constructive discharge, 273
Craig, Jim, 111, 112
Craig, Sally Keene, xix, 32, 71, 299, 381
Croyden, Stan, 22-25
CSC (Computer Sciences Corporation), 18, 19
Curzan, Mary, xviii, 206, 299, 334, 346, 368, 381
Curzan, Mike, 31, 32, 152, 299, 346

D.C. Human Rights Act, 170
D.C. Superior Court, 170, 171, 300, 301, 307
Danziger, Joan, 35, 299
Danziger, Martin B.
on ABH's lawsuit, 166, 381
on ABH's pregnancy, 44
ABH's work location, 35
attorney, 34, 37, 166
on Burroughs, 37, 39, 41, 42
director of Health and Retirement Fund for United Mine Workers of America, 34
on errors, 35
hires Dan Maceda, 39
personal characteristics, 35
relationship with ABH, 35, 166

at Supreme Court celebration, 299
Deloitte and Touche, 335
Deloitte, Haskins, and Sells, 335
Devaney, Bill, 65, 67, 122
Dondero, Joanne, 314-16, 319

Economist, 363
Edmondson, Jim, 115, 116, 165
Edwards, Harry
on authority to order partnership, 378
on Thomas Beyer's advice, 263
chief judge for appeal on liability, 262
circuit court judge, 262
circuit court ruling on remedy, 377
dialogue with Ted Olson, 369
on Susan Fiske's conclusion, 263
on Judge Gesell's review of the record, 369
on Judge Gesell's ruling on liability, 369, 370
John Gibbons on, 264
on giving ABH a partnership, 371, 374
judge for appeal on remedy, 368
on quality of evidence, 370
on role of the court of appeals, 263, 273, 369
on stereotyping, 373
EEOC (Equal Employment Opportunity Commission)
appeal on remedy, 372
argument at appeal on remedy, 372
Brenda Taylor complaint, xiii
discrimination claim, 157
dispute resolution, 164
harassment and retaliation claim, 164
interrogatories, 172
investigative process, 154
jurisdictional dispute, 161, 162, 164
process, 154
right to sue, 164
Epelbaum, Don
ABH's partnership proposal, 126, 201
on ABH's relationship with staff, 227
ABH to, on meeting with Joseph Connor, 227, 354
advice to ABH, 148, 227
commuting from St. Louis, 116
"Dandy Don," 148
deposition, 200, 201
discriminating official, 229
FMS project, 121, 227
Judge Gesell on hostility of, to ABH, 372
Karen Henderson on trust, 372
impression of, on Judge Gesell, 240
as interloper, 116
introduction to State, 113
meeting Ivan Selin, 116, 117
meeting with ABH, 200, 227

quality control review, 151
on socializing with managers, 201
testimony, 226, 227, 240
vote on ABH, 141, 197, 215, 225
on working with ABH, 201
Ernst and Whinney (one of Big Eight), 26,
   337
Ernst and Young, 337

Feldman, Gilda, 243, 251
Feldman, Roger B., 96
   Thomas Beyer on client satisfaction, 197
   comptroller, Department of State, xviii,
      85, 243
   cross-examination, 211
   and FMS, 85, 86, 97, 109, 117
   on Judge Gesell as Moses, 212, 299
   on loons, 299
   member Senior Executive Service, 97
   move to Florida, 381
   relationship with ABH, 85, 86, 89, 211
   relationship with Thomas Beyer, 85
   relationship with Howard Renman, 89
   relationship with Ben Warder, 86
   REMS proposal, 123
   as reviewer, 87, 106
   stipulation on technical competence, 211
   testimony on ABH, 211, 212, 243
   witness for ABH, 203, 210
Fennessey, Dennis, 33, 34, 37, 38, 52
Ferraro, John, 87, 100
Fiske, Susan,
   on critical mass of women, 237
   as expert witness, xiii, 194, 195, 204, 228-
      29, 232, 238, 275, 287
   Judge Gesell on testimony of, 351
   on stereotypes and stereotyping, xiv, 233-
      36, 238
FMS (financial management system)
   defined, 84
Forbes, 17
Fortune, 17
Freeman, Bob
   and ABH celebrate end of FMS competi-
      tion, 116
   ABH introduces staff of, 107
   ABH's impressions of, 113
   assigns FMS technical experts, 108
   delivers AMS proposal, 113
   FMS project manager for AMS, 107
   hired by Price Waterhouse, 116
   offers congratulations to Price
      Waterhouse, 116
   REMS proposal, 122, 123
Fridley, John
   on ABH's integrity, 141, 142, 201
   attributes time-recording and billing
      deficiencies to ABH, 220
   Don Epelbaum on ABH's comments, 227

FmHA proposal partner, 124
Roger Marcellin on comments, 220
partner in St. Louis, 123
vote on ABH, 141
vote on ABH's partnership proposal, 220

Gallagher, Margaret, 47
Gallagher, Rose, 55, 59, 206
Gallagher, Sheila, xviii, 73, 74, 78, 81, 266-
   68, 291, 292, 295, 299, 300, 316, 319,
   379-81, 387, 396, 397
Gallagher, Tela Margaret (daughter), 2, 20,
   47-55, 59-61, 64, 70, 71, 73-75, 78, 81,
   110, 119, 135, 145, 146, 188, 205, 206,
   244, 247, 249-51, 258, 265, 268, 270,
   278-81, 285, 286, 291, 292, 294, 295,
   297, 301, 302, 309, 311-14, 316, 318-21,
   336, 337, 345, 347, 356, 357, 359, 361,
   376, 380, 385, 386, 388, 390-97
Gallagher, Thomas Gilbert (son), 11, 54-56,
   58-60, 64, 70, 71, 73, 75, 78, 81-83, 88,
   102, 108, 110, 119, 135, 142, 145, 146,
   205, 206, 244-47, 259, 265, 267, 268,
   270, 278-81, 285, 286, 291-93, 295, 297,
   302, 309, 311-14, 316, 319, 345, 347,
   348, 350, 355-57, 359, 361, 376, 389-92,
   394, 395-97
Gallagher, Thomas Peter (son), 73, 75, 77,
   78, 81, 82, 108, 110, 112, 118, 119, 135,
   145, 146, 205, 206, 244-47, 256-60, 265,
   268, 270, 278-81, 285-87, 291-93, 295,
   297, 302, 310, 311-20, 345, 347-50, 355-
   357, 359, 361, 376, 391, 392, 393, 395-
   97
Gallagher, Thomas Peter, Sr., 29-32, 43-55,
   58-61, 63, 64, 69-71, 73-75, 81-83, 101,
   102, 105, 107, 110, 115, 116, 118, 135,
   138, 143-46, 152, 153, 155, 162, 165,
   166, 175, 177, 178, 185-89, 192, 205,
   206, 208, 230, 244-47, 256, 257-60, 266-
   69, 273, 285, 286, 300, 301, 308, 311,
   312, 321, 323, 329, 331, 334, 376, 379,
   388, 396
GD lawyers. *See* Gibson, Dunn, and
   Crutcher
Gellar, Marjorie, 215
Gentry, Lisa, 313
Gervasi. *See* Jerbasi
Gesell, Gerhard A.
   on ABH as star, 212
   on ABH calling Donald Epelbaum stupid,
      240
   ABH testimony in trial on liability, 208
   ABH too disagreeable to be a partner, 283
   ABH's appeal on constructive discharge,
      255
   on ABH's computer, 330
   on ABH's desire to return to Price
      Waterhouse, 209, 330

on ABH's forms, 217, 218
on ABH's job search, 322, 323, 325, 326, 328, 329
on ABH's meeting with Joseph Connor, 208
on ABH's misrepresentation of meeting with Joseph Connor, 354
on ABH's pretrial brief, 325
on ABH's qualifications to be partner, 330
on ABH's return as partner, 353
on ABH's returning as eligible partner candidate, 342, 353
age of *Hopkins v. Price Waterhouse*, 367
angry, 240, 241, 317
appearance, 207
on argument that women's comments are free of gender bias, 351, 352
asks help to interpret *Hishon v. King and Spalding*, 229
attitude toward attorneys, 230
background, xiv–xv, 207
on Thomas Beyer's handwritten notes, 214
on bifurcation, 254
burden of proof, 283
chivalry, 327
clear and convincing evidence, 306, 318
computing damages, 360
on confidentiality from the partners, 218
on constructive discharge, 253, 333, 334, 342, 344, 352, 353, 378
court of appeals affirms order of, 377
court of appeals on, 369, 378
court of appeals order to, 344
courtroom, 225, 241, 261, 317, 320
on criticism of dress, 213
definition of "clear and convincing," 351
on definition of "consultant," 208, 233
definition of "preponderance of the evidence," 350
on definition of "Staff," 208
on difference between man and woman, 213
discovery on remedy, 318
on discriminating officials, 229
evidence cross-referencing, 221
evidentiary standard, 283
expert testimony by economic statistician, 341
expert testimony on outplacement counseling, 341
failure to meet preponderant standard, 350
federal district judge, 191
"Findings of Fact," 242
"Findings of Fact" on remand, 349, 350
findings on liability, 263, 269, 273
on Susan Fiske's testimony, 204, 232, 233, 236, 238
on front pay, 343
frustration with court of appeals, 332
frustration with Supreme Court, 332
on Daniel Gervasi comment, 221

Jim Heller's belief in error on constructive discharge, 263
Jim Heller's argument on, 371, 372
Hopkins v. Price Waterhouse as precedent, 229, 230
Hopkins v. Price Waterhouse, oldest case on docket, 316
humor of, 212, 216, 221, 236, 321
impression of Joseph Connor, 216
impression of Don Epelbaum, 240
impression of ABH, 240
on interpersonal relations, 224
irritation with *Hopkins v. Price Waterhouse*, 317
irritation with the press corps, 309
Judge Edwards's comments on, 369, 370
Judge Henderson's arguments on, 372
judgement on liability, 317
on lack of client confidence in ABH, 212
legal mess dumped by court of appeals, 316
liability based on unconscious stereotyping, 283
on likelihood of appeal from his decision on remedy, 343
on long form, 217
on lost wages, 354, 384
on making a record after the fact, 210
managing attorneys, 191, 203, 213, 228, 317
memorandum, 377
on mitigation of damages, 331, 332, 353
as Moses, 299
motion to dismiss, 216
on no problems with clients, 224
on office visits by Admission Committee, 219
on opposing expert testimony, 351
on Price Waterhouse's failure to appeal constructive discharge, 333
on public proceedings in his court, 192, 335, 336
on quartile ranking of partner candidates, 216
on retrying facts, 324
on role of stereotyping in the ABH partnership decision, 233
on secondhand information, 209, 224
on statisticians, 228, 232, 239, 342
on staying at Price Waterhouse as non-partner, 209
on stereotypes, 238
on structured settlement, 343
on testimony by Joseph Connor, 339
on timing of informing partners about rejections, 218
on treatment of women, 228
on withdrawal of retaliation claim, 210
on women candidates, 219
on women managers, 213
on women partners, 216

opinion on liability, 250
opinion on liability (memorandum), 252-56, 277
opinion on remedy, 355, 357
partnership order, 355, 359, 360, 397
post-trial briefs, 230, 249
post-trial procedures and schedules, 343
press reaction to partnership order, 357
pretrial conference, 204
Price Waterhouse arguments on, 369, 370, 373
Price Waterhouse argument on error, 274-76, 283, 306
reversal by Supreme Court, 313
ruling on "back pay," 254
ruling on constructive discharge, 273
ruling on liability, 352
schedule to reconsider liability by new evidentiary standard, 316
schedules trial on liability, 191
scheduling conference, trial on remedy, 316
testimony of the Big Six, 335, 337, 338
testimony of Thomas Peter Gallagher, 331
testimony of Joseph Tryon, 335
trial on remedy, 277, 310, 316, 317, 322, 343
use of technical terms and buzz words, 208, 233
videotape of Joseph Connor deposition, 203
Gibbons, Elizabeth Antoinette (Toni)
art shop, 366
briefcases, 358
at celebrations, 299, 346
court of appeals, 261
death of, 387
dogs, 279
ear piercing, 249-51
entertaining, 257, 280
five-minute meetings, 168
FMS shadow, 96
FMS travel to Bonn, 97
FNPay project, 167, 168, 243, 247, 248, 250, 255, 258
health, 167, 280, 282, 387
High Knob, 268
lunch meetings, 205, 243, 251, 347, 348
member Senior Executive Service, 97
receiving line, 96
Ridgewell's, 257
U.S. Department of State, xviii, 96
Gibbons, John
attorney, 249
at celebrations, 257, 299, 346
on constructive discharge, 352
at court of appeals, 261, 262, 264, 368
dogs, 279, 280
on Jim Heller, 249

High Knob, 268
interprets briefs, 249, 253, 254, 282-84, 288
interprets opinions, 277, 380
reads briefs, 248
Gibson, Dunn, and Crutcher
appeal of liability, 256, 275
appeal on remedy, 318, 343-45, 351, 372
appeal to the Supreme Court, 282
attorneys for Price Waterhouse, 191
at end of litigation, 384
trial on liability, 191, 192, 195, 196, 198, 199, 202-4, 207, 208
Giere, Joseph M., 69, 73, 74
Glaberson, William, 288, 289
glass ceiling, ix, xi
Godwin, Mable, 3
Golding, William, 10
Goodstat, Paul B., 58, 61, 223
Gopol, 304
Green, Joyce Hens, 262, 263, 273, 274
Green, Tom, 124, 127, 128
Gulli, Ed, 85-88, 90, 91, 103

Haller, Ed, 225
Hardisty, Merrily, 244, 245
Hart, Peter, 202
Haskins and Sells (one of Big Eight), 26
Heller, Bobbie, 292, 293, 301, 345, 368
Heller, Jim
ABH's attorney, xviii, 172, 193, 364, 365
ABH's reentry to firm, 384, 385
appeal of constructive discharge, 255, 256, 273
argument before court of appeals, 261-64, 317, 370-72
on attorneys, 282
bifurcation, 254
on child custody, 286
computing damages, 360
on constructive discharge, 253, 276, 352
court of appeals celebration, 380-82
on difficulty of winning partnership, 318
divorce, 300, 301
on evidentiary standard, 288, 303
Harvard, 249
Hopkins v. Price Waterhouse, 173
on insincerity of promotion, 371
interview with Bo Wilmer, 312
on legal documents, 249
legal fees, 241, 253
on legal outcomes, 283
on liability for attorneys' fees, 306
on litigation schedules, 242, 271, 313, 376
on making peace with Doug Huron, 340
on media, 288, 289, 308, 310, 357, 358
oral arguments, 277, 278, 318
on poetry, 362
preparation for Supreme Court, 285, 286

preparation for trial on liability, 193, 194, 198-201, 203
preparation for trial on remedy, 317-19
on reinstatement as partner, 321, 340, 350, 360
relationship with John Gibbons, 249
on retaliation, 371
retaliation claim, 207, 210
ruling on remedy, 349, 350
ruling on remedy celebration, 359
on settling, 381
Supreme Court, 292-94, 304, 305, 309
Supreme Court celebration, 297, 299, 300
tax preparation, 301
testimony, ABH, 208-10, 241, 322-25, 327-29, 331
testimony, Bill Beach, 336
testimony, Big Six, 337, 338
testimony, Joseph Connor, 216, 223, 339-41
testimony, Thomas Peter Gallagher Sr., 331, 333
testimony, Bob Lamb, 212
testimony, Roger Marcellin, 225
testimony, outplacement counselor, 341
testimony, Joseph Tryon, 334, 335
trial on liability, 207, 215, 229, 239-41
trial on remedy, 320, 321, 340, 343-45
trial on remedy celebration, 345, 346
written briefs, 278
yellow Volkswagen, 286, 349
Henderson, Karen L., 368, 372
Herrmann, Bini, 32, 195, 299, 310, 381
Higgins, Steve
    FMS design project, 109
    FMS implementation proposal, 112
    FMS technical expert, 108
    opposition to ABH as partner, 215
    partner candidate, 120, 138
Hinkle, Tela O., 2
Hishon, Elizabeth Anderson, xii, 162, 163, 171, 269, 270, 287, 288, 290, 353, 378
Hishon v. King and Spalding, xii, 162, 163, 170-72, 229, 340, 353, 378
Hoffman, Corky, 202
Hollins College, 8-10, 12, 14, 15, 27, 30, 32, 245, 269, 274, 315
Homer, Nick, 108, 109, 112, 114, 125, 127, 128, 202
Hopkins v. Price Waterhouse, 170, 173, 229, 277, 288, 316, 317, 352, 367
Hopkins, Ann Branigar (ABH), 6, 11, 22, 47, 78, 91, 138, 187, 211-15, 220, 221, 223, 226-29, 234, 235, 237, 238, 274-76, 299, 305, 321, 324-26, 328, 329, 338-40, 350-54, 361, 362, 368, 370, 371, 372, 377, 378
Hopkins, Cathy, xviii, 118, 119, 316, 364, 366, 375, 376, 389, 396
Hopkins, Grace Branigar, 2, 3, 6, 9, 11, 91, 196, 303

Hopkins, John William, xviii, 4, 6, 12, 13, 19, 31, 118, 119, 121, 195, 271, 290, 291, 292, 294, 295, 296, 300, 316, 359, 364, 366, 371, 388, 389, 392, 396
Hopkins, John William, Sr., 1, 2, 4-8, 11, 15, 32, 105, 121, 165
Hopkins, William Branigar, 2, 9
Hopper, Ruth, xviii, 71, 72, 91, 107, 110, 206, 271, 284, 292, 297, 300, 304-6, 309, 311-13, 320, 349-51, 353, 355, 361, 363, 367, 369, 374, 380, 388
Hopper, W. David, xix, 71, 72, 91, 107, 110, 174, 175, 269, 271, 272, 284, 292, 300, 311, 312, 320, 350, 361, 363, 367, 368, 369, 374, 381, 388, 389
Hughes, Frank, 16, 18-20
Huron, Doug
    ABH's attorney, xviii, 153, 365
    on ABH's resignation, 157, 161, 163
    on amicus briefs, 288
    appeal of constructive discharge, 255, 256
    argument before the court of appeals, 261-63, 372
    bifurcation, 254
    computing damages, 360
    court of appeals celebration, 381
    court of appeals declines en banc, 284
    defines rebuttal witness, 204
    deposition, ABH, 198, 199
    deposition, Thomas Beyer, 196, 197
    deposition, Joseph Connor, 203
    deposition, Lew Krulwich, 201
    deposition, Ben Warder, 198
    deposition, Donald Ziegler, 200
    on depositions, 194, 195
    discovery, 191
    on evidentiary standard, 288, 303
    on experts, 194, 228
    files lawsuit in D.C. Superior Court, 171
    files lawsuit in federal court, 172
    and Susan Fiske, 195, 204
    on Judge Gesell, 191, 207, 239, 240
    on *Hishon v. King and Spalding*, 171
    interpretation of, 195
    interview with Bo Wilmer, 312
    introduces Jim Heller, 172
    joins Kator, Scott, and Heller, 172
    on legal documents, 192, 194, 195, 204, 277
    legal fees, 154, 157
    on legal fees, 194
    on legal outcomes, 264, 283
    on litigation schedules, 242, 376
    on media, 171, 288, 289, 308, 309, 357, 358
    at mock court session, 293
    office, 192, 193
    on partner compensation data, 192
    on reinstatement as partner, 360

on stereotyping, 193, 194
oral arguments, 278
preparation for lawsuit, 154, 157, 164,
    170-72
preparation for trial on liability, 193, 199
preparation for trial on remedy, 317-19
refuses to stipulate to Big Six partners,
    321, 322, 335, 338
retaliation claim, 207
ruling on remedy, 349, 350, 352
ruling on remedy celebration, 359
schedules pretrial conference, 191
Supreme Court, 305
Supreme Court celebration, 297, 299
Supreme Court grants cert, 284
testimony, ABH, 208, 210
testimony, Thomas Beyer, 212-16
testimony, Barrett Boehm, 226
testimony, Tim Coffey, 226
testimony, Roger Feldman, 211
testimony, Susan Fiske, 228, 229, 232,
    233, 236, 238
testimony, Roger Marcellin, 225
testimony, statistician, 230
testimony, Joseph Tryon, 334, 335
testimony, Donald Ziegler, 220-22
trial on remedy, 320, 321, 324, 327, 331,
    333, 337, 340, 343, 344
trial on remedy celebration, 345, 346
written briefs, 229, 230, 249, 256, 276-78,
    285, 287
Hutchings, Mary, 3

IBM, 12, 14-18, 25, 27, 34, 37, 44, 67, 110,
    111, 244
IBM (Big Blue), 18, 20, 37, 111
Ireland, Kathy, 196, 202, 226

Jenkins, George, 90
Jerbasi, Daniel W., 221, 238
Johnson, Lyndon B., 207
Jones, Hunter, 125
Jones, Mark, 92-97, 104
Jordan, John, 223

Kamen, Al, 289
Kaplan, Robert, 214, 215
Kator, Irv, 364, 365
Kator, Mike, 204, 365
Kator, Scott, and Heller
    appeal on remedy, 334, 344, 350, 360,
        362, 364, 365, 368
    appeal to the Supreme Court, 292, 304
    attorneys for ABH, 192
    at end of litigation, 384
    trial on liability, 195, 196, 198, 204
Kennedy, Anthony M., 305
Kennedy, John F., 14, 288
Kim, Yangja, 20

King and Spalding, 162, 171
King, Gilbert Wesmore, 11, 12, 31, 32, 54,
    55, 60, 118, 119, 189, 246, 270, 295,
    316, 389, 392, 393, 396
King, Martin Luther, 340
King, Stephen, 319
King, Tela Maurine Chiles (ABH's mother),
    1, 2, 4-9, 11, 12, 30-32, 45, 47, 51, 54,
    55, 60, 64, 69, 80, 118, 119, 178, 189,
    190, 205, 206, 246, 249, 270, 271, 295,
    316, 388, 389, 392
King, Tom, 22, 23
Kinsey, Sandy
    and ABH in Paris, 189
    ABH's deposition on, 203
    on ABH's interpersonal skills, 351
    on ABH's resignation, 163
    on ABH's return to Price Waterhouse,
        385, 386
    advice to ABH, 148
    Thomas Beyer's advice to ABH on, 208
    on GD lawyers, 197
    hospitalized in Paris, 186, 188, 189
    meetings with ABH, 330, 345
    quality control reviews, 149-51, 157
    REMS project manager, xix, 143
    REMS travel to Paris, 158-60
    replaces ABH on REMS, 163
    testimony, 228
    visits with ABH, 251, 318
Krulwich, Lew
    ABH deposition on, 199
    on ABH's failure to make partner, 137,
        140
    ABH's impression of, 62, 63
    on ABH's performance appraisal for
        FmHA, 126
    advice to ABH, 148
    assigns ABH to FmHA proposal, 123
    Bureau of Indian Affairs, 65-67
    conversation with Roger Marcellin, 225
    on Joseph Connor meeting, 137
    deposition, 200, 201, 209
    and Bill Devaney, 122
    discuss ABH's meeting with Joseph
        Connor, 142
    on John Fridley, 142
    helps ABH reenter Price Waterhouse, 384,
        389, 390
    hired from Office of Management and
        Budget, 62
    partner-in-charge, NY consulting, 384,
        389
    presence at ABH's deposition, 199
    on profanity, 225
    quality control reviews, 121
    sends ABH to St. Louis, 123
    sets record straight on ABH's integrity,
        141, 142, 220

on time-recording, 67, 68
time-recording and billing practices, 141, 220
vote on ABH, 141, 225

Lam, Bob
  employment contract, 143
  evaluation by ABH, 143
  REMS project manager, 73, 127-29, 133, 135, 142, 143
  REMS staffing problems, 142, 143
  REMS travel to Bonn, 129, 134
  replacement, 143
  transition to Sandy Kinsey, 143
Lamb, Bob
  ABH's deposition on, 203
  advice to ABH, 107, 108
  American ambassador to Nicosia, 381
  assistant secretary for administration, 168
  counselor for administration, U.S.
    embassy Bonn, 96
  foreign service officer, 96
  and Toni Gibbons, 96, 97
  testimony, 210, 212
  U.S. embassy, Bonn, 107
Lanhoff, Donna, 194, 287
Lee, Hyun Heh, 48
Lee, Kayong, 48-51, 55, 135, 319
Lee, Won Ju, 48
Lee, Won Kyung, 48, 135
Lewis, John L., 34
Liljekrans, Al, 65-67
Lindstrom, Kay, 202
Linnemann, Joe, 109, 110, 203
Lum, Henry, 227

Maceda, Dan, 39, 40, 42, 85
Mancusa, Bert, 103
Marcellin, Roger
  Admissions Committee, 201
  Don Epelbaum testimony about, 227
  Judge Gesell on contradicting Thomas
    Beyer, 274
  interview notes, 201
  interviews in OGS about partner
    candidates, 141, 218, 223
  testimony, 224, 225
Marshall, Thurgood, 31, 293, 305
Mayer Brown, 282, 283, 287
McClure, John L., 65, 66, 112, 215
McCoy, Jim, 34, 38, 44
McHale, Austin, 96, 107, 109, 197
McVeagh, Pete, 148, 156, 157, 199, 202, 323
Mikva, Abner, 368-74
Montefusca, John, 384, 385
Moore, Bert, 131-33, 158
Moore, Marjorie, 132, 133
Mornand, Brigette, 160, 161, 187-89, 248, 255, 258, 387

Mornand, Jean Charles, 160, 161, 187, 189, 387
Muhith, A., 174-77, 179-87
Myiang, Robin, 128, 135, 160

National Geographic, 101, 132
Nemerov, Howard, 10
nepotism policy, 51
New York Times Magazine, xvii, 288, 289
Nold, Karen
  ABH's deposition about, 203
  ABH's divorce, 257
  on ABH's failure to make partner, 138, 139
  ABH's impression of, 88, 89
  on ABH's interpersonal skills, 351
  ABH's testimony about, 330
  becomes partner, 228
  Thomas Beyer's deposition about, 215
  Bureau of Indian Affairs, 64
  climbs Talleyrand, 95, 132
  competition with AMS, 108
  and FMS, 86, 87-91, 92, 94-96, 104, 106, 107, 109, 112
  hired from Federal Reserve, 64
  on hospitalization of Sandy Kinsey, 186
  knowledge of State operations, 108
  senior manager, 108
  testimony, 227, 228
North, Oliver, 308, 309

Oakland School, 314-16, 319, 320, 347, 349, 376, 389, 391
Oberly, Kay, 293, 294, 317, 335
O'Connor, Sandra Day, 270, 293, 305, 369, 388
OGS, acronym for Office of Government
    Services, 64
O'Hern, Pat, 128, 129
Olson, Eldon, 368
Olson, Ted
  ABH's impressions of, 317
  argument before the court of appeals, 318, 368-70, 372-74
  computing damages, 360
  on constructive discharge, 333
  on employment experts, 344
  Judge Gesell on going to the Supreme
    Court, 333
  Ronald Reagan's attorney, 282
  replaces Kay Oberly, 317
  testimony, ABH, 323-30
  testimony, Bill Beach, 335
  testimony, Big Six, 335, 336
  testimony, Joseph Connor, 338, 340
  testimony, Thomas Gallagher, 334
  trial on remedy, 323
Otanazio, David Louis, 106

Parks, Rosa, 270

Parrish, Dawn, 265, 266
Peat Marwick and Mitchell (one of Big
   Eight), 26, 338
Pegues, Linda, 65-68, 122
Picciotto, Bob, 284, 285, 319
Policy Board
   decision memorandum from Admissions
      Committee, 224
   decision on ABH, 253
   disposition of Admissions Committee
      recommendations, 200, 218
   member Roger Marcellin, 223, 274
   membership, 200
   problems with ABH, 274
   report of the Admissions Committee, 225
   review of comments on women partner
      candidates, 276
   views on ABH, 274
   views on ABH as a partner, 340
   views on women partner candidates, 276
Popovich, Pat, 347, 348
Powell, Peter, 122
Presley, Elvis, 7
Price Waterhouse
   appeal on liability, 255, 256, 307
   appeal on remedy, 368-74
   appeal to Supreme Court, 283, 288, 293,
      294, 297, 300, 305, 306, 307, 352
   applicability of Title VII, 163
   award ceremony FMS computer system,
      117
   back pay award to ABH, 355
   Jeff Baldwin on, 58
   Big Eight, 26, 33
   briefs, 228, 242, 249, 282, 287, 358
   briefs (amicus), 287
   building FMS computer system, 114, 117
   Bureau of Indian Affairs, 62, 64
   change in business environment, 395
   changes legal representatives, 282
   circuit court ruling on constructive
      discharge, 276
   circuit court ruling on liability, 274-76
   circuit court ruling on remedy, 377, 378
   comments on charm school, 274
   comparable employment opportunities
      for ABH, 324
   competence of ABH, 211, 330
   competing to build the FMS computer
      system, 111, 210, 211
   competitive proposal to FmHA, 124, 128
   competitive proposal to RRB, 168, 169
   constitutional rights, 282
   constructive discharge, 253
   court costs, 307
   D.C. Superior Court, 301
   D.C. Superior Court complaint, 171
   Department of State client, 107, 211,
      212

   designing the FMS computer system, 84,
      86, 97, 103, 109
   discrimination policy, 222
   district court ruling on remedy, 350-54
   EEOC complaint, 154, 164
   EEOC discrimination claim, 157
   EEOC interrogatories, 164
   employment policy, 61, 105, 115, 199
   expert witnesses, 239
   federal district court complaint, 172
   federal district court depositions, 196,
      197, 199, 203
   federal district court interrogatories, 191-
      95, 220, 318
   federal district court ruling on remedy,
      351-54
   federal district court trial on liability,
      204, 208, 212, 216, 226, 227
   federal district court trial on remedy, 317,
      318, 321-24, 331, 332, 333, 335, 338,
      340-42
   female partners, 234
   fiscal year promotion celebration, 118,
      147
   FMS partners, 211
   Toni Gibbons on, 205
   hiring ABH, 58, 61, 162, 174, 232
   hiring employees of competitors, 116
   hiring Nick Homer, 108
   in-house cousel, 360
   managers who became partners at
      Touche, 335
   medical insurance, 189
   office location, 345
   offices, 390
   partner compensation, 192, 318, 335-37
   partner profanity, 198
   partnership decision on ABH, 138, 156,
      229, 252
   and Pinkerton Computer Consultants,
      110-12
   quality control review, 150
   quality control standards, 197
   Julie Randall on, 362
   removal of Ben Warder from FMS project,
      211
   request for rehearing en banc, 284
   resignation of ABH, 154, 163, 165, 167,
      174, 323, 329, 341
   resignation of Harry Barschdorf, 162
   retaining attorneys, 282
   return of ABH, 382, 385
   senior manager compensation, 338
   senior partner travel itinerary, 203
   settlement with ABH, 381
   staffing the REMS project, 126
   staff relationships with ABH, 212, 330,
      345
   tenacity, 288

troglodyte, 276
using computers, 330
videotape testimony, 223
women partner candidates, 221
world firm, 338
Price Waterhouse v. Hopkins, ix-x, xii, xv,
    287, 288, 290, 294, 303, 397
Procter, Mary, 57, 58
Psyck, Fred, 227
Pushaver, Ernest, 221

Ramakis, George, 48, 49, 53, 55, 60
Ramakis, Sull, 48, 50, 51, 53, 55, 60, 70, 74,
    75, 78, 110, 135, 270, 319
Randall, Julia Van Ness, xix, 10, 30, 196,
    363-65
Reach, Judy
    ABH's deposition, 203
    on ABH's failure to make partner, 138,
        139
    on GD lawyers, 197
    hospitalization of Sandy Kinsey, 186
    meetings with ABH, 330
    meets ABH, 78, 79
    technical skills, 79, 136
    works for Ben Warder, 148
Reagan, Ronald, 282
Rehnquist, William H., 293, 305
REMS (real estate management system)
    named, 123
Renman, Howard, xviii, 88, 89, 113, 166-68,
    203, 266, 299, 381
Richardson, Elliot, 35
Ridgewell's, 117, 257, 297, 298, 300, 356,
    359, 366, 375, 381
Riley, Susan, xviii, 244, 245, 299, 302, 366,
    368, 375, 381
Rimal, 185, 186
Robinson, Will, 92-94, 103, 104, 107
Rockwell, Norm, 96
Roe v. Wade, 270
Rosen, Mike, 20, 21
Russell, Rosalind, 12

Sand, George, 10, 29
Scalia, Antonin, 293, 305
Scheve, Tim, 126, 127, 129-35, 146, 162
Schneider, Rebecca and Sara, 300, 321, 345,
    368
Schneider, Vera, xviii, 206, 244, 245, 291,
    292, 302, 310-12, 320, 366, 368, 375,
    381
Schrader, Wayne
    computing damages, 360
    GD lawyer, 196, 262, 345
    testimony, Big Six, 321, 322, 335, 337
    testimony, Tim Coffey, 225
    testimony, Roger Marcellin, 223, 224
    testimony, Joseph Tryon, 321

testimony, Donald Ziegler, 216, 217, 219,
    220
Scientific American, 24
Scott, Joe, 344, 363-65
Seetheram, Sam, 128
Selin, Ivan, 108, 111, 116, 117
Shakespeare, William, 365
Shirley, Jack, 8
Shirley, Jane, 8, 9
Shirley, Susan, 8, 9
Slade, Grant, 175, 177, 186, 187
Smith, Essie, 1
Smith, Frances, 1, 12, 13
Smith, Julius, 1, 4, 12, 13
Smith, Junius, 1
Smith, Peggy, 55, 56
Smith College, 57
Snyder, John, 22-25
Snyder, Mitch, 356
Spanos, Anne, 111, 116
Spencer, Louie, 295, 299, 300
Sprague, Betty, 188, 189
Sprague, Christopher, 188, 189, 318, 386
Starr, Ms., 372
Statland, Norm
    ABH on, 202
    data processing partner, 67, 104
    on FMS report draft, 105
    negativism, 67, 105
    reviews FMS implementation proposal,
        112
    selection of technical experts for FMS,
        108
    snoring, 109
    testimony, Don Epelbaum, 227
    vote on ABH, 141
Stein and Huron, 152, 153, 157, 163, 192, 193
Stevens, John Paul, 305
Strickland, Bob, 310
Sullivan, Ric, 196, 199, 208, 360, 368
Supplee, Carol, 230, 291, 292, 295, 302,
    303, 310, 319-21, 336, 340, 345, 346,
    359-61, 366, 368, 375, 381, 387
Supreme Court
    argument before, 289, 294
    briefs, 287
    on burden of proof, 306
    dissenting opinion by Justice Kennedy,
        305
    dissenting opinion, joined by Justices
        Rehnquist and Scalia, 305
    dressing for, 294
    on evidentiary standard, 306
    judgment of, 303
    judgment of, by Justice Brennan, 305
    judgment of, joined by Justices Marshall,
        Blackmun, Stevens, 305
    judgment of, Justice O'Connor concurring,
        305

judgment of, Justice White concurring, 305
justices of, 293
on liability for attorneys' fees or damages, 306
reverses court of appeals, 307
ruling on *Hishon v. King and Spalding*, 171
seating, 292
sleeping in, 293
start of term, 289
writ of certiorari, 277

Tallent, Steve
ABH's impressions of, 196
argument before court of appeals, 262-64
deposition, ABH, 199, 200, 202
deposition, Thomas Beyer, 195-97
enters motion to dismiss, 216
on Susan Fiske as rebuttal witness, 232, 233
GD lawyer, 196, 240
replaced by Kay Oberly, 317
testimony, ABH, 209, 210
testimony, Joseph Connor, 223
testimony, Don Epelbaum, 226, 228
testimony, Roger Feldman, 211
testimony, Susan Fiske, 236-38
testimony, Bob Lamb, 212
Tandon, Evalyn, 304, 308, 357
Tarentino, Dom, 390
Taylor, Brenda, xiii
Thompson, Claude, 11, 12
Time, 195, 310
Title VII of the Civil Rights Act of 1964, xii, xiv, 157, 162-64, 170-72, 233, 240, 252, 283, 332, 339, 340, 352, 353, 370, 371-74, 377, 378
Totenberg, Nina, 308, 309
Touche Ross and Co. (one of Big Eight) 25-30, 33-35, 37-41, 51, 52, 54, 58, 60, 61, 70, 77, 101, 105, 115, 116, 166, 232, 308, 322, 323, 335, 358
Tryon, Joseph T., 321, 334, 335, 341, 346, 354, 355

Valdivieso, Sonia, 305, 308

W. R. Grace (Price Waterhouse client), 64
Wall Street Journal, xi, 17, 166
Walsh, Mary Roth, ix, xii
Warder, Ben, 202
on ABH partnership proposal, 125
ABH testimony on, 199, 210
Thomas Beyer's testimony on, 211
characterization of ABH, 148
deposition, 198
employment contract on Bob Lam, 143
at FMS orals, 79, 80

FMS partner, 86
FMS proposed partner, 79
FMS travel to Asia, 87-89
FMS travel to Canada, 86
meeting with ABH, 200
quality control reviews, 149-51, 153, 161, 163
reassigned from FMS, 92, 125
relationship with Feldman, 86
vote on ABH, 197
Warren, Robert Penn, 10
Washington Post, 243, 289, 356
Washington Times, 171
Wayne, John, 98
Weddington, Sara, 270
Welner, Steve, 116
Welty, Eudora, 10
Werking, Roger, 20, 24, 25
White, Byron, 31, 305
Whitehead, Alfred North, 109
Williams, Edward Bennett, 153
Williams, Judge, 262, 273, 276
Wilmer, Ami, 119, 316
Wilmer, Bo, 119, 312, 313, 316
Wilmer, Susan Hopkins, xviii, 118, 119, 268, 270, 271, 290-92, 294, 295, 299, 312, 316, 359, 363, 366, 375, 376, 389, 392, 396
Wilson, Diana, 221
Wind, Amy, 334, 346
Woodward, Bob, 31
World Bank, xviii, 71, 174, 175, 177, 185, 208, 209, 271, 281, 284, 285, 304, 305, 319, 327, 329, 334, 335, 344, 348, 357, 359, 362, 376, 381, 384, 385, 387, 389
World Court, 313, 380
Wortham, Gus, 12, 13
Wortham, Lyndall, 12, 13

Zagorin, Debbie, 110
Zagorin, Greg, 284, 288, 300
Zagorin, Karl, 110, 363
Ziegler, Donald R., 200, 201, 216-23
Ziegler, Ron, 200